PRAISE FOR *The Bibl*

"In this well-written, cogently argued, book, Alicia Johnston ~~~ strates that there is **strong biblical support for a theology that affirms** ~~~ than condemns non-heterosexual orientations and love-based monogamous same-sex marriages. Many, in and outside the Adventist Church, believe that it requires a liberal theology to conclude that LGBTQ people must be fully accepted in the church and must have the same privileges and status as heterosexuals have. **This book shows that a responsible conservative theology can lead to the same conclusion.** Her personal history as an ex Seventh-day Adventist pastor, who struggled to come to terms with her own bi-sexuality, has provided Alicia Johnston with the **empathy and the theological expertise** that went into this book. I believe it offers important insights that will help many readers to form or fine-tune their opinion and to support an affirming theology."
—Dr. Reinder Bruinsma, retired Adventist pastor
and administrator in the Netherlands, scholar, and author

"You love people and know something of the variations in human sexuality. You love the Bible and regard it as the Word of God. Is it possible to bring together those two loves? Yes. Alicia Johnston's book takes you deep inside the experience of real people and the actual meaning of the biblical text. **She demonstrates that a faithful, honest interpretation of the Bible supports a full welcome for LGBTQ people as members of the body of Christ.** If you are wrestling with how to reconcile your love for people with a high regard for the Bible, I urge you to read Alicia's book. We do not have to choose between loving people and honoring the Bible. Alicia helps us see the essential harmony between knowing people and rightly interpreting the Bible."
—John McClarty, Adventist Pastor at Green Lake Church

"Fair-minded and clear-eyed, Alicia Johnston targets with gracious care the Adventist Church's stance toward LGBTQ people. **The tone of the book is thoughtful, Scripture honoring, and redemptive.** If Adventists truly believe in our admirable aim of growing into Present Truth, **this is an excellent resource to move beyond damaging personal interactions, shallow reasoning, and blithe dismissals.** It turns out LGBTQ people can be biblically affirmed as wholly Adventist and fully human."
—Chris Blake, Pastor, San Luis Obispo and Morro Bay Seventh-day
Adventist Churches, Author, *Swimming Against the Current*
and *Searching for a God to Love*

"The Bible and LGBTQ Adventists is exactly as its subhead describes it: 'a theological conversation about same-sex marriage, gender, and identity.' In a church and society that is increasingly segmented, **this book is a wonderful invitation to participate in a conversation about sexual orientation that is respectful, informed, measured, and challenging** on both personal and corporate levels. Whether we agree or disagree, we cannot ignore this important topic. The church owes its members and its broader community a conversation that is thoughtful, gracious, and Christ-centered. This book provides it."

—Stephen Chavez, Adventist pastor and writer/editor

"The care, clarity, and thoroughness of Alicia's work here cannot be overstated. She demonstrates **the utmost love and respect** for the people in our denomination, our traditions, and the varied lived experiences of those in the LGBTQ+ community."

—Travis Sandidge, sabbath school teacher and engineer

"**This book is an answer to prayer.** Among the many strengths of Alicia's approach is that it does not require readers to agree with her conclusions to find it beneficial. Although her persuasive arguments further clarified my own affirming theology, I am confident it will help any Adventist reader to better appreciate why many of us believe that LGBTQ affirmation is a biblical imperative. I am eager to share the book with fellow Adventists because **I am convinced it will elevate the conversation about LGBTQ affirming theology** and help us reorganize our theological priorities around what matters most."

—Adventist Pastor in Atlantic Union

"This is a **significant contribution to the conversation**. Alicia Johnston has provided a very important and well-thought-out contribution to the ongoing discussion regarding the delicate relationship between the Seventh-day Adventist Church and our LGBTQ community. With an **exceptionally high view of scripture** and an extremely **competent, exegetical approach**, Alicia tackles some of the more challenging texts in scripture on alternative sexuality. In doing so, she invites us to re-examine some of our previously held assumptions. She challenged my thinking. She expanded my understanding. And she upheld the authority of scripture. Thank you, Alicia, for helping me along in my journey to **more effectively love and embrace the LGBTQ community**."

—Adventist pastor in the Southern Union

"'I wish I could be more open and accepting of gay people, but my beliefs won't let me—I can't ignore or get around what the Bible teaches, and I want to be faithful.' Stop wishing, and pick up this book! This is the theological explanation you have needed and hoped for. **Alicia doesn't 'get around the Bible,' she uses the Bible itself to offer the answers that so many have hoped they could find on this topic. Alicia writes like a scholar, reads like a researcher, and does Biblical exegesis with the ministerial training and professional ethics that those of us faithful to scripture must insist on.** If you've been looking for better Adventist theology on homosexuality, you just found it."

—Adventist Pastor in Pacific Union

A SPECIAL THANK YOU

I would like to extend a special thank you for the following supporters who helped make this book a reality:

Peterson Masigan	Esther Loewen
Dennis Skinner	Clifton Goff
Heather May	Scott Allen
Bryan Ness	Daniel Laredo
Kimberly	Carolyn Clayton
Debbie Masela	Sophie Webster
Matt Stevens	Portia James
Floyd Poenitz	Caroline Laredo
Paradox Church	Janna Chacko
Keisha McKenzie	Claudia dos Santos
Nayaliuqas Imxal	Heather & Zadok Calkins
Muyang Song	Alexander Carpenter
Lawrence Nelson	Kathy Baldock,
Randi Robertson	Canyonwalker Connections
Priscilla Flores	

A Theological Conversation
About Same-Sex Marriage,
Gender, and Identity

The
BIBLE&
LGBTQ
Adventists

ALICIA JOHNSTON

AFFIRMATION
COLLECTIVE

First paperback edition January, 2022

Cover and interior book design by Aphelandra

ISBN 978-1-68489-439-0 (paperback)
ISBN 978-1-68489-444-4 (ebook)

www.aliciajohnston.com

To those restless souls who are never satisfied with convenient answers.

To those who ache with loneliness and despair.

To those who clutch their Bibles with trembling hands, shoulders heavy under the shame they carry in their efforts to please God.

In wild hope that we may begin to grasp the truth.

The extravagance of God's love surpasses imagination.

———————

"There is no excuse for anyone in taking the position that there is no more truth to be revealed, and that all our expositions of Scripture are without an error. The fact that certain doctrines have been held as truth for many years by our people is not a proof that our ideas are infallible. Age will not make error into truth, and truth can afford to be fair. No true doctrine will lose anything by close investigation"

ELLEN G. WHITE (CW 35.2)

Contents

My Story

When I left my career as a counselor to become a pastor, people who loved me worried about me. It's not easy to get a job as a pastor when you're a woman. I don't come from a pastoral family and didn't have anyone to help me along the way. I was just getting out of the financial hole from one master's degree, only to go to seminary and dig myself into another one. No conference promised me a job or supported me through seminary. More people were graduating from the seminary than there were jobs to give them. Even qualified men were getting passed over. A lot could go wrong. The odds were never in my favor. I was making an impractical decision.

It turns out that odds don't matter to God. A few years later, I was pastoring a wonderful little church in my hometown. If you aren't acquainted with the world of Adventist ministerial hiring, you might not know just how unusual it is for a woman pastor, not long out of seminary, to pastor her own church. I felt like I was cutting ahead in line.

Not long after accepting the job, I spoke to a mentor from the seminary. She told me to be grateful and not question what the Lord had done. Good advice. I was grateful indeed. It was all I ever wanted. I looked forward to decades of pastoral ministry in the Adventist Church.

Fast forward 16 months, and it was all over. All because of something I thought I had put behind me. All for something I thought I clearly understood, but I hadn't. I was losing my career, financial future, and, more importantly, my entire support system and community.

The Adventist Church was more than a religion to me. Like many people, I was raised Adventist by Adventist parents and went to Adventist schools. More important than that, I made a personal decision to accept Adventist teachings and be an active part of the Adventist community. This decision was made over many years, through study and prayer, and came from a place of trusting in the mission and message of Adventism. The Adventist Church has something great to offer the world, and I wanted to be part of it.

In contrast, the LGBTQ community seemed like a group of people with whom I shared nothing. They had always been a separate group, distant from my friends, family, and church. They were characters on TV shows, people in raucous pride parades, and a person here or there I had known in college or high school who ended up leaving the church.

Then I fell in love with a woman. I could not have been more surprised if I'd sprouted a tail. It seemed impossible. I was committed to following God. I wasn't perfect by any means, but I was faithful to the church's teachings about sex. I'd also never been sexually abused, never used drugs, and never rebelled. I came from an intact, healthy, loving, Adventist family with a mother and a father who loved each other and me. God knows I'm far from perfect, but my life didn't fit what my church told me about gay people.

Yet my feelings were strong, seemingly from nowhere, and much later in life than I thought possible. I was 30 years old and hadn't been aware of these feelings before. Not only that, I was in the seminary, studying with unlikely hopes of becoming a pastor. It just didn't make sense that this was happening to me. It seemed crazy. I was at seminary, studying with hopes of becoming an Adventist pastor. Was this an attack from the enemy to keep me out of ministry? It seemed likely.

Many people I know now have similar stories, but it would be years before I met any of them. My experience felt unique and bizarre. I didn't realize that my entire life, others all around me had the same feelings. Most silently suffered and left the Adventist Church without a word. There was no one to listen to them, no one to understand.

When I finally did come out, person after person shared their stories with me about realizing their sexuality or gender while being part of the Adventist Church. In every case they were devastated, wanting to change, wishing they could be like everyone else. At this point, these stories are so well known they're cliché.

HOW DID THIS HAPPEN TO ME?

To me, there was nothing cliché about my situation. I didn't understand how this could happen *to me*. These feelings were unbidden and unwanted. They defied everything I believed was good and life-giving; the opposite of everything I strove to foster in my life. I just wasn't this type of person. I'd never thought of myself this way before. My feelings seemed to materialize from nowhere.

No wisdom or insight I'd received from my Christian experience seemed to fit or help me. I felt lost. I was unwilling to follow the values taught in the outside world. My church offered little other than bogeyman stories about gay people who lived very differently than I ever would.

Many pastors, professors, and even friends spoke about same-sex marriage as a sign that the end was near, that society was turning its back on God. I couldn't trust this problem to them. Finding resources was slow and painful. I struggled to manage these feelings and submit them to God.

Disorienting as the experience was, my faith also grounded me. I placed loyalty to God above all things. I hoped and prayed that my same-sex attraction would pass. At first, it only got stronger. Something long-dormant awoke in me, and I couldn't coax it back to sleep. I was drawn to women against my will. I kept noticing them in different ways. Sometimes in small interactions I felt an energy pass between myself and another woman and wondered with a sense of shame if she felt it, too.

Feeling exposed and out of control, I recall being almost uncontrollably drawn to a female friend, desperate for the slightest glancing touch on my skin. I spiraled emotionally and spiritually. Thanks to having few opportunities and high motivation to resist, I managed to restrain myself.

Loneliness was more than a feeling to me; it took residence in my body, and I could feel its ever-present weight. Privately, I was fighting what felt like a battle for my soul. Despite having many friends, my secret felt safe with few. It may have been paranoia. Perhaps more people were safe than I realized. Yet it wasn't only about trusting people to keep my secret; I simply didn't want people to think differently of me. I was the same person. I didn't want to be treated or thought about differently.

In my isolation, I wondered who had felt this way before me and what they had done. I needed help. I needed advice. I needed to talk to someone who had walked this road before me, but I didn't know of anyone I could talk to. At first, it seemed there was no help.

Besides, I didn't fit the boxes. I knew I wasn't gay. I was attracted to men and always had been, yet clearly I was also attracted to women. I didn't know what that meant. I also had no examples of people living good and holy lives who admitted to the kinds of feelings I had. My entire life in the church, and I didn't know a single person who admitted to feeling same-sex attraction.

This time in my life didn't last forever. I did find resources eventually, but it was difficult. I found ways to manage my feelings. I also confided in a few close friends. Life got much better. After a couple years, the occasional attraction I had for women was manageable. I still hoped to be married to a man one day. Overall, things were going well.

LGBTQ ADVENTISTS

When I was in the middle of my most difficult struggle, feeling alone and confused, I didn't know how common my experience was. We've done a disservice by painting sexual minorities as outsiders and painting this issue as originating in the outside world.

The church's challenge is not of LGBTQ people who are not Adventists showing up in our churches on Saturday mornings and asking to become members. I'm sure this happens occasionally, but it's not the church's primary challenge. It's not about a challenge from the outside with secular LGBTQ people.

LGBTQ people are already in our churches, silently observing, asking if they are wanted. We face the primary challenge of gay, bisexual, and transgender people growing up inside our churches and schools. The first challenge is about our own people. We aren't doing well at understanding gay, bisexual, and transgender Adventists. We certainly aren't adequately supporting them.

That problem begins with our framing of the question. We think it's the culture versus the church. Even the few visible gay or ex-gay people in the church speak of having gay lives outside the church, lives full of sin and addiction, and a dramatic return. It's as if church membership equates to being straight, and being gay, bisexual, or transgender makes someone an outsider, of a different culture or ideology. Even those who are committed to the Adventist Church for our entire lives can quickly become outsiders, viewed as opponents in an ideological struggle.

A large Adventist church I know discussed among the pastoral staff whether it was effectively ministering to gay, bisexual, and transgender people. Some feared their church's response had been inadequate, yet they weren't sure how to move forward.

After discussion, the senior pastor said, "I don't want to make this a political issue. I want to be pastoral. If we were to talk about it right now, it would just be political because we don't have anyone in our church who is LGBTQ. Since we don't have these questions pastorally, we should let it go for now."

I wish this matter could easily divide between the political and the personal. No one wishes that more than those of us caught between two fronts in the culture war. Feeling sympathy with both sides doesn't stop the bullets flying from every direction.

The pastor that day didn't realize that he had many LGBTQ people in his congregation. I knew one personally, even though I lived nowhere near his church. She wasn't open about her sexual orientation with anyone at the church because she didn't feel safe. They were waiting for her to step forward and announce herself, but they'd never given her any indication of what she could expect if she did. So, the senior pastor didn't know about her suffering or the suffering of other members, some of whom were LGBTQ, and some with close friends and family who are. Because he saw gay, bisexual, and transgender people through a political lens, he could not provide pastoral care.

It's even harder for gay, bisexual, and transgender kids growing up in our churches. A friend who was an Adventist teacher recalls being told by his principal, "There are no LBGTQ children at our school." This was one of the largest K-12 Adventist schools in the country, with hundreds of students. But in the Adventist Church, we don't often think about children growing up as sexual minorities in our midst. We think of this as a question of outsiders asking if they can be welcome in our churches, but it's first and foremost about those growing up in Adventists homes, schools, and churches.

We can't begin to help these children if we can't acknowledge their existence. Despite the principal's denial, here's what I know: There are likely children in his school who don't understand why they want to be one-of-the-girls so badly even though they keep getting treated like one-of-the-boys. These children don't know any transgender people and don't know what to make of this persistent and uninvited sense of identity that makes everyday life an exhausting, unpredictable, shameful burden. They don't even have the words to ask for help.

Girls in that school hide the secret that while their friends are crushing on boys in their class, they can't stop thinking about other girls. They feel that they are the only ones in the world with these feelings. Children grow up in oppressive silence, wondering whether they will ever belong in this church or even in their own families. They receive prohibitions, not support.

They also have no models. They don't know how they can fit into this church or their own families. The adults are afraid to acknowledge these kids because they know they don't have any real solutions. That's why there is so much silence in the first place. If the church offered livable solutions, it would be common to know visible, healthy, happy adult and middle-aged people with same-sex attractions. They would be role models of a plausible life for these kids. But so few exist in our churches that most of us have never met even one such person. If LGBTQ people were visible and in the church at the same rate as everyone else, there would be examples in nearly every church.

On top of this isolation, these kids are told the Bible says the desires they have are sinful. In private, when no one can see what they are doing, they look up Bible verses that say men who have sex with men are abominations and should be killed. They see indictments from Paul saying that people given over to "vile passions" and consumed with lust who receive shame in their bodies for their evil acts. They've heard that these verses are about gay people, so they wonder what kind of wicked creatures they must be. If they are particularly unlucky, someone comes through their church or school sharing a testimony of their past in the "homosexual lifestyle." These testimonies are inevitably filled with promiscuity, infidelity, and drugs. One of my dearest friends told me that growing up with these stories made him think he was a monster.

I myself was in deep denial about my repetitive dreams of marrying a woman and the intense, dysfunctional friendships I occasionally had with female friends. I was attracted to men, but I seemed unable to be the kind of woman Adventist men were looking for. Sometimes, a man might tell me that he was attracted to more feminine women than me. People thought I was gay, but I knew I wasn't. Something was wrong, and it was something about my basic personality that I seemed unable to change. Why couldn't I make this work? What did everyone see but me? Why did I experience such constant rejection?

These are the struggles that children silently face as they grow up in Adventist homes. They're afraid they are monsters. They don't know what's wrong with them. They try desperately to fit in when nothing seems to fit at all.

They hear mostly silence. No one gives voice to their struggles. But every time a word is spoken about the LGBTQ community, they listen intently. They try to understand what kind of life they might have in the Adventist Church, if any. What do they hear?

PULSE

In my last camp meeting as an Adventist pastor, I was asked to lead out in the Youth Department. It was an intense week. I worked nonstop for 14 hours a day, and it was gratifying. Our team was terrific, and the teenagers who came to our meetings stole my heart with their struggles and sincerity. I was in my element, sharpening my leadership skills and working with talented people for the sake of the gospel.

When the week ended, as we were all packing to go, I joined a group of fellow pastors and volunteers for an early breakfast in town. We were letting go of the pressures of the week, celebrating the victories, and thanking God for the privilege. Everything was going well in my life and ministry. My body was tired, but my spirit was renewed.

As we stood to leave, one of my friends asked us if we'd heard about the shooting the night before. With sadness in his voice, he said it had been at a gay bar. They didn't yet know any details about the shooter. Nearly 50 people were dead. It was the worst mass shooting in U.S. history at the time.

I couldn't know it then, but after hearing those words, my life would never be the same. Before I heard them, my personal struggle with my sexual orientation felt like a thing of the past. It had been a long time since I'd struggled with my attractions, and I didn't think of myself as part of the LGBTQ community. Yet my attraction to women had clarified a lot for me. I knew how gay, bisexual, and transgender people were thought of, how they were characterized, and the part that Christianity had played in making this country unsafe for them. It seemed plausible that an unstable Christian, jacked up on fear and hate, could have targeted the LGBTQ community. My first thought was, *I hope the shooter wasn't a Christian.*

As details emerged, it became clear that the shooter was not a Christian, and he had not deliberately targeted the LGBTQ community. None of this changed the impact of that moment for me. The tragedy of the Pulse shooting tore down a wall I had carefully constructed. When it stood, the wall kept me from feeling the pain, suffering, and rejection my church was causing. It helped me feel separate and complacent. When it fell, I was unable to tolerate our sins any longer.

I committed myself to a serious course of study. Something wasn't adding up; I was missing something. On the one hand, I knew who God was. I knew that being a Christian was not supposed to be easy, but it was supposed to be good. On the other hand, I knew people with same-sex attraction, people like me, were having a dramatically different experience of God and the church.

I also knew that same-sex marriage was equally capable of real love and commitment. It's not a sexual addiction or lust-crazed indulgence. Plenty of gay, bisexual, and transgender people live lives of integrity. For all the explanations I'd heard about why same-sex marriage is wrong, and for all the explanations I'd come up with myself, something was missing. How could love be a sin?

How do I reconcile all these things? A religion that promised one thing but delivered another to some of its members. A faith centered on love but opposed to relationships that seemed founded on love and commitment. A church that said it loved LGBTQ people, but I had been living a different reality for years.

There was a mystery here. As a pastor, I knew it was my responsibility to look for a better answer. I decided to thoroughly study the subjects of sexuality and gender as openly and objectively as I could.

I knew that God would lead me to greater truth, though I had no idea what that could be. I needed a solution. I needed a pastoral and theological solution that I could implement as a pastor. It was my responsibility, so I prayerfully and carefully began to study, willing to receive what God had for me.

It's good I was willing, because I never imagined the truth would demand so much.

THE COST OF CHANGE

When I finally engaged fully in the effort to understand, I was an Adventist pastor. Hard work and persistent faith were necessary ingredients, but I also knew my position was a gift directly from God. I knew I was where I belonged, and I was grateful. I had a fantastic church. My conference gave me wonderful support and unexpected opportunities. I appreciated them then, and I'm still grateful for the generosity they showed me in employment and when I had to resign.

For all these reasons, I didn't want to change my theology. The cost was too high. The attraction I experienced toward women was no longer overwhelming as it had been at first. Years of struggle had brought a kind of internal stalemate. I ignored those feelings, and they seemed far away. I was satisfied that I was doing just fine.

There was no way I wanted to give up everything I had worked for and the relationships I held so dear. Being attracted to men as well as women, I thought I could choose. It seemed insane to date women and risk everything I had. Even the thought felt strange, terrifying, and wrong. All my family was Adventist, all my friends were Adventist, and nearly every person I had any meaningful connection with was Adventist. Who would want to lose all that? In my mid-30s, I would be starting every aspect of my life over again from scratch.

On top of that, I believed the church was correct in its accepted theology of rejecting same-sex marriage. I'd read a couple books on the topic, all supporting this theology. Of course, I also read all the standard Bible verses. When it came up at seminary, I'd been satisfied with the basic theological ideas my professors taught. I had enormous respect for the intellect and compassion of my seminary professors, and they confirmed these beliefs. I had questions about how well they understood the LGBTQ community, but I respected their theological integrity.

So, I wasn't expecting a theological change, but unresolved dissonance plagued my mind and spirit. When the Pulse shooting happened, I couldn't push it aside any longer. LGBTQ people were suffering. Not only was the church not helping, we were making matters worse. My heart broke. I determined to understand the will of God for gay, bisexual, and transgender children of God.

Something was missing. There must be some mystery I didn't understand. Surely God would help me know what we could do to love these people better. I hoped and expected that whatever God revealed would be consistent with the accepted theology of the Adventist Church.

I began where I still believe everyone should begin, with studying affirming theology from those who believe it. Before we go about the difficult business of living up to our beliefs, we should vet those beliefs. I knew I hadn't—not as well as I should have. It was something I kept intending to get around to, so I would check that off the list first. Then I would get on to learning how to love LGBTQ people better.

I believed then, as I believe now, we can't go about the business of loving someone if we've never put in the effort to listen to them respectfully and thoroughly. I didn't think I would find affirming theology convincing. It was a shock when I did. After all this time in the Adventist Church, after turning my life upside down to become an Adventist pastor, I found myself in total disagreement in a way that threatened my very participation in the church.

Until then, I believed that if I ever came to a significant disagreement with the Adventist Church on a matter of theology, honestly owning up to my beliefs would be a simple matter of integrity. I would leave. I even thought it would be easier if I didn't believe in being Adventist. Being an Adventist can be challenging, especially when you're a woman in ministry. There is dysfunction, pain, stubbornness, and a fair dose of crazy on the fringe of this denomination I love.

There were days I thought, *wouldn't it be easier to walk away?* I now know the answer to that question. It's about as easy as cutting a limb from your body. At least it was for me. In some ways, I don't feel like I left. Maybe I didn't. Perhaps I'm still just an Adventist in exile, writing letters to the homeland, hoping someone will read them.

AN ADVENTIST VIEWPOINT

One summer, I was an Adventist pastor, pastoring my own church and enjoying the challenge and promise of local ministry. I led a Sabbath school class on basic Adventist doctrine. I preached regularly about why Adventism gives us a compelling and accurate picture of God. I supported the Adventist position on same-sex marriage. I was solidly in the fold.

The following spring, I came out openly and confidently as fully affirming and bisexual. As a result, I can never pastor in the Adventist Church again.

The battle that brought me there took place between summer and spring. The intervening months were a time of rapid change, filled with prayer, Bible study, and wave after wave of grief as it became clear that I was called to challenge the church I love.

The intensive study of those months made it impossible for me to continue in the church with the same legitimacy. Yet ironically, I only engaged in that study because of the values I learned as an Adventist member, pastor, and seminary graduate. The subsequent years in which I've delved deeper into these subjects build on that same foundation. I hope you can read this book in this spirit.

The Adventist Church opposes same-gender marriage and transgender identity, but that teaching is not part of the core belief system of the church. If we change that one belief, as I advocate in this book, there is no need to change any other belief. Opposition to same-sex marriage and transgender identity is not part of the baptismal vows. It's not integral to the structure of the belief system. Opposition is a second-tier theological conclusion, not a foundational assumption.

If I were to get the answer wrong on a math question, it would mean I made a mistake, not that math itself was to blame. Advocating for affirming same-gender marriage and transgender identity within a framework that is distinctly Adventist is entirely consistent. As such, you can expect an Adventist approach in this book:

- Scripture is honored as authoritative, relevant, and instructive for our lives today.
- Scripture is seen holistically, seeking to harmonize all of Scripture.
- The supernatural work of God and the reality of biblical accounts will not be questioned.
- The Law of God will be honored, not mocked or treated as irrelevant.
- Sexual ethics will encompass more than avoiding harm and ensuring consent, but also honoring the family, holding common values, having loyalty to each other, protecting one another, fairness and justice, holiness, sexual restraint, and the authority of God.
- Scripture will not be subject to modern culture but modern culture to Scripture.
- The ultimate goal is to understand and follow the will of God.

As you read each chapter, I hope that you will show me the generosity you would show any other Adventist, even if you disagree with me. I hope I will succeed in passing on some of the wisdom and theological insight I've worked so hard to gain. I hope you will find it helpful.

HOW TO READ THIS BOOK

This conversation is too often about scoring points or showing the absurdity of those who disagree with us. This is a reflection of the cultural moment in which we all live. Social media makes it easy to dismiss one another and rewarding to bombard our enemies with "truth bombs." It is essential to elevate the conversation above these dismissive tactics.

So, I wrote this book as a dialog. I start each chapter with two quotes. These quotes represent some of the most common reasons Christians oppose same-gender marriage and transgender identity. Some are actual quotes; some are my own words based on what I have read and heard many times. All represent common and sincere objections. Following the quotes, I've fleshed out and clarified the nature of those objections. I've worked hard to understand accurately and communicate fairly.

This also helps me elevate my communication. Writing this book was healing for me. It's helped me understand that even those who deeply hurt me didn't do so from malice. It held me accountable to integrity in communicating what my ideological counterparts are saying rather than being dismissive or inaccurate.

It helped me avoid constructing straw-man arguments or vague criticism. In short, it helped me respect, understand, and love those with whom I disagree consequentially and morally. This is the kind of dialog we need, and I hope I've made some contribution toward such ends.

This book may not be for everyone. I don't spend a lot of time debunking harmful stereotypes. Some still believe that sexual orientation is a choice and can be changed voluntarily or through treatment. Some see sexual minorities as fundamentally different from the rest of humanity. They see our sexuality in terms of sexual addiction or unrestrained desire. This book will not be compelling for such audiences because I spend very little time addressing these viewpoints.

Instead, this book is for those who see that gay, bisexual, and transgender people have the same flaws and virtue as the rest of humanity. Most of us care deeply about our communities and are asking for the same things others in the church already have. This book is written for those who won't disparage the LGBTQ community and won't ignore the Bible.

Readers should expect to be respected and never to have their motives or sincerity questioned. This is what I strove for, and all my early readers were quick to tell me I hit my mark. They reported being drawn to the consideration of ideas without feeling coerced or denigrated. I was happy to hear it because that was my goal.

NOTES ON WORD CHOICE

People in this book identified by first name only, unless otherwise clarified, are names that have been changed. I also routinely changed other identifying information so people could remain entirely anonymous. I sometimes compiled stories from incomplete recollections or took common occurrences and gave them a specific account for communication purposes. Though the details may be fictional, the substance is accurate.

I've had to make some choices about how to describe the two main sides of this debate (though in truth there are many more than two positions). Those who support same-gender marriage and transgender identity I have identified as "affirming theology." I am aware of objections to this word choice by those who contend that they affirm the humanity and equality of LGBTQ people, but not the behaviors of same-sex marriage or choices related to accepting a transgender identity. I've still chosen to use this phrasing for a couple of reasons:

First, I don't know of a better word. What better succinct summary is there? Second, most gay, bisexual, and transgender people believe that affirmation is the right word. Affirming our sexuality and gender in the same way cisgender heterosexual people are affirmed is (in the opinion of most of us) a necessary precursor to full affirmation of our humanity and equality in the view of most people in the LGBTQ community. So, in using this word, I am speaking from the perspective of the community.

I also want to be crystal clear: I recognize that those on the other side of the question often do their best to love and care for us. To clarify further, I have often opted to use a longer explanation throughout this book, speaking of affirmation in terms of affirming marriage and gender identity. I recognize that this answer won't be ideal for everyone.

The other side of the question was more difficult. Do I use the word "biblical"? No, because I'm making a biblical argument for affirmation. Do I use the word "conservative"? No, because conservative people can also be affirming. Do I use the phrase "non-affirming"? No, because that could be understood as a wholesale rejection of LGBTQ individuals.

Do I use the word "traditional"? That's probably the most common word choice, but I don't feel comfortable with it for a couple reasons. First, most hold their view in a way that isn't at all traditional. The idea that someone could be gay and celibate is not historical; it's a contemporary perspective. Throughout history, most people understood same-sex sexuality as sexual promiscuity, people roaming for new and exciting ways of degrading themselves under the complete control of lust. Historically, there was also no category for LGBTQ people. Today's Christians tend to recognize sexual orientation and not denigrate all LGBTQ people as sexual hedonists. So, I think they are too good for the word "traditional."

Second, using the word "traditional" seems a bit insulting, to be honest. Adventists hold that our theology comes from the Bible, not tradition. For those who are not Roman Catholics, this isn't about ecclesiastical authority but biblical interpretation. It's not our understanding of tradition but the Bible.

I settled on a word-choice that is not ideal, but I hope it is accurate: "accepted theology." I worry that this word sounds dismissive, and that's not my goal. This theology is accepted because it's what most conservative denominations and churches have accepted as true. I hope that it's a neutral word, that it insults no one, and that it accurately describes the present reality. This is the theology accepted by most conservative churches as biblical, and my goal is to communicate why some of us see a different conservative, biblical approach.

CHAPTER 1

Is the Bible Clear?

"The difference between you and me is that you think the Bible is hard to under-stand, and I think it's easy."

"It seemed very strange to us that if the Bible didn't teach anything certain about homosexual practice, then it didn't seem to us to teach anything certain about anything else. That anything the Bible taught could be subject to the oversight of whatever cultural winds or whims were blowing."[1]

This first quote is from a dear friend from college in response to my explanations of affirming theology. It may sound strange, but I can relate to her words. I've said similar words myself and in a similar situation.

It happened 15 years ago. A close friend, whom I'll call Ian, told me he was gay. Ian was and is a man I respect and even admire. I also had deep feelings for him. My heart was crushed and my mind was confused when he came out to me. We'd shared years of theology classes, served in the same ministries, prayed, and studied the Bible together. He was the last person I'd expect to tell me he was gay. Plus, I thought we were perfect for each other. I thought we could serve God together. Now he's telling me he's gay?

Questions and confusion crowded my thinking. How could this happen?

What did this mean for Ian? Was he going to leave God, too? What was God's will in all this? I took time to study and pray, reading any book that might help me make sense of a situation that seemed impossible.

Those books told me that homosexuality was a result of dysfunctional family dynamics, that it is often a result of sexual abuse, that it led to a life of disease and addiction, and that the only way to be whole and healthy was to address the problems underlying homosexuality. These books promised that, as same-sex attracted people healed, they would return to wholeness and heterosexuality. They would be the people God created them to be. They would be attracted to the opposite gender (even if some temptation remained).

This was the accepted understanding in conservative Christian churches back then. An abundance of testimonies from people who had once been gay and were now happily married to opposite-sex partners validated the perspective. There was strong institutional backing. Focus on the Family supported and promoted Exodus International, an umbrella organization for hundreds of ministries that promised change.

At the time, I didn't know about any of these connections. I only knew that when I tried to find a biblical Christian perspective on homosexuality, every source told me the Bible was clear and went on to elaborate on psychological theories of change. Warnings about the danger of homosexuality to destroy families and society were everywhere I looked.

Neither did I have a depth of understanding about Scripture or even the tools to understand Scripture that I have today. I don't remember ever addressing homosexuality in my undergraduate theology classes at Union College. When Ian came out to me, I was just googling and reading books, trying my best (without guidance from the Adventist Church) to understand what the Bible says.

But it's not only essential to understand what the Bible says, it's also necessary to know what we are asking of the text. On that point, I knew even less. Before Ian came out to me, I'd never had anyone tell me they were gay—not a friend, not a stranger, no one. It was difficult for me to understand. I'd known Ian for four years. After all our history together and countless conversations about God, I knew his sincerity.

But the books I read said homosexuality was brokenness—the result of trauma, sin, or both. They said it would lead to all kinds of dangerous and sinful behaviors. I began to worry about my friend.

Perhaps the most crucial bit of information I failed to understand at the time was that I am bisexual. I didn't fit these descriptions. My family life was remarkably stable and loving. I followed, loved, and trusted God in the halting, human way that all of us on the Christian journey do, sincerely with my whole heart.

Sadly, I didn't give Ian the same credit I gave myself. I say this to my shame. It was too easy to decide that his sexuality resulted from brokenness, that he could love women if he healed. I didn't handle it well. I was brokenhearted, confused, and afraid for him. I searched for and found what seemed to be the clarity I was seeking. I told him about the books I read and told him I thought he could change and should. I told him that the Bible seemed clear on the subject. Then I stopped talking to him.

Convictions backed up my actions. The Bible was clear. I'd poured over certain verses and sought texts that would give me clarity. I didn't want to guess. I didn't want to act from intuition, sympathy, or comfort. This is what I concluded based on my studies. It's basically the same conclusions I now hear from friends who push back on me since I've come out as bisexual.

1. The Bible says same-sex sex is wrong; therefore, all same-sex relationships are wrong, including marriage.
2. The Bible says marriage is between a man and a woman.
3. Gay people (and all people) must be celibate or marry someone of the opposite sex.[a]

BIBLICAL CONVICTION

How had I reached these three conclusions? When I began my study, I suspected that the church was wrong. A lot of that was probably because of my friend and the respect I had for him. I hoped that the Bible didn't condemn Ian's decisions after all. But I was disappointed.

---

a. When I originally asked the question, conservative churches almost universally understood that orientation could change and gay people should desire marriage to someone of the opposite sex. The change ministry, Exodus International, closed in 2013, admitting that people weren't changing. Many people still believe the failed promises of Exodus International and the conversion therapy movement, still teaching that prayer and correct treatment can remove the underlying psychological deficits that cause homosexuality. Coming Out Ministries is a prominent example of this in the Adventist Church. Through their examples, leaders of this ministry encourage LGBTQ people to accept psychosocial origins for their sexuality, origins rooted in Freudian psychoanalysis, to achieve healing and leave homosexuality. Yet more have moved on from this model, which amounts to conversion therapy. Many now recommend celibacy for gay people and require opposite-sex relationships only for bisexual people.

When I looked for biblical insights on the pro-inclusion side, they seemed to stretch the truth beyond breaking. They claimed that David and Jonathan were lovers, that Jesus and John the beloved were lovers, and that the Ethiopian eunuch was evidence for accepting same-sex relationships. None of it made sense to me.

I also noticed an unsettling theme. These perspectives didn't seem to take the Bible as seriously as I did. They seemed to be forming the text to their ideas, not being formed by the text. Instead of focusing on the author's intent, these liberal approaches focused on specific phrases, stretching them beyond what the author intended. For example, this verse of poetry from the future King David to Jonathan:

> I am distressed for you, my brother Jonathan; you have been very pleasant to me; your love to me was wonderful, surpassing the love of women (2 Sam. 1:26).[b]

Even at the time, as a young person with a theology degree, I could see that the literal words were being confused with the author's intent. Do the words sound romantic? Yes, but in context, they weren't. It's just not what we would expect historically. It *sounds* romantic on the face of it, but I didn't think we could believe that's what David meant. There is simply no biblical context for this kind of romance.

Other problems I encountered were vague claims about the importance of love. Scripture identifies love as the essential organizing idea, yet society uses love as a broad justification for almost anything. I knew love could not be sentimentalized and separated from the law and will of God.

And what about Creation? Didn't God create men and women for each other? Aren't we specifically designed to complement and fulfill each other? Aren't we also formed to procreate through sex?

Then there were other texts the proponents of same-sex relationships dismissed quickly.

> For this reason God gave them up to vile passions. For even their women exchanged the natural use for what is against nature. Likewise also the men, leaving the natural use of the woman, burned in their lust for one another, men with men committing what is shameful, and receiving in themselves the penalty of their error which was due (Rom. 1:26, 27).

---

b. Unless otherwise noted, all Bible texts come from the New King James Version.

I found these words from Paul compelling despite myself. They were the solid wall of scriptural truth preventing any movement in the direction of approving of my friend's "choice." I had to be faithful to Scripture. Scripture was clear: God must be obeyed.

DIFFICULT QUESTIONS

What is strange to me now is that I didn't stop to ask myself the same questions of Romans 1 that I had asked of 2 Samuel 1. Caught up in the face value of the verse in Romans, I had quickly dismissed the face value of David's apparent love poem to Jonathan.

Why not ask the same questions of Paul's words in Romans? What did Paul intend? Did he intend to condemn same-sex marriage? Was there such an equivalent of same-sex marriage in their society? What did he mean? What was the cultural understanding behind his words? I didn't ask. I chose the face value of one text and rejected the face value of another without any apparent reason.

Had I paid better attention to context, there's no guarantee that I would have affirmed same-sex marriage. There is no automatic conclusion that paying attention to context makes a person affirming. What strikes me now is not my conclusions. My inadequate study of Scripture strikes me. "The Bible is clear." That phrase quenched my thirst for Scripture.

Frankly, I'm not alone. I picked up on what others were doing. Anytime someone dismisses affirming theology as "liberal," they are doing the same thing. They say that affirming theology can't possibly be a reasonable conclusion for anyone who believes in the authority of Scripture. They say that they don't need to consider a liberal perspective carefully. It's just another way of saying, "The Bible is clear."

Now that I've become much more familiar with the topic, it's plain that conservative Christians fail to adequately wrestle with Scripture and the possibility of same-sex marriage or transgender identity. That's not okay. It's not an affirmation of the authority of Scripture but an abdication of our responsibility to search the Scriptures. God is not pleased when we say Scripture is clear and use that as a reason not to look more closely.

I hope this book can help elevate the biblical conversation. I hope conservative Christians can see the significance and legitimacy of theology that affirms same-sex marriage and transgender identity. It's not enough to acknowledge that we *should* look more closely at Scripture. We must *actually* look at Scripture more closely.

It's hard to do. It was hard to break out of traditional interpretations when surrounded by people who didn't challenge me. It was hard to consider that we could all be wrong. How could all these intelligent, compassionate, biblically minded, deeply spiritual Adventist pastors, scholars, and students of Scripture miss something so important?

My immediate circle had no reason to go deeper. There was resistance to challenging accepted doctrine or even talking about it. Being in such an environment soothed my doubts. It was easy to believe that I already understood all I needed to understand. The slight sense of guilt, guilt that I hadn't studied deeply enough, was easy to dismiss. I'd studied it more than most. I even had good intentions to study more. That was enough to placate my conscience and help me deny what I knew deep down; I hadn't studied for myself. Not really.

A REASON TO ASK

For a long time, nothing happened. I didn't think about it, and the whole incident was in the past. Then little things happened here and there. People I met or situations I observed raised questions. I still didn't study. I experienced my own attraction to women, and still I studied only a little and didn't seek out opposing views.

I didn't get serious until something serious happened that fateful night when a disturbed man killed 49 people as he terrorized a gay nightclub in Florida. The conversation that followed among my Adventist friends on social media clarified a few points for me.

First, we have many gun tragedies in the United States, but what I observed after this one was unique. Adventists felt a sense of pride for extending words of condolence or offering to do funerals for the victims. They would pass such statements around social media and even verbally praise each other for being "loving."

This was strange. It never happened after other mass shootings. No one ever felt proud to offer basic condolences to other victims. Neither did it seem impressive that churches were offering not to charge families for funerals. It seemed inconceivable that any church would charge a family to use their facilities after a national tragedy. Why was this situation different? The answer seemed all too clear. What would have been ordinary acts of solidarity were not taken for granted when the victims were at a gay nightclub. Common compassion was considered exceptional for these victims. The baseline was lower, so we felt pride over the smallest gesture.

Second, this seemed like an opportunity for Adventists to reflect on their complicity and discrimination toward gay, bisexual, and transgender people. Christians are often complicit, if not directly responsible, for this discrimination. Nothing could be further from the gospel, the character of Jesus, or the law's intention than the way Christians often treat gay, bisexual, and transgender people.

This seemed like an opportunity for self-reflection, repentance, and a renewed commitment to loving all people. Many Adventists I knew were already aware that there were problems. So, why were we not wrestling with our demons? Why were we congratulating ourselves for doing the bare minimum? I couldn't understand why we weren't addressing our stigma towards this community.

You could disagree. You might think stigma is uncommon in the Adventist Church. I understand that. The reason stigma was real to me is that my own same-sex attraction made me pay attention. I watched for signs. Was my denomination a safe place for me? Could I be understood and respected if people knew the truth about me? Or did I need to conceal this with every tool at my disposal?

With such questions in mind, I noticed every time I was told gay people were sex addicts, promiscuous, or a sign that the world is more sinful than it's ever been.[c] Gay, bisexual, and transgender people were usually described in precisely these terms. I heard stories of sex and drug addicts, of men who died of AIDS, and of people who renounced their "gay lifestyle" after decades of pain and disappointment.

No one talked about well-adjusted LGBTQ people living lives of productivity and happiness. Nor had I ever met anyone in the church who was openly gay and celibate. The picture my church painted was grim and full of stigma. I never heard people like me spoken of as well-adjusted and honorable. I could tell that there would be a lot of suspicion about me if I came out.

Third, I learned something about myself. This was personal for me. Even though I'd never set foot in a gay bar, I intuitively understood that gay bars were their places of safety. I felt the desecration of the violence in the very place where marginalized people felt most accepted. My visceral reaction was the same as the reactions of those in the LGBTQ community. The responses from churches felt just as empty to me.

For the first time in my life, I felt a real connection to the LGBTQ community. They didn't feel like enemies or aliens anymore. Even though I was completely separate, I suddenly realized that I was one of them, at least in some

---

c. I don't think it makes sense to argue that accepting gay marriage is worse than slavery, the genocide of Native Americans, or mass incarceration.

sense. Shared sexual orientation isn't what connected me; it was the shared experience of rejection from church and society. I didn't know what to do with that. It made me more than a little uncomfortable. It didn't change my beliefs at all. It didn't make me want to leave the Adventist Church or stop being a pastor. But it was the beginning of something.

Finally, with all these factors weighing on my mind, I knew it was time for thorough study and prayer. This time I would not allow myself to be easily satisfied. I would seek the will of God with all my heart, mind, and soul. I would seek that I might find. I would be willing to follow.

OPENNESS

Looking back, it's clear. My belief that "the Bible is clear" was standing in the way of understanding the Bible. It caused me to close my Bible on this subject instead of opening it. It didn't drive me toward greater understanding but to stagnation.

Some Christians work from a biblical basis to build the case for affirming theology. James Brownson, Matthew Vines, Kathy Baldock, Austen Hartke, and Megan DeFranza are important examples. Yet every Adventist book, publication, and statement I've read (and I've read everything I can get my hands on) refers to same-gender marriage affirmation and transgender affirmation as liberal. The arguments that they address are liberal ones. They often set up an explicit dichotomy between believing the Bible and supporting same-sex marriage and transgender identity.

From what I can tell, Adventist theologians have never read conservative affirming theology or considered its arguments. They certainly don't interact with these concepts meaningfully. I've seen only one reference to any of these authors, and the engagement was sadly superficial.[2] It's hard to believe, but it's true: Adventist engagement on this topic has been woefully inadequate. I hope this will change.

Adventists should carefully consider affirming theology. My education tells me that it doesn't oppose Adventist theology. Conservative principles of interpretation I learned at seminary are the same ones that apply to affirming theology. I have never had to take a liberal stance, disregard Scripture, or treat the text any differently than conservatives already do on other subjects to become fully affirming.

For some, that statement will sound as bizarre and unlikely as it would have sounded to me a few years ago. I get it. If you are anything like I was, your experience and knowledge of the text make it sound absurd. But further study was nothing short of shocking and disorienting. I realized how much we missed in our study of this topic.

We Adventists too often wear our biblical certainty as armor. We use it to protect ourselves from ideas that might threaten us. The result is that we protect ourselves from biblical knowledge itself. When I finally began studying, conservative principles of biblical interpretation fit perfectly with affirming theology.

Why had these same principles used for other topics never been considered for gay, bisexual, and transgender Adventists? In accepted theology, I found considerable leaps in logic. They were forcing texts about sexual assault or promiscuity onto the question of same-sex marriage, smoothing over differences instead of acknowledging them. There was very little wrestling with the text and the difficulties of applying it today.

I also found a darker side of accepted theology. Far too often, there was a mischaracterization of LGBTQ people. We were characterized as craven sex addicts, controlled by our impulses and worshiping at the altar of desire. Too often, the mischaracterization made it possible to apply texts about sexual exploitation or indulgence to all gay, bisexual, and transgender people. Not all theologians did this, but enough did to make me deeply concerned that some of our theology might be based on more than Scripture.

SEMINARY

Few experiences in life have been more disorienting than losing faith in accepted theology. It was about more than questioning a theological belief but about the system that produced that belief and the people who expounded it. The authors I was beginning to question were not unknown to me. Many of them were people I knew personally. Many of them were my heroes.

I got to know them while studying for a Masters of Divinity from the Seventh-day Adventist Theological Seminary at Andrews University. When getting my degree, I spent as much time as I could in the Biblical Studies departments, learning how to understand the Bible. I got to know many of the people whose work I critique in this book. They are people with deep compassion, kindness, and love for Scripture. To this day, I can't question their sincerity and commitment.

Even though I have critiques to offer, I can never lose my respect for these generous and intelligent people. They mentored and cared for me. They are brilliant theologians who dedicate their lives to understanding the text.

So, the question must be asked: why did I see things they didn't? I could never actually know the answer to such a personal question. But I have observed something helpful. When someone starts reading the *whole* Bible, it raises a lot of questions. We encounter slavery, genocide, violent tribalism, sexual assault, and all manner of challenging topics and moral problems. Serious students of Scripture are aware of this.

So, what do we do? Too often, we just ignore these texts. But my seminary professors weren't content with that approach. We learned to read the Bible better. We learned to understand the intent of Scripture and the movement of God to a better world. We learned to read the Bible not as detached verses recruited for proof-texting but as a cogent whole. I learned these things in seminary from the professors I was now questioning for not fully applying these principles.

In my conversion to affirming theology, every principle of interpretation I used was one I learned in seminary. Not one time did I use a method of interpretation that isn't already considered conservative when applied to other subjects. But it's easy to apply these tools to matters we already believe to be ethically wrong, like slavery or genocide. It's tough to use these tools when doing so cuts across the grain; it doesn't seem right because it goes against our established beliefs.

When we talked about slavery, the nuance was deep and the contextualization careful and thorough. When we talked about genocide in the Old Testament, the moral questions were complex and the textual detail intricate. Motivations, meaning, the movement of Scripture, the character of God, and ultimately the primacy of love and justice took center stage.

Yet when we talked about gay, bisexual, and transgender people, the nuance vanished. Instead, we spoke starkly, almost mathematically, about laws and behaviors stripped of cultural meaning. That it was consistently forbidden was enough.

There were questions we failed to ask or only brushed over. What was happening then that demanded a restriction? Who are gay, bisexual, and transgender Adventists now? What did the author want us to take away from the text, and how does that apply today? How did these laws reflect the character of God and the loving intent of Scripture? Questions about context, intent, and application were scarcely imagined. These were nuances we failed to acknowledge.

I know some will say that focusing on the plain meaning of laws is enough, especially when the laws all point in the same direction, in this case, towards prohibition. They will say that a deep, scholarly study of Scripture is dangerous. They prefer simplicity. They think academics are too liberal and susceptible to manipulation. They believe the whole problem is that these academics use cultural context for any interpretation of Scripture. They want a plain reading of every text. They think that by taking the plain meaning of a text, they can avoid interpretation.

But I've never seen these folks look honestly at morally difficult texts. Ironically, they dismiss these texts with superficial disregard. I've never seen them wrestle with understanding the Bible. I've only seen them proof-texting and explaining away or skipping over what's uncomfortable. If we want to avoid nuance and complexity, we must carefully ignore large portions of Scripture. If we ignore large portions of Scripture, we don't care about the Bible as much as we might think.

Questioning and learning is hard work, emotionally and intellectually. But why should we expect mining the Scriptures to be easy? I've returned to the text repeatedly, testing each idea against what I found in my Bible. I've compared Scripture with Scripture, struggling to understand the author's intent and the will of God. I've read all sorts of opinions and analyses. I've mined the original language and the cultural context. I've gone back again and again and done my best to be open. I'm still doing it. I'm trying to stay open and maintain curiosity. This is precisely what I believe God wants from us. Sadly, this rigor was missing when my seminary professors talked about sexuality and gender.

We can do better. Above all, we must pray for guidance. We must be mindful of God's love for all people, especially those impacted by our theology. Staying open to the Spirit is not easy on a topic so consequential. The Bible changed everything for me. I trembled as I turned pages infused with the potential to change my life and the lives of others. We must read Scripture through the Inspiration of the Spirit.

PEOPLE OF THE BOOK

My conversion to affirming theology through the study of Scripture may be the most Adventist thing I've ever done. Adventists are born of a movement that exists only through independent and relentless study of Scripture. The unique doctrines of the Adventist Church are a result of setting aside tradition in favor of biblical inquiry.

Starting as early as William Miller's conversion in 1816, the Bible was the hallmark of our movement in its early days. By studying the Bible with fresh eyes, we learned that the human soul is not immortal, the Sabbath is the seventh day, and the Sabbath commandment is still valid. We rejected views such as the rapture and adopted prophetic insights based on close examination of the text.

Our founders accomplished something extraordinary. This spirit of open biblical inquiry is perhaps the most critical Adventist value. Only because of this core virtue were we able to discover truths in Scripture that were obscured for centuries.

To be Adventist is to believe that traditional theology should never be taken for granted. To be Adventist is to be unsatisfied with easy proclamations about the clarity of Scripture and the value of continuing to believe the doctrine we have always believed. To be Adventist is to be willing to test every teaching against Scripture, even our teachings. *Especially* our teachings.

Ellen White reflected on the origins of the Adventist church, and lamented how far the church had strayed from these values even in her day. She wrote an article on the subject for *The Review and Herald*, July 26, 1982, that is worth reading in its entirety. Here is an excerpt:

> Long-cherished opinions must not be regarded as infallible. . . . Those who sincerely desire truth will not be reluctant to lay open their positions for investigation and criticism, and will not be annoyed if their opinions and ideas are crossed. This was the spirit cherished among us forty years ago. We would come together burdened in soul, praying that we might be one in faith and doctrine; for we knew that Christ is not divided. One point at a time was made the subject of investigation. Solemnity characterized these councils of investigation. The Scriptures were opened with a sense of awe. Often we fasted, that we might be better fitted to understand the truth. After earnest prayer, if any point was not understood, it was discussed, and each one expressed his opinion freely; then we would again bow in prayer, and earnest supplications went up to heaven that God would help us to see eye to eye, that we might be one, as Christ and the Father are one.

Ellen White's masterpiece, *The Great Controversy*, is nothing if not a record of the persistent willingness of God's people to question assumptions and authority, to discover anew the truths that God has been waiting for us to find. From the Waldensians to Luther to Zwingli to Wesley to Miller to those faithful followers of Jesus at the end of time, God's people are willing to go against the grain of traditional Christianity for the sake of faithfulness.

PEOPLE OF THE BOOK?

Have Adventists behaved like Adventists when it comes to same-gender marriage? Have we acted Adventist in our beliefs about gender identity?

Institutional leaders resist open consideration of affirming theology. Even when I check back through decades in my search, I can't find a single example of an institutionally supported, sympathetic explanation of affirming theology. Not one article. Not one institutionally endorsed sermon. Each time the church gathered to discuss sexual minorities or transgender people, traditional theology was explicitly assumed from the beginning and defended to the end. The institution isn't open to the possibility that it could be wrong. If we aren't open to our own fallibility, we can't trust our conclusions. That's what's happening right now on an institutional level.

The first official statement was in the 1985 *Church Manual*. The statement paired "homosexuality and lesbianism" with adultery as "obvious perversions of God's original plan." General Conference (GC) leaders at the 1987 Annual Council voted a similar statement, but this time added premarital sex, sexual obsession, abusive sex, incest, and pedophilia to the list of comparisons. They again used the phrase "obvious perversions." Similar statements were made in 1996. As same-sex marriage became a topic of national debate, the *Church Manual* was revised in 1999. The new statement was longer and stronger. It referred to creation, the lack of same-sex couples in the Bible, and biblical prohibitions.[3]

The election of Ted N. C. Wilson as General Conference president led to a more vocal stance by the church. The GC Executive Committee made the strongest statement yet in 2012, "Homosexuality is a manifestation of the disturbance and brokenness in human inclinations." In 2015 the Seventh-day Adventist Theological Seminary made a statement differentiating sexual orientation from behavior, welcoming all people, and welcoming sexual minorities to full participation if they follow the sexual ethics of abstaining from same-sex relationships in any capacity, including marriage.[4]

Administrators voted for all these statements. None were a result of an intentional study of both positions. Indeed, many indicate that this is an "obvious" matter and that there should be no two ways of thinking of the subject.[d] No statement was made on transgender identity until 2017.

The church sponsored two conferences on the topic of homosexuality. One was at Andrews University in 2009 and the other in Cape Town, South Africa, in 2014. At the Andrews University conference, one presentation was supportive of legalizing same-gender marriage. Other than this one presentation, every

---

d. A review of these statements and much more can be found in Ronald Lawson's exceptional four-part series, "The Adventist Church and It's LGBT Members." The first part is available at: spectrummagazine.org/news/2021/adventist-church-and-its-lgbt-members-part-1

theological, testimonial, and legal presentation was made in opposition to same-gender marriage. That one supportive presentation was excluded from the book published later based on the conference's presentations. In other words, there was no desire to consider alternate perspectives.

Opening comments by Nicholas Miller, a professor of Church History at the Seventh-day Adventist Theological Seminary, indicated that the purpose of the conference was to show that accepted theology is not only correct but also good. Mark Yarhouse, then a psychology professor at Regent University and one of the plenary speakers, agreed. "It was not so much a dialogue among people with radically different perspectives. In fact, with the exception of one panel that had one dissenting voice, it seemed to me that the conference provided more of an update and points of discussion for primarily conservatives within the community."[5]

In 2014, the church gathered in Cape Town, South Africa, for a summit addressing homosexuality. The conference was full of influential leaders and scholars from around the world, with at least 20 people from each of the 13 global divisions of the church. This conference was not to study the Bible or submit preconceptions to Scripture. The Adventist News Network clarified: "The summit organizers are clear that they intend no redefinition of the Church's historic opposition to all sexual expression other than heterosexual marriage between one man and one woman."[6]

If we begin with a theological assumption and double down for decades, critiquing that perspective through institutional channels becomes impossible. Fidelity to accepted theology is a requirement of employment.[7] Affirming theology simply hasn't had a hearing.

Where do we begin if we want to study this topic openly? Of course, when you bring people together with the precondition that they believe same-gender marriage and transgender identity are wrong, they will conclude that these things are wrong. It's an exercise in coming up with better reasons for the same predetermined conclusion. Even those who disagree face every incentive to keep their mouths shut.

Dwight Nelson, the long-time pastor of Pioneer Memorial Church and my preaching professor at the seminary, was asked about this in a seminary forum. What are we to do about those who believe same-gender marriage is biblical? Pastor Nelson was adamant that there is no room for theological difference. "Incredible scholarship has ascertained [that] we can stand here, with a univocal testimony."[8]

He shared his experience on the committee of 104 people who studied women's ordination. The church had intentionally brought together people on both sides. There was robust disagreement about whether to ordain women.

According to Nelson, the same was not true of same-sex marriage. He said everyone was unequivocally against same-gender marriage. There was only one mind among them on the matter.

When I heard this claim, I was skeptical. I looked over the list of 104 people and was more skeptical. So, I reached out to someone I know from the committee, and here's what I found: No such question was asked of each of these 104 people. If people had been free to share their viewpoints about same-gender marriage and transgender identity, there would have been disagreement. Nelson just wasn't aware of it.

This is what I expected to hear. I know people who are affirming at every level of leadership in the Adventist Church. I know many affirming pastors and teachers, seminary professors, administrators, and some well-known names in the church. A high-ranking Adventist administrator told a transgender friend of mine that they have no problem with transgender identity or medical transitioning.

Why does Dwight Nelson draw such a different conclusion? Why does he say there is no disagreement? My experience as a student of his was overwhelmingly positive. He is a sincere, dedicated, and intelligent man. Neither is he lacking in courage or conviction. He's not lying. This is simply the way he experienced the conference. No one told him any different. The scholars at Andrews University confirm this for him.

I could understand skepticism of the claim that many in the Adventist church are quietly affirming. Could I be making it all up? I have no way to confirm it without threatening people's livelihood, and this is precisely the problem. How can you rely on institutional agreement on a subject unless there is freedom of expression?

The situation is opaque because the institution forbids employees from sharing freely, particularly in public. At the committee Nelson referenced, it seems likely that the environment didn't encourage or solicit alternative perspectives on same-sex marriage or transgender identity. Because we haven't fostered free expression on this subject, our uniformity has little persuasive value.

How did we get here? It happened innocently enough. There were no nefarious characters in this story. There's no inquisition. In fact, because they do care, the Adventist Church in North America is making a good-faith effort to treat LGBTQ people better. But theological change remains taboo and organizationally threatening. It's a particular problem with how institutions work. It's difficult for them to self-correct and self-critique once they've taken a strong position.

This isn't all bad. It makes sense to conclude a theological matter after vigorous study. The Adventist Church did so with all her core theological tenets. But there has been no such study on same-sex marriage and transgender identity.

There has been no attempt to bring various viewpoints into the open for robust discussion. There has been no hard look at the possibility that we could be wrong.

How can a church that claims to be standard-bearers of biblical fidelity, which proudly proclaims no creed but the Bible, and which strives for the reputation of "people of the book," feel free to adopt theology without studying the Bible first? Why are they unwilling to do what William Miller did? Where do we find the confidence to say the Scripture is clear and dismiss the concerns of gay, bisexual, and transgender Adventists?

We are behaving as traditionalists. We are failing to center on Scripture. How can we in good conscience hope other Christians will re-examine closely held beliefs and accept our views if we don't do the same in our own church? How can we challenge others about the Sabbath, the state of the dead, the prophetic interpretations of Daniel and Revelation, and the ministry of Ellen White? How could we ever ask others to question their long-standing beliefs if we are closed to questioning our own?

Theological humility is needed, and not just on October 22. This is true both as individuals and corporately as a denomination. Humility doesn't happen easily. It begins by refusing to say, "the Bible is clear," and replacing that instead with biblical curiosity.

If you're still not convinced, if you still think it's entirely obvious, I will share one more story. Something interesting happened early in the Adventist Church's history with gay, bisexual, and transgender people. It was in the 1970s. The church hadn't yet made a single theological statement on sexual orientation. But the gay liberation movement was underway, and gay Adventists began finding one another. They formed a network that eventually became Seventh-day Adventist Kinship International (sdakinship.org). In 1979 they held their first gathering, called "Kampmeeting."

At the time, the church hadn't done much to advise gay people about living as faithful Adventists; so Kinship asked for help. Ronald Lawson reached out to the New Testament, Old Testament, and Theology departments of the Seventh-day Adventist Theological Seminary at Andrews University and two other pastors. Lawson asked them to study the Scriptures and give spiritual guidance based on this study. Kinship was open to hearing what they had to say and placed no restrictions on their conclusions.

Their advice? "Homosexuals, like heterosexuals, [are] called to faithfulness within a committed relationship and to chastity outside of such a relationship. The biblical proscriptions were the same for homosexuals as for heterosexuals: sexual exploitation, promiscuity, rape, and temple prostitution."[9]

I didn't learn about this until recently. After all the times people have told me I'm twisting Scripture, I felt vindicated. The first time Adventist scholars studied this topic, they concluded essentially the same thing I concluded in my study. They were affirming. Maybe accepted theology is not so obvious after all.[10]

A letter-writing campaign to the General Conference was organized in opposition to these scholars even attending Kinship Kampmeeting. People were concerned that their association implied support. I can only imagine how incensed they would have been if they'd known the theological conclusions of these scholars. Adventists just weren't ready to hear it.[11]

BASIC ADVENTISM

The institutional Adventist Church has struggled to live up to its values. Biblical curiosity is an Adventist value. Rather than relying on tradition, Adventists believe in progressive revelation and present truth. We say we will never stop learning, that there will always be more.

Ellen White wrote: "We shall never reach a period when there is no increased light for us" (*Advent Review and Sabbath Herald*, June 3, 1890). "In every age there is a new development of truth, a message of God to the people of that generation. The old truths are all essential; new truth is not independent of the old, but an unfolding of it" (*Christ's Object Lessons*, p. 127).

This doesn't mean that everything is up for grabs. Some doctrines are here to stay. These doctrines are called landmarks or pillars. They are foundational to Adventist belief and are historically the original revelations that gave rise to the Seventh-day Adventist Church. Ellen White is not vague about these truths but states them plainly.

> The passing of the time in 1844 was a period of great events, opening to our astonished eyes the cleansing of the sanctuary transpiring in heaven, and having decided relation to God's people upon the earth, [also] the first and second angels' messages and the third, unfurling the banner on which was inscribed, 'The Commandments of God and the faith of Jesus.' One of the landmarks under this message was the temple of God, seen by His truth-loving people in heaven, and the ark containing the law of God. The light of the Sabbath of the fourth commandment flashed its strong rays in the pathway of the transgressors of God's law. The nonimmortality of the wicked is an old landmark. I can call to mind nothing more that can come under the head of the old landmarks (Manuscript 13 1889).

There is no mystery about the original theological foundations of the Adventist Church. That's important for our current discussion. The early Adventist Church certainly did not affirm same-sex marriage or transgender identity, but neither was it opposed. Ellen White never said a word about it. It simply was not an essential part of the faith. Awareness of sexual orientation was new in Ellen White's time, and few had any concept of it.

Ellen White's quote here outlines the landmarks, beliefs that should never change, also known as "pillars" of the Adventist faith: (1) Salvation by faith in the righteousness of Christ; (2) the heavenly sanctuary; (3) the seventh-day Sabbath; (4) the state of the dead; (5) the three angels' messages; (6) the Second Coming; and (7) the Spirit of Prophecy.[12]

If the Adventist Church became fully affirming of same-gender marriage and transgender identity tomorrow, it would pose no threat to the theological pillars of Adventism. It would pose a danger politically and to the financial stability of the church, but not to its theological pillars. There is nothing inherently non-Adventist about same-sex marriage in terms of our foundational doctrines.

It's down to whether the accepted theology is better biblically or whether affirming theology is better. That's a question that needs to be studied. Considering our doctrine of present truth and progressive revelation, it's about time we seriously cracked open our Bibles.

I don't expect the institutional church will do so. There are reasons the church never has, and those reasons are still present. It has already committed to another course and has set out to prove this perspective. Seminary teachers are required to sign a statement saying they oppose affirmation of same-gender marriage.[13] Educators and pastors risk losing their jobs because of church standards that require fidelity to doctrinal statements. Any church-wide discussion is prefaced by reaffirming those doctrines before the discussion even begins.

At present, I'm not sure the church is ready to study this subject in a balanced way. Employees have position statements and requirements to follow. It's gone on for so long that I'm afraid any dissenters have been silenced or excluded. Ellen White warned about the danger of such a situation:

> The fact that there is no controversy or agitation among God's people, should not be regarded as conclusive evidence that they are holding fast to sound doctrine. There is reason to fear that they may not be clearly discriminating between truth and error.
>
> When no new questions are started by investigation of the Scriptures, when no difference of opinion arises which will set men to searching the Bible for themselves, to make

sure that they have the truth, there will be many now, as in ancient times, who will hold to tradition, and worship they know not what (*Gospel Workers*, p. 298).

Not long after coming out, I discussed this with a friend who is also an Adventist pastor. I challenged him about the reality that the Adventist church says it bases its theology on the Bible but has not studied this subject thoroughly. He said there was no point because the church would conclude against it no matter what, and it would be a political disaster. Church members would never accept it. People would withhold their tithe and offerings.

That's the sad reality, and church administrators are aware of it. But that's not what we are telling gay kids growing up in our churches. That's not the message we are sending to transgender children struggling with the fundamental nature of their existence. We tell them, "The Bible is clear" even though we've never considered the possibility that we could be wrong.

This situation may be our reality, but it is an abdication of Adventist values, not their expression. When someone says we do not need to consult the Bible, they aren't honoring the Bible or Adventism. We have our theological pillars, but outside of this, there is room for new understanding, progressive revelation, and even doctrinal change. As Ellen White says:

> There is no excuse for anyone in taking the position that there is no more truth to be revealed, and that all our expositions of Scripture are without an error. The fact that certain doctrines have been held as truth for many years by our people is not a proof that our ideas are infallible. Age will not make error into truth, and truth can afford to be fair. No true doctrine will lose anything by close investigation.[14]

In truth, "The Bible is clear" is an approach to Scripture that has never led to deeper study. It's a phrase intended to close Bibles, not open them. It's motivated by self-satisfied confidence that we already understand the Bible and need not study further. Besides, if the Bible is clear, there would be no threat to looking at it more closely on this subject. Learning more would only enhance this clarity, but that is never what I've found on this subject. In reality, "the Bible is clear" is not a phrase intended to affirm the authority of Scripture. It's a cliché designed to terminate thought and keep our Bibles closed.

Writing this book is the best way I know to move forward. The institutional church is simply not ready to have the conversation, but so many of us are. Many have questions and want to delve deeper into a biblical understanding of sexuality. This book will help us do so.

HAVE THE CONVERSATION

As you read, I trust that you won't change our views simply because I did. You won't take my word for it when speaking of what the Bible says. You will read, pray, and wrestle for yourself.

I know that my theology is not unique. I know a lot of gay, bisexual, and transgender Adventists who have fully reconciled their biblical faith with their sexuality and gender. I also know many heterosexual, cisgender Christians who support us. Many Adventist pastors quietly support this cause, and many don't.

Because the church has become so institutionalized, I don't believe we can count on the scholars and leaders of the church to broker an open inquiry on the topic. Employees could lose their jobs for trying to do so. That means it's up to church members. It's up to us. Conversations need to happen between us, our friends, and our fellow church members in small groups and local communities.

That's why I wrote this book. I hope it can help us have a better conversation, even though we won't all agree at the end of the day. For Adventists, careful study of Scripture is not optional, and tradition is not a compelling reason for belief.

What I hope for my church, even for those who reach the end of this book and think I'm wrong, is a revived passion for the Bible and a steady refusal to take it for granted. I hope we can all see how important it is to keep studying and learning from God.

As you read, I believe you will realize that the deeper you go, the more reasons there are for accepting affirming theology. When we look at specifics about scriptural context, cultural context, consistency in interpretation, historical teachings, and the original language, we will find that the case for affirming theology becomes stronger and stronger.

Let's begin at the beginning, Genesis 1 and 2. This is where humanity and marriage both have their origin, but we've been far too inconsistent in interpreting and applying these first two chapters of the Bible.

CHAPTER 2

Marriage, the Sabbath, and Creation

> *"The texts I believe that speak both clearly and strongly against same-gender sexuality are those in Genesis that describe the creation of humanity (male and female) and the institution of marriage."*

> *"God designed marriage from the beginning to be between one man and one woman, to fit together sexually and to make babies. We can't make marriage whatever we want it to be. There is no such thing as a marriage between two women or two men."*

Key to the moral reasoning of the accepted view of sexual orientation is the conviction that heterosexual marriage is rooted in creation. God established the definition of marriage at the beginning: one man, one woman. Following God's will is simply a matter of faithfulness to God's established order and plan for humanity.

This view is critical to Seventh-day Adventists, one of the few Christian denominations that keeps the seventh-day Sabbath modeled in Eden. Creation is the starting point, the moment at which all was "very good" and shining in the light of holiness. There was no shame, no sin, no brokenness. It is this state to which God's people will one day return.

The importance of Eden echoes throughout Scripture. The holy and most holy places of the sanctuary include symbols of creation. The Song of Songs is full of the language of the garden; Jesus Himself prays in the garden before being sent to the cross. It's no accident that Jesus is mistaken for a gardener after the resurrection. Revelation is full of references to Creation, the Garden of Eden, the Tree of Life, and the River of Life.

This grand narrative of Scripture that begins in the first two chapters of the Bible concludes dramatically in the last two. Revelation 21 and 22 tell of the return to a new Eden. The New Earth will bear the marks of the original creation. Once more, the Tree of Life will stand with roots sunk deep into the River of Life. This is Eden restored, but this time with the Lamb of God and the great city, New Jerusalem.

Bookending the whole Bible is the perfect creation and the perfect recreation. The rest of the story is about how we lost and regained paradise. For now, we are caught in the middle.

In this middle space, everywhere are reverberations of Eden and foreshadows of heaven. But the fullness eludes us. Life has a not-quite-satisfying quality. We are torn between the lives we are created for and the reality we are living. This is the story of people expelled from Eden and waiting for New Jerusalem.

These are the lives we have, and we must do our best to live them well. What does it mean to live them well? If Eden teaches us what it means to be fully human, it gives us a worthwhile path to follow. We should model ourselves after paradise, becoming like Adam and Eve. When it comes to marriage, as the over-done joke puts it, it's Adam and Eve, not Adam and Steve.

There are also references to creation in the central statement of Revelation, from which we gain our identity as Adventists. The seal of God is for those who continue to "worship Him who made heaven and earth, the sea and springs of water" (Rev. 14:7).

Adventists know this worship to be closely associated with the Sabbath. The Sabbath is the weekly celebration of creation. It also memorializes redemption (Deut. 5:12-15) and the grace we receive from God when we rest from our works (Heb. 4:1-7).

The Sabbath affirms that it matters how the world was created. Just as creation shows how vital the Sabbath is, the Sabbath shows how vital creation is. Adventists emphasize creation more than most Christians. When God laid the foundations of the earth, God also laid the foundation of the Sabbath. Ellen White wrote:

I was shown that if the true Sabbath had been kept there would never have been an infidel or an atheist. The observance of the Sabbath would have preserved the world from idolatry (*Testimonies for the Church*, Vol. 1, p. 76).

This close connection between creation, the Sabbath, redemption, and our prophetic identity as Adventists means we do not ignore the Creation narrative. We find our identity in Genesis 1 and 2. I'm not speaking only of our identity as Adventists, but our identity as humans.

When I was a literature evangelist, I had frequent conversations with all kinds of people about doctrine and theology. I often referred to the first two chapters of Genesis because so many of our doctrines are found there. The Sabbath is in Genesis 2. Genesis 1 tells us the origin of the world. The true nature of the soul—not an immortal spirit but a body animated by the breath of God—is explained in Genesis 2:7. It's even true that Adam and Eve ate a vegetarian diet (Gen. 2:9).

So, while it may be easy for others to set Genesis 1 and 2 aside, not so with Adventists, there are layers of meaning and importance for us. When an Adventist like Richard Davidson, a professor of Old Testament at the Seventh-day Adventist Theological Seminary, highlights the importance of Eden, we take notice:

Only two institutions have come down to us from the Garden of Eden: the Sabbath and marriage. It is not surprising that in the last days both of these divine institutions, these sacred gifts to humanity from the Creator's hand, are under attack.[15]

Indeed, Davidson is only drawing upon Ellen White, who said, "[In the] blessed days of Eden, when God pronounced all things 'very good,' Marriage and the Sabbath had their origin, twin institutions for the glory of God in the benefit of humanity" (*The Adventist Home*, p. 340).

Though Ellen White didn't have same-sex marriage in mind when she made her statement, Davidson did. When he says marriage is under attack, that attack is, according to him, the legalization and increasing acceptance of same-sex marriage. In an official statement, the Seventh-day Adventist Theological Seminary said the following:

The sacredness, beauty and relevancy of marriage is diminished as never before in contemporary culture, society, and law, because the growing influence of a secular sexual ideology . . . various alternate sexualities, including homosexuality, bisexuality, and the variety of transgender identities have become increasingly mainstream.[16]

If we are created for heterosexual marriage, honoring and protecting heterosexual marriage means protecting our very humanity. Violating God's intention for marriage is a threat to life. Affirming theology claims to be an affirmation of the humanity of gay, bisexual, and transgender people. But if accepted theology is believed, the opposite is true. Same-sex marriage is a violation of God's design. Such a violation doesn't affirm our humanity but diminishes it.

Christians who oppose same-gender marriage usually don't do so because they hate gay and bisexual people. They believe all of us are better off if we trust and follow God. Some of us struggle to acknowledge it, but those who oppose same-gender marriage often have compassionate intentions rooted in trust in Scripture and the will of God.

BROKEN MODELS?

What does affirming theology seek to do with the Creation narrative? Affirming theology does not throw out Genesis. The objective is greater understanding. If we are to find knowledge of our very humanity from Adam and Eve, if they reveal what it is to be whole and good, we should be crystal clear about what we mean.

We begin with ensuring a consistent approach to the text. If we pick and choose aspects of their story to apply to our lives while ignoring others, we're imposing our own ideas on the text and not treating it as authoritative. If God's original creation is our present aspiration, we need clear and consistent methods for applying their story to our lives.

Adam and Eve worked in agriculture, tending a garden. This garden wasn't like gardens we might have outside our homes; the garden was their home. They presumably lived in the open air and slept under the stars. There was no profession other than caring for land and animals. Even after the fall, Adam worked the ground (Gen. 3:17-19). So did his sons (Gen. 4:2).

The first person to break from this model was Cain, after committing the first murder (Gen. 4:17). He didn't live outside or even in the countryside. He founded the first city. Cities are defined not only by buildings but also by specialization of labor. The first people to break from Adam's divinely appointed profession were Cain's descendants, who made musical instruments and worked as blacksmiths. One of Cain's descendants also bragged about being seven times as vengeful and murderous as Cain (Gen. 4:17-24).

The next city to appear is Babel, after the flood. Those who built this city wanted to challenge the authority of God. God ultimately destroyed their city, scattered the people, and separated humanity by creating different languages (Gen. 11). Lot chose to live in the city of Sodom instead of living in tents and living off the land as Abraham did (Gen. 17-19); we all know how that turned out.

In short, cities are bad news. If Genesis is a model, cities are not okay, and neither is the specialization of labor that comes along with them. If all men are to be like Adam, they'd better all be farmers, living and sleeping in the open air or tents at most.

But things changed. Did the authors of Scripture believe Eden was a model for all time? When it came to how they lived and what professions they engaged in, the answer seems to be no. Otherwise, cities would still be forbidden. Instead, things change without explanation or deliberation. They didn't understand Genesis that way. There is no indication anywhere in the Bible after Genesis 19 that there was tension around the construction of cities or divisions of labor that are quite different from Eden.

For example, building the tabernacle in the wilderness was accomplished as God called individuals to do specialized labor that was quite different from Adam's tasks in Eden (Ex. 35:30-35). But the wilderness was not the final resting place of God's people because God promised to establish them in the land with a city of their own. God gave Israel the city of Jerusalem (Ps. 48:1-3; Heb. 11:16). In the end, even God's kingdom will be manifested on earth in the enormous city of New Jerusalem. Even God will live in this city (Rev. 21:9-27).

The issue is not only that these changes took place, but that there is no need to explain them. There is no theological shift because the mere fact of life in Eden was not a mandate or a constraint for the future. Eden is not the pattern for all time. There are no statements or wrestling with the meaning of new developments. It just happens.

That indicates that the life of Adam implied no moral command. His life was descriptive, not prescriptive. All men were not required to live under the stars or work the land like Adam. So, can we be sure that all men are commanded to marry like Adam? We are inconsistent if some aspects of Adam's life become rules and others don't.

I've never heard a man criticized for pursuing a career he believes in instead of being a farmer like Adam. But I have seen people look at two men getting married and shake their heads at the wickedness of our world. Adam fell in love with Eve, and we made a rule out of it. But when they were placed in a garden to work the land and raise animals, we didn't make a rule out of that. We're selective about those aspects of the narrative that become rules and those that don't. Why?

SABBATH AND MARRIAGE

If we aren't supposed to make rules from the events of Genesis 1 and 2, what do we take from the text?

What was established in creation remains. All that was good then is still good today. Marriage between a man and a woman doesn't go away or diminish. Neither does agricultural work cease to exist because not everyone does it. Marriage between a man and a woman doesn't have to be exclusive to be meaningful. Like all good beginnings, creation lays a solid foundation that makes room for new things.

Let's look again at the other institution established at creation, the Sabbath. The first marriage is in Genesis 1:26-28,[17] and five verses later is the first Sabbath (Gen. 2:1-3). The first couple was created in time to celebrate the first Sabbath together.

The two institutions, marriage and Sabbath, are closely related. Understanding the Sabbath helps us understand marriage and interpret Genesis consistently. We won't do with marriage what others have done with the seventh-day Sabbath.[a] Instead of dismissing the creation of marriage, I want to look more closely at both marriage and the Sabbath, paying attention to the similarities and the differences.

In most translations, the first time the word "Sabbath" appears in the Bible is Exodus 16. Genesis 2:2 says God "rested on the seventh day." But that hides a nuance of the original language. The Hebrew word for "rested" is the verb *shebeth*, the same word translated as "Sabbath" when it appears as a noun. Not only does the idea of resting on the seventh day come from Genesis 2:1-3, so does the word Sabbath. God "sabbathed" on the seventh day.

When they sabbathed, they called the day "holy" (Gen. 2:3). As Abraham Heschel points out,[18] the Sabbath holds the honor of the first blessing of holiness. God's sovereignty exists not only over objects and people, but over time itself. Just as God speaks and the world is created, when God speaks, the Sabbath is created. We Adventists believe this holiness never leaves the Sabbath, no matter how much time has passed. What God has called holy will always be holy.

There are implications for same-gender marriage. If Sabbath cannot be changed, neither can marriage. Adventist theologians have linked the two together. Àngel Manuel Rodríguez, former director of the Biblical Research Institute of the General Conference, wrote:

---

a. I will never understand how evangelicals say marriage was created in Eden between a man and a woman but ignore the seventh-day Sabbath. It's hard to follow that reasoning.

The transfer of the sanctity of the biblical marriage to same-sex marriage is like trans-
ferring the sanctity of the seventh-day Sabbath to Sunday. What God has not explicitly
sanctified cannot be sanctified by theologians in opposition to His will.[19]

Same-sex marriage is like changing Sabbath to Sunday. I see the appeal to
this argument. The text has a common thread of obedience. Everyone on each
Sabbath is called to acknowledge its holiness.

On the other hand, Rodríguez says the sanctity or holiness[20] of biblical marriage is transferred in same-gender marriage. This might sound like a minor
point, but the Bible doesn't say this. Marriage in Genesis is not called holy or
sanctified, so there is no holiness to transfer. The text says that God blessed
them (Gen. 1:28) and that they were naked and unashamed (Gen. 2:25). But
the word holy was reserved only for the Sabbath. The uniqueness of that statement is meaningful. The first time God calls something holy is when God rests
on the Sabbath, showing God's sovereignty not only over the physical world
but also over time itself. The parallel between Sabbath and marriage deserves
consideration. Still, we shouldn't jump ahead and equate the two institutions
or apply the language and theological reasoning from one directly to the other
when it's not that way in the Bible.

INSTITUTIONS AND CREATION

Marriage and the Sabbath are institutions in different ways. The Sabbath is an
institution for everyone, for all God's creation to participate indirectly. Even
cattle are to be part of Sabbath rest (Ex. 20:8-11). Even non-Israelites are to keep
Sabbath (Isa. 56:3). On the other hand, marriage is only an institution for some.
Other parts of Scripture encourage avoiding the institution of marriage (Matt.
19:10-12; 1 Cor. 7:8, 32-35). There are certainly no such texts about avoiding
the Sabbath.

Jesus Himself opted out of the institution of marriage, but not the institution of the Sabbath. To opt-out of marriage doesn't harm marriage as it does the
Sabbath. That's because Adam and Eve are our examples of marriage, but God
is our example of the Sabbath, which is holy. The call to follow the same path as
Adam and Eve is not for everyone. But everyone is supposed to follow the path
of God and rest as God did, celebrating the seventh-day Sabbath (Heb. 4:1-13).

The establishment of the two institutions in Genesis was also a bit different.
The word "Sabbath" is used in its establishment. The word "marriage" isn't used

when Adam and Eve come together, nor is there any kind of wedding. The word marriage only came to describe relationships after the fall.

There is some irony in saying the institution of marriage was established in a passage of Scripture that doesn't include the word "marriage." In its most literal form, Genesis 1 and 2 describes two people falling in love and living together for life. They didn't make vows or call themselves married.

Of course, this doesn't mean that marriage didn't start in the garden; it certainly did. But the same intentionality was not present as the intentionality we find with the Sabbath. We can compare marriage and the Sabbath, but we shouldn't equate them.

It's not surprising there was no marriage ceremony. There were no family and friends in Eden to attend a wedding ceremony or hear any vows. There was no community to acknowledge and honor Adam and Eve's marriage. There was no legal or religious system to recognize their status change. Only later was anything as formal as marriage established because only later was it needed. As a social institution, marriage requires a society to celebrate and honor it.

Marriage in Eden doesn't come to us fully formed. It wasn't even called "marriage." That shouldn't make anyone less confident in marriage. It's because marriage is integral to human societies that it requires a society. It's not only about the two people getting married, but also about the community that recognizes and respects that marriage.

Sabbath is more straightforward. We can rest and honor Sabbath if we're only two people. We can sabbath solo. I spent a recent Sabbath praying and studying alone all day. It was lovely. That type of Sabbath is present at creation, but there is no description of a wedding or marriage vows.

Still, the absence of an actual wedding in Eden doesn't mean it wasn't the first marriage. It doesn't mean there was no commitment or permanence to their relationship. When Adam said of Eve, "bone of my bone and flesh of my flesh" (Gen. 2:23), he spoke of a permanent relationship. Bone and flesh is a Hebrew way of referring to family.[21] Yet many details about how that would work out over time didn't come to us in Genesis 1 and 2.

Even more important is the object of imitation. In keeping the Sabbath, we are imitating God. We rest because God rested. In getting married, we are imitating Adam and Eve. We are marrying as they married. It seems evident that following God as our example is infinitely more consequential than following Adam and Eve.

OTHER SABBATHS

With all these differences, what are the similarities? The Sabbath was given with an important specificity. It was on the seventh day. One could say the first couple also had specificity, with a man and a woman. Since there is a problem with people ignoring the specificity of the Sabbath and changing it to Sunday, what about the specificity of marriage?

Let's look at the logic itself more clearly presented:

- The first Sabbath is made holy, so only Sabbath should be holy. Keeping Sunday as a holy day violates the Sabbath.
- The first marriage was between a man and a woman, so only men and women should be married. Same-sex sex violates marriage.
- Therefore, no other day but Sabbath is holy, just as no other marriage but heterosexual marriage is ordained by God.

The problem with this reasoning is subtle. According to the Bible, the seventh-day Sabbath is not the only holy day. The Sabbath is the *first* and most *enduring* holy day, but not the *only* one. There are many holy days. When the Israelites were reminded of the seventh-day Sabbath on Mount Sinai, they were also given other days and years to keep holy (Ex. 23:10-17; Lev. 16, 23, 25).

These holy days were also called sabbaths. In English, we distinguish between the two by capitalizing Sabbath when referring to the seventh day, but even this is not something we get from Scripture. There is no capitalization in Hebrew or Greek.

There were seven annual sabbaths throughout the year. The Day of Atonement is a sabbath that Christians understand as foreshadowing the sacrifice of Christ and the reconciliation of humanity to God (Lev. 16:31; 23:32). Pentecost is a sabbath that we understand as foreshadowing the movement of the Holy Spirit in God's people (Lev. 23:15).

It wasn't only days that were sabbaths. The entire year of jubilee was referred to as "sabbath: because it marked rest and rejuvenation for the land and its people (Lev. 24:2, 4, 6; 26:34, 35, 43; 2 Chron. 36:21). The word "sabbath" is used generally to refer to ceremonial holy days given to Israel through Moses (Isa. 1:13; Hos. 2:11).[22] It's as if the goodness of the Sabbath could not be contained, and it spilled out into other days and times.

This is not to say there is no distinction between sabbaths and the Sabbath. There certainly is. One is established at creation, the other at Sinai. One is for all time; the other may be long lasting, but it's not forever. The Sabbath is in the Ten Commandments; the other sabbaths are not.

Yet despite the supremacy of the seventh-day Sabbath, it's not the only sabbath. Even the lesser sabbaths are holy. God also gives them. They are also days of rest. They also teach about the will of God. They even share the same name. The goodness of creation in Eden remains, but it was not the only sabbath that would ever be good. It was the creation of something good, not the elimination of all other possibilities for good.

Though these other sabbaths are temporary in their literal observance, they are eternal in their fulfillment. This is the foundation of the Adventist doctrine of the heavenly sanctuary. These sabbaths reveal God's plan for the salvation of humanity. The fulfillment of one particular sabbath, the Day of Atonement, which Adventists believe began in 1844, is the climax of salvation history and the reason for the existence of the Seventh-day Adventist Church. It is indeed an important and holy day.

Let me return to the question: Is keeping Sunday as a holy day the problem? Not really. The problem isn't making Sunday *a* holy day; it's making Sunday *the* holy day. Other holy sabbaths were continuations and expansions of the meaning of the Sabbath. They didn't interfere with the keeping of the seventh-day Sabbath. They enhanced it.

The problem with observing Sunday as the Sabbath is not that it adds another holy day; the problem is that it *replaces* the Sabbath. The problem is that instead of enhancing the Sabbath, it's abolished and becomes merely Saturday. No longer are we resting on the seventh day in imitation of God and celebration of creation.

In truth, we already keep additional days holy by dedicating them to the Lord. The things we do on those days could be the same things we do on Sabbath. We can set any day aside for meditation and prayer. We can fast. We can worship. Congregations can gather at other times.

No specific activity God commands us to do on Sabbath is forbidden on any other day. The problem is not having other holy days that we set aside for rest and worship; the problem is abandoning the holiness of the Sabbath.

So, we should correct that argument we made earlier:

- The first Sabbath is made holy, so it can never lose its holiness. There may be other holy days, but they must never abolish the seventh-day Sabbath.
- The first marriage was between a man and a woman, so male-female marriage must never end.
- The creation of the seventh-day Sabbath and of marriage established these as good, without excluding other goods.

Since the creation of the seventh-day Sabbath didn't exclude other sabbaths, why does the relationship between Adam and Eve exclude other marriages or lifelong commitments? What about celibate communities? What about other formations of extended family? What about same-sex marriage? The key is not whether new ways of doing things arise, but whether these new things abolish and replace what was established at creation, and ultimately whether these new things are moral and good in their own right.

REPLACED?

But wait, aren't same-sex marriages replacing heterosexual marriage? The person who gets married to the same sex is now not married to someone of the opposite sex. Isn't heterosexual marriage replaced for them? Isn't this like someone who replaces the seventh-day Sabbath with Sunday?

Heterosexual marriage is unlike the Sabbath in that we've already established that not everyone is called to heterosexual marriage. In the New Testament, lots of people opted out of marriage.[b] So, since heterosexual marriage is not a requirement, we don't have to participate directly to support it. Let's consider how this reality has played out in Scripture.

In the Garden of Eden, Adam was created first. "And the Lord God said, 'It is not good that man should be alone; I will make him a helper comparable to him'" (Gen. 2:18).

In a sly trick, God then made the host of animals. Adam searched the animal kingdom but was unable to find a partner.[c] After allowing this struggle, God placed Adam under a deep sleep and removed a piece of his body. From this piece, God made the first woman (Gen. 2:19-23). Finally, someone suitable to Adam! "Therefore a man shall leave his father and mother and be joined to his wife, and they shall become one flesh" (Gen. 2:24).

---

b. In the Hebrew Bible (Old Testament), only physical eunuchs and Jeremiah (who was explicitly called by God to be celibate for the sake of prophetic witness) seemed to see themselves as exempt from marriage.

c. Commentators often argue that what made Eve compatible with Adam was the complementary nature of their anatomy. The male part inserts into the female part. This text does not support that. If that's what Adam was looking for, he would have found it in the animal kingdom. Yes, I know, it's gross. It just exposes the inconsistency of this argument. Adam was looking for more than a compatible organ. Yes, Adam's partner is a woman, but the text emphasizes that his partner is a fellow human being. That's what Adam was looking for and was unable to find in the animal kingdom. Sometimes we are told that the story shows that Adam was looking for someone similar (human) but different (a woman), but the text only supports the similarity aspect. Adam did not see and reject a male human partner for being too similar, only animals for being too different.

This passage states: "it is not good that man should be alone." For Adam, the solution is to have a life partner, one he searched for and recognized as suitable for him. Today, this text is used to forbid all same-sex marriage. Yet never does it explicitly say that it's not good for man to be with someone of the same gender. It says explicitly and plainly, "it is not good that man should be alone."

If the text said, "it is not good for man to be with man," this would be understood today as an explicit biblical prohibition of same-gender marriage. Yet this is the kind of direct statement we have about celibacy. It's a straightforward statement that it's not good for man to be alone, followed by that man being given a heterosexual spouse, further clarifying that a sexual relationship is the statement's intent.

Despite this apparent clarity, New Testament authors have no problem with celibacy. They seem utterly unconcerned that their approach seems to be contradicted by the words of Genesis 2:18. They don't even feel the need to reconcile the encouragement of celibacy with Genesis. They feel no need to explain or even acknowledge it.

Only in the modern world do we feel a need to explain what we believe is a dichotomy. We do so with disingenuous interpretations, saying that it's possible to be celibate and not alone. That's certainly true in a broad sense, but Adam's aloneness was about wanting a sexual and romantic partner. His aloneness was satisfied by a wife.

In the Bible, authors had no problem with celibacy. This wasn't because they didn't believe Genesis 1 and 2 were authoritative. Quite the contrary. It was because they understood Genesis 1 and 2 differently than we do. It wasn't a moral template; it was a starting point. We should never abandon heterosexual pairing; we find it in Eden. But it's not a universal command.

THREAT TO MARRIAGE?

Yet many people seem to think same-sex marriage is a threat to heterosexual marriage, that affirming same-sex marriage will undermine heterosexual marriage. Let's look again at a quote from an official statement from the Seventh-day Adventist Theological Seminary at Andrews University:

> The sacredness, beauty and relevancy of marriage is diminished as never before in contemporary culture, society, and law, because the growing influence of a secular sexual

ideology . . . various alternate sexualities, including homosexuality, bisexuality, and the variety of transgender identities have become increasingly mainstream.[23]

Remarkably, we don't see any threat to heterosexual marriage in a celibate man who opts out of heterosexual marriage. Yet if that celibate man were to opt out of heterosexual marriage differently, by marrying another previously celibate man, we see a seismic threat. Where does this fear originate? How does the existence of same-sex marriage pose any risk to heterosexual marriage?

Gay and bisexual people do not want to destroy marriage. We want access to marriage. We see its value, and we want to be part of it. That's why we fought so hard. That's why so many rushed to courthouses to get married the moment it was legal in the U.S. and why many continue to do so in every country where same-sex marriage is legalized.

David Blankenhorn, founder of the Institute for American Values, says it best. He used to oppose same-gender marriage. As a vocal advocate of traditional marriage, he traveled the country and the world with his message. He believed same-sex marriage undermined the institution of marriage.

But the more he learned and the more he came to respect and better understand gay and bisexual people, the more he realized that excluding them from marriage did nothing to help heterosexual marriage or families. He was particularly influenced by a friendship with a gay man who challenged his preconceptions. In an interview with Krista Tippett, he shared why he finally changed his mind:

> We're in this funny situation. We've got 2 or 3 percent of the population, a tiny number of Americans, who are sincerely saying, "Let us in this institution. This means everything to us." Meanwhile, the vast majority of Americans are exiting the institution quickly. If you go to Middle America now, blue-collar America, working-class America, you will find marriage in shambles.
>
> So it's weird. [To] the people that want in, we say no, and the people that are already in are just rushing out, and I was Mr. Anti-Gay-Marriage.
>
> How is this helping strengthen what really matters to me? And the answer is, it wasn't. It wasn't. If fighting gay marriage was going to get heteros to recommit to the institution, we would have seen a sign by now, I think.[24]

Those of us who are affirming in our theology want to be included. We want the blessing and help of society. We want the legal protections of marriage for ourselves and our families. It's not only for us, but to help us support, serve, and care for one another. We believe full inclusion is the right and Christian choice for heterosexual Christians to make.

We're glad to have protections for many families in the West, but there are so many more worldwide who need it. The Adventist Church is one of the most influential global institutions in the world and has thus far thrown its influence in the direction of opposing marriage rights for same-sex couples.[25]

More than legal protections, we crave the support of our churches and families. Marriage is hard enough without support. We see how heterosexuals grow up with models of (hopefully) good and stable marriages. They know pastors and teachers they respect who experience relationships the way they do. They hope that they can one day have that kind of marriage and know the church will help them and their spouses stay together and raise children.

We see all that is happening for heterosexual kids, and we want it for gay and bisexual kids, too. It's hard to go it alone, to try to build a healthy life without the support of our Adventist family or our families of origin. It's hard to leave our Adventist family to find the supportive communities that can help us live up to our responsibilities to one another. It's hard to construct families of choice once we've lost the support of our families of origin.

Giving us this support and helping us have solid marriages and families would not harm heterosexual marriage; it would strengthen marriage for everyone. We would be there to remind you of just how important marriage is. And frankly, heterosexuals need the reminder.

IN THE BEGINNING

What is the story of creation if it isn't a model of how to live?

I think of Genesis first and foremost as telling me who I am. I'm a child of God, given the gift and responsibility of this world. I'm created for dynamic relationships with God's creation and my fellow humans. I have a loving Creator who created me and called me good. All things created in Genesis 1 and 2 are good. This is not a limitation but a down payment. There are good things for us to discover and create that aren't mentioned in Genesis 1 and 2.

The first two chapters of the Bible were never intended to explain the full range of what is possible and what is good, nor could such a small portion of Scripture take on such a responsibility. Genesis was not supposed to be the whole story. We do have the rest of the Bible, after all.

Neither were the circumstances of Adam and Eve's lives meant as a set of laws and rules for timeless application. Instead of being a set of rules, Eden was a beginning. The evidence for Eden as the beginning rather than the model for all people at all times begins in Genesis 1:1:

> In the beginning God created the heavens and the earth.

The text describes itself as the beginning. This leads me to wonder, *What would have happened had there never been an end? What was God's intention for the human race as it matured and grew?* There are clues.

> The Lord God planted a garden eastward in Eden, and there He put the man whom He had formed (Gen. 2:8).

God planted the garden in a specific place. The garden wasn't everywhere, just in one place. He called that place Eden, a word that translates "delight." God planted this garden as a delight for them. The rest of the planet was not a garden, maybe not even a delight.

Most of us are disconnected from the ground. It can be hard to understand the significance of a garden. A garden in Hebrew was not a planted field, but more like what we call an orchard with perennial plants that produced year after year without needing to be replanted. It was different than a field that had to be worked, sowed, cultivated, and harvested year after year. Once established, gardens are easier to maintain, but they take years to develop. Because of this, gardens were precious in the ancient world.

After the fall, the first couple is expelled from the garden.

> Therefore the Lord God sent him out of the garden of Eden to till the ground from which he was taken. So He drove out the man; and He placed cherubim at the east of the garden of Eden, and a flaming sword which turned every way, to guard the way to the tree of life (Gen. 3:23, 24).

If they were expelled, there was a world to be expelled into, a world outside of the garden. That world was difficult, wild, and untamed. So, what we have in Genesis 1-3 is a picture of a large world with a small garden. Before everything went wrong, what was the plan exactly?

> Then God blessed them, and God said to them, "Be fruitful and multiply; fill the earth and subdue it; have dominion over the fish of the sea, over the birds of the air, and over every living thing that moves on the earth" (Gen. 1:28).

The garden wasn't a place created for eternal, quiet repose. It was a place for meaningful work. The garden could and should expand to contain the whole of a planet that was yet wild and inhospitable.

What would that have looked like had it happened? Hard telling. Was the goal a planet that was nothing but garden? I doubt it, but who's to say? There might have been many innovations along the way. We don't have these kinds of details in the text, though we can imagine possibilities based on our knowledge of what humanity is capable of, even in our fallen state.

Eden was not the end of the story. It was a starting point for a couple that would grow into a family, then a community, then a society, then a species inhabiting and cultivating an entire planet.

There would be changes through such a process. Gardens may have given way to cities full of artists, trade workers, and scholars. Maybe there could be additions to what already existed. Gardens wouldn't cease to exist, but not everything would be a garden.

Wouldn't this growing society develop in different ways? The first couple must be male and female. They also must have children. Without those two factors, there isn't any humanity and no filling of the earth. But what about later? Are all couples commanded to have children for all time?

Perhaps somewhere in that movement from two people to a species inhabiting the entire planet, there is a point at which procreation of the species no longer requires procreation by every couple. What happens when the earth is filled, and there's no death? Doesn't procreation become a problem?

I'm only speculating about things we can never know. But it seems from the text that God had something else in mind other than humanity simply repeating the existence of Adam and Eve forever. There was a growth and maturing intended from the beginning.

EDEN-TO-EDEN

What do we make about the crucial Adventist value of an Eden-to-Eden ethical framework? As Adventists, we believe that God created us perfect in Eden, and the New Earth will be a New Eden. What was lost will be restored. So if that is true, we should embody the ethics of Eden as much as possible. Therefore, isn't same-sex marriage excluded?

I am in favor of the Eden-to-Eden model. The only way to support the Eden-to-Eden ethical framework is to view it biblically. It must harmonize with all of scripture. If we make the ethical framework literalistic, it collapses. This is perhaps nowhere more true than it is for marriage. If we anticipate that marriage in the New Eden will be just like it was in the beginning, we quickly run into problems.

We are told in Revelation 14:4 that in the throneroom of God, there are men who have been celibate their whole lives and follow Jesus wherever he goes. These last-day men, the 144,000, are characterized by their celibacy and lack of connection with women. They are not returning to the Eden model of marriage. Their departure from marriage is a sign of holiness.

This text in Revelation is a continuation of New Testament principles. Far from a return to the Eden marriage model, there are indications that there will be no marriage in the New Earth. In Matthew 22:23-33, the Sadducees tried to stump Jesus by asking him about a woman who had been married and widowed multiple times. Whose wife will she be? Jesus responds that in the resurrection, there will be no marriage. Luke 20:34-36 adds further insight:

> Jesus answered and said to them, "The sons of this age marry and are given in marriage. But those who are counted worthy to attain that age, and the resurrection from the dead, neither marry nor are given in marriage; nor can they die anymore, for they are equal to the angels and are sons of God, being sons of the resurrection.

When we read Revelation 21-22, we find a huge city. There is no sea. There is no sun and moon. There is no night. And possibly, there is no marriage. The Eden-to-Eden ethical framework is not a replay of Eden. That doesn't mean it's not a valid framework, just that it's not literalistic, and the authors of scripture never treated it as such.

But couldn't we say that the Eden model still applies, but only when there is marriage? Only if we use two separate and distinct standards. Only if Eden applies to same-sex marriage, but not to celibacy. If we apply Eden so indiscriminately, our inconsistency invalidates it as an ethical framework. Fortunately, there is a better way.

FROM BIRTH TO MATURITY

Eden was a beginning, not an ending, and not a template for all time. When we say that the Bible is a story of paradise lost and paradise regained, we should remember that paradise is not static but dynamic. This doesn't change the value of Genesis 1 and 2. It places this weighty passage of Scripture in its proper place. Beginnings are crucially important, even if they don't tell the whole picture. Eden is not the entire Bible.

Think about birth stories. My parents told me several things about my birth. I was born on the Sabbath, which my mother always told me was special. I was born in Lincoln, Nebraska, to a doctor who wanted to delay my birth until the Huskers' game was over. They weren't in a big hurry until I managed to speed things up by trying to come out feet first. Then they rushed my mom into surgery for a C-section.

Those things are intensely interesting to me because they are my story. I could draw from them that I'm destined for a spiritual life, which would seem true, but only because of what I've done with my life. Or one could decide I'm a born Huskers fan, which would be a fabrication. Or perhaps there is significance to the fact that the very first thing I did in life was to make a mistake, a dangerous one at that, by trying to come out feet first. Or maybe that tidbit has no significance at all. All those things are what I've made of them, or the value placed on them by others.

But some things are continually relevant: my mother's name, my father's name, and the fact that they did nothing but stare at me for hours on end because they were so amazed and in love with their tiny baby. These details tell me I am loved, and I have value to my parents. My father told me again and again about holding me on the elevator and being the happiest man in the world. My father is gone now, but he was there, and his love was true.

I carry this history with me as evidence of who I am and that I am loved. I treasure those events. They are significant, not merely interesting. People who don't have such beauty in their birth stories, I pray, will learn those lessons other ways— through adopted parents, through healing relationships, and through their heavenly Parent. But my story has real and lasting significance to me.

In the same way, I carry with me the knowledge that my heavenly Parent loves me. The biblical origin story I have received tells me I am created in the image of God. I was "very good" in my creation.

Still, beginnings are a mix. In some ways, they're about what we make of them. The story will unfold. Much of who I am as an adult is yet to be revealed even now. On the other hand, in some ways beginnings are foundational. They reveal truths about where we come from and who we are. I'm not trying to go back to the state in which I was born, but I carry my parents' love with me wherever I go. Perhaps the birth of the world is a lot like that.

BLUEPRINT OR BEGINNING?

The significant difference between seeing Genesis as the model and seeing Genesis as the beginning is this: Models are rarely built upon and added to, but beginnings always are. Models should be strictly followed. Beginnings tell us something about who we are. Beginnings guide us; they teach us about realities that can never change, but not every detail is a rule or prophecy.

Those who believe in affirming theology believe that Adam and Eve are not models to be emulated. Jesus is our model to be emulated, and each of us has a unique way of doing so. The first two humans lived differently than most of us, and that's okay.

We shouldn't all be farmers. Living in a house is just fine. Not everyone will get married. A small number of people might even marry someone of the same gender. Adam and Eve give us a way of understanding how this whole thing started and some of the beautiful gifts we've been given—gifts like nature, meaningful work, the Sabbath, and marriage. Most importantly, they tell us that we are created in the image of God. As such, they also speak to what the New Earth will be like, with a restoration of these gifts.

Even though there will be echoes of the beginning at the end, and the restoration of innocence will return much of what was lost in the garden, the end will not be a replica of the beginning.[26] Eden isn't a picture of exactly how things will look in the end. It's a reminder of what things were like "in the beginning."

To say that Genesis was a beginning does not negate its moral value. Beginnings teach us what is good. God declares many things good in the garden, and those things remain good forever, but they are not the sum of all that ever will be good. There is more goodness in the world than was mentioned in Genesis 1 and 2.

When I see Genesis 1 and 2 in this light, I can do something difficult to do when we see it as a model. I can be clear about which parts of the books have continuing meaning and which don't. I can be consistent in my application.

Those who see Genesis as a model struggle to give specific, textual reasons for applying parts of the narrative as rules while not applying other parts. Why don't we all live in nature under the stars rather than in cities and houses? Why do the specifics of Adam and Eve's genders constrain marriage, but the specifics of their professions don't? Even though Genesis says, "it is not good for man to be alone," why is celibacy acceptable? Why is same-sex marriage forbidden simply because it's not in Eden when so much of our daily lives were not literally present in Eden either?

When I see Genesis as a beginning, I can be clear that it teaches us about our nature, the stuff we are made of. We are God's good creation, created in God's image. I can be clear about who God is. God is our Creator, our Mother and Father who birthed us, loves us, and sustains us. We were good in our creation, so the truest part of our creation must still be good. After all, we are made in the very image of God.

We also have commitments to our planet. We have the task of caring for and loving the world. We don't all need to fulfill this legalistically as farmers and agricultural workers, but we have "dominion." It's not a rule or a restriction. It's a responsibility and a gift. It defines the obligations we have to the world.

When it comes to our obligations to one another, I see Adam and Eve not as a model not only for how married people should relate to one another, but how all people should relate to one another. Adam was looking for someone who shared his humanity, and he found that in Eve. Eve came from his very flesh and bones. All other people who have come after them are from this same flesh and bones.

Our beginning reveals that we are one human family. What I find so compelling about the origin story of the Israelites is that it isn't a story about how Israelites were created, but of how all people were created. We aren't meant to be at war with one another, separate, angry, and afraid of our brothers and sisters.

I don't believe God meant Adam and Eve's relationship to be interpreted in narrow terms as a blueprint for all future behavior, but in the broad sense of the obligations we to love one another. The human family is one family. With all the national, religious, and cultural forces that separate us, there is a sense in which we share a common substance. We all breathe. We all bleed. We are all born. We all die. We all feel fear, pain, joy, and love. We are all human. We all share the same bone and flesh.

Dehumanization is at the heart of oppression and hate. Those who are different are robbed of their humanity and treated as if they don't share common human emotions and relationships. In the origin story of Adam and Eve, I find the most important moral principles in the Bible: Love God, love all people, and love all creation. We are all connected. Jesus taught us to love our enemies, pray for those who hate us, and love others as we want to be loved. I see this truth ringing out from the first chapters of the Bible.

MOVING FORWARD

Still, some might feel torn. What I'm saying may sound consistent, but something about it doesn't seem quite right. I remember the first time someone challenged me with this theological approach to Eden. It was a conversation I had with Matthew Vines.[d] He simply said that he thought Genesis was the beginning, not the model, and my brain froze. It was oddly destabilizing. I remember thinking that he didn't know (not being Adventist) how important Genesis is. Yet, I also didn't know how to tell him what he was missing. I'm afraid I stumbled over my response without really knowing what to say.

As I look back, I understand my reluctance. I'd held the theology for so long and connected it to my thinking about God and the Bible in so many ways that the idea that Eden was the model to which we would one day return had acquired theological weight. It was heavy and not easily moved. Even though this new perspective made more sense, it took time to think it through enough to make the shift.

For those reading right now, I'm going to guess that two main forces are pulling you away from seeing Adam and Eve as a beginning and not a definitive example of what marriage is. First, it seems like working in agriculture and living in nature rather than cities are not moral issues, and the gender of marriage is a moral issue. Second, the rest of the Bible echoes the idea that marriage is between a man and a woman (though sometimes men had multiple wives).

On the question of morality, moral issues are moral issues until they aren't. For some Adventists, living outside the city is a moral issue. At many times and places, agricultural pursuits have been seen, if not as the only morally allowed profession, at least as morally superior. Thomas Jefferson's moral vision of America was as an economy based on family farming. Alexander Hamilton wanted to base the economy on industry by establishing a federal banking system. These were considered moral issues at the time. Gender and marriage will be regarded as moral issues until they aren't. It might feel intuitive for us to determine what's moral and what isn't. We might be tempted to simply assume we understand this, but it has more to do with what we bring to the text than what we take from it.

On the question of consistency with the rest of Scripture, the fact that there is no same-gender marriage in the Bible is a question to hold on to as we proceed.

---

d. You should read his book if you haven't. It's called *God and the Gay Christian*.

I will address it. One huge open question from this chapter is how we interpret Jesus' words about creation and gender in Matthew 19 and Mark 10. I've dedicated an entire chapter to that question. We'll delve deeper into the meaning of "bone of my bone and flesh of my flesh." We'll also talk more about the meaning of creation as male and female created in the image of God.

In the next chapter, we need to look at something even more fundamental. We'll look at gender itself and what Genesis 1 and 2 tell us about maleness and femaleness.

CHAPTER 3

The Creation of Gender

"God doesn't make mistakes, and God created us male or female. If God made you a man, you're a man. If God made you a woman, you're a woman."

"No one can change their gender any more than we can change our height or age. We learn in kindergarten that there are men and women. It's not something based on feeling. It's just how you're born."

Controversy about transgender people has moved to the front line of the culture wars. Transgender people have become the subjects of national debate, whether in bathrooms, classrooms, or the military. It can all be exhausting—even for those of us who aren't transgender.

I don't want this chapter to be about politics or the culture war. We're often too busy fighting each other to listen to one another or open our Bibles and study together. I'm much more concerned with talking about the topic itself. I want to get beyond the rhetoric to real people and the words of the Bible.

Many Christians are genuinely concerned by what's happening. Something as basic as gender has always seemed like an unchangeable reality. We're born female or male, and we're stuck with it. That's just how it works. We can't choose or change our gender.

Then we hear about or know someone who is transgender. For many people, Caitlyn Jenner was the first trans-person they'd heard about when she came out in 2015. Many people struggled to understand this. Why would someone change something about themselves that seems so obvious?

The most common statement I hear from Adventists who oppose gender transitions is simply, "I don't agree." They don't believe people can change their gender. They believe gender is determined by anatomy. They don't believe someone can change that or that they should try.

Behind this concern is a broader concern about reality itself. How can we decide what's true and untrue? Can a person just say whatever they want about themselves? Can an Asian person choose to be European? Can we identify as something other than our actual age or our actual height?

These questions misunderstand what it means to be transgender, but that doesn't mean that those who ask them aren't sincere. There's a lot of confusion and uncertainty around this topic. There's also a lot of misunderstanding. When any issue becomes this political, it's bound to get complicated quickly.

Let's begin by defining our terms: Transgender people describe themselves as having an internal sense of gender that doesn't match their birth sex or assigned gender at birth, as defined by their external reproductive anatomy. In other words, the baby is born, the doctor looks down and says, "it's a boy" or "it's a girl," but as that child grows, they have a persistent and unchanging internal sense of identity that contradicts the doctor's declaration at birth. The word itself comes from the prefix "trans," meaning "on the other side," indicating their gender is on the other side of their reproductive anatomy.

"Cis" means "on the same side." "Cisgender" refers to most of us. Our gender matches our anatomical presentation. For cisgender people, doctors look at us when we are born, announce our sex, and that matches the way we feel about our gender for our entire lives. In practical terms, this means a transgender woman was born with typically male anatomy, was announced as a boy, but as she grew up, this did not match her unchosen neurological gender identity. A transgender man was born with typically female anatomy and transitioned his gender to male. What may or may not be included in "transition" will be discussed later in the chapter.[a]

So, how do Christians approach a situation in which individuals say they are transgender and transition their gender identity? How do Adventist churches approach it? What do we do when we are asked to use different pronouns and a

---

a. For more in-depth explanations, see: https://transequality.org/issues/resources/understanding-transgender-people-the-basics

different name? Or maybe you are transgender yourself. Perhaps you experience gender dysphoria, a sense of depression related to your sex and gender. Perhaps you long to live your life differently. What is the best choice for you? What does the Bible say about it?

The Seventh-day Adventist Church has produced two official statements on the subject. The Ethics Committee of the Biblical Research Institute (BRI) of the General Conference wrote a "Statement on Transgenderism" in 2014.[27] Basing much of their statement on the BRI's work, with some changes and omissions, the General Conference (GC) Executive Committee voted to affirm their "Position on Transgenderism" in 2017.[28] I'll refer to these throughout the chapter as the BRI statement and GC statement.

The GC statement says God established gender at creation in clear categories of "male and female." It points out that "the human being is a psychosomatic unity." This leads it to conclude that "the Bible does not endorse dualism in the sense of a separation between one's body and one's sense of sexuality. . . . A human being is also meant to be an undivided sexual entity, and sexual identity cannot be independent from one's body."

In its statement, the GC acknowledged that transgender people experience gender-related psychological distress. Sometimes they are diagnosed with related depression called gender dysphoria. This depression is often behind decisions to transition genders, though not everyone who identifies as transgender experiences gender dysphoria.

It can be difficult to decide how something like gender dysphoria fits into one's theological understanding. The position the GC takes is that "our emotions, feelings, and perceptions are not fully reliable indicators of God's designs, ideals, and truth (Prov. 14:12; 16:25). We need guidance from God through Scripture to determine what is in our best interest and how to live according to His will (2 Tim. 3:16)."

How should we think about the struggles that people sometimes have with their gender identity? The answer for the GC is that the primary lens for thinking about gender identity should be physiological, not psychological. From a theological perspective, the GC statement views the psychological difficulties of gender dysphoria and those who identify as transgender as a sign of the fall and human brokenness.

> The fact that some individuals claim a gender identity incompatible with their biological sex reveals a serious dichotomy. This brokenness or distress, whether felt or not, is an expression of the damaging effects of sin on humans and may have a variety of causes. Although gender dysphoria is not intrinsically sinful, it may result in sinful choices. It is another indicator that, on a personal level, humans are involved in the great controversy.

The statement asserts that when transgender people want to live their lives as a different gender than what is indicated by their external anatomy, this desire is sinful. In its view, external anatomy determines the gender intended by God. The desire to change gender is no worse than any sinful desire any of us have. The GC statement expresses that to give in to those desires by transitioning one's gender would be an act of sin, just like giving in to any temptation is an act of sin. Transgender people should be guided by God's original creation rather than their feelings. The GC statement says this is accomplished by living one's gender consistent with external sexual anatomy.

What is the solution for those with gender dysphoria? The statement acknowledges that "transgender people may suffer silently, living a celibate life or being married to a spouse of the opposite sex."[b] Yet it hopes that a transgender person might attain some peace through faith without transitioning.

Because I know something about silent suffering, it's hard for me to read these words. They seem dismissive. I want this needless suffering to end. I don't believe transgender people need to suffer or do so silently. I have a difficult time understanding the purpose of such suffering.

If you have a similar reaction to mine, keep in mind some ideas about suffering itself. We all must accept suffering in the Christian life. This suffering is balanced by the belief that we can trust God. God knows who we are. God knows how to heal us. We hope that through faith in God, contentment and joy are attainable even while suffering. Nothing is automatically wrong because it produces suffering.

Yet, suffering is not without theological significance. The lived experience created by our theology does matter. It matters if our theology produces needless suffering. We need a better theology of suffering and of healing, and I hope we can work toward this end. We can hopefully all agree that Christians should be prepared to suffer for their faith, but also that the Great Physician is interested in our healing and not in perpetual and needless suffering.

Ultimately, many conservative Adventists believe that those who struggle with gender identity await restoration in the earth made new. Because of these beliefs, the Adventist Church does not support transgender identity. The official stance from the GC statement is that people who transition their gender should not remain members of the Seventh-day Adventist Church.

The BRI statement provides additional reasoning. It focuses particularly on gender confirmation surgery, also known as sex-change or sex-reassignment

---

b. Presumably, this last statement about being married to a spouse of the opposite sex assumes the sexual orientation of a transgender person. Yet, transgender people can have any sexual orientation.

surgery. They oppose surgical intervention not only on theological grounds but also on humanitarian grounds claiming that "such treatment may disturb the patient even more." It also questions the motives of people seeking such surgeries. "In some cases, sex-change surgery may be motivated by a sophisticated desire for homosexual activity."[29]

To summarize, the BRI Statement holds that surgery might not work, it's irreversible, and the motivations for pursuing it are rooted in brokenness and fallenness. The best chance a person has is to trust God "while leaning on the Lord for constant help" and not pursue these interventions. This is the only way they believe a person can be faithful to God and the Bible.

GENDER AND CREATION

The first and most important text is in Genesis: "So God created man in His own image; in the image of God He created him; male and female He created them" (Gen. 1:27).

Here we find a binary of gender. There is male; there is female. Both genders flow from the existence of God. They reflect the image of God. From a God who encompasses all, we have the creation of male and female.

If gender is binary, and this is the basic nature of our creation, then we should conform to that binary. Some trans people identify as non-binary, with an internal sense of gender that is not wholly male or female. Others are raised one gender and transition to another. Accepted theology teaches that transgender and non-binary people shouldn't defy the gender binary taught in Genesis 1:27. These individuals should accept and try to live as the gender that matches their reproductive physiology.

But what about those whose physiology may not be consistent with the binary? There are intersex people who have physical characteristics of both male and female. Are intersex people created in the gender binary? What does it mean for them to follow God's will?

The accepted interpretation of Genesis 1:27 raises these questions. Let's take a closer look and see if we can find clarity. How does the Bible represent God's Creation? Do binary concepts show up elsewhere in the Creation account? Looking at the rest of creation in the same chapter, we find that gender is not the only binary.

God separated the light of day from the darkness of night (Gen. 1:4, 5). But we know there is also an in-between time of twilight when the sun sets and rises.

These emerge from the spaces of overlap, when one aspect of God's creation touches another. Does that mean sunsets and sunrises are outside of God's will? Of course not. These words were not intended to exclude sunsets from God's creative intent simply because they aren't day or night. Neither were sunsets an accident. The author simply did not include every possibility. Day and night are excellent examples of God's creation, not the only options.

God separated the land from the sea (Gen. 1:9, 10), yet springs come up from dry land, and islands rise in the sea. Through shifting and change, lakes, rivers, and islands have taken their place in God's good creation.

God created the sun to rule by day and the moon by night (Gen. 1:16), but of course, the moon is often seen during the day, is sometimes absent at night, and occasionally eclipses the sun's light in the middle of the day. There is no problem here because these are general descriptions, not exhaustive.

God created sea animals first, fish and all kinds of swimming creatures. The next day God created animals that lived on dry land (Gen. 1:20-25). So, what about amphibians such as frogs or newts? What about animals that are sea creatures part of their life and land creatures the rest? When were they created? What about birds that swarm in the water like penguins or live on the land like ostriches. No one knows when they were made, but the fact that they don't fit into the categories given doesn't mean newts and penguins are sinful or a sign of God's displeasure.

God gave us a creation story with all the highlights. It wasn't intended to exhaust all possibilities. It wasn't supposed to be a physical model of all things, let alone a moral one. Sunsets, islands, moonless nights, and bullfrogs are not products of the fall or of the sinfulness that has infected humanity. They are good gifts from God.[30]

In fact, this is the way the Hebrew language works. Hebrew language communicates the whole by stating the two most exemplar examples or the two ends of the spectrum. It's called a "merism."[31]

An example of merism is saying "heavens and earth," and meaning all creation, including the sun and moon, which they understood as between the heavens and earth. Another example is describing all of the Hebrew Scriptures as the "Law and the Prophets," when in fact they also include a third section described as the "Writings." The intention is not to exclude the Writings but to include them.

The New Testament book of Revelation often uses Hebrew thought and language. Jesus is described there as the "Alpha and Omega," "the beginning and the end." When he wrote these words, John did not think that Jesus was only the beginning and the end but absent in between. Jesus is everything and everywhere. Jesus is the beginning, the end, and everything in between.

Many use Genesis 1:27 to indicate that "male and female" is all God created. This interpretation ignores the possibility of a Hebrew merism and is inconsistent with the rest of the creation narrative. The creation categories simply are not intended to explain all that can be, all that should be, or all that can morally and ethically be considered good.

The text is open, not closed. The mentioning of "male and female" does not create a mandate or limit future possibilities. Like the rest of the creation narrative, it only gives the high points.

This doesn't mean that the author of Genesis intended to say specifically that there would be intersex or transgender people. I don't believe that. I wouldn't use Genesis 1:27 as a proof-text for affirmation.

Nor should it be used as a proof-text for accepted theology. The author was not intentionally *excluding* intersex or transgender people. The use of language simply does not support the gender binary because of the Hebrew merism and the extensive use of merism in this chapter. It can't teach that gender exists in two discrete, unchanging, and unambiguous categories and actually hints at the opposite.

This text says that all of us are created in God's image regardless of gender. That was quite the revolutionary statement not only for the days of Moses but for all human history. That applies to transgender people as much as it applies to anyone else. We don't need to stretch the text beyond this universal statement of human value, and we shouldn't make that human value contingent on sexual orientation or gender identity.

In fact, there is something else worth noting about Genesis 1:27. If both male and female are in the image of God, what does that say about God's gender? Is God male? Female? Both? Neither? It would be silly to be literalistic about precisely what this means, but it must at least mean that God's gender contains (at a minimum) all that it is to be male and all that it is to be female. God both transcends and contains all good things. Therefore, it's not a strict binary of gender that reveals God because no such binary exists in the personality of God.

GENDER AND THE FALL

I recently had a conversation with a friend about this. William told me that he had a hard time believing that hormones and surgery were God's intention.

We were talking about an interview I'd recently had with an intersex person named Geoffrey[32] for my podcast, *Open Bible Podcast.*

William was moved by his story and felt that he had no right to tell Geoffrey how to think about his own life. Geoffrey had been through horrible agony and a near suicide before making changes in his life and discovering and embracing that he was intersex and transgender. But William couldn't help but have questions when Geoffrey said he was created the way God intended. How could that be? Geoffrey being intersex involved a potentially dangerous medical condition.

William's question extends beyond Geoffrey's story. How could it be God's will that someone needs hormones or surgery? Whether they are transgender, intersex, or both, if a person is exactly how God intends them to be, why would these interventions be necessary or desirable?

These questions are worth considering. They are sincere questions from a desire to understand. What is God's intent? Are transgender and intersex aspects of a person's existence as God intended them? For that matter, are gay and bisexual people as God intended? Or are we a result of the fall? And what are the implications?

There are a few different ways to think about the creation story and divine intent. Here are four:

Descriptive: "Male and female" describes what happened in Eden. It's the divine starting point. It is about what happened with Adam and Eve. It's not a mandate or a prescription in any sense. It's not a command.

Diverse creation: God created "male and female" and every combination of the two. God didn't intend everyone to fit the gender binary, and gender diversity is part of God's good creation and original intention. It may have been there from the beginning. Or perhaps God set in motion a reproductive mechanism that would inevitably produce these results.

Moral fallenness: God created all people to be either male or female. There is moral value in this ordering. Part of our ethical responsibility is to live out our gender as God intended, and the desire to do otherwise is temptation. Intersex people should conform to the binary as much as possible. Transgender people should recognize their sense of gender as a mistake and a departure from God's moral will (instead of merely a departure from God's natural will).

Natural fallenness: God created all people to be male or female, but things got dicey after the fall, and we have to adapt as best we can. Our adaptations aren't moral or immoral, just an attempt to function well and live faithfully given the bodies we have.[33]

Of these four options, all are potentially affirming except the third, moral fallenness. I believe in a combination of the first, second, and fourth options. I don't think God intended people to need medical interventions, but neither do I see any sense in withholding them.

In the model of natural fallenness, being transgender is a matter of adaptation, not of morality. Withholding medical interventions from someone who is transgender would be no different from withholding any other medical or adaptive intervention. Hormones or surgery could be an excellent way to treat gender dysphoria. They could help people live well and contribute to their communities rather than silently suffering under an unnecessary weight.

Natural fallenness is only valid if being transgender is not a choice or a sinful desire. If it's biological, transgender people don't deny their gender but reconcile a biological reality that is a matter of natural fallenness. Wires were crossed, and something other than genitalia is the best determination of one's gender. If all that is true, natural fallenness makes sense. There is no biblical imperative to moralize the situation.

Jesus gives guidance about how we should approach natural fallenness. His disciples asked if a man born blind was suffering for his sins or the sins of his parents. Throughout time people have ascribed moral failure to physical difficulties. Non-disabled people have historically regarded people with disabilities as stricken by God.

Jesus saw disability and physical challenges differently. He didn't see sin when He looked at natural fallenness in a man born blind. "Neither this man nor his parents sinned, but that the works of God should be revealed in him" (John 9:3).

GENDER AND THE FETAL BRAIN

What is the physical and medical evidence? Is gender determined by more than our genitalia? What do we know? What don't we know?

During gestation, hormones wash through the fetal brain. Most experts believe that gender identity begins in the brain after conception and before birth through this process. But they have yet to work out the details of exactly how this happens. The specifics remain unclear, and there is no brain scan to externally validate the feelings transgender people describe. We have to take them at their word. Still, the evidence favors an unchangeable neurological and biological reality.[34]

In other words, being transgender is not a choice. Our brains have an innate sense of gender. Gender is not purely about reproductive organs or socialization. It's a biologically coded innate sense of identity. There has long been evidence for this.

In 1965 a tragic accident with a circumcision tool damaged the penis of Bruce Reimer just eight months after his birth. His twin brother, Brian, was unharmed. Bruce's parents heard about a medical psychologist named John Money at Johns Hopkins when they saw him in a TV interview. Dr. Money said he was helping children born with ambiguous genitalia.

Taking on their case, Dr. Money recommended altering Bruce's genitalia to female, giving him female hormones, changing his name to Brenda, and raising him as a girl. He said Bruce would then believe he was a girl and have no difficulty. The parents agreed to most of his recommendations but didn't allow the full surgery.

Before he met with the Reimers, Dr. Money was already performing surgeries on newborn babies, sometimes without consent from their parents. When he altered the genitalia of intersex infants, he based it on a simple rule of thumb. If the penis was more than an inch, they were male. If less than an inch, they were female. Surgeries to make their genitalia more typical were considered simple corrections of a birth defect.

Dr. Money did this because he was confident that gender was not neurologically predetermined. He believed the gender of a child wasn't determined until age three. Before that, gender was malleable. So, by raising children appropriately, these babies would grow into their assigned gender, matching their surgically altered genitalia. Like many today who oppose gender transition, he believed there were psychological answers.

When Dr. Money heard about Bruce's case, he saw an opportunity to obtain his needed proof. He would be able to demonstrate his theories about gender development. Genitals and social development are the drivers of gender identity.

Unknown to the Reimers, as Dr. Money oversaw treatment, he published the case in professional journals. Dr. Money told the professional community in medical journals that his treatment was a wild success. It was a lie. Brenda felt like a boy, persistently and unchangeably. Brenda also acted in stereotypically male ways and wanted to dress like a boy. Finally learning the whole story as a teenager, Brenda changed his name to David.

Eventually, David found out about Dr. Money's dishonest publication of his case. David made a brave choice. He exposed the fraud in an article in *Rolling Stone*.

By this time, the damage was done. Dr. Money's fraudulent theories had been accepted and propagated throughout the professional community. For decades, genital surgeries on infants with ambiguous genitalia had been the standard of care for intersex babies. Tragically, Dr. Money's fraud wasn't exposed until 1997.

Only after David Reimer's exposé did the research progress to more data-driven and accurate understandings of gender. Gender specialists now believe there is a strong, built-in neurological component to gender.

I wish this story had a happy ending, but neither David nor his brother could withstand the pressure and disappointment. Brian committed suicide first, then David. You can read more about David's story and similar stories in Kathy Baldock's book, *Crossing the Bridgeless Canyon*.[35]

The impulse to make people clearly male or female led to tragic choices in the medical community. Misunderstanding the nature of gender has caused pain and death for an untold number of people. The surgeries on infant genitalia were cosmetic and not medically necessary. They can cause a lifetime of pain and struggle. Though these surgeries are no longer recommended, they still happen.

Why did David experience the psychological difficulties he did? Why do intersex babies who are surgically altered as infants often grow up to struggle with the results of that choice? It must be because a person's sense of gender isn't driven by their genitals or socialization. Gender doesn't come from life circumstances, personal desire, or choice.

Instead, a person's sense of gender is natural, enduring, and unchangeable. God psychologically stamps gender on the psyche of a person. In scientific terms, the brain is neurologically hard-wired with a sense of gender that cannot change through any technology or psychological treatment at our disposal.

I fear we've misunderstood what happens with transgender people. There could be cases in which the hormones that impact the neurological sense of gender don't match the hormones that influence the development of reproductive organs. Most likely, the fetal brain and body are exposed to hormones at different times in development. This explanation is the most feasible and matches the evidence, but there is still much to learn.

Though we can't point to a specific biological indicator, we can listen to what transgender people tell us. They tell us that they have a persistent sense of gender—unavoidable, unchosen, and unchangeable. Their brains send signals that don't fit expectations based on their external anatomy at birth. Their internal and external anatomy are misaligned. Transgender people have said this all along, and it fits the best scientific understanding we have today.

IDEOLOGY

I've often heard that there is a "transgender ideology," a kind of philosophical "transgenderism." This ideological position is rooted in postmodernism and subjectivity. It's a denial of essential truth. Transgender people, they say, make a particular kind of statement about reality. They say they can choose their reality by choosing their gender.

That's why many people respond to transgender people by saying, "I just don't agree." If you think of transgender identity as an ideological stand, it's subjective, and you can disagree. Being transgender would be a fanciful exercise in self-expression and ultimately absurd.

If we can choose our gender, why can't we choose our race? Why not choose our height? Why can't a 27-year-old white man identify as a 63-year-old Asian woman? While I understand how absurd this sounds, I have to point out that the real question is not about whether gender is a choice but how gender is determined.

Is it like height and age? Does having a vagina mean someone is a woman, just like being 5'7" means someone is 5'7"? Or does having a vagina only mean that someone has a vagina? Do other factors also influence gender?

Having heard the story of David Reimer and learned more about the neurological nature of gender, we can see that being transgender is not an ideology. Transgender people don't choose their gender. Why would they choose to be transgender? The world is unkind to them. It's a difficult path. Every transgender person I have ever met resisted being transgender. They've fought against it for many years in many ways.

Being transgender is not an ideological stance about the subjective nature of truth. It's a description of how a small number of people experience gender. Gender is real. It's not just external. It's not about personal choice or preference. On this question, the evidence is in. Gender is in the brain, stamped on the psychological makeup of every person. When people say they are transgender, they are saying that there is more to gender than genitalia.

THE "FALLEN" LABEL

Perhaps this situation is a result of the fall. But before rushing to that conclusion, we need to consider the tragic history of labeling people "fallen" and drawing moral conclusions about them because of this label. It's been disappointingly easy to disparage people with this label when they don't fit the mold and don't have the power to fight back. Victims included left-handed people, dark-skinned people, and women.

These beliefs in the fallenness of these groups were theologically justified by referencing Genesis 1 and 2. As far as we know, no one in the garden was left-handed. For a long time, lefties were considered deviant, a perversion of God's good creation.

Women were allegedly responsible for sin coming into the world. Our gender was associated with the fall. But even in Genesis 1 and 2, many theologians believed women were not entirely created in God's image but were more of an afterthought to serve men and satisfy the requirements of procreation.

Ostensibly, dark-skinned people didn't manifest the image of God. Europeans and white Americans pointed to their impressive cities. They considered themselves "civilized" Christians who had inherited the blessings of Adam as manifest in their ability to have dominion over the earth (Genesis 1:26). They didn't view other people as fully human. Instead, others were labeled "savages" whose humanity was unrealized. They applied this reasoning to African people and Native Americans alike. This theological justification enabled genocide and enslavement.

We have a terrible track record deciding who is and who isn't morally fallen. These mistaken and prejudicial judgments were all rooted in assumptions about the fall. They were all based on theological perspectives that ascribed moral defect and inferiority to people who were different.

I know it's a lot to ask, but could we consider the possibility that those of us who are not transgender are in danger of repeating this mistake? Maybe we've made a moral issue out of a simple difference. Perhaps it's been too easy for us to consider intersex and transgender people as products of the fall. Maybe it's been too easy for us to prescribe moral value to that fallenness.

All humanity is flawed. We are all prone to selfishness and sin, centering ourselves to the detriment of others. That's the real fallenness we need to be concerned about. It seems plausible that the fallenness of cisgender people has led us to moralize natural fallenness. We've made transgender people the sinners and ourselves the judges without really understanding what we were doing.

THE BASICS

If we were to think of intersex and transgender aspects of people's identity in terms of the natural fallenness, what would that look like? What are we seeing and hearing from people who have a transgender and/or intersex experience? What interventions could the church support?

Today, of 1,000 adults in the United States, six identify as transgender (0.6%). That's 1.4 million souls. Seven in 1,000 of 13–17-year-olds identify as transgender (0.7%), a total of 150,000 youth.[36] The number of people who identify as transgender is increasing as transgender identity becomes more visible and sometimes more socially acceptable. Because the issue is politicized transgender people are sometimes at greater risk of harassment and assault. This is similar to what happened with increasing acceptance of left-handedness. The numbers increased for a while, then plateaued. We can expect the same for transgender people.

Intersex people have sexual traits that do not fall uniformly into either male or female categories. Estimates of intersex people are much more challenging. That's because there's disagreement on what exactly constitutes an intersex person.

The broadest definition includes people who have any kind of reproductive, genital, genetic, hormonal, or otherwise identifiable biological differences. These differences may not manifest until adolescence. An estimated 1.7 percent of people fall into this category, about the same as the number of redheads. Most of this group doesn't have difficulty with their sex and gender. They feel clear about both and consider themselves cisgender even though there is some (often minor) variation in their sex characteristics.

Another way of estimating is based on how many babies are born with genitalia that is not obviously male or female. This method doesn't account for all intersex people. It excludes people who grew up and later discovered an aspect of their sex that isn't binary, such as variation in hormones, chromosomes, or internal sex anatomy like testes that never descend, undetected ovaries, or reproductive cells that never developed into male or female. The American Psychological Association estimates that one in 1,500 babies fit this category (0.07%). The most restrictive definitions estimate that only 0.018 percent of the population is intersex,[37] but this estimate probably doesn't count people we would think of as intersex, such as Geoffrey, mentioned earlier in this chapter.

By any estimate, only a small number of people are intersex. But the small number shouldn't matter to us as followers of Jesus. We must not be content letting a small number of people struggle without consolation or understanding. We don't dismiss people because they are few in number.

When Jesus told the parable of the lost sheep, He told it as an indictment of those who would ignore the plight of some just because they are few. The 99 sheep who were content with the suffering of the one sheep were left in the "wilderness" together. Meanwhile, Jesus went after the solitary abandoned sheep (Luke 15:3-7).

It doesn't matter if gender variation is rare. We are called to brave the wilderness to invite those people back to the fold. We are called to risk our safety and comfort for the sake of their safety and comfort.

Maria Jose Martinez-Patino was a female athlete, a hurdler from Spain. Despite female external anatomy and identifying as a woman her whole life, she was given genetic testing and found to have XY chromosomes. She was banned from sports in 1986 but fought the ruling and eventually won. She wasn't the first to experience this rejection, but she was the first to fight it and win.

More recently, South African runner Caster Semenya drew scrutiny when her race times dramatically improved. After winning the 2016 Olympic Gold Medal for women's 800-meter race, her testosterone levels were tested. Despite being a woman and having female anatomy, her testosterone levels were more consistent with a man's. Only then did she learn she had hyperandrogenism, which elevated her testosterone levels. She was initially stripped of her medal. Later it was restored. But recently, she has again been denied from performing in her sport. She's never publicly identified as intersex, her external anatomy is female, her sex organs are female, and her gender identity is female, but her hormone differences disqualify her from women's sports.[38]

Some intersex people also identify as transgender, some don't. Laura Beth Buchleiter is a trans friend of mine. As an adult, she transitioned to living as a woman. She worked with an endocrinologist for several years about hormone imbalances, and they decided to increase her estrogen. She also grew out her hair, changed her name, and got a new wardrobe. Since she and her family were conservative Christians, it was a strain on everyone. They felt she was going against the Bible and the will of God.

Only later, during an unrelated medical procedure, did she learn something about her body that no one had known. She had underdeveloped internal ovaries. She'd been intersex all along and hadn't known. She would never have known without the privilege of decent medical care and persistent advocates on her behalf, as well as a fair bit of chance. Perhaps there were biological reasons for her internal sense of gender that hadn't been immediately apparent. Laura Beth now travels the country sharing her story with churches and has written her memoir called *Shattering Masks: Affirming My Identity, Transitioning My Faith*.

Another intersex condition is complete androgen insensitivity. These individuals are born with XY chromosomes, but they don't respond to male hormones at the cellular level. As a result, they develop female genitalia. They are usually identified as girls at birth and raised accordingly. It often isn't until adolescence or later that they learn about their condition. Sometimes they only learn as adults when they cannot conceive children because they have no ovaries and no uterus, though they usually have a female gender identity.

In partial androgen insensitivity, the path is more unpredictable. With XY chromosomes, the individual has a mixed ability to respond to male hormones. They may have male genitalia, female genitalia, or ambiguous genitalia. Their gender identity may be male, female, or non-binary. They could have alignment between their genitalia and neurobiological gender, or they might not.

I recall a pastor friend telling me about a doctor in his Adventist congregation. This man is a solid conservative and takes the conservative side on most questions. But when transgender people were brought up, he became emotional and spoke with frustration of the church's misunderstanding. He said patients came to him expressing gender dysphoria, only to discover that they had strong intersex biology. He was convinced that there was a biological component the church was ignoring.

Anecdotally, I've met several people with similar experiences from conversations with trans people. I've also heard from doctors that it's not uncommon for patients to present as transgender, only to discover that they are intersex after medical testing. Some people initially identify as gay, lesbian, or bisexual, and as they learn and grow, they shift in their self-understanding, perhaps questioning their gender identity. Later, they may find that they are intersex. By this point, the church has already rejected them based on their initial self-understanding. The link between intersex conditions and the whole of the LGBTQ community has been poorly understood.

Identifying someone as intersex rather than transgender is a moving target. We couldn't always do genetic and hormone testing, ultrasounds, and surgeries. Many intersex people could never have been identified as such for most of human history. In the future, it's feasible that we will find an identifiable difference between cisgender and transgender people.

Someday we might be able to run a scan or test that will tell us if someone is transgender. There may already be progress in this,[39] but the research is inconclusive so far. Will we change our minds if science does find a reliably testable difference? If so, why not change our minds now?

Not all intersex people have variance between their anatomy and gender. Most have minor differences that are easy to reconcile. But for those who do have variance, there is ultimately one difference between intersex and transgender people. Intersex people have an identifiable biological difference they can point to. Many transgender people don't have any biological evidence explaining their sense of gender. They have no way of verifying what they are experiencing internally. All they have is the information being given to them directly by their brains, and many people consider that information subjective, without biological significance.[40]

But why do we consider this information subjective? If there were a real neurological difference, we would expect it to show up as a persistent internal sense of gender. And since our brains are certainly part of our bodies, the question itself is different. It isn't about feelings versus physiology. The organ between our ears is still an organ. How can we justify privileging one part of the anatomy (the genitals) over another part (the brain)?

THE UNITY OF THE BODY

This helps us clarify one of the theological questions. What does unity of the body mean for transgender and intersex people? What does holistic theology mean for them?

Adventists have always held a firm belief in the unity of body and soul. While most religions teach dualism, that the soul is separate from the body, Adventists never have. We cannot be disembodied. The soul is the body, and the body is a living soul. "The Lord God formed man of the dust of the ground, and breathed into his nostrils the breath of life; and man became a living being" (Gen. 2:7).

Because of this teaching, Adventists care for our bodies. We care about what we put into our bodies. We care about how we present our bodies. We care about what we do with our bodies. Our bodies are to be cared for and protected because they are the means through which we experience God.

The GC statement said that transgender identity is a violation of that unity. The authors believe transgender people do not honor the realities of the body. They argue that this community chooses their feelings instead of honoring the bodies God gave them.

That's probably why I was so interested to find that transgender Christians speak of the theology of the body a lot. They speak in ways that are remarkably similar to Seventh-day Adventists, even if they aren't Adventist.[41]

At first, I found this puzzling. Why are these two groups starting in the same place and arriving at such different conclusions? I realized that transgender Christians who weren't Adventist were discovering the theology of the body through necessity. They can't separate their spirituality from their bodies. They must think clearly about their bodies and the unity of body and soul. This leads them to discover scriptural teachings that are remarkably Adventist.

Transgender people talk about making peace with their bodies. They do the work of harmonizing their bodies, learning to accept all of themselves. Through this experience, they know that our relationship with God is inextricable from our bodies. Accepting, loving, and living into their embodied experience is psychologically and spiritually healing.

It's not surprising that for transgender people, their physical bodies loom large in their spiritual experience. Yet, there is one critical difference from accepted Adventist theology. For so many transgender people I've spoken to, this process of embodiment didn't replace medical interventions but worked in harmony with them. Hormones and surgery often helped them experience gender alignment and, therefore, spiritual peace.

The GC statement says that "a human being is also meant to be an undivided sexual entity, and sexual identity cannot be independent from one's body." Most transgender people would ultimately agree with that statement. They just see a different path for achieving this goal.

A lot of transgender people have achieved this peace. Yet, in decades of being an Adventist, I've never met a single transgender person who reached this peace without transitioning. Perhaps that's not the best way to determine right from wrong, but one has to wonder why the solution the church proposes doesn't seem to work for anyone.

It could be that the church's theology is misplaced. The holistic theology of the soul is about the oneness of body and soul enlivened by the Breath of Life. Without the body, there is no soul. That oneness means that the way we inhabit our bodies has spiritual significance. It does not mean that our bodies will have no difficulties and need no medical interventions or social adaptations.

The duality of the body that the Adventist Church opposes is the duality of body and soul, not duality of genitalia and neural biology. Since nothing about gender transition implies that we have an immortal soul distinct from our bodies, there is no real problem here. The GC statement seems to have conflated categories. The unity of the body and the soul are different than the unity of external sexual anatomy and gender identity.

INTERVENTIONS

In seeking gender congruence, transgender people first transition socially. This means they live in the world in a way congruent with their internal sense of gender. Broadly speaking, there are both social and medical transitions. Social transitions include name changes, pronoun use, and gender presentation. Medical transitions include hormones and surgeries.

There is no one way to be transgender. While all trans people transition socially when they come out, not all transition medically. Before transitioning medically, there are psychological, social, and medical assessments to ensure interventions are indicated and safe. No one decides to transition on a whim. It's a process that usually takes years of reflection and stable indications of its importance. Some people get hormones; some don't. Some people get surgeries; some they don't.

An abundance of false information exists about the transition process, particularly for children, and it's helpful to go to the source. For those interested in learning more about how the medical community approaches transitions, that information is available for free from the World Professional Association for Transgender Health (WPATH.org). Information is also available from the Endocrine Society (endocrine.org).

I remember an older transgender woman I met through PFLAG[42] talking to me about how things had changed. She'd transitioned decades ago. Back then, bottom surgery (to change genitalia) was a sign of legitimacy. It was the ultimate goal. But now, she said, younger trans people feel more freedom to make decisions based on what's best for them, and sometimes they opt-out. Bottom surgery may be crucially important for some transgender people, but for others, it's not important at all.

These decisions are personal. No one should ever ask a transgender person about surgical interventions they have had or are planning to have. To do so is as invasive as asking anyone for specific information about their genitals. Transitioning means different things for different people.

The Adventist Church opposes bottom surgery for transgender people. This is no surprise. For intersex people, the GC statement says, "Those born with ambiguous genitalia may or may not benefit from corrective surgical treatment." This concerns me. Earlier in this chapter, we referenced the inhumane surgeries performed on the genitals of intersex infants. The GC has never opposed such surgeries, and I'm concerned their position could be perceived as endorsing them.

The viewpoint of the GC statement, that bottom surgery is wrong for trans people but acceptable for intersex people, is problematic. They determine gender based on a person's genitals to the exclusion of their neurobiology. But since that gender should be unambiguously male or female, if it's ambiguous, they advise operating. Why are ambiguous genitalia an acceptable reason to operate, but severe gender dysphoria isn't?

Consider how confusing this becomes in light of the reality that many trans people later discover they are intersex. Is their surgery retroactively morally acceptable? If they get the surgery without ever knowing they are intersex, but it turns out they are, are they guilty of sin, or are they innocent retroactively? And if in 20 years we learn to scan the brain for gender identity, do all trans people become intersex, and are they retroactively innocent?

After reading and rereading both statements from the GC and the BRI, I see that they are struggling. Both documents state early that "we recognize the uniqueness of their existential situation and the limitation of our knowledge in such issues."

The BRI document struggles to understand what to do about transgender people who join churches post-transition and what to do about existing marriages. It states that transgender people who have had bottom surgery should be treated consistent with that surgery. A transgender man would be considered and treated as a man, the same with a woman. Yet, a church member is not permitted by church standards to transition in the same way.

Things get more difficult in the BRI document. The church does not allow a transgender man to be with a cisgender man because that would be a "homosexual relationship." This statement recognizes the gender identity of the transgender person, but only to restrict a relationship. On the other hand, they discourage single transgender people from marrying someone of the opposite gender but stop short of forbidding it.

The document also identifies itself as "a current position." This language demonstrates an admirable willingness to grow and learn and a recognition that their understanding is evolving. This is hopeful. They are struggling and hopefully open to growth.[c] They aren't clear on what to do. They don't seem to have agreement on their committees. It's difficult for them, and it's good to see that wrestling.

And no wonder they wrestle. It's hard to know pastorally what to do in the reality of the local church. It's easier to consider moral stands about biology and gender abstractly, but since biological realities are complex, how does the church enforce its moral perspectives? Do they require medical examinations? Chromosomal testing? Evaluations from endocrinologists? If someone comes out as lesbian, do they ask them to get testing for intersex conditions?

---

c. This uncertainty may be why there is such a difference between the GC statement and the BRI statement. The BRI statement includes a long discussion about practical and pastoral concerns for transgender members who have had surgery. The GC based its statement on the BRI statement but left that entire portion of the discussion out, choosing to focus more on the theological instead of the more complex pastoral questions.

This is absurd. The church would never take such an invasive stance towards its members. But it only underscores the complexity of the questions and the impossibility of imposing moral conclusions on the local church level. Like many topics, gender, sex, and sexuality are not as simple as what we learned in kindergarten.

Applying these moral rules in the real world breaks down in the details. What too often happens is that those who don't fit expectations are misunderstood and reflexively required to accept moral standards that the church itself struggles to understand. Perhaps this reality alone is enough to merit liberty of conscience for the transgender and intersex people who embody these questions. Maybe we should allow them to take the lead when it comes to questions about their bodies.

COMPLICATED

There is no biblical advice about gender identity. If the Bible was clear, it would be easier for the church to be clear. Besides, hormone and surgical treatments options weren't available in Bible times, so that guidance could never be present.

Though we crave simplicity and clarity, it's not always as simple as we'd assumed. Sometimes it is simple. It's simple for those of us who are cisgender and whose sex presents in a typical way. Our interior biology and exterior biology are aligned. But this isn't true of everyone. In situations in which it's legitimately more complicated, we should let it get more complicated.

I fear we are trying to force simplicity both onto people and onto the text. When we try to force simplicity onto the text, we make mountains out of molehills. If the text says, "man and woman," we say it certainly means God created no variation in sex or gender and that we have a moral obligation to enforce this clarity. But is that what the author intended to say? I don't believe so. The author was not making commentary on intersex and transgender people. The text is simply being descriptive.

When we force simplicity into the complexity of people's lives, the consequences are devastating. Even with good intentions, the outcomes can be tragic. We abuse people when we try to force them into a box that doesn't fit.

"Abuse" may sound like a harsh word, but consider the following statistics. In K-12 school, transgender people recall being harassed (78%), physically assaulted (35 %), and sexually assaulted (12%). They have twice the rate of unemployment and four times the rate of extreme poverty, with 90 percent experiencing workplace harassment, mistreatment, or discrimination. They are fired, denied promotions, or not hired in the first place (47%) because of being transgender. They often try to hide that they are transgender to avoid discrimination. Homelessness is experienced by a staggering 19 percent of transgender people. Significant family rejection is shared by 57 percent of transgender people. Forty-one percent of transgender people attempt suicide, compared with 1.5 percent of the typical population.[43]

These numbers represent a reality that should be front and center for all of us. What we are doing as cisgender people is devastating the lives of transgender people. This is what happens when people are forced into a life they can't inhabit.

We've been talking so much about what the Bible says about gender; we should never forget that compassion is biblical. Caring for the lives of others and making decisions that lead to their thriving and health is a central concept in Scripture (Ps. 82:3, 4; Matt. 25:40; Col. 3:12). We should love others as we love ourselves (Matt. 22:39).

Transgender people have been clear about what they need to live healthy lives, and so have the scientists and professionals who work with and care for the medical, psychological, and spiritual well-being of transgender and intersex people. They ask for support and access to medical interventions. We should pay attention to what they say about their own lives. We would do well to listen and accept their influence on this topic.

GENDER AND EUNUCHS

There is biblical guidance. We are given examples of physically different people, including when that difference includes sexual variation. Eunuchs were a well-known category from the Hebrew Bible to the New Testament. Many transgender and intersex people find hope in the way God restored and honored eunuchs.

This isn't to say that eunuchs can be equated to trans or intersex people. Though some eunuchs were probably intersex, they were considered male. It's not a one-to-one correlation, but it guides us about how God has worked in the past for people who didn't conform to gender and sex expectations.

The category of "eunuch" was broader than I initially thought. Eunuchs were not only made eunuchs through castration, such as Daniel and his friends who were likely made eunuchs as adolescents by their Babylonian captors. Eunuchs were also "eunuchs of the sun" who were eunuchs from birth. We would probably classify at least some of these people as intersex today.[44]

Eunuchs were important people in the Ancient Near East and were often outside of typical gender norms. They were sometimes trusted advisers since they didn't have ambitions for their own progeny. The Hebrew word for "eunuch" is the same as the word for "trusted adviser." Eunuchs often watched over women in the court, guarding and helping them (e.g., Esther 2:14) because there was no concern that they could produce an illegitimate heir.

A religion that requires circumcision on the eighth day, as Judaism does (Gen. 17:12), is one in which the genitalia of all children are examined. Eunuchs were inevitably be identified, and decisions were made about intersex infants. The legal code of the Torah provides guidance. Eunuchs were excluded. Even if they were Levites, they were not allowed to serve as priests. Being a eunuch was considered a "defect" (Lev. 21:16-20). More seriously, they were excluded from "the assembly of the Lord" (Deut. 23:1).[45] Yet we Christians should find it instructive that Leviticus and Deuteronomy were not the last word:

> Do not . . . let the eunuch say, "Here I am, a dry tree." For thus says the Lord: "To the eunuchs who keep My Sabbaths, and choose what pleases Me, and hold fast My covenant, even to them I will give in My house and within My walls a place and a name better than that of sons and daughters; I will give them an everlasting name that shall not be cut off" (Isa. 56:3-5).

In Isaiah and also in the New Testament, eunuchs are not only restored but honored. One of the first converts to the church was the Ethiopian eunuch (Acts 8:26-40). He was reading the scroll of Isaiah just after the chapter we just quoted. Not understanding the prophecy, he asked God for guidance. By the hand of God, Philip appeared from nowhere to explain that the text was a prophecy about Jesus. The eunuch, learning about Jesus, wanted to follow him. Coming across a body of water, the eunuch proclaimed: "See, here is water. What hinders me from being baptized?" (Acts 8:36)

I wonder if that question wasn't rhetorical. The Ethiopian eunuch was doubly excluded from the assembly of God. First, he was a Gentile. Second, he was a eunuch. Perhaps he desired baptism and was waiting for all the reasons he couldn't be. But Philip, knowing he'd been divinely transported to this man, wasn't about to question whether the eunuch was fit for the kingdom. He baptized him then and there.

Indeed, Philip may have been following in the footsteps of Jesus. He advised that all should accept the status of eunuch if they are able (Matt. 19:11, 12). He suggested someone might make such a choice for the sake of the kingdom of heaven.

Jesus wasn't calling cisgender people to castrate themselves as a sacrifice to God. Yet, some literalists in the early church took His words much too literally. The early church was already developing an unhealthy demonization of sexual desire. They read Jesus' instructions that his followers should become like eunuchs if they are able, and they responded by castrating themselves.[46]

Jesus seemed to mean that the preferable state of His followers was celibacy, to live as eunuchs. This is quite the turn of events. Once excluded from the assembly of God's people, eunuchs are now an example to be emulated in the kingdom of heaven. Despite the first commandment of God in Genesis 1:28, "be fruitful and multiply," Jesus held eunuchs as exemplars in God's eyes. Jesus himself was a eunuch in this sense, never marrying or having children.

Transgender people are not eunuchs. Intersex people only sometimes are. The key difference was that eunuchs had a gender identity that matched society's understanding of their gender. Transgender people and some intersex people do not. But the fundamental similarity is that they didn't conform to societal expectations for their gender through physiology and behavior. This inability to conform led to their exclusion.

Yet later, God restored eunuchs and gave them a place of honor. This is just like God. The first shall be last. When we are weak, we are strong. As Rachel Held-Evans said, "The folks you're shutting out of the church today will be leading it tomorrow. That's how the Spirit works. The future's in the margins."

Were eunuchs part of God's original creation in Eden? Not according to Genesis 1 and 2. When God commanded Adam and Eve to be fruitful and multiply, that was a command eunuchs were physically unable to heed. Yet Jesus later chose to live as a eunuch, never having a wife or fathering children.

This brings to mind something important about the theology of the fall. We reactively think of the result of the fall as unfortunate, negative, and less-than. But that's not how the Bible views things.

The results of the fall can also be morally exemplary in the kingdom of God. Eunuchs are one such example. The incarnation itself is another. The incarnation, life, teachings, suffering, and crucifixion of Jesus all resulted from the fall. The greatest revelation of God's person, and the greatest revelation of God's love, all exist because of the fall.

In truth, everything around us is a result of the fall. The Bible itself is a record of fallen people striving to know God. The Bible wouldn't exist without the fall. All this is part of the mess we live in, but all of it is how God chose to reveal goodness, love, and mercy.

This is the nature of God: to bring beauty from ashes, strength from fear. This is what we find in the restoration of eunuchs. It's what we see in the incarnation of Jesus. It's also what we can see in the lives of intersex and transgender people. The Bible doesn't picture people always trying to live as if they are in Eden but living courageously and virtuously in the face of suffering, pain, and difficulty.

VIRTUE IN ACTION

A friend of mine, Randi Robertson, was an associate professor of Aviation at an Adventist university. Earlier in life, she'd done what so many transgender women do when they're trying to be men. She chose a hyper-masculine career. If there was any way of embracing her masculinity, it was becoming an Air Force pilot. She served in the military for 22 years.

After retiring, she was hired to overhaul the university's aviation program. Still living as a man, she hadn't told anyone she was transgender, but she'd always felt and known herself to be a woman. By not transitioning, she spared herself from the heartache of direct rejection and lived up to her responsibility to care for her spouse and two children. She maintained her place, respect, and job in the Adventist system, but ultimately it wasn't worth it.

Robertson chose to resign from her position with the university, knowing that her transition would inevitably lead to her termination. She also preemptively resigned for the sake of the university, knowing her transition would cause significant controversy. When she resigned, she communicated her reasons for leaving and the reasons, as an Adventist, she believed transitioning was the right thing to do.

Reflecting on the response of her colleagues, Robertson says she felt no judgment from most in university leadership nor from fellow professors who worked with her and her wife. Many were very supportive. There were, of course, notable exceptions.

Despite relative support and goodwill on a personal level, she was never invited to return as a guest speaker at this or any other Adventist school. Yet, she made it clear on her departure that she would be happy to do so. As one of the most eminently qualified aviation educators within Adventist circles, her expertise would normally have been sought after.

What happened? When Robertson finally decided to align with her internal sense of gender, she was institutionally barred from leadership or employment.

The Adventist Church judged Robertson's internal sense of gender as a "defect," just as Leviticus 21 spoke of eunuchs. No matter what the personal convictions of university employees, she was no longer acceptable for Adventist employment. She knew this would happen.

She told me, "I left because I knew that leadership would be forced to terminate me if I didn't leave on my own. People within the community would have tried to stop it and raised hell for the university leadership and my department, which I worked so hard to improve. It wouldn't have made a difference. Understanding the SDA hierarchy and the political forces, we took the course of action we did."

What impresses me so much about Randi is how intentionally, persistently, and compassionately she chose to come out. She knew she would never really be at home again in her church. Yet coming out was important, not only for herself but for others who would come after her.

She patiently explained herself to Adventist colleagues. She spoke to them about the difficulties of being transgender in the Adventist Church and of the importance of affirmation. She explained her position theologically with both depth and humor.

When I asked about her experiences, it was plain to see that she chose her course of action not because it would be easy but because it was the right thing to do. It was an act of compassion for those who would come after her and those who failed to understand.

For gay, bisexual, and transgender people who affirm their gender or sexuality, holding onto one's faith can be difficult, particularly as an Adventist. It's a narrow path. Most people abandon either their sexuality or their faith. Increasingly, those of us who hold both are finding support and community, but only by the grace of God is this a path any of us can walk.

When I was preparing to come out, I attended support groups where I met quite a few transgender people. I'd never really thought about their experience. Now I tried to put myself in their position, and I couldn't project what it would be like or feel like. I felt stuck. Their experience was so alien to mine, and it was difficult to understand.

Then I realized I don't need to understand. I don't need to imagine feeling the way they feel. That would only be my imagination, not reality. It wasn't important that I understand, but that I accept. So instead of struggling to understand when transgender people spoke about their experiences, I received and believed what they said.

I heard heartbreaking stories. I was shocked at the callous attitudes from families, friends, coworkers, employers, and congregations. I was also surprised at the integrity they displayed throughout their lives, the persistence with which so many worked to make the lives of others better.

I met Karry, who had been on the police force for her entire career in a conservative city with a lot of religious influence. "I was a man's man," she told me. But all that time, she was hiding that she was transgender. No one would have guessed. She maintained this for her entire career until she was eligible for retirement.

By this time, Karry had finally decided to come out and live her life with congruence. She could easily have retired and then started her new life, but she made a surprising decision. She decided to come out as a transgender woman and work one more year. Her attitude was defiantly optimistic, but it was apparent to me that she'd been harassed and denigrated by her colleagues.

When I was getting ready to come out as bisexual to my community— parents, church, family, and friends. I was terrified. I had no idea how I would do it. My heart was already breaking. The thought of doing what Karry did seemed overwhelming. I didn't understand how she could do it, let alone why. I asked why she chose to work that extra year. She said, "So the next person wouldn't have to be the first."

This is the strength and love I've found in the transgender community. Before I met them, I regret to say that I was too busy thinking about them as sinful and broken to see their humanity and virtue. These are now people I admire, perhaps more than any others. They taught me so much about what it means to sacrifice for others. They lead the way.

Robertson tells me that no matter how hard she tried or how long she tried, she couldn't change her internal sense of gender. I accept it as truth. When a transgender person says to me (as many have said) that the difficulty of trying to pretend every day that they are someone they aren't became so intense that they had to choose between transitioning or dying, I believe them. When they talk about the pain of rejection, of people who refuse to call them by their new name or use their correct pronouns, I take them at their word. I trust that they understand what is happening in their bodies and brains better than I do.

I also trust that they are strong, capable, and intelligent people because I've come to know them as such. I trust that they love God and pursue goodness and holiness in their lives because that's who I know them to be. I know they are strong, capable, and willing to sacrifice for the sake of others.

FEELINGS

This is how I see transgender people now. But I remember when I felt quite differently. Years ago, I was listening to a pastor make a case for affirming transgender people. He talked about these same difficulties I'm describing. As I listened to him, I experienced growing discomfort.

His words sounded compassionate. But didn't they deny God's Word? Besides, I was attracted to women, and I was able to live with it. I thought of my attractions as feelings that I could ignore. I tried to listen and stay open as he was preaching, but I struggled.

Later, I interrupted as he was talking to someone else about these ideas. I couldn't take it. If transgender people could do whatever they felt like, what foundation was there for ethics? I butted into their conversation. "We can't just do whatever we feel," I said, exasperation in my voice.

He was unimpressed. "As a straight cisgender person, you can't possibly know what it's like."

This was too much for me. He had no way of knowing that I wasn't straight, but I sure did. Later, I tried to make him understand. It seemed so important that he understand. I knew it was reckless, but I said it anyway. "You shouldn't assume everyone is straight."

Of course, I felt like I said too much. I had told almost no one about my attraction to women. It was a secret that still felt like it could destroy me. Here I was foolishly implying I wasn't straight to someone I barely knew.[d]

I intensely believed that our feelings couldn't take the driver's seat. I was convicted, convicted so clearly I was willing to sacrifice personally. We can't just follow our feelings. That seemed like the essential principle.

Controlling our impulses is part of being Christian. Indeed, controlling our impulses is what separates us from animals. We learn to make informed, moral decisions, denying many of our desires when they don't align with God's will. We don't live by instinct. Why should LGBTQ people play by different rules?

Today I want to make the case that there is enough room here for us to hold two things at once, even though they might seem contradictory at first blush. We can affirm the legitimacy of the internal sense of gender that transgender people

---

d. I later tried to backpedal. I didn't feel that I was part of the conversation since I was attracted to men. I didn't know what it was like to be lesbian and certainly didn't know what it was like to be transgender. At the time, I hadn't unpacked the impact on my life of being bisexual and didn't consider myself part of the LGBTQ community.

have. Simultaneously, we can also affirm the importance of subjecting our feelings and impulses to God and God's will.

In fact, we are talking about steering a course between two extremes. Our feelings don't control us. Neither do we suppress and ignore them. Feelings are information we use to think rationally and prayerfully. The Bible is not void of feeling. Flip through the Psalms, Lamentations, Job, or any prophetic books, and the pathos is moving and vivid. Nor is it biblical to center our lives towards the gratification of feelings. Feelings, and the enduring emotions behind them, can be intelligently understood for the information they provide.

Sometimes transgender, bisexual, and gay people are characterized as being ruled by feelings. We are portrayed as worshipers at the shrine of desire. Affirmation of transgender identity or same-sex marriage is described as making an altar of emotions and worshiping gratification. That's what I thought when I dismissed the value of feelings, as if considering feelings was the same as being controlled by them.

In the case of transgender people, what they experience is more than superficial feelings. So many transgender people I know display an impressive ability to do and feel hard things. They make unthinkable sacrifices for the sake of others. They know that feelings come and go and that even our more persistent emotions change.

Yet, that doesn't mean that emotions are to be suppressed. Emotions have value as information. Understanding them and thinking theologically about our emotions is a better path. If we cease to care about how people feel, if we refuse to take mental health into account, we become less compassionate and loving. We become less like Jesus.

I've learned to be open to learning from feelings and emotions. Transgender people have told me that their feelings and emotions aren't primary. They are secondary to their sense of identity that they can't change or outrun. Their emotions respond to their enduring sense of self. No matter how their emotions might come, go, and change over time, the enduring sense of self remains.

As Robertson explained to me, "When people say, 'I feel . . .' they then go on to presume that a transgender person's sense of self is similar to when they feel happy or sad or angry. They are not remotely similar. Those feeling or emotions are not remotely like my sense of self." Randi and others describe their internal sense of gender as separate and distinct from the feelings and emotions they experience daily.

As I understand it from the conversations I've had and the testimonies I've heard, when a transgender woman tries to behave like a man, she can only act the part. No matter how good she gets at acting, she still feels as if she's acting. When a transgender man plays the part of a woman, he can never let down his guard, the role never fits, and the awkwardness never goes away for long.

My transgender friends have described a sense of feeling like outsiders in their own lives, longing for belonging but instead working to fit in. They've also explained the sheer exhaustion that comes from constantly faking their gender year after year, decade after decade. They describe a constant sense of their being and existence that is at variance with what is expected by society.

This sense of gender doesn't shift and change through faith, therapy, and maturity. It might abate for a while, only to come back stronger than ever. For whatever reason, it's not transformed by God or channeled in a manageable direction. For many transgender people, it's a persistent knowing that has to be constantly denied.

When this charade continues indefinitely, the result is often persistent and pervasive gender dysphoria. Dysphoria varies from person to person. Some people can withstand it for many years, distracted by other things in their lives. Some can live as themselves in some small part of life, which alleviates their gender dysphoria enough to get by. Others can't, as hard as they try. Still, others don't want to. They don't believe it's holistic. They don't see the point. But for none of them is it a matter of self-gratification or fulfillment. It's about survival, authenticity, and integrity.

Now I know that I was wrong. Transgender people aren't just doing whatever they feel like. I was dismissive, not only of transgender people but of myself. It's not just about feelings. People who follow the Adventist Church's guidelines usually experience persistent mental health problems, depression, anxiety, and suicidal thoughts. To call such experiences "feelings" is dismissive.

It's also about the other side of the coin. It's about the joy we experience and the contributions we can make to the world when we no longer have to ignore the truths we know in our bodies. It's not about bowing down to our feelings, but about rationally understanding them, with the help of God, and making decisions that help us live well and do good in this life.

INFORMED

I hope that at least the church can move forward on this topic with better information. The question we are asking is not about feelings versus biology but neural biology versus genital biology. Does the Bible have anything to say about that?

What appears at first blush to be clear statements of the stability and inviolability of gender are not. Genesis 1:27 teaches us that all human life has value because we are created in the image of God, "male and female." But this doesn't mean that intersex people don't exist any more than it means that frogs don't exist. Intersex people have traits of both "male and female"; frogs have traits of both "land" and "sea" animals. Perhaps transgender people also have diverse neurobiological features.

The Bible speaks of humanity with gendered language, but that doesn't erase the existence of either intersex or transgender people. The only biblical example we have of people who don't entirely fit the gender binary are eunuchs, and these people were accepted and given honor by Isaiah (Isa. 56) and Jesus (Matt. 19; Mark 10). This fits the biblical theme of justice for the vulnerable and love for those who are despised.

Adventist theologians acknowledge the reality of gender dysphoria. Their solution is for transgender people to accept the gender that matches their external biology, yet they recognize that it may not be possible. Transgender people themselves, and the medical community that serves them, agree that one's neurological gender identity cannot be changed by any means known at present. Being Christian and praying for this transformation doesn't seem to change this.

Then what's the solution? Adventist leaders have concluded that transgender people should endure the suffering of gender dysphoria. They should hope that God will transform them at the Second Coming. But what would that look like? Would God change the neurology of the transgender person? Or would God change the physical exterior?

Theologically, we've made a mistake by prioritizing the external body. The external may matter to us, but it's the mind and heart that matter to God (1 Sam. 16:7). What is the meaning of the resurrection if not that our minds will still be our own, but our bodies will be changed? (Rom. 8:10, 11; 1 Cor. 15:35-49; 2 Cor. 5:1; Phil. 3:2) And if it's our bodies that are changed, not our minds, wouldn't a transgender person's body be transformed to match their neurological gender identity? By emphasizing external biology, theologians have looked at transgender people through the eyes of fallen humanity, not through theologically informed eyes.

There are mysteries here. We don't understand exactly what we will be like in the resurrection. Yet, we have still undergone all kinds of corrective surgeries for physical defects and diseases without the slightest fear that we are disturbing God's design. A woman with a mastectomy gets reconstructive surgery. A person with imbalances or age-related decline takes hormones. A child going into early adolescents is often given puberty blockers. We don't blink at these medical interventions, but these same procedures are withheld from transgender people.

If we are to cooperate with the work of God, we will continue to transform our bodies when we have difficulties and sickness. Even our attempts at transformation will be fallen, incomplete, and faltering, but we won't let our imperfection stop us from doing our best. We'll fight disease, death, and emotional or relational problems with medical interventions. We'll do the best we can to be the best people we can, people who can serve God and one another. We will continue the work of Jesus, the great Healer of bodies. And we'll learn from Jesus to stop stigmatizing and judging those who need medicine. We'll acknowledge that eunuchs are among the greatest in the kingdom of God and that even those who are blind may be blind to bring glory to God.

There is biblical precedent for this expansive Christianity. God honors those who were formerly considered "defective." As a revelation of God's goodness and power, God privileges people we once pitied. We shouldn't be surprised to see God making a way for intersex and transgender people, just as God did for eunuchs, those who were blind, and other misunderstood people. This is what God loves to do.

Transgender and intersex people have a lot to give. So many are kind, strong, and willing to sacrifice to make the world a better place. They could edify the church. They could minister to us and help us be better people, as they have done for me. I hope the church can consider the possibility that we have fundamentally misunderstood them. We have misapplied vitally important biological and theological information. I hope we can step away from politics and culture wars and reconsider our choices about people and their lives.

CHAPTER 4

Did Jesus Define Marriage?

"I believe marriage is between a man and a woman because that's how Jesus defined it."

"Whenever Jesus talked about marriage, He talked about marriage between a man and a woman. Any sex outside of this is sinful because it's fornication, something Jesus often spoke against."

People point out that Jesus never talked about homosexuality. That's true in a strict sense. But Jesus did talk about marriage. Many see in His words an understanding or even a definition of what marriage is. When speaking about marriage, Jesus referred particularly to two verses.

Have you not read that He who made them at the beginning 'made them male and female' [Gen. 1:27], and said, 'For this reason a man shall leave his father and mother and be joined to his wife, and the two shall become one flesh'? [Gen. 2:24]. So then, they are no longer two but one flesh. Therefore what God has joined together, let not man separate (Matt. 19:4-6).[47]

Jesus is combining two texts from Genesis 1 and 2. Many people believe that Jesus does this to be clear about the definition of marriage based on Eden. That definition is "one man and one woman."

If it's a definition, it can be used in all kinds of situations. Definitions are less dependent on context. They are a quick way of understanding something in a universal sense. If Jesus is giving a definition, that definition will apply to same-sex marriage whether or not that was the topic of the conversation.

This passage also has implications for how Jesus interprets and applies Scripture. They ask Jesus about divorce: "Is it lawful for a man to divorce his wife for just any reason?" (verse 3)

Jesus responds by quoting from Genesis 1 and 2. But the Pharisees are unhappy with His response. It is much more restrictive than they expected. Plus, it doesn't fit with other parts of the Bible. "Why then did Moses command to give a certificate of divorce, and to put her away?" (verse 7)

Jesus' response shows that He has a method for interpretation. "Moses, because of the hardness of your hearts, permitted you to divorce your wives, but from the beginning it was not so" (verse 8).

Moses' law was not the final word but an accommodation for "the hardness of your hearts." The law of Moses is in Deuteronomy 24:1.

> When a man takes a wife and marries her, and it happens that she finds no favor in his eyes because he has found some uncleanness in her, [he shall write] her a certificate of divorce, [put] it in her hand, and [send] her out of his house.

Many people, theologians and pastors alike, have concluded that Moses wasn't trying to make divorce readily available. Men were already divorcing their wives. Moses was moderating divorce, telling them they at least had to give a certificate to make it official so the divorced wife could move on unencumbered.

In the Old Testament law, it's apparent that women did not have the same autonomy or legal rights as men. They had few choices in life. They were usually married off by their fathers to men who could drop them at any time.

This is a reflection of not only Israel but all the surrounding cultures in the Ancient Near East. Many have argued that the Hebrew Bible represents a dramatic improvement of conditions. They say that while it wasn't a good situation compared to today, it still would have been better to be born a woman in ancient Israel than in any of the surrounding cultures.[48]

Jesus' statement fits right in with this interpretation. According to Jesus,

Moses gave this commandment because the men in Israel had hard hearts. To whom were their hearts hard? Their wives.

Instead of focusing on these laws that accommodated an already bad situation, Jesus suggested focusing on a time when a husband's heart was not hard toward his wife. He asks His listeners to think instead of the binding commitment that Adam and Eve had to one another. That commitment was called "one flesh" (Gen. 2:24, Matt. 19:6).

Those who oppose marriage for same-sex partners make a theological point here that is worth hearing. We need to listen to this reasoning and understand its implications. Jesus was not only teaching about divorce. He was giving us insight into how to understand the text. Jesus was saying that the original creation takes priority. When a later law seems to violate the original creation in Genesis, we can fall back on God's original creation when everything was as it should be.

This also means, more broadly, that even though every text of the Bible has weight, not every text has the same weight. We should consider not only what is said, but why it is said, and its place in the whole of the Bible. We should take a broader view of Scripture, and as far as possible discern how, when, and why certain texts apply to certain situations.

In this situation, Jesus wants to bring a new awareness to His listeners. That awareness means a softening of hard hearts. By identifying with Moses' teachings on divorce that accommodated hard hearts, religious leaders showed that their hearts were also hard.

Since Jesus' strategy was to refer back to Genesis 1 and 2, the original couple, some believe this passage forbids same-sex marriage. Jesus is saying that our understanding of marriage is that it should be as it was in Eden. Jesus is giving a definition of marriage that is rooted in creation.

Because it's rooted in creation, it's morally superior, reflecting a time when life was unspoiled. This is the interpretive strategy they believe Jesus was using. It can also apply to the gender of marriage partners. Because Adam and Eve were male and female, the original creation models marriage as heterosexual. Not only this, but Jesus also pointedly used the phrase "male and female" to refer to marriage, making it even more evident.

QUESTIONS AND ANSWERS

As we have already seen, the grounding in original creation is a point that is central to accepted theology. In fact, in each text that speaks to same-sex erotic behavior, accepted theology sees moral reasoning based on original creation. In most cases, my study leads me to conclude that the references to Eden are debatable at most. This is the only text in which it's undeniably clear. Jesus is quoting Genesis 1 and 2 and naming "male and female."

Less clear is whether Jesus' interpretation applies to the gender requirements of marriage at all. This is not one of the texts of the Bible that refers to same-sex erotic behavior. Gender and sexuality are *our* question, but not Jesus' question. We are understandably looking for a direct answer to our question, but Jesus was asked about divorce.

But didn't Jesus sometimes answer questions He wasn't asked? Of course He did. We see this particularly in the Gospel of John, where Jesus often gives spiritual answers to tangible questions. For example, in John 4, the woman at the well asks a simple question about physical water. Jesus responds with a spiritual insight; she should ask for living water to never thirst again. He's directing her to higher spiritual realities, and this is common in John's Gospel. He is answering a question she never asked. Yet in we know from the text that this is happening. The text clarifies the double meaning. In fact, it's the point of the text.

That's not what we find in Matthew 19 and Mark 10. To demonstrate that Matthew 19 and Mark 10 apply to same-sex marriage, accepted theology must show that Jesus was answering more than the question at hand. How would we know this? The text itself would give a compelling reason, as it does elsewhere. That's the only way we'd know that we are not injecting our own ideas.

Also, it would have to be a reason that was relevant to the original audience.

In the absence of a compelling reason to understand the text differently, it's reasonable to assume that when they asked a question, and Jesus gave them an answer that makes sense to them, this is the intent of the text. When the further dialogue later in the chapter continues to focus on the original question, we have more confidence still. Without this safeguard, we are begging questions the text never intended to answer.

The question of their day was, "When can a marriage be dissolved?" Jesus answered that question. He was not asked, "Can people of the same gender get married?" Nor does anyone in all of Scripture ask this question. It's our question, not theirs. To substitute our question for theirs is a misreading of Scripture, even if well intended.

Even broadening the subject isn't indicated in the text itself. Jesus wasn't asked, "What is marriage?" Nor did Jesus respond by saying "marriage is…" We know that "the seventh day is the Sabbath" (Ex. 20:8). We know that "faith is the substance of things hoped for, the evidence of things not seen" (Heb. 11:1). No definition of marriage is given in Scripture with the words "marriage is…"

An example of what can go wrong when we apply a text beyond its intended meaning is in the Parable of the Rich Man and Lazarus (Luke 16:19-31). In this parable, Jesus uses the imagery of Lazarus and the rich man dying and going directly and immediately to heaven and hell, respectively. In heaven, Lazarus is in the bosom of Abraham and has all he could want or need. In hell, the formerly rich man is tormented for his failure to care for the needs of Lazarus.

Christians who believe we go directly to heaven or hell when we die say that in this parable, Jesus taught this very doctrine. We Adventists object. We say that we can only draw from the text the meaning that the text itself gives. Jesus was using a familiar story and common phrasing; He wasn't trying to make any point outside of the topic at hand. The point is, "If they do not hear Moses and the prophets, neither will they be persuaded though one rise from the dead" (Luke 16:31).

Adventists have already accepted the idea that we need to be cautious about drawing extra conclusions when we already know the main point. Otherwise, we would have to conclude that Luke 16:31 directly contradicts Adventist doctrines about the nature of death. It's not a leap to apply the same principle to Matthew 19 and Mark 10. It's a matter of consistency.

As another example, we don't take all of Jesus' statements to be universal. It's important to pay close attention to context. Later in Matthew 19, after speaking about divorce, Jesus is asked how to be saved. Jesus' response? "Go, sell what you have and give to the poor, and you will have treasure in heaven; and come, follow me" (Matt. 19:21).

If we focus on context, we will be cautious about making broad applications. Jesus isn't saying all Christians need to have a big garage sale, sell their homes, cash out their 401Ks, and donate all the proceeds to ADRA. He isn't saying we need to leave behind our communities and families to follow Jesus. We're careful to point out that this command was given to a specific person. Because we are careful about context here at the end of Matthew 19, we should also be careful at the beginning of the same chapter. We should head the context.

JESUS AND CREATION

But what about Creation? Isn't the reference to creation what makes it universal? That is a crucially important question. Since Jesus is showing priority for the original creation in these verses, is that an indication that when speaking about marriage, we should always prioritize God's original design?

I would love to do a complete investigation of this question. What is Jesus' methodology for applying Genesis to the present day? How does He use Genesis 1 and 2 to interpret other texts? What do we find when we compare various passages in which He does this? Unfortunately, there is too little to go on.

Matthew 19 and Mark 10 both tell the same story and are the only places in all of the Gospels in which Jesus explicitly quotes the original creation in answering any question. It's also the only place where he references Adam and Eve. For Jesus, using creation as a moral template is an uncommon approach.

There are three possible allusions to something from creation. Our creation in the image of God (Mat. 22:21; Mark 12:17; Luke 20:25) and perhaps he speaks of the existence of the serpent in Eden when he says "he was a murderer from the beginning" (John 8:44). These are hardly evidence that the creation of Adam and Eve are moral templates for marriage today.

In Mark 2:27 we find a reference to creation that I would argue is more persuasive on the affirming side. Jesus says, "The Sabbath was made for man, not man for the Sabbath." Comparing this to Genesis 2, we find that the creation account only says that God "rested" (the literal Hebrew word "sabbathed"), not that God made the Sabbath for humanity. Jesus draws a conclusion based on the design for Sabbath, but he gives a meaning that isn't explicit in Genesis 2. Sabbath was created for us because it was part of creation. What broader conclusion can we draw? Creation is for us.

When we accept this teaching on creation, that it is for us, the principle can be applied to marriage. "Marriage was made for man, not man for marriage." This in no way prioritizes heterosexual marriage. In fact, it might imply that the institution should be open to all God's creation.

In fact, Jesus refers to the laws of Moses much more frequently than creation as an indication of what is good and what is the will of God.[49] I am not saying that there is no meaning in Eden. It does mean that overall, Jesus didn't treat Genesis 1 and 2 as a moral template of immoveable realities. Jesus' moral center is easy to locate, and it isn't the Creation account, though it does flow from the two principles Jesus quoted from creation: that we are in God's image and that the law is for our good.

Something else about this passage gives me reason to doubt that Jesus was drawing on the description of Eden as a moral prescription. Just a couple verses later, Jesus contradicts Eden. Adam wanted a spouse, and Genesis says that "it is not good for man to be alone" (Gen. 2:18). Genesis implies that celibacy is not good. Yet Jesus says it is good. Not everyone can be celibate, but "he who is able to accept it, let him accept it" (Matt. 19:12).

This actually makes perfect sense. As we've already discussed, Genesis is not a universal rule but a narrative describing creation in general ways. For most people, it's not good to be without a spouse. Jesus agrees with this. But for those to whom "it has been given," celibacy is good. That's because Adam is not our example; Jesus is.

God blesses the life-choice of celibacy even when it doesn't align with the original creation. That should give us pause. There is a risk of over-generalizing Jesus' Creation statement. Jesus didn't see the original creation as the moral imperative in all situations.

So why mention creation at all? The text answers this as well. Jesus' main moral concern is "the hardness of your hearts." Adam and Eve are an example of two people who did not have hard hearts. That's why they represent the better approach.

Taken as a whole, the moral imperative of Jesus' teachings throughout the Gospels is consistent. He always prioritizes the same principle. Jesus cares about where our hearts are toward one another and toward God.

When asked pointedly about the most significant law (Matt. 22:36-40), Jesus didn't refer to Genesis. He referred to the Law of Moses, citing two verses: "You shall love the Lord your God with all your heart, with all your soul, and with all your strength" (Deut. 6:5), and "You shall love your neighbor as yourself" (Lev. 19:18).

These laws were guiding lights for Jesus, the interpretive lens to apply the law. He said, "On these two commandments hang all the Law and the Prophets" (Matt. 22:40). There was no place for any law to find its moral grounding if not in these two principles of love.

Our text is no different. It's the hardness of heart that Jesus cares about. The problem with divorce is that it shows a hard heart rather than an open and soft heart of love. It's not a question of *whether* Jesus thinks Adam and Eve are important, but *why* they are important. They are important because they were open-hearted and loved one another, as demonstrated by Adam's spontaneous love-poetry expressing the forever bond he had with Eve.

This is now bone of my bones
And flesh of my flesh;
She shall be called Woman,
Because she was taken out of Man (Gen. 2:23).

Jesus is telling people that Moses' model is not the only one. Their hearts should be soft toward one another, as Adam's was. That's the primary moral principle and the moral point that Jesus consistently makes throughout the Gospels. His moral point is not that Eden is the legal template but that the law exists as a framework to support the love (the soft hearts) that should guide our treatment of one another.

SOFT HEARTS

When discussing the question of same-sex marriage, this should challenge all of us. When we engage in this discussion, are we doing so with hearts that are hard toward one another? Or with hearts that are soft and loving? Do we have soft hearts for those who oppose us? When we feel uncertain, confused, or challenged, do we resist the temptation to harden our hearts? Or do we strive to have hearts that are open to one another?

The challenge for the church is never to lose sight of the reality of LGBTQ lives. We are not a problem to be solved. Hearts can be hard in many ways. The church sometimes forgets that this is a tender conversation about people's lives, not a controversial, divisive, hot-topic. Sometimes LGBTQ people are seen through the lens of perceived sin or even disgust. In our churches, LGBTQ people are often treated as a problem or project. There are many ways to have hard hearts.

Since I came out and expressed my disagreement with the accepted theology, one of the most painful aspects of this conversation is that many people began treating me as an outsider. I knew it would happen. It's still painful being written off as someone who no longer belongs in the Adventist community, especially since Adventists tend to pay extra attention to other Adventists.

On the other hand, those of us who believe in affirming theology also need to be careful. It can be easy to write off people who oppose something so basic to our lives. It's easier to walk away. Sometimes we need to walk away for our own sanity. However, Jesus' words challenge us to strive for soft hearts, even as we maintain boundaries that protect us.

I've often wanted to lash out at people who disagree with me on this subject, and sometimes I have lashed out. In my pain, I've often wanted to judge, dismiss, and even hate those who make my life difficult. When Jesus speaks about loving the enemy, Jesus is speaking to me. It's so much easier to harden our hearts to one another than to remain soft.

Have we submitted ourselves to the softening power of the Spirit of God? That is the most critical question Jesus is raising in this passage. That's the moral heart.

DIVORCE IN THE TIME OF JESUS

Seen in this light, Jesus' moral reasoning is sharply focused on the question at hand. Jesus wasn't asked to define marriage. Jesus wasn't asked whether people of the same gender could get married. Jesus didn't use the language of definition by saying "marriage is." Jesus addressed the topic of divorce.

> The Pharisees also came to Him, testing Him, and saying to Him, "Is it lawful for a man to divorce his wife for just any reason?" (Matt. 19:3)

Jesus explicitly draws a hard line on divorce, much more restrictive than most churches follow today. He says divorce for any cause but fornication forces the other party to commit adultery.

> Whoever divorces his wife, except for sexual immorality, and marries another, commits adultery; and whoever marries her who is divorced commits adultery (verse 9).

The disciples found this rule extremely difficult. They lamented that Jesus' prohibition makes them think it might be better not to marry at all.

> His disciples said to Him, "If such is the case of the man with his wife, it is better not to marry" (verse 10).

Even so, Matthew's Gospel is permissive compared to the account of Jesus' words in Mark's Gospel. In Mark 10:2-12, Jesus entirely forbids divorce for any cause at all—including sexual immorality. Divorce is also totally restricted in Matthew 5:31, 32, and Luke 16:18.

When asked about His teachings on divorce, they wanted Jesus to take sides in a contemporary debate between two Rabbis, Hillel and Shammai. Hillel said it was lawful for a man "to divorce [one's] wife for just any reason" (verse 3). Shammai forbade divorce for any reason.

It's easy for us to transfer this discussion directly to our context. The question we ask is whether or not it is okay for people to divorce. Jesus was primarily asked whether it was okay for a husband to divorce his wife (Matt. 19:3, 7, 8), and only secondarily whether it was okay for a wife to divorce her husband (Mark 10:11, 12).[a]

DIVORCE, MALE, AND FEMALE

This helps us understand why Jesus used the phrase "male and female" when speaking of divorce. Jesus wasn't looking ahead 2,000 years to when people would want to marry someone of the same gender and answering this question even though it made no sense to the people in front of him. He was commenting on the question being asked by those in front of Him.

This was about divorce because men put women in a difficult position when they divorced them. Most women, especially Jewish women, did not have financial resources. They couldn't provide for themselves. They often had to remarry to survive.

This is about the human cost of divorce. Jesus' answer immediately impacted the lives of vulnerable women. Were Jesus to side with Hillel and allow divorce for any and every cause, real women would be on the streets begging for food. Jesus had to know that. This is not only about marriage; it's about caring for those who are vulnerable.

This is also consistent with Jesus' overall message. Jesus prioritizes human need. More often than I can count, Jesus talks about the need to care for and love one another. Jesus was intimately concerned about the way we treat one another, so He prioritized this in His response to the question of divorce.

Jesus also responds to the way that patriarchal culture harms women. Cheryl Anderson describes patriarchal cultures, particularly the patriarchal culture of Bible times. She summarizes the values as "women are objects to be controlled."[50] Patriarchal societies prioritize the thriving of men and the use that women have for furthering the objectives of men. Men have the power of choice, and women do not. We would be naïve to believe that there were no such attitudes in Jesus' day. Such a situation is born out in the question, "Is it lawful for a man to divorce his wife for just any reason?" (Matt. 19:3).

---

a. Matthew is writing to a Jewish audience, and Jewish people did not allow women to initiate divorce. Jesus was also speaking primarily to Jews. For most of His listeners, this was about whether men could divorce their wives for any reason (or no reason at all). Romans did allow women to initiate divorce, though this may have been more common with wealthy women only, women who could afford it. Women were also less likely to divorce their husbands because it meant losing their children, who would stay with the husband. Mark is writing to a Roman audience, and in Mark's gospel, the question also includes whether wives can divorce their husbands.

Jesus not only affirms the importance of fidelity in marriage, He affirms the humanity and significance of women. Jesus begins his discourse by affirming this dignity. "Have you not read that He who created them at the beginning 'made them male and female'?" (Matt. 19:4).

Women are in their creation equal to men in value, dignity, and importance. All of us are created by the hand of God. His Jewish audience knew their Bibles backward and forward. They would have immediately known that Jesus refers here to the creation of humanity in the image of God. The full text reads, "God created man in His own image; in the image of God He created him; male and female He created them" (Gen. 1:27). Jesus chose to quote the part of the message that specifically emphasized the equal value of women.

This is relevant. It mattered practically and immediately. Divorce laws carried stark implications for women and their dignity and worth. They may as well have asked, "Can a man throw his wife out on the street, destitute without recourse, because she burned his toast?"

Jesus is saying that women are not objects to be acquired and discarded at the whims of the men in their lives. They are not lesser creatures who exist for the convenience of men. They are filled full of the image of God: full of dignity, full of value, and fully human.

Jesus' response brims with moral implications. He reminds them that women were also created by God and in God's image. Jesus' statement highlights gender to remind His listeners that men are not the only image-bearers. Women are image-bearers too. Therefore, you men shall not idly cast aside the image of God. You shall not divorce your wife for any reason. You shall not leave her vulnerable and alone.

This is precisely the use of the Genesis narrative that we highlighted in chapter 2 about creation. Creation tells of our inherent worth, heavenly parents, and value as people loved by God.

DIVORCE TODAY

Divorce has such a different context today. Our culture isn't perfect, but most women are less vulnerable than they were 2,000 years ago. Jesus' values still apply. We are still called to care for one another. We are still called to have soft hearts and love one another. From a literal perspective, today's church has taken a much softer stance on divorce than Jesus did.

Someone once told me about her mother, Susan. Susan was active in her Adventist church in the 1950s. The church was her life. She was involved in children's ministry and faithfully attended and served every week. All that changed when she divorced her husband. She'd divorced him because of abuse and alcoholism. I don't know whether her church realized this, but it wouldn't have mattered. They relied upon Matthew 19 and Mark 10 to determine Susan's guilt.

The church gathered all the members, people Susan had known for decades, and they voted to disfellowship her. They took away her membership. They never again allowed her to teach their children or participate in any kind of ministry.

I can't imagine the shame she experienced. In her moment of greatest need, Susan's church family turned on her as if she was morally depraved. They treated her as if her depravity was contagious to their children. I can't understand how she continued to attend week after week, but she did.

Susan is one of many. The Bible was used to disfellowship people who divorced, forbid people from being remarried, and fire church employees who divorced or remarried. The church did so because, as they interpreted Jesus' statements, divorce was a violation of Jesus' teachings.

But things changed. They changed not because of the discovery of a Greek word that no one understood before but because of lived experience. As more and more people divorced, the problem became more personal. Like grains of sand, thousands of stories piled up in their midst until the weight of suffering finally caused peoples' hearts to soften.

This softening happened to a friend of mine. She once told me that she always looked down on people who were divorced. She thought they weren't good Christians. She laughed, then said, "until I got divorced." That story has repeated itself again and again in Christianity until it's happened at a church-wide level.

We made room for divorced people because we care about them and their stories. It happened slowly, but it happened. Beginning in the 1960s, more and more sincere followers of Jesus were either divorced or saw people they respected go through divorces. Slowly and painfully, policies began to change.

Divorce is not encouraged, but it is now generally recognized that good and sincere followers of God get divorced, remarry, and remain members in good standing. I even know several divorced pastors who remained pastors through the entire process of divorcing and remarrying. Even some of the best-known and most conservative pastors in our denomination are divorced and remarried. Depending on the circumstances, divorce alone doesn't disqualify someone from church membership or pastoral leadership, nor should it.

This change didn't happen because of new insight into Matthew 19:3-12, Mark 10:2-12, Matthew 5:31, 32, or Luke 16:18. No new theological understandings or new truths were revealed in the Greek language. It happened because Christians learned to better embody the character of God in the reality of divorce.

The change came because of new awareness, not new information. If we've allowed such experiences to change the way we treat divorced people because of our love for them, shouldn't we be open to new understandings of these texts for others as well?

How can we allow for grace and understanding for the divorced people Jesus spoke to plainly and directly, but not for gay and bisexual people who Jesus wasn't addressing? How can we relax strict literalism for those who were the subject of the text but hold firm literalism for those who were not the subject of the text?

We are too prone to rush to conclusions. We need to slow down and take our time. We need to discern prayerfully. We can read the text with real people in mind, applying Jesus' principles. We can also look at the text more closely than we have. Here are some valuable questions:

- What is the intent of the text?
- Where is the moral force?
- What is the underlying reasoning?
- How can we find an interpretation that is consistent in its moral reasoning?

Literalism makes it far too easy to read more into the text than was ever intended while simultaneously missing the moral point. That's especially easy when that reading aligns with our church's accepted understanding.

Before we are too literalistic, let's remember that people have used literalistic readings to explain away Adventist doctrine. They've quoted Romans 14:6: "He who observes the day, observes it to the Lord; and he who does not observe the day, to the Lord he does not observe it." They rightly said that the grammatical meaning free from context says people can choose their own Sabbath day. Adventists have responded by saying that the subject at hand was fasting, not the Sabbath. We say that we shouldn't take words out of their context but rather pay attention to the question asked.

They've quoted Luke 23:43: "Assuredly, I say to you, today you will be with me in paradise" to say we go straight to heaven when we die. We've noted that there is more nuance and possibility in Greek, and John 20:17 says that even on the third day, Jesus hadn't yet gone to heaven. We should be open to more contextual readings.

They've quoted Mark 7:18: "Do you not perceive that whatever enters a man from outside cannot defile him" to say the categories of clean and unclean meat are no longer valid. We said that the context was ceremonial washing, not a universal statement.

One of the beautiful aspects of Adventist theology is the careful attention to the context of these texts. Adventists are good at paying attention to the passage, not just the verse. That's the same principle we should apply here.

There's no harm in stopping to pay more attention to the text. What was the context? What were the meanings of the words? What did the author intend to say? I ask for nothing more than that kind of attention to detail in Matthew 19 and Mark 10.

We're also good at comparing Scripture with Scripture. I want to do that in this chapter. We need to look at the big picture, understand the verses Jesus quotes, and pay attention to context if we want to understand what Jesus is saying.

Here's why that's so hard in this situation: same-sex marriage is a huge issue. We want God to speak to us directly and clearly on this topic. We want Jesus to be asked about same-sex marriage. We want to hear what Jesus says. In our eagerness to hear clarity from God, we force this text beyond its biblical meaning.

To understand the text, we need to set those anxieties aside, leave them in the hands of God, and give ourselves space to be curious. This kind of trust is a big part of what it means to read the Bible under the influence of the Holy Spirit. We don't need to be afraid. Perfect love casts out even this kind of fear.

THE IMAGE OF GOD

When Jesus quotes Genesis 1:27, we should look at the full text:

> God created man in His own image; in the image of God He created him; male and female He created them (Gen. 1:27).

Ty Gibson, an Adventist pastor, has clarified the gospel for many people. He often emphasizes grace, forgiveness, and justice. Gibson communicates the love of God as our theological center. When speaking of the image of God, Gibson says:

> When the Bible says that human beings are creatures of the divine image, it means that we possess the capacity to love like God loves. . . . It lies within our power as human beings made in God's image to actualize events and relationships of everlasting beauty that cannot come to pass apart from our individual choices.[51]

This makes sense within the context of Jesus' words. Jesus wants His listeners to remember their capacity to love as God loves. He wants them to remember the choices they are making and align them with the love of God for all people, male and female. They shouldn't cast their wives out of their homes and give no thought to their survival.

Gibson goes further, pointing out what may be the most important theological point about the image of God:

> Fast forward to the New Testament, we encounter strategic uses of the word again, this time pertaining to Jesus Christ as a new and restored manifestation of what it means to be human. In 2 Corinthians 4:4, Paul tells us that Jesus 'is the image of God.' Hebrews 1:3 states that Jesus is 'the brightness of [God's] glory and the express image of His person.' Jesus now carries the descriptive title, 'the image of God,' because He is, in His humanity, the new pattern man. He is, as it were, a fresh enactment of the human experience, living once again in God's love as originally intended.[52]

Jesus is the fullest expression of the image of God. It doesn't matter that Jesus was never married and never had children. This single person is the greatest representation of God on earth.

Gibson alludes to another important New Testament theological concept. Jesus is the new Adam. The first Adam ultimately brought only destruction, but as the second Adam, Jesus brought life. Adam sinned and threw the world into death. Jesus was righteous and sacrificed Himself so we could be righteous. Jesus is the new leader of the human family (Rom. 5:12-21; 1 Cor. 15:21, 22, 45-49).

While the image of God tells us about our most basic nature as creatures created by God, there is also an aspirational element. That aspirational element is not that we aspire to be like Adam, but that we aspire to be like Jesus. Our model is not Adam, but Jesus. We would not conclude that this means all people should be celibate any more than we would assume that Adam's creation in the image of God means all people should be heterosexually married.

In general, Adventists are clear that this is the meaning of being created in God's image. See, for example, this passage from Ellen White's book *Patriarchs and Prophets*:

> Man was to bear God's image, both in outward resemblance and in character. Christ alone is "the express image" (Hebrews 1:3) of the Father; but man was formed in the likeness of God. His nature was in harmony with the will of God. His mind was capable of

comprehending divine things. His affections were pure; his appetites and passions were under the control of reason. He was holy and happy in bearing the image of God and in perfect obedience to His will (page 45).

The image of God is about our essential value, and aspirationally it's about our ability to be followers of Jesus. Before the Fall, Adam was flawless and in complete harmony with God. Yet this side of the cross, where we live our lives, Jesus is the full embodiment of that image.

REDEFINING GOD'S IMAGE

I am 100 percent on board with this theology of the image of God. It makes sense for the text. It's all there. It seems that it was on the mind of Jesus, the original writers, and the original hearers. It makes sense that Jesus would remind His hearers of human dignity and the value of both genders as He speaks of divorce. The rest of Scripture also supports this meaning. It's manifestly true, good, and righteous.

It usually seems like we agree on this meaning of the image of God. But when I start reading Adventists writing about same-gender marriage, I find a different take. This is what Ty Gibson says about the image of God when engaged in the debate about same-sex marriage:

> Man was only *half* of the masterpiece, *half* of a relational equation, *half* of God's image. *Half*, not the whole. The total image of God is constituted in the union of the male half and the female half in order to compose a single relational identity. This is evident from a rather casual examination of the male anatomy and the female anatomy . . . in their fitting together, the two bodies constitute a single entity, or 'one flesh,' capable of producing life.[53]

Remember the movie, *Jerry Maguire*? The movie's punchline is when Tom Cruise's character, Jerry, makes the smitten proclamation, "You complete me." The idea is that before the romantic union, each party is incomplete. Is this sentiment what God intended when He created man and woman in God's image? Are men and women incomplete until they become one flesh in marriage and sexual union?

When Gibson speaks of the male and female anatomy being a completion of the image of God, I must confess it feels like a stretch. I understand that sex is a beautiful gift, but I don't see even a hint anywhere in Scripture that human genitalia is what is meant by the image of God. I certainly disagree with the theology that male and female genitalia, when involved in the act of sex, is the image of God.

Such an interpretation seems painfully reductionist and excludes single and childless people such as Jesus and Paul. Are we to believe that when God said humanity was created in the image of God, it meant men and women have appropriate genitalia for sex and procreation?

Jesus is the apex of the image of God. Jesus was single, celibate, and childless. That means even procreation does nothing to increase the quality of God's image we embody. It must be possible to fulfill God's image completely without heterosexual sex, marriage, or biological procreation.[b]

Heterosexual marriage is not a moral principle. It's certainly a blessing, but it's not morality. It doesn't complete the image of God. As hard as I try, I can't reconcile Gibson's two very different statements. The best example of the image of God isn't heterosexual marriage; it's Jesus. How can we imagine that heterosexual marriage was the image of God? We can't. And the truth is, unless talking about same-sex marriage, we usually don't define the image of God this way at all.

Historically, this is also a new interpretation. Genesis 1:27, "God created man in His own image; in the image of God He created him; male and female He created them," wasn't imagined as a reference to marriage until Karl Barth popularized the idea in the twentieth century.[54] This interpretation is interesting but not necessary to understand the text, nor can it fully explain it.

I'm not even sure that those Adventists who define the image of God as heterosexual marriage are totally on board. I only ever hear the image of God described as a heterosexual pairing in one context: the exclusion of same-sex marriage. If we're on any other topic, the image of God means no such thing.

As an LGBTQ Adventist, it sometimes feels as though there are two versions of Adventism. One is the version I fell in love with. The other is the version for those of us who are gay, bisexual, and transgender. I can sense and feel this in many areas, but it may be strongest here.

---

b. The New Testament reveals a shift in the meaning of procreation. In the Hebrew Bible, God promises Abraham that his children will be as numerous as stars. Biological procreation was the way to expand the number of God's people. Religious leaders at the time of Christ were secure in their status as "sons of Abraham." But Jesus thought of family differently. Jesus said, "My mother and my brothers are these who hear the word of God and do it" (Luke 8:21). Paul often made faith the signifier of the family of God, not biology (Gal. 3:26). The New Testament emphasizes belief over biological relation and conversion (the new birth) over physical birth (John 3).

Here's another example of how theology sometimes shifts when discussing gay and bisexual people. The late Miroslav Kiš, a professor of theology at the Seventh-day Adventist Theological Seminary, wrote this about the image of God:

> At the highest level of life on earth—the human level—there are no classes, categories, or value distinctions. Both male and female humans are equally privileged to reflect God's image.[55]

This is what I believe about Jesus' use of the text in Matthew 19. The image of God is about human dignity. It's leveling and inclusive, showing the value of all women and men. But Kiš said something different when speaking about gay and bisexual people who affirm their sexuality:

> It is a formidable project indeed to reinvent oneself once the Creation pattern for humanness has been discarded. It is equally an impossible task to match the image of the reconstructed human with one which would incorporate fully the image of God.[56]

In a broader sense, I understand what Kiš and others are saying. Any act of sin is incompatible with the image of God within us. Those who believe same-sex marriage is a sin also think it tarnishes the image of God.

But among all sinners, only gay, bisexual, and transgender people are singled out this way. Only LGBTQ individuals are told we cannot reflect God's image. As some people define it, the image of God is essentially and inseparably heterosexual marriage. That should be a problem for all of us. It may be appropriate to say this is heterosexist theology and certainly not Jesus' point.

Kiš went too far. Gay, bisexual, and transgender people who believe in affirming theology are not "reconstructed human[s]" who fail to "incorporate fully the image of God." For the sake of our essential humanity, Kiš should have been unwilling to say such things because we also have the original grace of being created in God's image.

ORIGINAL GRACE

Religious men in Jesus' day prayed a ritual prayer that included thanking God that they were not born a woman. They excluded women from the inner temple court. They couldn't testify in a trial. They couldn't be a rabbi or a rabbi's disciple (Jesus also challenged this in Luke 10:38-42). Jewish women couldn't divorce their husbands. Even today, women don't count toward a quorum in Orthodox Jewish meetings and also don't count in many of the more conservative branches of Christianity.

That's why Jesus' first and foremost concern when speaking of divorce was to remind His listeners that God also created women. He wasn't talking about the gender configuration of marriage. He referred to Genesis 1:27 to remind everyone that women have value, dignity, and worth.

Single, divorced, and widowed people embody the image of God as much as anyone else. The image of God is imprinted on us in our creation. No matter how we live, no matter what mistakes we make, this original grace of our creation will always remain.

This is why all human life has equal value. We are each stamped with the image of God. We cannot erase it. It is in our essential nature. It's grace.

This is also how the image of God is understood elsewhere in Scripture. Each person is born in the image of God. Marriage as an institution is not the image of God; we are. We are shaped in God's image (Gen. 5:1; 9:6; Eph. 4:24; Col. 3:10; James 3:8-10).

This very principle has been the salvation of Christianity in many dark periods in which Christendom degraded humans because of their gender, ethnicity, religion, or social status. Religious leaders used theology to strip people of dignity, excluding them from the image of God to perpetuate injustice. Patriarchy, the crusades, slavery, and serfdom all depended on weakening the universality of the image of God. Christians even developed theological ideas for why certain people didn't bear God's image.[57]

God's creation calls us to recognize our shared humanity, which we obscure when the image of God is equated to heterosexual marriage. It takes away from the dignity of gay, bisexual, and transgender people. It makes the image of God a matter of human works, not of God's power. This is a line no person should be willing to cross, regardless of whether they support or oppose same-gender marriage.

I submit another statement from an Adventist institution that reminds us of the dignity of LGBTQ people. This is from the North American Division of Seventh-day Adventists in 2015:

> As imitators of Jesus, we welcome all people, inviting them into our faith communities and sacrificially serving them. Followers of Jesus, regardless of their views on alternative human sexualities, treat people with dignity and respect and extend hospitality and grace to all.[58]

I am grateful for this acknowledgment, even as I'm sad that it was necessary. From the least of us to the greatest, the image of God remains. This is the basic foundation of human dignity. This is the heart behind all the best movements and moments of Christianity.

ONE FLESH

After Jesus quotes Genesis 1:27 to say that men and women were both created in the image of God, Jesus quotes Genesis 2:24. "Therefore a man shall leave his father and mother and be joined to his wife, and they shall become one flesh."

The image of God is about basic human dignity for both sexes. The two becoming one flesh is about the permanence of the marriage connection. Separating flesh wounds the body. When two people commit and unite with one another, relationally and sexually, to become family, breaking this bond causes pain and injury.

Some proponents of accepted theology teach that the reference to "one flesh" is a sexual reference in the context of heterosexual marriage.[59] One flesh is seen as the uniting of male and female sexual anatomy.

Of course, there is a sexual element in Adam and Eve's marriage. Does this mean that Adam is referring to this sexual aspect of marriage? Let's look closely at the words from Genesis 2:23.

> And Adam said:
> "This is now bone of my bones
> And flesh of my flesh;
> She shall be called Woman
> Because she was taken out of Man."

It seems that these words aren't referring to sex. This flesh connection is because "she was taken out of me" (Gen. 2:21). She was actually formed from his body; therefore, they are forever connected as one body. But it's also true that she is the companion he couldn't find among the animals (Gen. 2:20). Adam and Eve share one flesh; the animals have a different flesh.

The terms Adam uses here are familiar in Hebrew Scripture. For example, Laban calls his relative, Jacob, "my bone and my flesh!" (Gen. 29:14). Of course, Laban isn't referring to sex. The words simply refer to the fact that they are related. Yet Laban's words echo Adam's words.

We find the phrase used the same way in Judges 9:2; 2 Samuel 5:1; 19:13, 14; and 1 Chronicles 11:1. "Bone and flesh" is never used to refer to a romantic couple except in Genesis 2.[60]

It seems more consistent with the rest of Scripture and the story itself to interpret the phrase "one flesh" as referring to their familial connection, not the act of sex. That's exactly how the writers of Scripture interpreted "flesh of my flesh." That's why they used it to refer to male relatives. It wasn't a euphemism for sex.

However, in the case of married people, the act of sex could signify the initiation of their familial relationship. This connects the act of sex with the bond of family, the bone and flesh bond. This doesn't rely on genital difference but on a willingness to unite in kinship.[c] Of course, they would have thought of men and women, but they also wouldn't have been intending to exclude or comment at all on the possibility of same-sex marriage. The concepts themselves aren't rooted in anything necessarily heterosexual.

This gives new meaning to Jesus' words:

> "For this reason a man shall leave his father and mother and be joined to his wife, and the two shall become one flesh"? [Gen. 2:24] So then, they are no longer two but one flesh. Therefore what God has joined together, let not man separate (Matt. 19:5, 6).

There's no reason to believe Jesus or Genesis referred only to heterosexual sex. The language emphasizes kinship, the unbreakable family bond (which, sadly, is sometimes broken). It applies to spouses and other family members as well.

Even the one text of Scripture in which "one flesh" does appear to refer to sex, closer examination of the surrounding texts tells a different story. The apostle Paul says in 1 Corinthians 6:15-20 that we can't be part of the body of Christ and "one flesh" with a sex worker. He is referring to sex. He uses a Greek word usually translated "prostitute" with a literal meaning of "fornicator."

But a careful reading of the passage shows that Paul is drawing a contrast. He begins by saying, "your bodies are members of Christ." Because of this, they shouldn't become "one flesh" with "a fornicator." The contrast tells us that sex is only one way to unite our bodies. We can't be one body with both Christ and with fornication. Therefore, this uniting can happen either through sex or with participation in the Christian community.

---

c. Other than genital fittedness, the other argument for understanding "one flesh" as exclusively heterosexual sex is procreation, but this doesn't work either because there is no reference to procreation in Genesis 2.

Sex might be one way to unite in body, but it's not the only way or even the truest way. According to Paul, we can and should experience that oneness through union with Christ and community. This excludes the idea that heterosexual genital sex is the exclusive fulfillment of "one flesh."

In fact, when Paul says paying for sex is incompatible with the body of Christ, I'm pretty confident this would apply regardless of the gender of the sexual partner, so I don't think it's a statement on heterosexuality. Paul is talking about the connection between sex and kinship. The absurdity of the man who pays for sex is that he is trying to have a sexual relationship without having a familial one. Paul says this is incompatible with a familial relationship with God and God's people.

The creation narrative is about more than heterosexually married people having sex. It includes more people and more stories than this one story alone. We should have a familial, "one flesh" bond with the community of faith. We can fulfill the longings of our hearts and our desire for companionship with more than heterosexual marriage. That's good news indeed.

WHAT IS JESUS SAYING ABOUT MARRIAGE?

So how are we to understand Jesus' words? I began this chapter by looking at moral arguments that take issue with same-sex marriage. They believe that Jesus is giving us a definition, that Jesus is saying marriage is between one man and one woman. But we've seen that this interpretation changes the context. It favors the question we want an answer to instead of the question Jesus was asked and answered.

I propose instead that Jesus is forbidding divorce for two reasons. First, because of the humanity and value of each person. This applies especially to the spouse who may be more financially and socially vulnerable.

Second, because marriage is a familial relationship, it creates a bond that is as visceral as the connection of our flesh and bone. Separating flesh and bone can only be done with pain and loss.

Yes, there are relationships in which the flesh has already been irreparably torn, and divorce is only an acknowledgment of vows already broken—some experience these divorces as a welcome relief. Abusive relationships should end immediately. But that only means that the damage happened before the paperwork was filled out. It doesn't mean there was no harm and pain.

I believe that Jesus said these words because His hope for all of us is that what is joined together should never be torn apart because our hearts remain soft.

This is no different than the hopes of the couples themselves when they choose to marry one another. The moral foundation Jesus draws on isn't heterosexuality. Jesus' foundation for marriage is human dignity, the deep connective tissue of family, and the soft hearts He hopes we have for one another. I also suspect that while Jesus acknowledged that Moses' permissiveness was due to the hardness of their hearts, He would recognize with grace that sometimes our hearts are also hard today. Jesus accepts our imperfections and offers us restoration.

After thinking about Jesus' words, we are left to wrestle with what it means to be married and a family. Is it legitimate to think of marriage and family in ways other than heterosexual? It's that question we turn to next.

CHAPTER 5

"One Man, One Woman"

"Once we understand that human beings were designed for other-centeredness, something brilliant dawns: we realize that there is an ingenious divine rationale for creating the man and the woman different from one another and yet complementary in the way their bodies and minds are able to interlock with one another. Men and women are different by design—intentionally, deliberately different."[61]

"The biblical definition of marriage is one man and one woman. God created it that way so there would be a balance of similarity and difference. It's been broadly recognized throughout time and in many different cultures."

Part of the purpose and meaning of marriage is bringing difference together, opposite ends of the gender spectrum. Indeed other-centered love is found in bridging the space between a man and a woman. That is a rationale and moral reason for forbidding same-sex marriage.

The first quote above, by Ty Gibson, expresses this idea. Marriage is stronger when both partners understand its gendered nature. Many conservative churches teach specifics about how husbands should treat their wives and how wives should treat their husbands, drawing on texts such as Ephesians 5:21-33. They don't see these roles as interchangeable; a man is always a wife's husband

and vice versa. In Scripture itself, those who married always married someone of the opposite sex. Even in polygamous relationships, wives are married only to their husband, not to each other.

Marriage is also a metaphor for the relationship between God and God's people. In the prophetic book of Hosea, an unfaithful wife symbolized God's people. Her husband, who represents God, faithfully loves her husband (see also Isaiah 54 and Ezekiel 16). Revelation is full of prophetic imagery of the church as Christ's bride (Rev. 12; 17; 21:9).

If marriage between a man and a woman follows the pattern of Christ and the church, where does that leave same-gender marriages? How do these relationships reflect Christ and the church?

In Scripture as well, from the beginning, marriage was described in these terms: "Therefore a man shall leave his father and his mother and be joined to his wife, and they shall become one flesh" (Gen. 2:24). This pattern was followed throughout Scripture.

The definition of marriage as one man and one woman is important. It's important not only because that was the configuration of marriage in Eden; male and female is also the basic nature of marriage almost universally. This applies to both Scripture and human societies.

Marriage is also a remarkably universal human institution. It is present in every corner of the globe, and nearly every society sociologists have ever sought out and documented in their attempt to understand humanity. In most societies, marriage is between a man and a woman, or possibly a man and multiple women. There are exceptions, but the exceptions are rare.

The Adventist Church has examples everywhere of beautiful, faithful, life-giving relationships between men and women. I grew up in one such home, with a mother and father who loved each other very much and whose love brought my brother and me into the world. I love marriage. I love marriage between a man and a woman. It's a beautiful thing.

This understanding of marriage as an institution fundamentally composed of a man and a woman is nearly ubiquitous. According to most conservative churches, those are the two basic ingredients of the recipe God made for the human family. They are like the flour and oil the widow used to make bread and feed the prophet (1 Kings 17:8-16). Both are necessary. Otherwise, we are stuck eating a pile of flour or drinking a glass of oil. There is creative energy in the recipe that goes beyond oneself.

All these objections boil down to one central point: the uniting of a man and a woman is essential to the institution of marriage.

The operative word here is "essential." It's not enough to be normative, typical, or good for a marriage to be a man and a woman. It must be that a marriage cannot be a marriage if both spouses have the same gender. That's what Gibson was getting at when he spoke of the sameness and difference of marriage. Without gender difference, it would be all sameness. Therefore, same-gender marriage is disqualified. The partners are too similar.

WHAT IS MARRIAGE?

I'm not alone in feeling frustrated when this conversation is condensed to bumper-sticker theology. Conversations about marriage have been egregiously over-simplified. I believe we can take a deeper look at the subject of marriage. What is it? How has it shifted and not shifted over the years? Let's begin with the foundation and work our way up.

What do we mean when we say marriage is an institution? According to *Merriam-Webster*, an institution is "a significant practice, relationship, or organization in a society or culture, e.g. The institution of marriage."

Interestingly, most dictionaries use "the institution of marriage" as the example for "institution." It's literally true that if you look up "institution" in the dictionary, you will find marriage. That's how important marriage is for our societies and our language. Marriage is foundational.

Notice that the institution of marriage doesn't exist as an abstract concept but in the reality of human lives. It is "a significant practice, relationship, or organization in a society or culture."[62] Marriage is part of "society or culture." This sounds simple enough, but it flies in the face of more recent understandings of marriage.

Today, people often describe marriage as a private institution, a choice two individuals make on their own that is all their own. One of the arguments in favor of same-sex marriage is simply that it's nobody else's business. It's something two people choose, and everyone else should stay out of it. It's a personal choice.

This personal understanding is not without merit. There is a private aspect. No one else is privy to the intimacies shared by partners when they are all alone in their home. In no other relationship are two people given this level of privacy with so much time spent behind closed doors. Couples can form their own ways of living, speaking, and being together. Marriage is a private culture of two.

But that's not the whole story. Social aspects of marriage are also powerful.

Marriage integrates more than the lives of the two people who get married; the entire community acknowledges and supports this primary relationship. Society recognizes that these two have chosen to intertwine their lives and futures, making each other and their children their first loyalty.

That's why married couples can share health insurance and tax returns. It's why married people don't need legal documentation to visit each other in the hospital or inherit property from one another. It's why we get time off from work to grieve when a spouse dies. It's why the federal government gives spousal visas. It's why everyone understands when we drop everything because of an emergency with our spouse. Society collectively recognizes that when our beloved is in danger, nothing is more urgent. It's understood that for married people, their first loyalty among billions of people in the world is to each other, and society supports that ordering of priorities.

This makes marriage a social institution. It's a special relationship in society. Communities gather to celebrate marriages. Marriage licenses even require witnesses. It's written into our laws, our religion, and our culture.

It's also why, when married people decide they no longer want to be married, there are laws and social expectations for divorce. Marriage is supported by society, and even divorce is mediated by law and social expectations. What happens to the kids? The house? The business? The debts? The ripples of a decision two people make grow and widen, touching society broadly. Marriages need to be disentangled legally and intentionally. We have social systems to help with that process as well.

BEGINNINGS ARE BEGINNINGS

This is what marriage is. Yet none of this was present in Genesis 2. Adam and Eve didn't have a wedding with all their friends and family because they had no friends and no family. They didn't sign a marriage certificate in the presence of two witnesses, ratified by an officiant, because no one else was there. There was no society to whom they could announce their marriage. Only as society became society did marriage begin to flesh out its meaning as a social institution. Only then was it given the name marriage.

When Moses delivered the law to Israel thousands of years later, for the most part, his laws would have had no relevance to the Garden of Eden. Most laws about sex and marriage regulate complex social relationships that didn't exist in Eden, where there were just two people.

When we speak of marriage as an institution, we speak of something that has matured with the development of society and unfolded throughout Scripture. It wasn't delivered in its fullness in Eden.

Had there been no sin, marriage would still have matured as society formed and developed. Marriage would still have provided the foundational relational unit on which society is built. It's hard to imagine what culture would have looked like without sin, but we can bet it would still have supported this institution.

THE SAME BUT DIFFERENT

What does it mean for this institution to develop along with society? Does marriage change when society changes? Or does it stay the same? People tend to take strong positions on this question.

Accepted theology usually stands on the side of marriage being fundamentally the same. Sometimes it concludes that if marriage were to change, it would shatter and cease to exist. Marriage is timeless and unchanging, established in the perfection of Eden. Therefore, same-gender marriage is a threat to marriage as an institution. It's a departure from Eden.

Advocates for same-gender marriage roll their eyes and say that the stability of marriage as an institution is an illusion. The only constant for marriage is change. It has no stable definition.

Neither extreme captures reality. Marriage is an institution with both remarkable universal meaning and remarkable capacity to adjust itself to the needs and values of any society. It is cogent and pliable at the same time.

In that sense, marriage is like the written word. Throughout time it's been recorded in different ways. It was chiseled in clay, impressed on scrolls of flattened animal hide, painted on thick, handmade paper, stamped with movable type, and laser printed on reams of paper. Now words flicker across the screen as ever-shifting forms of light. Yet, in every language and on every medium, writing is writing, and words are words.

So it is with marriage. In every culture, through every technology, in any place and time, and despite drastic changes in particulars, there is continuity. Marriage is marriage. It's always recognizable. When we see Egyptian hieroglyphics, we recognize it as writing. Likewise, when we see a family represented in an ancient text, we recognize it as a family and recognize that their marriages have continuity with our own.

Because marriage is foundational in all societies, it must be recognizable by consistent elements. It also must have flexibility to be able to fit all societies. Marriage has always managed to be what we need it to be, yet remain marriage.

There are many examples of this resiliency. If constant war decimates a society and most young men die, marriage needs to be polygamous so that enough children can be born to replace the men who died. If women cannot provide for themselves financially and are in constant physical danger, marriage becomes a way of protecting them even if this situation is less than ideal. In agrarian societies, marriage becomes a way to pass the family land and name from one generation to the next. In monarchies, it's a way to pass the dynasty from one generation to the next and provide stability for nations. In modern societies, where each partner has increasing autonomy, marriage is a place to experience love and partnership and the ideal way to raise children and experience financial prosperity. Marriage has proven elastic enough to meet the needs of shifting economic, social, and political realities.

The trick is to figure out what part of marriage is stable and what aspects change. Is there an essential essence to marriage? Is that essence unbending? What do we recognize that enables us to identify a marriage across the centuries?

MARRIAGE IS...

There is substance to marriage. It means something. That something can be described in terms of several different and related foundations. There is a universal aspect to these components. There are foundations to marriage.

Man and woman: People who get married are male and female, complete with social roles within the given society. The specifics change, but the presence of roles remains.

Unrelated couple: They should come from two different families and not be related to one another. The required distance of the relationship has shifted. Cousins were considered good marriage candidates not long ago, but not brothers and sisters. They could not marry or have sex, even if one or both were adopted.

Sex: Though many societies have had situations where sex could happen outside of marriage without disapproval (especially by men but sometimes by women), marriage is the only universally socially approved relationship for sex. In marriage, a sexual relationship is publicly formalized. Marriage is consummated by sex and can be annulled by the absence of sex.

Biological children: As a result of sex, children are an expected part of marriage. Marriage is a cradle of new life and the foundation of a family for the survival of humanity.

Financially joined: Married people generally share finances and financial goals. However, the financial choices were historically almost always entirely the husband's, particularly in Western countries.

Enduring unto death: The intention of marriage is a partnership that lasts a lifetime.

Community recognition: Marriage includes the recognition, participation, and blessing of society. This is true whether a society is secular or religious. This is why weddings often occur in churches and in front of family, friends, and community. This is why they are announced and celebrated within communities. The surrounding culture should recognize and respect this special commitment.

Legal status: Beyond simple recognition, married people have legal status that gives them access to privileged relationships with each other. Legal protections help with financial sharing, medical decision-making, even protection against testifying against each other in court.

Love: In today's Western society, love is the center of marriage; a loveless marriage is considered a tragedy. Love wasn't always this important, but that doesn't mean love hasn't always been part of the conversation about marriage.

We see that the definition of marriage is more complex than "one man, one woman." That's not precisely a definition at all. There are many scenarios under which a man and a woman are not married. What makes a man and a woman married? To get a definition, we must state the assumptions clearly:

Marriage is one unrelated man and one unrelated woman in a legally and socially recognized relationship that includes sex and forms a loving family with shared finances to raise biological children until the death of one spouse.

DOES MARRIAGE CHANGE?

These are the basic foundations of marriage as a social institution. Let's return to the original objection to same-gender marriage. *The uniting of a man and a woman is essential to the institution of marriage.*

It's not enough to establish that "one man, one woman" is normative or even foundational to marriage. It must be essential. There can be no exceptions, even if those exceptions are as rare as 3 percent of the population.[63]

Let's look again at the social elements of marriage. What foundational aspects of marriage are essential?

Unrelated couple: The first marriages post-Eden were presumably between brothers and sisters; otherwise, there would have been no marriages since everyone was a child of Adam and Eve (Gen. 4, 5). This is not only a post-fall matter. God's command to be fruitful, multiply, and fill the earth (Gen. 1:22, 28) came before the fall. The only way to carry out this command would have been marriage between brothers and sisters.

Yet many of the laws in Leviticus 18 were about preventing marriage to immediate family members. In modern society, we have further limited marriage, often making it illegal for cousins to marry, even though this was widely practiced as recently as 100 years ago.

We may be disgusted by the types of marriages implied in Genesis 1:28, between brother and sister. This disgust serves a purpose since today we have concerns of genetic disease, but this is certainly not the only reason. Even for adoptive siblings who have grown up together, marrying and having sex is usually illegal.

We recognize the invariability and importance of a person's family of origin. Brothers can't become husbands, and sisters can't become wives; the two relationships are incompatible. To say the least, the possibility of romance between siblings would be disruptive to family dynamics. It's worth pointing out that even though this is a value on which we agree today, it was foreign to the world of Eden.

How can we reconcile ourselves to this reality unless we acknowledge that marriage as an institution gains strength from its adaptability? Shifts in some of the foundational meanings need not abolish the institution. It's good that Eden isn't the model in this instance.

Sex: Definitely part of the core meaning of marriage, the command for a married couple to have sex is the very first command of God (Gen. 1:22, 28). The Song of Songs, an erotic love poem, celebrates the sexuality of marriage. Paul even says partners should not withhold sex in marriage (1 Cor. 7:3). He says marriage is where sexual desire can be expressed. "But if they cannot exercise self-control, they should marry. For it is better to marry than to burn with passion" (1 Cor. 7:9). There are no examples of sexless marriages in Scripture.

Yet, would a pastor refuse to perform a wedding ceremony if one partner was physically incapable of performing sexually? Would someone be ineligible for marriage if sexual capacity had been stolen through injury or a medical condition? Would it void a marriage that already existed? Would we consider such people to be genuinely married before God?

More to the point, if such a marriage did happen, would it change the definition of marriage? Does the exception nullify the rule? Certainly not. We recognize many exceptions, but these exceptions do not change what is normative and foundational.

Biological children: The first command in Scripture was to have sex. It wasn't sex for the fun of it, but to make babies (Gen. 1:22, 28). For the sake of the human race, Adam and Eve were under a lot of pressure to produce children. If they didn't, humanity would be a one-hit-wonder. They couldn't opt out of marriage, sex, or children. Celibacy was not an acceptable option in Eden.

Now that society exists, and marriage takes place in a fuller sense as a more mature institution than the nascent state of Eden, the rules aren't so strict. Whether by choice or infertility, a couple doesn't have to have children to have a marriage. People who marry with no intention of ever having children are still married. Pastors don't generally question the validity of such marriages. Families and friends might pressure the couple to have kids, but they don't withhold their blessing if they don't intend to have children. The same is true in cases in which the children in a marriage are not the biological children of both parents. Adoption may not be typical, but it is beautiful.

These exceptions don't threaten marriage. No one would question the validity of a marriage because it's childless or because children are adopted. Neither is the presence of childless marriages any threat whatsoever to the foundational association of marriage and children. As part of a larger society, marriages don't all have to be the same. Children are still a foundational aspect of marriage, even if they aren't part of all marriages.

Non-biological children even help us understand God's love. God's love is not only the love of a biological parent but the love of an adoptive parent (Rom. 8:15-17; Gal. 4:4, 5; Eph. 1:4-6). So even though biological offspring are normative for marriage, there are exceptions. These exceptions do not threaten marriage itself.

Financially joined: You see where I'm going with this. You may or may not see the wisdom in prenuptial agreements that prevent a couple from being financially joined, but that doesn't mean such marriages aren't marriages. They exist without changing the nature of marriage.

In fact, this is one area in which marriage has probably changed most dramatically. The level of financial agency for wives ranges widely. Many women (though not all) in wealthy nations have financial autonomy. They are less likely to be financially dependent on their marriages. (Yet many women around the globe still experience legal oblivion and total dependence.)

Historically, coverture existed in England for several centuries as a legal part of marriage. Married women had no legal standing, could not own property, and could not enter into any contracts but were considered covered by their husbands. Their legal identities were subsumed by his. Few of us would want to return even to the laws of the Torah that were similar to coventure (e.g., Num. 30). Most of us now consider this a result of cultural sexism, yet we don't think that those marriages were not marriages.

Enduring unto death: This was the original intent of marriage, with exceptions because of human frailty. Jesus calls us to the higher ideal of maintaining life-long commitment as God's original intention except for infidelity (Matt. 19:4-9; Mark 10:2-12), to which Paul adds abandonment (1 Cor. 7:10-16). Yet today's church continues to recognize that human frailty often results in divorce, and we have decided to meet this failure with grace, even in our leaders and pastors.

Community recognition: Communities sometimes recognize marriage; sometimes they don't. When they fail to recognize a marriage, the enterprise becomes exponentially more difficult. There are few ways to undercut the stability of a marriage more effectively than withdrawing social and religious recognition.

Legal status: This can be controversial. I know a man and woman who live together and consider themselves married, but they chose not to be married legally. They chose this because it's the only way they can afford health insurance that's needed for one spouse's survival. They did this despite being deeply committed, conservative Seventh-day Adventists. I've also heard of elderly couples who consider themselves married but don't marry legally because of the loss of social security benefits they need for their financial health.

Sometimes the state doesn't allow couples to be legally married. Biracial couples experienced this historically, enslaved people experienced it, same-gender couples experienced it, and in many countries, they are still excluded from marriage.

When two enslaved people chose to commit to each other in marriage, knowing their marriage couldn't be legal, knowing they could be torn apart at any time and their children stolen away, were they still married? Of course they were.

Sometimes marriages involve only the sanction of the state, sometimes only the sanction of the church, sometimes only the sanction of the party being married and their community of choice. This is something gay and bisexual people understand well.

Love: When Adam met Eve, he burst into a spontaneous love song (Gen. 2:23). Scripture, poetry, and literature are filled with odes to love. God created us to fall in love. We have the capacity to carry that love in a relationship throughout our lives. I must admit, it's my favorite part of marriage. But sadly, it's not part of every marriage. Yet, a marriage doesn't cease to be a marriage when there is no love.

In Genesis 30, we find the sad story of Leah, the unloved wife of Jacob. She does all she can to earn his love, but it's never enough. Jacob loves his second wife, Leah's sister Rachel. It's a tragedy. There are other, less tragic manifestations of loveless marriages, such as marriages for convenience, survival, or levirate marriage (Deut. 25:5-10), based on preserving the family name and inheritance. Even without love, there can be marriage.

WHAT'S MARRIAGE REALLY ABOUT?

None of the characteristics of marriage we've been talking about is always essential for every marriage. Yes, Adam and Eve are the typical, normative example of marriage. But as marriage matured beyond this embryonic point into a mature social institution, marriage took on an adaptive quality, even as it maintained its core meaning. In fact, it's perhaps because of this adaptive quality that it has preserved its core meaning.

People in a marriage between two people of the same gender are only a tiny part of the population. We are an exception to one of the normative categories of marriage, that of gender difference. But exceptions aren't the same as a total change. An exception that proves the rule is not a revolution or an attack; it's just an exception. Maybe there's a good reason for the exception.

For example, a couple could have solid reasons for not having children, but that doesn't mean marriage is unrelated to childbearing. Ushering in the next generation has always been a primary reason for marriage and continues to be, even if it's not part of every marriage.

Same-gender marriage is often characterized as a precursor to the total collapse of marriage as an institution. This fear, like many fears, is overblown. Like the death of God, the demise of marriage is repeatedly announced, even as marriage marches steadily on. Marriage will always involve one unrelated man and woman in a legally and socially recognized relationship that includes sex and forms a loving family with shared finances to raise biological children until the death of one spouse. And there will always be exceptions.

The institution of marriage has give and flexibility even as it persists. Perhaps it persists *because* of this give and flexibility. A tree stands in heavy winds if it can flex and sway. A rigid tree breaks under the force of heavy winds.

That doesn't mean society should welcome any and every adaptation in the definition or understanding of marriage. Some have absurdly argued that same-gender marriage will lead to child marriage or marriage to animals, as if allowing for one new possibility requires automatic approval of all conceivable possibilities. We can still use our minds. Exceptions happen only for good reasons.

The point is not that we should welcome any exceptions with mindlessly open arms. The point is that being an exception, in and of itself, is not a threat. The substance and reason for the exception are crucial. There are many exceptions. Any exception must have merit, but it must be judged by its merit, not automatically dismissed based on a rigidly essentialist definition.

With these exceptions in mind, how do we recognize marriage when we see it? When two people of the same gender have a wedding, make vows, and share a life, do we recognize this as a marriage? I argue that it is easily recognizable. It takes intentionality to deny that this is a marriage. Recognizing it as a marriage comes naturally, even if it feels new and strange for those who are unaccustomed.

GENDER ROLES AND SCRIPTURE

What about gender roles? From God's perspective, are gender roles necessary for marriage? Same-gender marriage is based on love, fidelity, monogamy, and commitment. Is that enough? In many ways, culture is moving in this direction by emphasizing love in marriage instead of gender roles. But are these principles enough? Are gender roles also necessary?

What do gender roles mean? It certainly isn't wrong to have a marriage where a man and a woman take traditional gender roles. It isn't wrong for a woman to be primarily focused on home and children. It isn't wrong for a man to be the breadwinner. But is this necessary for all marriages? Or are there exceptions?

The role of men and women in marriage and society is complicated, controversial, and beyond the scope of this book. I can't provide a comprehensive perspective. What I can and must do is interrogate the exclusivity that makes these gender roles normative and required. When I look at the Bible for gender roles, I admit quite a few exceptions.

If men are supposed to take leadership, particularly outside the home and particularly the leadership of women, and if Eve's usurpation in Genesis 2 leads to the fall of humanity, what do we do with Judges 4 and 5? The leadership of Deborah, one of the judges of Israel, was God-ordained and led not to the fall of Israel but to its triumph. God even delivered the life of the enemy into the hands of the woman, Jael, who killed him by driving a stake through his temple (Judg. 4:17-21). Why is Jael never mentioned as an example of biblical womanhood? She did what God called her to do. Even before the battle, Deborah was the political and spiritual leader of Israel. People didn't make big decisions without her blessing and guidance, not if they were following God. Elsewhere the judges of Israel are called "shepherds," another word for "pastor" (1 Chron. 17:6).

Men are the pursuers in relationships. Yet Ruth pursued Boaz, even going to him in the middle of the night and pulling back his garment. The woman in Song of Songs pursued the king more often than he pursued her. She initiated by being first to seek him out.

Another foundational role of men was inheriting property. But the daughters of Zelophehad received an inheritance even though it meant changing the law itself (Num. 17:1-11; Josh. 17:3, 4). Kings sought guidance from Huldah, the prophet (2 Kings 22:14-20; 2 Chron. 34:22-28).

In the New Testament, Junia, a woman, was an apostle (Rom. 16:7). The woman at Jacob's Well was the first woman called to preach (John 4). Men were called as disciples and called to learn from rabbis, yet Jesus commended Mary for behaving like a disciple instead of caring for her home. Meanwhile, her sister, Martha, was reprimanded for urging Jesus to follow the gender roles and saying that Mary's place was in the kitchen (Luke 10:38-42).

Women were the first at the empty tomb, bearing witness to the most momentous act of God, even though women were not legally legitimate witnesses (Matt. 25:5-8; Mark 16:2-8; Luke 24:1-8; John 20:1). When they told the male disciples that Jesus had risen from the dead, "their words seemed to them like idle tales, and they did not believe them" (Luke 24:11).

Paul entrusted his most important letter to a woman and referred to her in Greek as a "deacon" (Rom. 16:1, 2). Paul saw no problem enlisting a group of women to start a church without a male leader (Acts 16:11-15). I've heard pastors say that men should provide for their wives financially, yet women financially supported Jesus (Luke 8:1-3).

We Adventists have another prominent figure to consider, Ellen White. It's fair to say that the Seventh-day Adventist Church would not exist in its current form without her leadership. To say that she had less authority than a local church pastor, or even her husband, is disingenuous.

In the face of so many exceptions, it seems that the only way to make gender roles a universal mandate is to be vague about what we mean. That is exactly what is happening today. Definitions of gender roles in churches get more and more flexible and ambiguous. Even gender complementarians, who claim to teach traditional gender roles, often ignore the reality of what gender roles were in Christian tradition (and mercifully so).

HISTORICAL GENDER ROLES

Historically, the founders of Christianity held teachings about gender roles that are shocking to even the most conservative Christians today. Consider the following examples.

Do you not know that you are each an Eve? The sentence of God on this sex of yours lives in this age: the guilt must of necessity live too. You are the devil's gateway. . . . You destroyed so easily God's image, man (Tertullian, 155-220 A.D.).

It is improper for a woman to speak in the assembly no matter what she says, even if she says admirable things, or even saintly things, that is of little consequence, since it came from the mouth of a woman (Origen, 185-254 A.D.).

Woman was given to man, woman who was of small intelligence and who perhaps still lives more in accordance with the promptings of the inferior flesh than by superior reason.

Is this why the apostle Paul does not attribute the image of God to her? (Augustine, 354-430 A.D.).

Paul looks . . . to God's eternal law, which has made the female sex subject to the authority of men. On this account all women are born, that they may acknowledge themselves inferior in consequence of the superiority of the male sex (John Calvin, 1509-1564 AD).

Early Christian leaders were clear that gender roles were based on the natural inferiority of women. That is the historical teaching of the church. Today's Christians who support gender roles insist that men are not superior. They also insist that women are not less intelligent, less important, or less moral than men. Yet, that was not the case historically. The submission of women was always based on a belief in their inferiority.

Lumping all ideas about gender roles together as equivalent, as if they are one unified and historic Christian teaching, is simply false. Contemporary advocates of gender roles, no matter how conservative, have more in common with feminists than with the church fathers.

This may sound extreme to those who are accustomed to thinking of feminists as ideological opponents. It may seem extreme, but it's true. Both today's conservative Christians and today's feminists believe in the fundamental equality of men and women in being and capability, but this concept is mostly foreign to the church fathers and most of historical Christianity.[64]

It will be no surprise that I believe marital roles should be based on who people are, their gifts and passions, not their gender. The person who fixes the roof (or calls the roofer) should have the most skill and interest in the task. The same is true of the person who fixes dinner. The same is true of the person who preaches. We are human beings first, men and women second. The calling God has given us matters more than our gender. I see this in the Bible as well, in the passages cited above.

Yes, many conservative Adventists will disagree with some of this. But the reality of their marriages is often egalitarian. Most conservative men don't order their wives around or believe men are intellectually and morally superior to the women in their churches. They don't expect their wives to call them "lord" (1 Pet. 3:6).

This is especially true in the Adventist Church. We are indebted to the ministry of Ellen White. As one of the founders of our church, her influence on our thinking about gender is ever present. I find more appreciation for the gifts and callings of women in our church than what is present in most conservative Christian churches.

With all this in mind, the case for mandatory, universal, culturally transcendent gender roles is difficult to make. What is the meaning of such roles? What would they even look like? We are so different from the historical church that it's hard to tell. We no longer believe women are inferior, and that was the foundation for their complementarianism.

The Bible never offered the gender roles of marriage as the reason for prohibiting same-gender relationships. These roles themselves shifted a lot within Scripture and were often broken. Historically there is little continuity. I wonder how anyone can be confident they've figured this concept out and know just how and when it applies. Even when Scripture speaks of roles in a marriage, we will see we have reason to question their universal applicability.

LOVE AND RESPECT

What about the Bible verses that describe gender roles in marriage? Doesn't the Bible say that men and women should have different roles? Wives are instructed to respect their husbands and husbands to love their wives. There is supposed to be a give and take, with each person having different roles. The main passage supporting this viewpoint is Ephesians 5:22-28.

> Wives, submit to your own husbands, as to the Lord. For the husband is head of the wife, as also Christ is head of the church; and He is the Savior of the body. Therefore, just as the church is subject to Christ, so let the wives be to their own husbands in everything. Husbands, love your wives, just as Christ also loved the church and gave Himself for her, that He might sanctify and cleanse her with the washing of water by the word, that He might present her to Himself a glorious church, not having spot or wrinkle or any such thing, but that she should be holy and without blemish. So husbands ought to love their own wives as their own bodies; he who loves his wife loves himself.

This is a crucial part of the reasoning against same-gender marriage, especially in evangelical and Roman Catholic churches. Yet, I've rarely seen it cited as a primary reason in Adventist thinking. It's probably been less prominent for Adventists because our views on women tend to be more open than those of evangelical, Baptist, or Roman Catholic churches. We tend to recognize that to some degree, Paul was speaking to what was already happening in his culture, modifying it in a way that functioned to make marriages closer to God's ideal than they were at the time.

The evidence is strong that this is the case. The text we just cited, Ephesians 5:21-6:9, was one passage of four that made up what we call the "household codes." Two others were also written by Paul: Colossians 3:18-4:1 and Titus 2:3-4:1. One set of codes was written by Peter (1 Pet. 2:12-3:6).

These instructions were a Christian version of household codes common in Rome. The foundation of Roman life was the household. Wealthy Roman citizens ruled their households and functioned as the government within their walls. They had complete authority. Households were composed of the wife, immediate family, extended family, children (adopted and biological), enslaved people, freed people, and servants. Ruling over Roman citizens, and by extension over households, was the local governor and, ultimately, Caesar himself. The household had a vital place politically and socially as the first building block of society and government.

Christian household codes taught values that were somewhat different. They didn't end the ultimate authority of the husband who ruled the household. Paul's and Peter's codes still called everyone to submit to the patriarch. But they also called the patriarch to a higher standard. He was expected to love and care for all those in his charge. The church could presumably hold him accountable for doing so, but they did not remove his role as governor of his household.

Who was called to submit and obey the patriarch? In all four passages, both wives and enslaved people are called to this.[65] In 1 Peter 2:18-21, enslaved people are called to submit even when unjustly beaten by slaveholders. Note that this translation uses the word "servant" instead of slave. The Greek word *doulos* is also the word translated as "slave." Though it could have a dual meaning, in this context, it certainly includes enslaved people. Enslaved people are beaten mercilessly, not servants who have the freedom to find another employer. Here's what Peter had to say:

> Servants [or enslaved people], be submissive to your masters with all fear, not only to the good and gentle, but also to the harsh. For this is commendable, if because of conscience toward God one endures grief, suffering wrongfully. For what credit is it if, when you are beaten for your faults, you take it patiently? But when you do good and suffer, if you take it patiently, this is commendable before God. For to this you were called, because Christ also suffered for us, leaving us an example, that you should follow His steps (1 Pet. 2:18-21).

What are we to make of this? What is the purpose of these codes? Fortunately, in several instances, the authors give us the stated purpose. In 1 Peter 2:12, 1 Peter 3:1, Titus 2:5, and Titus 2:11, we are told that the purpose of submission is for the sake of the Christian witness to the world, not because these household codes were inherently and transculturally moral.

Ample evidence indicates that these household codes speak to a specific cultural context that is vastly different than our own. They were doing what was right for their time and place. It's inconsistent to apply texts about husbands and wives as rigid concepts that must stand for all time yet support the abolition of slavery. The same passages that told wives to submit to their husbands told enslaved people to submit to those who enslaved them.

If we are willing to abolish slavery altogether, we shouldn't point to texts such as Ephesians 5 as God's eternal definition of marriage. They were a response to Roman codes, critiquing Roman culture while remaining part of it. We have a lot to learn from them within the proper context, but they aren't universal laws.

If gender roles in Scripture are not as transcultural as we once thought, we should use caution. How can we know that we are importing the morality of the Bible and not the culture of Bible times? If gender roles were the foundation for excluding same-gender marriage, they would need to be presented clearly, decisively, and universally for all times and all places. This is simply not done.

PSYCHOLOGICAL COMPLEMENTS

For some, the last vestige of gender roles is that God created men and women to be the perfect psychological complement to one another. Maybe men aren't superior. Maybe women are equally capable to men. But some might say that men and women fit psychologically.

In most cases, that is entirely true. But male-female marriages don't work well for gay people and sometimes don't work well for bisexual people. They are bereft of the natural psychological complement that draws men and women to each other. Gay people experience this love with someone of the same gender. Bisexual people span both experiences.

As a bisexual person myself, what I experience psychologically for men is no different than what I experience psychologically for women.[a] They aren't different types of impulses. They aren't even different impulses. It's one impulse. My desire is for a life partner.

It would take a lot of mental contortion to convince myself that my desire for women is psychologically warped and that my desire for men is psychologically

---

a. Not all bisexual people would describe themselves this way.

healthy. I know because I was deeply engaged in these contortions for a long time. They required maintenance, effort, and self-deception. And because we can't selectively numb our feelings, when I rejected part of myself, I also detached from my own tender heart. I was trying to numb only my feelings for women, but I numbed myself to many experiences of vulnerability and love. We can't cut ourselves in half, rejecting one half as evil and embracing the other as holy. Nothing is psychologically whole or healthy about convincing oneself that desires for love are evil.

For people who are exclusively attracted to the same gender, it's evident that someone of the opposite gender can never be the psychological complement they need. Relationships that don't include natural romance and sexuality are rarely sustainable. Many gay men have married women, and many lesbians have married men because of accepted theology. These relationships are difficult and usually unsustainable.

Sadly, I have often heard gay men who were married to women recount that the only way they could perform sexually was by imagining a man while they were with their wives. Would those who have daughters want them to have this kind of marriage? Should they marry a man who loves them deeply and passionately or a gay man without the natural marriage impulse for a woman?

ABOUT LOVE

This chapter began with a quote by Ty Gibson about how the difference of male and female is a strength that God designed into marriage.

> Once we understand that human beings were designed for other-centeredness, something brilliant dawns: we realize that there is an ingenious divine rationale for creating the man and the woman different from one another and yet complementary in the way their bodies and minds are able to interlock with one another. Men and women are different by design—intentionally, deliberately different.[66]

I agree with him. There is beauty in love that crosses the gender divide when a man and woman learn to love someone of a different gender. Marriage is a unique gift for helping us foster other-centered love, and even in demanding it. I see the beauty of it.

What Gibson misses is not the beauty of male and female marriage, but that other types of marriages can also be beautiful and other-centered. He says that while opposite-gender marriage is other-centered, same-gender marriage is self-centered. "Each would see the other merely as an image of himself, or herself, and the sexual act would be an act of *self-love* rather than *other-love.*"[67]

This one is hard for me to get behind, even on a commonsense level. When a woman loves her wife, it's not self-love. Even if their anatomy is more similar than that of a man and a woman, they are still entirely different people, and they know that. When a man kisses a woman's lips, he knows he is kissing someone other than himself. He doesn't need different anatomy to tell him that. Nor do same-sex couples need different anatomy to know that they love someone other than themselves.

It's not hard for same-sex couples to figure out that their partner is not themselves. Same-gender marriages face the same challenges of two different personalities, opinions, and desires that need to be negotiated. These marriages demand sacrifice like any other marriage. They also teach people to love someone other than themselves, just as Gibson's marriage teaches him to love someone other than himself.

Marriage demands compromise, loss of autonomy, and a level of selflessness that single life doesn't demand. This doesn't mean single people are more selfish; that depends on the person, of course. A person can choose to be selfless and single. A person can choose celibacy for selfless reasons, to serve others. A married person can refuse to compromise with their partner and instead exploit and control them. Yet, it remains true that marriage calls forth selflessness in a way that singleness and celibacy do not. Joining your story and your life with another person in marriage demands sacrifice, including sacrificing many preferences and dreams, large and small.

Yes, marriage calls us out of ourselves to love someone different than ourselves. I agree with Gibson on this entirely and wholeheartedly. It is beautiful theology. That marriage produces this only for heterosexuals is simply false. Those in same-gender marriages also know other-centered love.

In fact, same-gender marriages embody these challenges in unique ways. We often must embark on our marriages without the support of friends, family, church, and community. We must make our commitments while being told by some that our love is selfish and that our marriages aren't real. To love the other without the support of the Adventist community requires more faithfulness, not less. What is lost in community support creates a greater need to choose faithfulness, self-sacrifice, and trust in the divine purpose that holds us.

THE CALL TO LOVE

I see God calling us to other-centered love through same-gender marriage. Just as Gibson said, this is the nature of God, to create difference to help us learn to love better. That difference pulls us out of our selfishness. So why is the church not allowing the difference of same-gender marriage to pull them out of their own selfishness? Why will heterosexuals not embrace couples that are different?

Four years ago, I chose to stand with the LGBTQ community. It's been harder than I expected. It's taken more courage than I knew I had. It's taken me out of myself and my self-interest. Before I decided to come out, it seemed easier to keep quiet, date only men, and stay in the church. But it didn't seem right.

I know I'm not perfect, but I humbly and sincerely share with you that my motives were unselfish. I knew what I was sacrificing. I knew what it demanded. It demanded more of me than celibacy, more sacrifice than being baptized, and more sacrifice than going into ministry. Losing my place in the Adventist Church was like experiencing the death of a loved one; the grief was, and continues to be, just as heavy. But God, being God, has also made this sacrifice into the greatest gift of all.

I imagine the importance of vocally supporting affirmation would be less intuitive for those who are straight and cisgender, without the personal benefit of being able to come out. What is the cost of vocally supporting same-sex marriage and transgender identity while their livelihood and community depend on the Adventist Church? I don't have to imagine it.

Many people have lost jobs or careers to be allies of gay, bisexual, and transgender people. One person I know lost $4,000 a month in donations for sharing my story. Another evangelical in the United States went from having the largest church in his city to having about 200 members. It's impossible to be both a vocal ally and an employee of the Adventist Church. I've seen it. I've experienced it myself. I've sat in a room of people who paid this price as we commiserated about our unemployability in the church we love.

Remembering this helps me keep statements about the selfishness of LGBTQ people in context. Those making these statements probably sincerely believe them, but they are also benefiting from that belief. Greater other-centeredness would be required of them if they accepted affirming theology. If they embraced an understanding of other-centeredness that included affirming same-gender marriage, the cost would be high.

God blessed the church with gay, bisexual, and transgender people to give us an opportunity for other-centered love. My challenge for Gibson and anyone who resonates with his theological understanding of same-gender marriage is to apply this love of the other to LGBTQ people. Learn to love the love you see in us. Learn to support marriages that are different than your own. Don't close your eyes to the genuine love of people who are different.

My challenge to the church is to spend more time reckoning with how well LGBTQ people have fared in church and society. Have they experienced the dominant heterosexual culture of the church as one that has other-centered love for their gay, bisexual, or transgender neighbors?

A RECOGNIZABLE MARRIAGE

I once spoke with two lesbians who had been together for decades, Sonia and Jane. Before their marriage was legally recognized, they made sure they had legal documentation in place to be there for one another in emergencies. One day, Jane went to get the mail from the box by the street just as a car veered off the road. She was hit and thrown 30 feet into a ditch.

Sonia got a call that Jane was in the hospital. Because they had no legal relationship, Sonia couldn't just go to the hospital to see Jane. She first had to go home and get the paperwork to visit her wife in the hospital. I can only imagine how her hands trembled as she rushed home, afraid she would lose the love of her life while she was getting the paperwork she needed because society wouldn't recognize her marriage.

Sonia ended up taking several days off work while her wife was in the hospital. This leave of absence was not officially allowed. She could have been fired for taking the time because her wife was not considered family. Fortunately, her workplace allowed it. Not all workplaces would.

When Sonia did return to work, she felt frustrated and fed up with the inhumanity of it all. Plus, as a college professor, how would she explain her sudden absence to her students? She could be fired for telling them the truth.

There was a happy ending for Jane and Sonia. Jane fully recovered. Sonia was open with her students and suffered no consequences. Today they are legally married. But so many moments could have gone differently for them.

These two lives demonstrate something important about the nature of same-sex marriage. It's quite easy to recognize it as a marriage. Legal approval doesn't make it a marriage; it's just a recognition. Whether it's legal, social, or religious, community recognition of marriage is there to support two people who have already made a private commitment to one another, a commitment we call marriage.

I have difficulty understanding why recognizing the marriage of Sonia and

Jane is a threat to anyone else's marriage. Who is harmed if Sonia can go immediately to the hospital to see Jane? Who is harmed if same-sex couples can take family medical leave to support one another in illness? Who is harmed if we speak openly about our marriages without fear of losing our jobs? For that matter, who is harmed if our churches also recognize and support these marriages?

The issues at stake with religion are different, of course. But when Jesus was asked what the central, beating heart of the law was, He said again and again that it was love. Love says Sonia should be able to rush immediately to Jane's side. She should be able to stay at her side without fear of losing her job. She shouldn't have to lie and say her wife is her roommate to avoid being fired. Her marriage should not exclude her from a church community. Her marriage shouldn't mean she can't be a member, can't get married in her church, or can't serve God in ministry.

Perhaps I'm being simplistic, but maybe we need to look at this with simplicity for a moment. Perhaps we need to peel back the layers of theology, sociology, and law and ask ourselves what is humane and loving.

The status-quo harmed Sonia and Jane. Where is the harm in changing our approach? Where is the damage in offering social and religious support to people like Sonia and Jane? Fortunately, they attend a church that offers complete understanding and support for everything they went through. They attend a church that doesn't want to see them divorced. In fact, they are pillars and leaders in their congregation. Who is harmed by this? Whose marriage is threatened because their marriage is supported?

I understand the fear and hesitation based on current biblical understanding. I don't want to diminish or ignore that. I also know there is a place for stopping to consider the human element of this question. I'm convinced that Jesus would want us to take a moment and think about the burdens we are placing on people whose only interest is to love and support one another.

I remember my friend Peter. He told me that from the time he was in academy he wanted to marry a woman and have kids, but he couldn't fall in love with a woman; he had no desire for women. I'll never forget the sad way he told me how much he wished he could have had all those things.

People don't want to be different and despised. They don't want to be unnatural and excluded. While none of us can help or choose our sexual orientation, we can choose how we respond. The church has an opportunity to respond with other-centered love.

Some might immediately think, *Yes, that's true. But we can't just throw out God's law.* If God says it's wrong, it's still wrong. I'm glad you brought this up. That's the next chapter.

CHAPTER 6

Preserving God's Law

"The law shouldn't be dismissed. Just because it's in the Old Testament, doesn't mean we can just throw it out."

"One way you can tell that it's a liberal perspective to approve of the homosexual lifestyle is that they don't pay attention to the law of God."

One Adventist who vocally opposes same-sex marriage says that clarity matters. Sex between men is a sin. Anyone who says otherwise must rely on "interpretation." For him, interpretation is unnecessary when we have clearly stated Bible verses. Interpretation is just a way of explaining away what's clear.

> You shall not lie with a male as with a woman. It is an abomination (Lev. 18:22).

> If a man lies with a male as he lies with a woman, both of them have committed an abomination. They shall surely be put to death. Their blood shall be upon them (Lev. 20:13).

Notice the specificity and economy of words in these texts. There is no mention of mediating circumstances. No excuse is available for those who look for exceptions. It doesn't matter how we were born; what matters is what we do. The plain meaning is that sex between two people of the same sex is wrong. Period. End of story.

Yet others might dismiss these arguments simply because Leviticus is in the Old Testament. Doesn't it include many laws that we pay little attention to today? They often say that we eat bacon and lobster and work on Saturday, so we're already breaking the Levitical law.

These attempts at dismissing the law are especially unsatisfactory for Adventists. Like other Adventists, I've never eaten bacon or lobster, and I don't work on Saturday. I'm unsatisfied with discrediting or dismissing Leviticus and the Old Testament law in general.

The Hebrew Bible, which we call the Old Testament,[a] is brimming with meaning and wisdom. It was the Bible Jesus read and quoted. It was the language Jesus used to explain the Father to us. The words that were always on Jesus' lips were the words of the Hebrew Bible that we (somewhat dismissively) call the Old Testament. Since Jesus found in it guidance sufficient to understand the will of God, so should we.

More than rituals and symbolic acts appear in the Torah. There are moral laws. These laws are not simply a collection of outdated rituals and ideas that were never correct and should be dismissed or discarded. They have meaning. If carefully discerned, they help us understand how to live more holy lives. They help us understand what it means to be human in the way God intended.

The Israelites did not believe the laws were burdensome, arbitrary, or capricious. They were a blessing. King David waxed eloquent about the goodness and gift that is the law of God, "The law of the Lord is perfect, converting the soul; the testimony of the Lord is sure, making wise the simple; the statutes of the Lord are right, rejoicing the heart; the commandment of the Lord is pure, enlightening the eyes" (Ps. 19:7, 8).

Even in the New Testament, Paul said the law is "holy and just and good" (Rom. 7:12); and said, "What advantage then has the Jew, or what is the profit of circumcision? Much in every way! Chiefly because to them were committed the oracles of God" (Rom. 3:1, 2). What were these great oracles? The Hebrew Bible, particularly the Torah, including Leviticus 18:22 and 20:13.

---

a. "Old Testament" is not a great name because it downplays the importance of the Hebrew Bible and, some would say, of Jewish people and their religion. I will use the term in parallel with "Hebrew Bible." The other reason it might be appropriate to use the term "Old Testament" is that some Christian interpretations of that collection of books are not Hebrew in their approach. They reflect Christianity, not Judaism. Using the phrase "Hebrew Bible" to interpret from a Christian frame seems confusing.

We should resist skimming over or dismissing the Hebrew Bible. These texts are substantive and meaningful but often neglected. I hope that through this chapter we will arrive at a greater appreciation of the Hebrew Bible, a greater understanding of how to interpret it, and a sense of why it absolutely must be interpreted.

WHAT IS LEVITICUS?

In order to understand this text, it helps to understand the book of Leviticus. How does Leviticus fit into the whole of Scripture?

Leviticus is one of the first five books of the Bible, a section known by two names: the Torah and the Pentateuch. Pentateuch simply means "five books." "Torah" in Hebrew. The Hebrew Bible has three sections: the *Torah* (translated "Law"), the *Nevi'im* (translated "Writings"), and the *Ketuvim* (translated "Prophets"). Of the three, the Torah is preeminent, first in order and importance. The Writings and Prophets build on the foundation of the Torah.

Keep this in mind when reading the New Testament. When biblical writers refer to the law, the English translation of "Torah," they are not necessarily referring to the legal code with its rules. They often refer to the first five books of the Bible—Genesis, Exodus, Leviticus, Numbers, and Deuteronomy.

Even someone new to the Bible probably realizes that these five books contain a lot more than laws. Yet, they are called the "Law." How could this be? It's because the Hebrew concept of law is dramatically different from our own concept. Their concept is Hebrew; ours is Roman.

Hebrew law is more than a collection of rules and regulations. It contains many different genres, such as narrative, poetry, and legal code. Leviticus 18:22 and 20:13 are in the Hebrew genre of legal code.

Hebrew legal code isn't the same as modern legal code. It's not intended to be applied impartially and context-free. No congress passed these laws. No judicial branch enforces them; that was never their intention. We have no example anywhere in Scripture of rules being applied that way.

The Torah is a unified body of work. It explains, interprets, and contextualizes itself. There is narrative in every book, including Leviticus. As a whole, they give us an understanding of God's self-revelation through a specific people (Israel) in a particular time and place (the Ancient Near East). Scattered throughout the legal codes are affirmations that this law is intended for a specific time and place. The purpose of these laws is to reveal God to the nations that surrounded Israel in the Ancient Near East (Deut. 7:6-8; Isa. 43:10).

As a true revelation of God, the Torah has indispensable value. To use the legal codes as a set of modern statutes is to misunderstand them. This doesn't diminish the law but clarifies it. The Torah is a goldmine of insights into who God is, what a good and moral life is, and how people have wrestled to understand God and morality through the millennia.

TENSION

Interpretation is essential because there is another side to these laws, a difficult side. Of the 613 different rules in the legal codes of the Hebrew Bible, it's difficult to reckon with the morality or applicability of many of them.

Some of them include ceremonial rules that might seem strange to us. Some laws relate to corpses, mold, rashes, and other substances that make a person ceremonially unclean. There is an intricate and cumbersome process for becoming clean. There are elaborate ceremonies, descriptions of robes, and strict plans for building a temple, right down to the correct thread for the curtains (e.g., Ex. 25-28).

Then there are rules about executing people. According to these laws, execution was appropriate for many violations. Idolatry was punishable by death (Ex. 22:20; Lev. 27:29; Num. 25:1-9), as was false prophecy (Deut. 13:1-10; 17:2-7; 18:20-22), adultery (Lev. 20:10), cursing your parents (Lev. 20:9), breaking the Sabbath (Ex. 31:14; 35:2), persistently disobeying parents (Deut. 21:18-21), and disregarding a court order (Deut. 17:8-13).

At least, the letter of the law demanded execution. Whether or not these violations actually resulted in death is more uncertain. The law wasn't enforced with objective and automatic penalties but with deliberative contextual understanding. These were not like modern mandatory sentences. When we read the narrative, we see that violations are considered on an individual basis. No story in the Hebrew Bible exists in which a judge applied and enforced these laws without regard to context.[68]

But perhaps even more disturbing, there are laws about how to lawfully enslave people. People could be enslaved through war or be purchased from foreigners, but not through kidnapping (as Joseph was in Gen. 37). Fellow Israelites could only be temporarily enslaved. But as long as enslavement came through lawful means, and they were not Israelites, they could be kept forever, with their descendants, and passed down to children and their descendants as inherited property (Lev. 20:44-46).

It's often said that these laws were there to regulate an existing practice, not to condone that practice. But such an interpretation is not in the text itself. I think it's accurate, but it comes from our assumption that slavery is wrong. There is no explicit or implicit statement to this effect in the text. The language of the text simply explains that it is legal to enslave foreigners and how it can legally happen (Lev. 25:44-46). What is crucial is whether there is a biblical reason for this assumption.

Women were also on the losing end of Old Testament law. In Deuteronomy 22, we find scenarios where women are "seized" by a man who "lies with her." In one scenario, she is betrothed to be married to one man, and another man seizes her and lies with her; the man who seized her is executed. But if the same thing happens, and the woman is not engaged, the man simply has to pay the bride price, and she will be married to him (her rapist) for the rest of her life.

First, it's horrific to imagine a woman made to marry a man who forcibly raped her. Like slavery, this attributed to cultural differences. Because a raped woman would have no place in society, it was merciful for her to marry her rapist. Of course, it's the same law that gives her little autonomy in society. Men are representatives of the family, inheritors of property (Num. 26:55; 27:11; Joshua 18:10), and the only ones who can enter into binding legal agreements (Num. 30:3-17).

Second, an even more insidious injustice exists in the discrepancy between these two scenarios. The rapist is only punished if the woman is betrothed to another man. The violation the law seeks to remedy is not against the woman but her fiancé. The problem is not rape but a disturbance in a woman's chain of custody. Women had value according to their relation to men.

Third, this law also incentivizes rape. If a man wants to marry a woman who won't marry him (or whose father won't allow the marriage), all he has to do is find her alone, rape her, and pay the bride price. Then she is his wife.

This is only one example of difficult passages. There are more problematic passages that devalue women and allow slavery. In other passages, retributive justice is encouraged, "life shall be for life, eye for eye, tooth for tooth, hand for hand, foot for foot" (Deut. 19:21). Foreigners are sometimes subjected to exploitation that Israelites are protected from (Deut. 23:20). Some commands demand genocide, killing not only soldiers but also women and children: "You shall let nothing that breathes remain alive" (Deut. 20:16).[69]

WHAT IS YOUR READING?

Let's pause for a moment. Can we be candid? No moral person today would approve of these practices. It doesn't matter how adamant someone is about

taking the plain word of Scripture without interpretation. It makes no difference how firmly they believe that God gave us every word of Scripture. The face
value of these passages has no hearing. No one is interested in entertaining the
idea that raping a woman is only a problem when she's engaged to another man,
that she should marry her rapist, that slavery is acceptable, or that genocide is
God's will.

Neither does anyone come to Scripture asking whether or not slavery is
okay. No one is doing a Bible study to determine if rape is a sin against a woman.
No one is trying to determine the conditions under which genocide is acceptable. Even though there is (at best) ambiguity about these subjects in the Old
Testament, we aren't ambiguous in our interpretations.

Why? I know this is going to sound a bit extreme, but hear me out. No matter
what the Bible says, it's not changing what people believe on these topics today.
And there is a good and biblical reason for that.

Let me demonstrate with a scenario. Let's say we studied the Bible and concluded that slavery was biblically moral when done biblically. This isn't a crazy
conclusion to draw if one emphasizes the plain meaning of Scripture on the
texts that speak of slavery. It's been the most common conclusion for most of
Christian history. If we did that study and determined that the Bible supported
slavery, would we then support slavery? Would we believe we were wrong
to end slavery? Would we support reinstating legal slavery? Would we find it
acceptable for the United States to invade Canada and enslave Canadians? No,
we wouldn't.

Instead, we see the moral absurdity and the degradation of humanity that is
slavery. We consider it evil. We have eyes to see this because we live in a society
that has outlawed slavery. We understand that everyone deserves basic rights.
We wouldn't even entertain the idea that slavery is acceptable.

That's why no one even considers these texts at face value. I've been an
Adventist my entire life. I studied theology for four years as an undergraduate
at Union College. I earned my M.Div. at the Seventh-day Adventist Theological
Seminary at Andrews University. I'm a reader. I've read a lot of theology and
Christian thought. Never have I seen a modern pastor, theologian, or layperson
approach Scripture to determine whether or not slavery is wrong. They always
begin with the assumption that slavery is wrong. That's as it should be. We outlawed slavery because of human dignity and compassion. Compassion is biblical; dignity is biblical.

I have seen plenty of wrestling, trying to understand *why* these words appear
in the Bible *even though* we all know they are wrong. I have read, experienced,

and personally engaged fervently in this activity. It's a type of apologetics, and it's valuable.

Because we do this automatically and unconsciously, we fail to reckon with the implications. On subjects like slavery, we automatically ignore the surface meaning of texts because of the moral principles of compassion and human dignity. It's easy to explain why the plain meaning is inapplicable because we are predisposed to accept that explanation regardless of whether it is in the text or not. There is no real theological wrestling with the possibility that the text's plain meaning could be correct.

On other subjects, we apply the surface meaning universally, bemoaning any attempt to "interpret" or "justify" a different understanding. But it's not the texts that are changing. We are changing our approach to the text based on the moral code we bring to the text.

Take, for example, Deuteronomy 22:5: "A woman shall not wear anything that pertains to a man, nor shall a man put on a woman's garment, for all who do so are an abomination to the Lord your God." Roy Gane, a professor of Old Testament at the Seventh-day Adventist Theological Seminary whose work we will be looking at closely in this chapter, says this verse "would encourage a transgender person to prioritize physical gender as the factor that determines one's place in society, as indicated by what one wears."[70]

On what basis do we decide this plainly stated verse is a universal mandate? Couldn't it be an expression of their culture like slavery was? This verse could refer to a half dozen different scenarios that have nothing to do with gender identity. We have no reason to believe it referred to gender identity.

We've been changing our hermeneutic based on how we feel about the content. I suggest we learn to read Scripture consistently. Not only that, I want us to learn to read the text with moral clarity. Our hermeneutic should be consistent enough to make us oppose slavery even when slavery is culturally acceptable. It's easy today, because of our society, to say the Bible doesn't support slavery. It wasn't so easy in the eighteenth century when slavery was widely accepted. Can we be certain our hermeneutic would have made us 18th-century abolitionists?

It's easier to use compassion and dignity as our moral compass on a subject with no modern ethical debate. It's entirely different on a topic for which there is debate. On these subjects, we tend to talk a lot about compassion and dignity in our attitude but are reticent to allow these principles to touch our theology. I want us to have a deeper understanding of Scripture and apply it ethically even when compassion and dignity are difficult choices.

DELIBERATIVE PROCESS

Fortunately, this idea is not foreign to the Hebrew Bible itself. According to the Torah, the Torah should be applied in a deliberative way. We should sift out its meaning. We should understand the impact of what we are doing and not blindly follow the letter of the law. This is what God's people have been doing with the law from the beginning.[71]

Conservative Adventist scholar Roy Gane acknowledges this. Gane is an eminent, respected scholar, one of the top Christian theologians on Old Testament law, not only among Adventists but in the world. He is a passionate defender of Adventist theology, particularly the doctrine of the heavenly sanctuary.

As a defender of the accepted theology, I'm sure he won't agree with the use I'm making of his approach. I've never heard him speak a word to challenge any Adventist doctrine. He was my professor at the Seventh-day Adventist Theological Seminary. I know him as someone who immerses himself so thoroughly in the text that he almost seems to inhabit it. He has a mind for detail and adeptly parses symbolic meaning and legal intent. He was an editor for the book that was published by Andrews University opposing same-sex marriage.[72] He was one of the earliest voices to speak against same-sex marriage in the Adventist Church.[73] Yet when speaking on other topics, he says that the law is not always applied directly in its plain meaning, even within the text itself.

> The Israelites did not feel obligated to use the O[ld] T[estament] law collections to directly dictate their judicial verdicts, at least not in every case, and these laws point beyond themselves to an authoritative source (the character of YHWH).[74]

Gane wrote a critical book for our subject, *Old Testament Law for Christians: Original context and enduring application*. He explains these principles in chapter two in particular. As a conservative Adventist scholar, he isn't trying to explain away the text or engage in higher criticism. He is simply explaining what we find in the text, how we should interpret it.

> In Deuteronomy, after the Lord has given many laws at Sinai, judges are to judge justly because the judgment belongs to God as the source of justice, and they should refer to Moses any case that is too hard for them, but Moses does not instruct them to make their decisions according to the modern law collection (Deut. 1:16, 17; 16:18-20). . . . No biblical narrative includes consultation of a lawbook in a description of a judicial deliberation.[75]

Even when the laws of the Torah were fresh and modern, they were not consulted as judicial law is today. The Torah is supposed to be different than the modern legal system. The strict application of the Torah as a modern objective legislative code is unbiblical. This is an approach to the law used by Romans many centuries later. It wasn't the Jewish approach then or now.

Allow me to share a few examples. The story of the daughters of Zelophehad is one of the most remarkable and least appreciated stories in Scripture (Num. 27:1-11). The Zelophehad sisters were like a Jane Austen novel, always waiting for a brother to receive the family inheritance and care for his sisters. But he never came. Without a son to be heir, the family property would fall into the hands of a different family. A family's name and property were everything for ancient Israelites. God freed Israel from bondage in Egypt so they could possess that land. It was their birthright. It was literally the "promised land." Through this land, they fed themselves and carried on their family name. To lose the land was to love everything.

So, the sisters, Mahlah, Noah, Hoglah, Milkah, and Tirzah, sought an exception to the clear, explicit, unambiguous law of God. They asked to own the land even though they were women. And they got it. Moses took the case to God, and God said they should receive the land. Moses changed the law for them.

What does that tell us about how people in the Bible saw that law? Does it not demonstrate that to Moses a deeper principle was at work than a rigid keeping of the letter of the law? We tend to think that we can't do this today, that we can't go to God when the surface meaning of the law doesn't work as intended. The daughters Zelophehad were not so tentative. They boldly pursued justice for themselves.

There are other examples of Moses or those in the Hebrew Bible changing the law to accommodate a higher principle. Most of the book of Deuteronomy was Moses retelling the law at the end of his life, and it's not exactly the same as that recorded in the book of Exodus. For example, the law about temporarily enslaved people who get married and have families during their captivity was modified sometime between Exodus 21:2-11 and Deuteronomy 15:12-15.[76]

Among other changes, women in Exodus were enslaved for life, even if they were Israelites. In Deuteronomy, Israelite women went free the seventh year, as did men. In Deuteronomy, the freed person was also to be liberally supplied with resources to start a new life, but in Exodus, they left empty-handed.

The interpretation, application, and specifics of the laws were modified. In some of those cases, it was because the law was not comprehensive enough to cover new situations. In other instances, direct exceptions were called for by context. As Gane explains, this raises questions:

How could the O[ld] T[estament] law be normative if they were not comprehensive and if they can be flexibly applied to individual cases? First, the laws are paradigmatic examples that give positive behaviors, and when problems arise, the laws are to serve *as starting points for deliberation* of cases that are related but present variables. Second, . . . while the letter of the law was important, it was to be sensitively and contextually applied in light of the spirit of the law as a whole, recognizing that no law code can explicitly account for all the complexities of the human life.[77]

There we have it. The laws are not to be applied inflexibly but flexibly. When problems arise, they are to be seen "as starting points for deliberation." I can't emphasize the importance of this enough. Deliberation is crucial, absolutely crucial.

Let's return to Deuteronomy 22:5. Gane said that the prohibition against men wearing women's clothes should inform transgender people that they shouldn't identify as a gender different than their "anatomy." There are problems with this statement immediately. Gane assumes the only valid anatomy is genitalia, not neurology. Also, to our knowledge, none of this was a matter of discussion in Ancient Israel.

Still, going with Gane's assumptions, how would we deliberate on this? The daughters of Zelophehad had the law changed for them because, in their case, it wasn't carrying out its original intent. As we know from chapter 3, transgender people often suffer terribly if they don't transition. They can contribute to the world and accomplish more for God's kingdom if they aren't constantly fighting their neurological gender.

Was limiting transgender people the purpose of Deuteronomy 22:5? Of course it wasn't. Was preventing transgender people from transitioning the intended outcome of this text? It couldn't have been. The text might have referred to pagan rituals. It might have prohibited deception. It might have referred to the symbolic separation that forbids using different seeds in the same vineyard, plowing by joining different animals together, and mixing fabrics. These laws were given just a few verses later (Deut. 22:9-11). We don't know the purpose for sure. But we have no reason to believe the prohibition was intended to prevent transgender people from transitioning and every reason to think that it didn't.

Even if the plain meaning of the text forbids gender transition, deliberation leads us to different conclusions. For the sake of justice and love, it shouldn't be applied that way to transgender people. But are these deliberations sentimental and permissive? Or are they based on something substantive? Here is Gane again:

The source of justice that guided any Israelite, especially a judge (Deut. 1:16, 17; 16:18-20), was not the particular law that addressed the situation before him. Normative justice was revealed by YHWH's own character of justice (e.g., Ex. 36:6, 7), as revealed by the entire corpus of available divine law, including motive clauses and accompanying exhortations. In other words, while the letter of the law was important, it was to be sensitively and contextually applied in light of the spirit of the law as a whole, recognizing that no law code can explicitly account for all the complexity of human life.[78]

Sometimes circumstances mean going against the surface meaning. The intent is always more important. From day one of the law, this has consistently been recognized, especially within the text itself. It's difficult to become a serious student of the Hebrew Torah without seeing this reality.

I'm not quoting a liberal scholar. Gane takes a very high view of Scripture. The truth of what Gane says is unavoidable for those who have carefully studied the Torah.

All I need to do to arrive at affirming same-sex marriage and transgender identity is apply these principles. The difference in conclusions isn't because I'm approaching the text in a liberal way, and Gane is approaching it in a conservative way. The problem is that conservatives haven't been consistent on this topic. On this particular subject, a literalistic approach is used that is not used on other subjects. I think it's simply a blind spot, to which we're all prone.

THE TEN COMMANDMENTS

The narrative and historical context of these laws must be first and foremost in understanding them. The context is not the same for each law. Let's begin with an example particularly relevant to Adventists.

The Ten Commandments have a history, beginning with God calling Abraham. Eventually, Abraham's descendants are known as the nation of Israel, people favored by God. But these people are seized and enslaved in Egypt, where they had made a home. This enslavement continued through many generations of suffering and shame. Finally, and mercifully, God liberates them.

Only then does Israel gather, a nation of freed people huddled and trembling at the foot of Mount Sinai as God's voice announces these moral edicts as thunder from the peaks through a wall of clouds and mystery. These commandments are to be as a marriage covenant between God and Israel. They keep them as a sign of gratitude and covenant for the freedom they received. They are a kind of seal, binding the people to God.

Only by understanding this history can we understand the Ten Commandments in Exodus 20. The story tells us that the commandments are a gift. They help Israel form a relationship with God even though God is powerful and mysterious. Yet God is also nearby, merciful, and protective of Israel. God saved them, and in that salvation is a foundation for the law.

So biblical rules aren't like laws passed by legislators. They aren't a system of rules independent of context. They are laws that emerged from the grand narrative of God's intervention in the world. In fact, the first five books of the Bible are one connected narrative.[b]

The Torah is a single narrative that spans creation, the antediluvian period, the flood, the emergence of Israel, the story of Joseph, slavery in Egypt, the exodus from slavery, the Sinai encounter with the Ten Commandments, the legal code from Sinai, the wilderness wandering, Moses' reframing of the law (Deuteronomy), and the entrance into the Promised Land. The legal codes emerged as part of this narrative and tied to it.

Distinct from the Ten Commandments, many believe the legal code serves as a specific application of the Ten Commandments. This application helps the nation of Israel embody the Ten Commandments and the greater commandments of love in their context (Matt. 22:36-40). They help Israel witness the goodness of God to the surrounding nations (Deut. 4:6-8).

Perhaps this helps us understand a challenging aspect of Jesus' Sermon on the Mount. Jesus was willing to modify the legal code (Matt. 5:38-48) while maintaining adamantly that He was not changing one iota of the law (Matt. 5:17, 18). Jesus understood that the Torah itself tells us that it was given to a specific people for a specific time. For example, Deuteronomy was written on paper and placed outside the ark of the covenant (Deut. 31:24-26). It was a local embodiment of the universal principles of the Ten Commandments. Yet the Ten Commandments themselves were spoken directly by God (Ex. 20), written on stone (Ex. 34), and placed inside the ark of the covenant (Ex. 25:16).

Despite not being directly communicated by God and not having the same written on stone permanence as the Ten Commandments, the legal code is still morally illuminating. The Ten Commandments are concise but thin in their

---

b. Besides the unity expressed in the grouping of "Torah" itself, we also see that the Torah is one connected narrative that fits something called a chiasm. Chiasms were common Hebrew ways of connecting ideas and narratives into a single unit.

explanation of morality. They are more of a basic framework that leaves many moral questions unexplained.

The legal code makes up for this. Its explanations are thick. They give Israel detail and clarity about how to live out the full meaning of the Ten Commandments. They are explanations for Israel, designed for a particular time, place, and culture. This is clear in the narrative and also in the law itself.

Many factors indicate that these rules were for a specific time and place, yet it's easy to miss. For example, the legal code addresses excrement in terms of keeping it outside the camp (Deut. 23:12-13), not in terms of keeping it in the toilet, because it was for them, not us. There is advice on horses and cattle, not cars and cell phones. They were written for a different time.

As we've discussed, there are more than technological differences. There are also social differences. Women were not generally considered independent legal agents of their own lives as they are today. Slavery is permitted and regulated. Today we believe it immoral for us to behave as they did in these areas.

So, the legal code portions of the Torah are a significant expansion, from which we can learn a lot. Yet, they are only helpful if we keep in mind that they are also specific and time-bound. We don't apply them to our time uncritically. As much as we can, we must understand what they meant to them and not make too hasty an application to our world today.

PUTTING IT TOGETHER

When we think about interpreting Leviticus, many of the rules still apply, as do all the underlying principles and purposes. The best way to begin understanding how we should interpret Leviticus and other legal codes is to understand how they were understood and applied within Scripture itself.

For example, on two occasions (1 Cor. 9:9; 1 Tim. 5:18), Paul applied a principle from a specific law. The law allowed oxen to obtain sustenance from the grain they tread (Deut. 25:4), presumably rather than only grazing on grass. Based on this law about oxen, Paul said pastors should enjoy abundant sustenance from their congregations. They should be compensated generously, not meagerly. Pastors are obviously not oxen. Paul isn't taking this passage literally; he sees a principle with broader applications.

As another example, Jesus has no problem directly contradicting the plain meaning of some texts based on a principled approach. The Levitical law said that if someone harmed someone else, intentionally or even by accident, they would be maimed with the same injury. Jesus plainly contradicted this rule. He said we should return kindness to those who harm us.

> You have heard that it was said, 'An eye for an eye and a tooth for a tooth.' But I say to you, do not resist an evil person. But whoever slaps you on the right cheek, turn the other to him also. And if anyone wants to sue you and take away your tunic, let him have your cloak also. And whoever compels you to go one mile, go with him two. Give to him who asks you, and from him who wants to borrow from you do not turn away" (Matt. 5:38-42; cf. Lev. 24:19, 20).

The Levitical law of an eye for an eye was not meant to be the final word. It improved the situation from what it had been, but it was not yet what it could be. Jesus saw what it could be. Jesus was teaching the ideal. Jesus was moving in a redemptive direction.

The idea of an eye for an eye makes sense in context. At the time, vigilante revenge and feuding tribes were standard practices in the Ancient Near East. The original law was an example of retributive and proportional justice, which improved on standard practices when the law was written. It stops the escalation of violence.

Jesus looked at this law of retributive justice and saw the movement. He paid attention to the direction and intention of the law in a broad way, interpreting the law based on those principles.

In understanding what Jesus did, it's helpful to think not only of what the law said but of what it would have accomplished. How would a particular law have functioned in that world? If we live in a society in which rich people can get away with maiming poor people, the wealthy are free to abuse the poor. If people are free to pursue vengeance, violence quickly escalates.

However, if suddenly the eye of a wealthy person is demanded in payment for destroying the eye of a poor person, those who are rich will behave differently. With limits in place, disproportionate revenge is discouraged. The law is proportional, though it is still retributive and based on punishment. Because it is proportionate, it prevents escalation and reduces violence. Because it is still retributive, it does not fully embody the character of God. It's an increase in justice, but not the final word.

This isn't to say that we are better than ancient Israelites. We are just as flawed, and they were just as capable. The issue is that all knowledge is incremental. You can't learn about division until you've learned to count. Socially and legally, proportional retributive justice paved the way for the teachings of Jesus. Yet even today, we fail to implement Jesus' teachings in our legal system and usually opt instead for our own version of retributive justice.

That movement and growth are why it was legitimate for Jesus to flatly contradict this rule. There is a deeper meaning: Don't seek vengeance. Seek the good of all. Had people cared for the needs of each other from the beginning, there would have been no need for an eye for an eye justice in the first place.

Jesus is getting at something beyond a stopgap measure to improve the situation. He doesn't want His followers to get stuck. These measures eventually no longer increase justice and safety. The same rule was now encouraging revenge. Jesus said it was time to move beyond this. In so doing, He was faithful to the intended function of the law, not the plain meaning.

This reinterpretation of Leviticus 24:19, 20 is part of the Sermon on the Mount, which was a retake on Moses' law. It speaks to both Jesus' moral vision and Jesus' authority (Matt. 5-7). Jesus' reinterpretations show that He didn't prioritize the surface meaning of the text. He was doing what Moses did and giving the people a fresh understanding of the function and purpose of the law founded on love for God and love of neighbor.

We looked at another such interpretation of the Torah in a previous chapter. Jesus modified divorce laws, making them stricter than Moses had. By doing this, Jesus moved the needle in a redemptive direction. It served to give vulnerable people greater protection than they had under the old law. It highlighted and improved upon the intent of the law.

When I studied Old Testament law at seminary, my professors distinguished between restorative laws and creation laws. Restorative laws bring improvement; creation laws reflect God's moral intention and the ultimate goal of restoration. Jesus' Sermon on the Mount is full of renewals of the supreme ideal of the law. It's a valuable frame for understanding Scripture, and an approach like this is necessary for anyone who studies the laws and ethics of the Bible seriously and systematically.

Before going forward, let's summarize the legal code:

- The legal code comes from a narrative that explains its meaning.
- We know that the legal code at least partially explained the Ten Commandments, giving fuller explanations that were also appropriate to their time and place.
- Most of these laws were restorative. They helped Israel get closer to being the nation God wanted them to be. They were growth-oriented, but applying them directly in a different context doesn't always mean growth.

- Some of these laws also reflect God's Creation ideal and ultimate moral intention. These are creation laws. They may also be present in the legal code.
- Even when they were written, the laws were not meant to be applied as objective legal mandates. They were a "starting point for deliberation" even in Ancient Israel, and even more so today.
- Though the laws were written for Israel, they each have meaning for us. That meaning must be evaluated on a case-by-case basis, especially considering the following:
  - How did the law function in its original setting? What does this reveal about its purpose?
  - How does this law relate to God's ideal? How does it reflect the character of God and the major themes of Scripture?

Following these principles, we gain clarity about how to understand and apply the laws of the Torah. In fact, when we step back and look at the entire narrative context of the Torah, we have a lot more to go on than we might at first realize. Once we get to the end of the next chapter, I dare say we'll have a much clearer picture of the purpose of the Torah forbidding same-sex eroticism.

CHAPTER 7

Forbidden

> *"The Hebrew understanding of sexual ethics and the definition of fornication is found in Leviticus 18. This is what Jesus would have been referring to when He spoke about fornication. This is what Paul was referring to as well."*
>
> *"God told us homosexuality was a sin as far back as Sodom and Gomorrah. He burned the city to the ground because of it."*

In the last chapter, we talked about reading the Hebrew law as it's intended to be read. The law comes with a narrative context. It was important for Jews to ask how implementing laws would impact people and the community. There was supposed to be deliberation about their impact and intent before they were applied. Now we ask, how do we deliberate about these texts?

Many who believed in the accepted Adventist theology argue that deliberation makes their case stronger. The context of Leviticus 18 is the Bible's most complete explanation of sexual fornication. Jesus was a Jewish rabbi, Paul was an educated former member of the Sanhedrin, and they both warned against fornication. Every time they used that word, they would have had Leviticus 18 in mind. If that's true, these texts are not just footnotes but are essential to Hebrew thinking about sexual ethics:

You shall not lie with a male as with a woman; it is an abomination (Lev. 18:22).

If a man lies with a male as with a woman, both of them have committed an abomination; they shall surely be put to death; their blood is upon them (Lev. 20:13).

What accepted theology consistently highlights is how these statements are unambiguous. Here is Roy Gane, whose work we referenced in the last chapter:

The Old Testament does not refer, even in a descriptive narrative, to same-sex marriage or any equivalent to it, such as exclusive, committed, same-sex cohabitation. Does this mean that such an arrangement, outside the scope of possibilities covered by the Old Testament, is therefore permissible for Christians? Such a conclusion would overlook the comprehensive nature of Leviticus 18:22 and 20:13, which categorically forbids homosexual practice without any exceptions. *If marriage is a relationship that includes sexual relations, and if God prohibits sexual relations between members of the same gender, no room exists for discussion of the possible legitimacy of same-sex marriage, at least according to God.* . . . The Creator has always known more about human beings than science ever will, no matter how modern or sophisticated (cf. Ps. 139). He was the one who gave biblical laws, and He did not see fit to make legal distinctions that take orientation into account.[79]

According to Gane, the prohibition is universal and applicable regardless of context, culture, or situation. Part of the reason is that Leviticus 18 and surrounding passages are considered moral laws. They aren't related to ceremonial uncleanness but to morality. I tend to agree with this interpretation with some exceptions. There is evidence that laws against same-sex eroticism[a] are moral. They aren't about the sacrificial system or civic laws for running the theocratic government (at least not primarily).[b]

---

a. I'm using this term because it's specific and accurate. The law addresses erotic behavior. Using the term "homosexuality" would be confusing. That word implies that the behavior flowed from a particular sexual orientation. All scholars agree that this was not the meaning of these texts. There is every reason to believe that most people engaging in these acts were men who were sexually attracted to women.

b. I could be wrong in my interpretation. If I am, the next most likely explanation is one from Jewish tradition. Some Jews believe these texts are related to ritual impurity, since semen could make one unclean or because of the wasting of seed. See Robert Alter, The Five Books of Moses, p. 623, 624. This reasoning probably wouldn't apply at all in Christian interpretations since ritual impurity is not considered binding. Of course, this moral reasoning would also mean that birth control is forbidden. Interestingly, it also means this text wouldn't apply to women. Most Jewish interpreters agree that there is no prohibition of female-to-female sexual activity in the Hebrew Bible. Their focus was usually in some way on the wasting or impurity of semen. Rabbis mostly agreed in the Talmud that women who had sex with other women had not lost their virginity (though it was still a minor offense) and were still eligible to marry a priest.

In fact, these laws may have been used to make the most critical decision the early church had to make. In Acts 15, early Christians decided to allow Gentiles to become Christians without requiring them to be circumcised, despite the fact that Moses required it and Jews had been circumcising men on the eighth day for centuries. They asked the Gentile believers to keep three other requirements instead. Did the early church have any biblical basis for making this decision? Or was it based solely on the movement of the Holy Spirit?

Some scholars believe the early church based its decision on Scripture. When they allowed Gentiles into the church without being circumcised, the church left four laws for Gentiles to keep. They told them to "abstain from things offered to idols, from blood, from things strangled, and from sexual immorality" (Acts 15:29). Where did these rules come from?

In Leviticus 17 and 18, we find a set of laws that apply to non-Israelites living in Israel. The requirements extended to Gentiles by the early church could be a summary of these rules. They even appear in the same basic order. It makes sense that while not requiring Gentiles to become circumcised, they might still retain requirements that bound Gentiles in Leviticus.[80] For all these reasons, many Adventist scholars believe Leviticus 18 still applies. They believe that Jesus and the early church used Leviticus 18 to define the meaning of sexual fornication. They believe that if Leviticus 18 applied to Gentiles even after Jesus' death and resurrection, it applies to us.

IDEAL CREATION?

Why do they believe this text has such permanence? Leviticus 18 applies to Christians today because it reflects God's ideal for sexuality.[c] It's a reflection of how God set things up at creation. It's a creation law meant to return us to our true humanity, meant to bring us to exactly the behavior for which we were created.

The rationale of the prohibitions in Leviticus 18—including homosexual practice—rests upon the foundational principles of Creation order in Genesis 1:27, 28: the creation of

---

c. This argument is ubiquitous in accepted theology, from Adventist to non-Adventist sources. The idea is that sex was rooted in gender difference at creation, and all verses in Scripture about same-sex sexual contact refer back to this original creation. It's argued by many, including Robert Gagnon, Preston Sprinkle, the Seventh-day Adventist Theological Seminary, the Biblical Research Institute of the General Conference, and ordinary Adventist sermons on the topic.

all humanity in the image of God as "male and female"; the call for a man and his wife to become "one flesh," and the command to "be fruitful and multiply, and fill the earth."[81]

This creation ideal contrasts with redemptive law. Redemptive laws are partial measures. Creation is the ideal that God intends for us. Many Christians view laws about polygamy, slavery, and the legal dependence of women as redemptive laws. They place limits on the harmful practices deeply embedded in the culture in the hope that one day those harmful practices will cease entirely. It seems like it should be simple, but it's not always easy to tell the difference between creation law and redemptive law.

Accepted theology argues that these laws transcend all cultural considerations because they are rooted in God's original creation. They believe God created man and woman, and only man and woman, for sexual union in marriage. Physically and psychologically, they match each other. Therefore, this text is universal because it refers back to the creation story that's relevant to all of us. That also answers why the early church recognized the universality of these laws in Acts 15.

But there are no direct references to creation in either of these passages, no allusions or quotes from Genesis 1 and 2. Their connection to Adam and Eve or the creation narrative is debatable. So why the connection?

Roy Gane wrote a three-part series titled "Old Testament Principles Relevant to Consensual Homoerotic Activity" for *Ministry Magazine* (Sept. 2015, Nov. 2015, Jan. 2016). This article outlined why the prohibitions are related to God's original creation and why they are moral.

I take no issue with his analysis of the moral nature, but I can't agree that these laws refer to creation. Let's look at Leviticus 18 as an explanation of sexuality in Genesis 1 and 2. Does it make sense? Is this chapter of laws designed to restore the same sexual behavior that God would have had in mind for Adam, Eve, and their children?

By my count, there are 20 laws in Leviticus 18. They are supposed to apply to Genesis by teaching that sex and marriage create "one flesh," are male and female, and involve procreation. Most of those laws are about sex, but almost none of them apply to the original creation. Fifteen laws prohibit incest. "None of you shall approach anyone who is near of kin to him, to uncover his nakedness: I am the Lord" (Lev. 18:6).

How does this reinforce the teaching of "one flesh"? It doesn't reinforce "one flesh" in the sense of one man marrying one woman. If this was the intent, it could have said to have sex only with your wife. The prohibitions indicate that there is an allowance for sex with other women, just not family members. It assumes polygamy and moderates male sexual license. It doesn't prohibit polygamy. It's a redemption law, not a creation law. Conspicuously absent are any references to Genesis 2:24 or the concept of "one flesh." The rationale in these texts is not about creation but about not bringing "dishonor" or "uncover the nakedness" of others or oneself.

Leviticus 18 doesn't return the Israelite man to an exclusive relationship with one wife. Common sexual practices were not prohibited. He is still permitted to have sex with an enslaved person, a concubine, a foreigner, or a sex worker. Neither do these laws prevent polygamy, but instead, they set limits on polygamy. These laws are not telling a man he can only have sex with his one wife.

We can quickly identify these as redemption laws. They are adaptations to the conditions of polygamy and concubines. More broadly, they were restrictions on the absolute power a patriarch exercised over those in his household.

There is yet another reason that these laws can't apply to Eden. According to the Creation account in Genesis, Adam and Eve's children would have had no way of populating the earth other than having sexual relations with direct family members. We now call this incest. Yet on a strict reading, the procreation commanded in Genesis 1:28 would have been impossible to accomplish under the restrictive laws from Leviticus 18. Leviticus 18 cannot be about restoring sex to the creation ideal.[d]

Genesis and Leviticus address different challenges in different societies. At their core, these two passages of Scripture are concerned with the same things. They both want to make the world a better reflection of the loving character of God, but the way that happens is different in different times and places.

Leviticus 18:1-18 addresses the male head of household, who would sometimes take multiple wives and concubines. Within the household, the patriarch had absolute authority. Think of the type of leadership Abraham, Isaac, and Jacob had within their families. They enslaved people and could force them to have sex with them and bear their children (Gen. 16:1-4). They could favor one wife and leave another starving for love (Gen. 29:31-35). They could bless one son and disinherit another (Gen. 25:27, 28). They could make those they'd enslaved risk their lives in battle for them (Gen. 14:14).

---

d. Another rule from Leviticus 18:19 forbids a man from having sex with a woman during her menstrual period. It's hard to know how this could come from the first two chapters of Genesis. Yet another forbids child sacrifice, which I'm sure wasn't practiced in Eden, but it's hard to connect this law to those texts. The prohibition on child sacrifice doesn't naturally come to mind when reading Genesis 1 and 2. It seems clear that this is a response to problems that had arisen in the real world, not a commentary on Genesis 1 and 2.

In Abraham's willingness to sacrifice his son Isaac, it seems that Abraham believed he had the authority to take his son's life without fear of retribution (Gen. 22). After all, who would have been able to hold Abraham accountable? He was the law for his household.

In this family structure, Leviticus 18 does bring much-needed accountability for men who otherwise had none. It essentially makes standard practices by these wealthy men less messy and difficult for vulnerable members of their households. It forbids a patriarch from having sex with some extended household members, such as his mother, a woman and her mother, a woman and her sister, his daughter-in-law, and others.

What about the other five laws in Leviticus 18? They prohibit sex with a woman in her "impurity," meaning during her period (verse 19); sex with your neighbor's wife (verse 20); sacrificing children to Molech (verse 21); a man lying with a man as with a woman (verse 22); and a man or woman having sex with an animal (verse 23). All these could relate to procreation, because while having sex with a neighbor's wife could result in a child, that child would not be considered one's own child. The other prohibitions are either types of sex that aren't procreative or the direct destruction of one's progeny through child sacrifice.

If we base these final five laws on procreation and the assumption that Genesis 1:28 gives a mandate for procreation, there are other implications. This interpretation says something about the intent of sex. Sex is supposed to be for procreation. If sex is unlawful while a woman is on her period because it won't lead to a child, is it also unlawful to use condoms or other forms of birth control? That's a logical conclusion.

Interestingly, the Adventist Church has an official position on birth control.[82] It thoughtfully mentions several factors to consider in deciding whether to use birth control. Could using birth control help someone avoid having a child they can't afford? Could birth control manage population growth as a matter of stewardship? While acknowledging the importance of procreation in Genesis 1:28, it concludes, "Scripture never presents procreation as an obligation of every couple in order to please God."[83]

Is the church's statement correct? For the sake of consistency, if we believe Leviticus 18 forbids same-sex sex because it's not procreative, all forms of birth control should also be off-limits. If non-procreative sex is sinful, it's sinful for all of us, and Adventist teachings should adjust.[84] I believe that such a change would be a huge mistake in our society. It would lead families into poverty, limit women's freedom, contribute to continued overcrowding, and increase abortion rates (whether legal or dangerous illegal abortions) since more women would be desperate to avoid unwanted pregnancies. It's okay to acknowledge that the world has changed in the last several millennia and that laws that might have accomplished a redemptive purpose then don't do so today.

But there is also reason to doubt that these verses are rooted in creation or procreation. There are 20 laws in Leviticus 18. The first 15 don't expound on principles from creation. Only the last five are arguably related to creation. There are no direct allusions or references. The moral reasoning stated in the text isn't about Genesis 1 and 2 but shame, honor, and holiness.

I don't believe Leviticus 18 attempts to define sexual ethics in terms of God's original creation. Instead, these laws addressed the real-life situation of the Israelites. They were attempting to restore some degree of justice and holiness to a specific social and cultural situation. They were a substantial improvement that would have been appreciated by members of Jewish households in the Ancient Near East.

Therefore, when we come to verse 22, "a man shall not lie with a man as with a woman, it is an abomination," we shouldn't rush to the conclusion that it's related to Genesis 1 and 2. Another context connects more directly.

PARTIAL REMEDY

If Leviticus 18 isn't intended to restore the purity of Eden, what ills was it seeking to correct? The easiest way to address that is by asking what it accomplished when written. It sets firm boundaries about family relationships that forbid the patriarch of the family from sexually exploiting family members. It prohibits sacrificing one's progeny on the altar of the god Molech. It forbids bestiality. It prohibits sex with a woman on her period. It forbids a man lying with a man as with a woman.

These things must have been forbidden for a reason. The command not to sacrifice one's child is chillingly specific, naming the specific god who demanded children as an offering. This could only be in response to a real problem. Indeed, later the people of Israel did offer their children as sacrifices to Molech (Jer. 32:35).

So how do we understand the context of Leviticus 18:22 and 20:13 without simply imputing our ideas? We can look at Scripture to see what real problem these texts would have solved. This is the first step in our deliberative process. We have to understand what questions they were concerned about before we start asking our questions.

In my experience, Adventists are much better than most at speaking respect-fully and intelligently about Hebrew Law. Conservative Adventist scholars do an excellent job of clarifying and interpreting the context of the law. Those are principles we can use.

> A law provides a kind of normative skeleton of a "story" that responds to a previous story and guides future stories. . . . Although the Bible does not record stories/situations that created the need for all of its laws, it seems likely that real-life circumstances were behind many of them.[85]

Gane's emphasis on the need to pay attention to "real-life circumstances" is reinforced in our text. Two verses later, Leviticus 18:24 says, "Do not defile yourselves with any of these things; for by all these the nations are defiled, which I am casting out before you." These laws are there because God doesn't want the Israelites to repeat the behavior of others. They address actual behaviors that took place in real space and time.

While we don't have the history behind all of the law, we have some of it. Does biblical history help us understand what problem Leviticus 18:22 and 20:13 were solving? Yes. Stories on this exact subject appear in the very Torah in which these laws were written. The stories came before the laws. The actions took place in the time and place the text indicates. They are the situations into which the laws speak.

By understanding the stories, we understand how the law functioned. We can answer the all-important question: What would have been the real-life impact of these laws on the lives of the people who received them?

THE SIN OF HAM

A strange story appears in Genesis 9. After the flood, Noah and his three sons started their new lives. Noah promptly planted a vineyard, made wine, got drunk, and lay naked in his tent.

His son, Ham, went in and saw Noah naked. Not only that, the original lan-guage conveys the idea that Ham's eyes lingered on his father's nakedness. There are sexual overtones to this description.

In a seminary ethics class, the teacher described how Ham, a homosex-ual, was turned on by his father's naked body. I remember being aghast at this suggestion. Being gay doesn't mean someone is sexually attracted to their own father. How did my professor so easily reach this bizarre conclusion?

I can only speculate, but I imagine the respectful relationships she'd had with openly gay people were few to none. She seems to have been exposed to stereotypes, not people. There are far too many stigmatizing narratives about gay, bisexual, and transgender people that I was regularly exposed to at seminary, which regularly informed theological conclusions such as these. Unfortunately, my professor's thoughts on this text are an example of reading a mistaken understanding of LGBTQ people into the text.

Rather than reflecting the LGBTQ community, Ham's behavior likely had nothing to do with sexual orientation. Same-sex erotic behavior in itself is not always an indication of someone's sexual orientation, particularly when there are other motives for that behavior.

After this incident with Noah, Ham told his brothers about Noah's nakedness. The brothers were appalled by Ham's behavior. They returned to the tent and entered, walking backward with a blanket between them. They covered Noah's nakedness without seeing him naked for even a moment. By doing this, they showed respect that contrasted Ham's shame.

No one is sure what happened here. Uncovering someone's nakedness is a euphemism for sex, but Noah uncovered his own nakedness. It's not the same, yet it evokes the same ideas, especially in connection with Ham's gaze and Noah's humiliation. It's fair to say there is something less than rape and more than nothing going on here. There is a definite sexual tone, and it's aggressive. In verse 24, Noah sobers up and realizes what Ham "had done to him."[86]

One thing we know for sure is that Ham's brothers reacted very differently than Ham did. After Ham further shamed his father by telling his brothers he had seen Noah's nakedness, they wanted to show their father respect. Their treatment of their father was the opposite of Ham's. It restored his honor.

Ham was interested in humiliating his father, not in a private moment of sexual gratification. That's the indication of the narrative; that's why he immediately bragged to his brothers. Perhaps he hoped humiliating his father would allow him to claim family headship for himself. By contrast, his brothers' behavior was about restoring their father's honor.

This is an important lesson. In the Bible and in our time, sexual acts aren't always about sexual desire. They are often about power and humiliation. Even today, sex acts can be driven by motives that are more sinister than attraction and relationships.

THE SIN OF SODOM

This story is about more than Ham. Ham's descendants were the Canaanite people, and this story is the first in a series that justifies why Canaanites were evil and had to cede their land to the Israelites (Gen. 9:22). We next encounter the Canaanites when Abraham and his family, including his nephew, Lot, are called by God to the land of Canaan (Gen. 13). God tells Abraham He will give him all the land Abraham can see. Abraham settles in the countryside, but Lot decides to live in the Canaanite cities of Sodom and Gomorrah. We soon find that the behavior of Ham has escalated in the Canaanite people.

The story of this escalation appears in Genesis 18 and 19. I suggest a quick read. The basic story goes like this:

1. Angels show up at Abraham's tent. He doesn't know they are angels. He invites them in, feeds them his finest food, ensures they are safe, and ensures their needs are met. He honors them and protects them.
2. The angels tell Abraham who they are and that they've come to destroy Sodom. Abraham pleads with them not to, and they agree that if they find even five good people there, they will spare the city.
3. The angels show up in Sodom and announce they are going to sleep on the street. Lot sees them and realizes this is a dangerous idea. He invites them into his home.
4. Every single man in the city, young and old, gathers outside Lot's home, demanding he hand over the visitors so they can gang rape them (demonstrating that there are not five good men in the city).
5. Lot asks the mob to take his daughters instead. They refuse. They start forcing their way into the house.
6. The angels blind the men of Sodom and rescue Lot. The Sodomites still try to get at the angels even though they're blind, but they can't.
7. The next day, Lot and his family flee for their lives as God rains down fire from heaven, destroying the city.

Long before I had affirming theology, back when I was still trying to be straight, I remember what people said about Sodom and Gomorrah. One instance sticks out in my memory. I was sitting in the seminary chapel, surrounded by friends, fellow pastoral hopefuls, and professors. The speaker that day, speaking about Genesis 19, chose to describe the men of Sodom as "a group of gay men."

It's difficult to understand how this could be true. This group includes "the men of the city, the men of Sodom, both old and young, all the people from every quarter" (Gen. 19:4). Are we to believe that all of them are gay?

Further, Lot knows these men and offers them his daughters. As despicable as this act is, it shows that Lot was aware that these men had a sexual appetite for women. This wasn't about sexual appetite, though.

Sodom had been attacked before (Gen. 13, 14). It was vulnerable. While Abraham showed himself to be an exceptional host, Sodom showed itself to be bloodthirsty and violent to strangers. They craved a reputation that would strike terror in their enemies, perhaps because they themselves felt vulnerable and afraid. Gang raping visitors was the ultimate act of humiliation and domination.[e]

Unlike the "gay men" described by the speaker in seminary chapel, this explanation considers the whole text. Abraham provided safe harbor, excellent food, respect, and care to the strangers who showed up at his doorstep. In Sodom, they were first left on the street, and later the men of the city tried to gang rape them.

I've often heard this story explained in terms of good hospitality versus lousy hospitality. That's too mild an explanation.

For us, hospitality is a matter of being a good host. It's about comfort and kindness. For them, hospitality was a matter of life and death. When someone traveled, if strangers were hospitable, they lived. They found the rest, food, and safety. If the citizens were aggressive and gang-raped strangers in their city, the traveler died.

That is the message of Genesis 19, and it helps us understand the cultural meaning of homoeroticism in the Bible. The narrative of the Torah sheds light on the legal code of the Torah. By understanding what happened, we understand what the laws prevented. Just in case we aren't sure about this explanation, Leviticus 18:24, 25 draws the connections directly:

---

e. Roy Gane objected that Genesis 19 should also be informed by Judges 19, a parallel story in which Israelites engage in the kind of behavior the Sodomites did in Genesis 19. Gane argues that the lack of hospitality was not the only concern. The offering of the female servant in place of the Levite indicates that the patriarch of the household was trying to avoid homosexual intercourse as the greater sin. He says that this wasn't a matter of social status because the male servant was not offered. But there is a simple explanation for this. Bible writers and biblical culture weren't thinking in terms of "homosexuality" as a construct or concept since it didn't exist. The rapists were intent on harm and humiliation, and the best way to do that was to treat a man like a woman. It was a patriarchal culture, much more so than our own, and nothing was more humiliating or struck more fear in the hearts of enemies than treating men like women through rape. So yes, the offer of the young woman was an attempt to avoid the rape of a man, and they did see it as a greater evil, but we have every reason to believe that was because of the gender dynamics of patriarchy. The rape of a man was worse than the rape of a woman. This doesn't mean same-sex marriage is wrong. They were not trying to stop same-gender marriage; what happened here was something radically and categorically different. Roy Gane, "Same-sex Love in the 'Body of Christ,'" Christianity and Homosexuality, (eds. David Ferguson, Fritz Guy, and David Larson), pp. 4-66.

"Do not defile yourselves with any of these things; for by all these the nations are defiled, which I am casting out before you. For the land is defiled; therefore I visit the punishment of its iniquity upon it, and the land vomits out its inhabitants."

Leviticus 18 identifies these laws as addressing behaviors that came before Israel on the land Israel would occupy. The land was the land of the Canaanites; the behaviors were described in the Bible through the narratives of Ham and Sodom. The line is direct. The moral purpose of these laws is to prevent the violence used by the citizens of Sodom to intimidate their neighbors and the behavior of Ham to humiliate his father and gain power for himself.

HOW DOES IT FUNCTION?

When we understand the purpose of the laws, we are much better able to ask how they apply to us. Using the same law directly would have dramatically different results in our context, which is a strong indication that it was meant for different situations. This often happens when the questions asked in the Bible differ from the questions we ask today. If we don't recognize this difference and go simply on the face value of the words, we risk seriously misapplying the Bible.[f]

What similarity is there between gang rape and marriage? What connection is there between humiliating someone and nurturing someone? What sympathy exists between the tactics of intimidation and the sacrifice of commitment?

These laws would not have stopped any same-gender marriages. We've looked closely at the text, and that should be clear. They were not asking that question. We don't find it in the Bible. Such relationships would not have made sense in a society like Israel's, which was based on patriarchal power, male biological heirs, lack of female autonomy, and polygamous families.

Deuteronomy 22:8 says that if you build a house, you should put a parapet on the roof. A parapet is a wall on the sides of the roof that keeps people from falling off. In the arid terrain of Israel, where snow is rare, flat roofs make sense.

---

f. William Webb's book, Slaves, Women, and Homosexuals, is one we spoke about often when I took an Old Testament Law class at the seminary. He does not support same-gender marriage, but I would argue that many of his principles could accurately support same-gender marriage. He provides support for the idea I'm talking about here, the practical function of the law. "A component of a biblical imperative may be culturally relative if the pragmatic basis for the instruction cannot be sustained from one culture to another. The converse is that a biblical command is more likely to be transcultural in its articulated form to the extent that the pragmatic factors are themselves sustainable across various cultures" (p. 109).

It was customary to use the roof as a living space. A parapet was there for safety, so that people didn't fall off to injury or death.

Yet the law doesn't say it only applies to flat roofs that are used as living spaces. No exceptions are mentioned. No extenuating circumstances. No special cases. No reason to justify ever building a roof without a parapet. The language is plain, nontechnical, and clear.

We understand this easily today, even though it is never plainly stated. We build our roofs differently. They aren't meant as living spaces, and they are usually pitched so the rain and snow will find their way to the ground. We don't think the steep roofs of a New England home, built to shrug off massive snowfall, need to have fences around them because God commanded it in Deuteronomy 22:8. We don't worry about going against the plain Word of God. We don't need any explicit statements in the text saying there can be exceptions. The broader context is evident, and the specific laws are meant to be "a starting point of deliberation," as described in the last chapter. It's easy to see that this text speaks to a different time and a different way of doing things.

There was only one way of building a roof back then. There was also only one way of having a marriage. The one way was with a man who inherited property, represented the family, made contracts, and had legal autonomy. This man would obtain a wife by negotiating with her father, perhaps with her input, perhaps not. It was the father's choice whether or not to include his daughter's wishes about her own destiny. Women had laws to protect them but little autonomy.

That's how ancient people understood marriage. It was necessarily heterosexual. An uncomfortably misogynistic version of gender hierarchy was all they knew. God gave laws to limit, constrain, and improve these conditions, but not to overturn them, at least not for the time being.

It worked for them. Survival was difficult. They were vulnerable to war and famine in a way most of us can't imagine. Repopulating society after men were killed in battle was necessary for survival, and polygamy made that possible. Having children to care for the land was an important priority. Had their society functioned as ours does, they might not have survived.[g]

It wasn't all necessary for survival. There was slavery, excessive capital punishment, and genocide. We do not need to pretend this system was just. We

---

g. Though I see these benefits to the survival of humanity, I also know that it could have been possible to survive without male dominance. Other cultures have done so in ways that were more humane for women. While our twenty-first-century social systems wouldn't have worked for them, there are other systems. Yet God met them where they were.

shouldn't try to justify it or pretend that it was better than it was. The laws at this time were not meant to be the last word; they were meant for a specific time and place. We should be aware of the limitations of uncritically applying them to our time and place. If we aren't, we risk accidentally exporting their culture instead of God's will.

We should also remember that we are no better than they were. What's different is that we know better. We see the value of women and see that women should have legal rights. Women need not be under the stewardship of a man who alone has legal rights. Women should be able to own property, enter into contracts, vote, and have bank accounts.

When we know better, we should do better. That is no indictment of them and no reason for us to be proud. We are where we are, and we know what we know because of the people who came before us, kept humanity alive, and paved the way.

Neither is it an indictment of biblical authority. The problem is not with the law; it's with our desire to apply a legal code that is now 4,000 years old without understanding how the intervening 4,000 years have changed law, custom, culture, and language. It's about our desire to read the Bible in the way that makes us most comfortable instead of paying attention to how it interprets itself. The law was written for the Israelites first. It was written by them, written for them, and written with their understanding of what and how things were.

When Leviticus speaks of men having sex with other men, they only have one understanding of what that means. That understanding is revealed in Scripture; it's there for all to read. It's a power move by one man humiliating another by lying with him "as with a woman."

Within that same patriarchal system in which women have no legal autonomy, treating a man like a woman was the most degrading act of aggression possible. It was a power play. That's what we find in the narrative of the Torah through the stories of Ham and Noah and of Sodom and Gomorrah.

In their most basic forms, these two rules aren't different from roofs and parapets. They had no concept of what a New England roof was. They didn't know people who had to deal with many feet of snow at a time. God didn't give the law for a situation they didn't understand, but for the needs they had in their time and place. God knew about all kinds of weather and all kinds of possible ways of building roofs. But God didn't explain all that in Deuteronomy. There was no need to give desert dwellers an index of all roof types or explain different places in the world with climates that created a need for different roofs. The Torah would be a very different book if it explained the moral law for all geographies and all time periods.

So why would we expect an index of sexual laws for all people and all time periods to be delivered to the Israelites and recorded in Leviticus? We don't have such expectations on other topics, and indeed we don't get such exhaustive explanations in any of the laws. All the laws are relevant to the context in which they are given, not every context that has or ever will exist.

Leviticus 18:22 and 20:13 didn't stop a single same-sex marriage or partnership when written. Not one. If we want to take Leviticus 18:22 and 20:13 seriously, we should look to the prison system in the United States. This is where the acts of Sodom are perpetuated. We should seek justice and safety in our incarceration system. This would accomplish the purpose of these laws. Excluding same-sex couples from marriage does not.

WHAT IF I'M WRONG?

Maybe you're nodding along with me right now and find my arguments compelling. Maybe not. To me, this approach to the text makes the most sense. It aligns several of the interpretive clues I look for. It's a good explanation of the words in context. It reflects the way of thinking of the Bible, particularly the Torah. It also aligns with the values of Scripture and the character of God.

Yet, I could be wrong. Other reasonable interpretations are out there. Jewish tradition tends to see these texts a little differently. Some Jews believe their purpose is to prevent ritual impurity, since semen could make one unclean. Another reason would be a "wasting" of seed. Sex should be with women so that more children will be born. In this line of moral reasoning, the purpose of sex is to reproduce.[87]

Most Jewish interpreters agree that the Hebrew Bible has no prohibition of female/female sexual activity. Neither ritual impurity from semen nor the wasting of the seed would apply to women. Rabbis mostly agreed in the *Talmud* that women who had sex with other women had not lost their virginity (though it was still a minor offense), so they were still eligible to marry a priest.[88]

Though perhaps still compelling within some Jewish interpretations, the idea of ritual impurity wouldn't apply in Christian interpretations. Ritual impurity is not considered binding after the death and resurrection of Christ.

The wasting of seed is a compelling argument. The verses surrounding Leviticus 18:22 seem to reinforce this idea. Having sex with a woman during her menstrual period is unlikely to result in pregnancy and wastes seed (verse 19). Sacrificing children to the god Molech is a violent way to destroy the result of seed (verse 21). Having sex with an animal won't result in children either (verse 23; though this verse also applies to women engaged in bestiality, and there is no wasting of seed in that scenario).

The only verse that doesn't fit the pattern is the prohibition of sleeping with one's neighbor's wife (verse 20). This might be satisfied by shifting the argument slightly. Maybe it means the man's seed should be used for his own family line and no others. But one would wonder why sex with a sex worker is not included on this list since it was a common practice. In fact, it was probably the most common way men would spend one's seed on something other than their own family line. And, of course, masturbation isn't mentioned either.

Still, this moral reasoning also has the benefit of being consistent with many centuries of Christian tradition. For most of Christian history, sex has been valued primarily as a means of procreation. Often, Christian thinkers believed sex for enjoyment was sinful. Sex with one's wife was a necessary evil to produce children and accommodate desires that would have been better off denied. That's Christian history. Intentionally preventing pregnancy was morally wrong, an indulgence of lust.[89]

Only recently has this shifted. I know it's uncomfortable to admit, but this shift is directly related to birth control and the sexual revolution. Of course, Christians don't endorse everything about the sexual revolution, yet its influence is felt. Before the sexual revolution, Christians who spoke or wrote about the beauty, joy, and gift of sex were difficult, if not impossible, to find.[90]

Forbidding birth control would not be a radical idea or a departure from historic Christianity. If the moral reasoning behind Leviticus 18:22 is to prevent wasting seed, it shouldn't only be used to keep same-sex couples from marrying; it should also prevent heterosexuals from using any form of birth control.

I don't believe birth control is wrong. Even if this is the correct interpretation of Leviticus, society has changed dramatically. Our problem is too much reproduction, not too little. Also, the production of heirs to inherit the land and preserve the family line are not an issue in today's society as they were in Ancient Israel.

Plus, the New Testament had dramatically different ideas about family and reproduction, even encouraging celibacy. After all, even the command in Genesis 1:28 says, "be fruitful and multiply; fill the earth." The earth is full of people today. Maybe the commandment has been achieved.

It's okay to apply these texts differently than their surface meaning and in harmony with the law's purpose and God's character. It's okay for heterosexuals to use birth control. It's also okay for same-sex couples to ask the church to bless their marriages.

WHAT ABOUT ACTS 15?

What about the New Testament? As mentioned earlier, Acts 15 may call us back to Leviticus 17 and 18. The church in Jerusalem sent a letter stating that Gentiles should "abstain from things offered to idols, from blood, from things strangled, and from sexual immorality" (verse 29).

These categories broadly match Leviticus 17 and 18, laws for Gentiles living in Israel. Does this mean they are universal and literal? Should a direct reading of Leviticus 18 be taken as the definition of sexual fornication?

Rather than an illustration that Leviticus 17 and 18 should be applied in their most literal sense, these texts turn out to be yet another example of a deliberative process.

Despite the requirements of the Jerusalem Counsel, Paul advised the church in Corinth not to be concerned about eating food sacrificed to idols. The gods aren't real, Paul argued, so it doesn't matter. The only reason for concern is if the conscience of a Christian who was "weak" in faith was bothered (1 Cor. 8; 10:25).

What are we to make of this? Did the Jerusalem Council think these laws were applicable and did Paul disagree? How are we to sort out such a disagreement when both texts are part of the Bible? Whose side do we take?

Or we could consider another option. Perhaps we have drawn the wrong conclusion. Maybe the Council in Jerusalem was not commenting on the timeless application of Leviticus 17 and 18 but trying to figure out how to live in peace with Gentiles, who were now part of their faith.

This is precisely what Leviticus 17 and 18 helped the Israelites do: live in peace with the Gentiles in their midst. Such an explanation would resolve the apparent conflict. It also explains why they spoke so cautiously, "it seemed good to the Holy Spirit and to us" (Acts 15:28).

They were speaking of what "seemed good," which would help them move forward as a community that included Gentiles. Before this decree, a strong line of separation existed. Jews and Gentiles wouldn't so much as share a meal. Gentiles were unclean. By comparison, these three restrictions were minimal.

RETROSPECT

Maybe you disagree with my interpretation. That's fine. But for whatever reason, Paul did not believe the laws for Gentiles found in Leviticus 17 and 18 were applicable universally and literally. He didn't think they applied to the Gentiles he served, who shopped in markets run by pagans, but who didn't believe in idols. Even if Acts 15 took place after Paul's letter to the Corinthians, it still represents a different theological understanding.

When we think about it, today's Adventist Church doesn't follow all the laws for the Gentiles found in Acts 15. I was studying with Jehovah's Witnesses a few years back, and they brought up Acts 15. They understood it as referring to Leviticus.

We turned to Leviticus 17:14, where the rationale for not consuming blood was found, "You shall not eat the blood of any flesh, for the life of all flesh is its blood. Whoever eats it shall be cut off." The Jehovah's Witnesses said this is why blood transfusions are wrong; it's a way of consuming blood. They refuse to accept transfusions for themselves or their families based on this text, even if that means death.

I scratched my head because they refuse blood transfusions but don't refuse to eat food with blood. But we have to give them the point that they are making about transfusions. They take Leviticus 17 and 18 at face value, based on Acts 15. They argued that it is a transcultural law, which they apply directly to our culture without deliberation. Even though there were no blood transfusions in Moses' day, they believe Scripture is clear. Their object is to obey, not explain it away because it's inconvenient or because health professionals say it's harmful.

The woman I spoke to that day told us she'd had a premature child who risked death without a transfusion. She chose to trust God even though the doctor pled with her to accept the treatment. Her child lived, and she saw it as a reward for her faithfulness. My friend was silent as she listened, but I could feel her anger and see her clenched jaw. She told me later that it takes babies six weeks to replace lost blood and that though she was fortunate that her child lived, the brain didn't get the nutrients it needed. This woman's displaced faithfulness likely caused a lifetime of cognitive deficits for her child.

Is this God's will? For me, the answer is clearly "no," not because of how I define the Hebrew word "eat" or "consume," but because I know that law wasn't meant to prevent blood transfusions that would only be available thousands of years later. Taking the words on their plain meaning without thinking about their contextual meaning, and harming a child as a result, is morally evil. Treating a child that way is against everything I know about God's character.

Such treatment feels familiar to LGBTQ Adventists, particularly when we think of what we experience in childhood. As children, we are expected to live our lives and anticipate our future with a literalistic interpretation of Leviticus 18:22 and 20:13.

If the LGBTQ community, medical doctors, psychiatrists, psychologists, counselors, social workers, and adoption specialists are believed,[91] our teachings are wrong. They are harmful to children. Refusing to support transgender kids is harmful. It leads to psychological pain, depression, anxiety, and alienation.

As Adventists, we are so close to recognizing this. We already reject putting ourselves and our loved ones in harm's way for the sake of the plain meaning of the text about blood. We already deliberate. We already recognize that shifting meaning often means words don't apply with a one-to-one correlation.

But we take it further. Except for kosher meat, slaughtering practices intentionally keep the blood in the meat for flavor. While the Adventist Church encourages vegetarianism, eating a steak is not sinful. We treat vegetarianism as an ideal, but violating the laws from Acts 15 by eating meat with blood doesn't disqualify anyone from membership or ministry, except in the most legalistic environments. We don't think this part of Acts 15 is universal.

If anyone says differently, I challenge them to advocate for the same treatment of meat-eaters in the church that they give to people in same-gender marriages: fire employees, disfellowship members, and refuse to baptize the rest. Most of us would recognize this as fanaticism, and some of us have (sadly) learned that some think this way.

Three laws in Acts 15 may come from Leviticus 17 and 18. Two are related to food sacrificed to idols and to blood. They are categorically not considered applicable to all time. Perhaps that means that even according to New Testament standards, we aren't supposed to apply Leviticus 17 and 18 uncritically, directly, and literally to all situations. And even if Leviticus 18 does apply, would it mean the same thing now that it meant then? Wouldn't it apply to the same scenarios described in the Torah and not to entirely different situations?

And here's yet another wrench to throw into the cogs. The connection between Leviticus 17 and 18 and Acts 15 isn't certain. Some doubt it. The three requirements that might be from Leviticus are stated twice, and in different orders (Acts 15:20, 29). Once, they seem to follow Leviticus 17 and 18, and once they are in a different order. If it was an intentional reference to Leviticus 17 and 18, it seems likely that it would always follow that order.

Also, Jewish interpreters don't associate Leviticus 17 and 18 with laws for Gentiles. They find that instead in the "Seven Laws of Noah" taken from Genesis 9. This was a covenant made with all humanity before Abraham was born, so it applies to Gentiles and Jews. It also follows the same basic principles of Acts 15, but it doesn't include same-sex sexuality.

The Noahic Covenant applies to Gentiles in the Babylonian Talmud, which includes teachings from an oral tradition reaching back as far as the time of Christ. We don't know whether this understanding was present in Israel when Acts was written, but we know Jews today don't rely on Leviticus for laws for Gentiles. Indeed, laws in Leviticus that were intended to help sojourners live with Israelites in their wilderness wanderings might not be as universally applicable as the laws given to Noah and his descendants in Genesis 9 when the world was a blank slate.

If that's the case, the Jerusalem Council was not trying to give universal moral laws for behavior. It was trying to figure out how to function as a community. This means that Paul wasn't contradicting them at all. Paul was trying to figure out how to help his churches function as a community in a different context, in the Gentile world and not Jerusalem.

In other words, by assuming that Acts 15 intended to encompass all the commands of Leviticus 17 and 18, and by assuming that these laws were meant to be applied universally and literally, we've been missing the forest for the trees. We got so technical that we missed the point. We tried so hard to make solid and irrefutable rules that we missed the purpose of the rules in the first place. By doing so, we misunderstood the whole thing, much to the harm of LGBTQ people.

I hope this gives us pause about the simplicity of applying passages in literalistic ways. In the Hebrew Bible, they used a deliberative process to understand the law. The law came with a narrative that explained it. That narrative teaches us that Leviticus 18 addressed behaviors described in Genesis 19. Namely, it forbade the use of rape to humiliate men by treating them as women. There was a moral purpose behind these laws. They showed God's justice.

In the New Testament, believers also used a deliberative process. They also sought the wisdom and will of God. In Acts 15, they weren't making stuff up. They understood the Hebrew Bible correctly. They read it as it was meant to be read. They read it deliberatively, respecting both the text and their concern for the real-world outcomes of their decisions. They came up with something that made sense and "seemed good to us and to the Holy Spirit." Their wisdom helped hold the early church together. Without their wisdom, we might not be Christians today.

We can learn from their decisions and how they made them. This same process applies to the questions we ask now about same-gender marriage and transgender identity. Striking parallels exist between the inclusion of Gentiles and the inclusion of LGBTQ people. The question of LGBTQ inclusion today threatens to tear churches apart, just as Gentile inclusion threatened to tear the early church apart.

We can seek God and deliberate now as they deliberated then. We must read the text as carefully as they did. We must remember the character of God and the intent of the law as they did. If we keep the main thing the main thing, instead of trying to create universal rules from specific scenarios, we can trust God with our conclusions just as they did. But it will take bravery and courage for us, just as it did for them. It's not easy to try to be like our spiritual forbearers, learning from the Bible and seeking God in prayer to make decisions during times of change and uncertainty. But that's what the Jerusalem Council did. That's what Paul did. That's what ancient Israelites did. We can trust that God will guide us as God guided them.

In fact, we have much more to learn from the Council in Jerusalem. Choosing to accept uncircumcised Gentiles was a decision with stakes as high as they come. They couldn't have known it then, but their decision to be inclusive paved the way for a radical reshaping of the church itself, and eventually of the entire world. How did they make their difficult judgment call? How did God guide them? How did they deliberate? How did they come to the radical decision to accept "unclean" Gentiles into their churches? That's our topic in the next chapter.

CHAPTER 8

Love Doesn't Require Approval

"I don't understand why LGBTQ people think we have to approve of them in order to love them. It's like we have to agree with everything they say. I love them, I just don't agree with their lifestyle."

"Love the sinner, hate the sin."

Rick Warren probably summed up the view of so many when he said:

"Our culture has accepted two huge lies. The first is that if you disagree with someone's lifestyle, you must fear or hate them. The second is that to love someone means you agree with everything they believe or do. Both are nonsense. You don't have to compromise convictions to be compassionate."

These words once rang true to me. At the time, I felt torn in several directions. I suspect many might feel this tension:

- You have some idea of how difficult it is for someone who desires romantic love with the same gender to be told it's a sin, yet you believe it to be true.
- You know that transgender people face many difficulties, but you believe gender is biological and not determined by choice or feeling.
- You also believe that God loves all people, and everyone is deserving of love no matter what. Period. End of story.
- You love LGBTQ people because you know God loves them. You want them to know that you love them.
- Speaking out when convicted is important to you, and ignoring your beliefs to get along seems shallow, unloving.
- You may also experience gay, bisexual, and transgender people resisting this approach. You may feel frustrated and misunderstood when people characterize you as unloving for your sincerely held theological convictions or when your church is criticized as an unsafe place for LGBTQ people because of theological beliefs.
- It feels unfair to be judged by those who say they don't want to be judged.

This is how I felt for a long time. It's a lot of tension to bring into any conversation. I remember coming across Rick Warren's statement, and it served as a tonic for my tension, affirming that speaking against someone's choice does not mean we don't love them.

Back then, I wanted people to know that love should not require denial of truth. Instead, love is a principle that flows from the nature of God and is in harmony with how God created us. Cheap acceptance, approval, and dishonesty are poor substitutes for love.

The reality for those living under the authority of Scripture is that if God communicates that something is wrong, we trust the assessment of God. The reason many Christians believe same-sex relationships are wrong is not that they hate gay, bisexual, and transgender people; it's because they trust God and believe God said these relationships are wrong. They trust that if God has forbidden anything, there is a good reason. It's neither safe nor wise to disobey the will of God.

"If God is for us, who can be against us?" asked Paul (Rom. 8:31). "The Lord shall fight for you, and you shall hold your peace," said Moses as the Israelites prepared to cross the Red Sea (Ex. 14:14). Peace and safety ultimately come from trust in God, so rejecting God's view on marriage is the risky choice.

Also, many Christians feel it's a double standard for gay, bisexual, and transgender people to demand acceptance of their sexuality and gender without extending acceptance to them. In short, they feel that they have been rejected, hated, and judged. Yet they know their own hearts. They know they want what is best for gay and transgender people.

This all amounts to a general belief that gay, bisexual, and transgender people misuse the idea of love. Many people see the LGBTQ community this way, demanding love from others in the form of banal acceptance while asking others to set aside their sincerely held convictions. Compounding the problem, many believe LGBTQ people distort love to justify their desires.

This is a sincere complaint, and it comes from a difficult place. It's challenging to enter into conversation with someone if we believe they judge us as homophobic before opening our mouths. I've never met anyone who thinks they are homophobic. How can we ever have the conversation if that type of judgment exists before we even get started?

I know there is genuine love in the hearts of many who oppose my sexual orientation. I've seen and experienced it. I felt that love for LGBTQ people myself even when I wasn't affirming. I don't want to challenge the love people feel.

Still, we need to explore more closely the relationship between beliefs and love. What demands does love place on our theology and our praxis, if any? If our theology is correct, does that help us love one another better? If our theology is wrong, does it make it more difficult to love one another? And does it matter whether our theology makes it more or less difficult to love one another?

ALL WE NEED IS LOVE?

The word "love" is often misused. Those who are affirming have been guilty of using love in vague and sentimental ways. In our impatience and pain, we sometimes don't care about the sincerely held beliefs of others. We just want ourselves, our relationships, and our gender to be accepted. Speaking candidly, I don't judge anyone who reacts this way when hurting from the sting of rejection and expulsion from their family and faith community. Still, I recognize how difficult it makes these conversations. Those who have shifted theologically to affirming theology often forget that we condemn people who believe the same things we ourselves believed not long ago. No one is so intolerant of opposing views as those who recently changed their mind. I am guilty of this.

Those who are non-affirming of same-sex marriage and transgender people have often been guilty of superficial understandings of love. They assume they love LGBTQ people without self-reflection and sometimes with little effort.

It's tempting to stop talking about love or to lean instead on a concept of truth that seems firm, something we can stand on, something clear and solid. It's easy to become defensive when accused of not caring about the difficulties faced by the LGBTQ community. It's hard to hear someone accuse you of having a theology that is incompatible with love. It's hard to listen. It's easy to begin defending ourselves as loving people instead of striving to be loving people. It's easy to use professions of loving the LGBTQ community as a rhetorical shield against criticism rather than as an essential value and aspiration.

One thing that unites us all is that this conversation can cause confusion, tension, pain, and defensiveness. How do we love one another? How do we get back to the reality that love is at the center of everything? That's a theological truth. Backing away from love is backing away from God's character and the foundation of all ethical teachings. Love is the origin and theological center of the law, the Bible, and Christian life (Deut. 6:4, 5; Hosea 6:6; Matt. 22:36-40; John 13:34, 35; 1 Cor. 13:13; Col. 3:14; 1 John 4:8; and many more).

Avoiding love or pretending that love isn't serious theology would be like tending to a plant without caring for the soil. If we are to understand God, we must understand love. If we are to understand our own creation, we must understand love. If we want to understand God's will for Christians who are attracted to their own gender, we must understand love. Love must be the center and beating heart of our theology, or our theology is not of God or the Bible.

The solution for accepted theology is articulated: The church loves and accepts gay, bisexual, and transgender people. It has no problem with the people themselves. The people can be involved in the life of the church at all levels. Simply having attraction to the same gender doesn't disqualify anyone.[a]

However, agreement with the church's sexual ethics is a required part of membership, especially leadership. This applies to everyone. LGBTQ people are no exception. We love the people; we forbid the lifestyle. We love the sinner; we hate the sin.

---

a. The Adventist Church is far from consistent on this subject. In many Adventist churches, LGBTQ people cannot be members if they are open about their orientation, even if they are celibate. I know people who wanted to be pastors and were candid about being gay but celibate. Job offers were rescinded or never given. In theory, LGBTQ people can minister if gay and celibate or transgender but living as a cisgender person, but it's vanishingly rare in practice. The same is true for church members. Very few local churches have members who openly identify as LGBTQ or describe themselves as having same-sex attraction in the present or past. To their credit, from my conversations with leaders of my conference when I was coming out to them, they might have allowed me to continue pastoring had I followed the church's teachings, even though identifying as bisexual. This should be standard practice. The North American Division of Seventh-day Adventists differentiates between orientation and behavior. It allows people to identify as LGBTQ, but it forbids same-gender romantic relationships or gender transitioning.

Most of us who are gay, bisexual, and transgender push back against this thinking. We have questions. Can we always separate the person from the behavior? Or are there some situations in which restricting a particular behavior also excludes a whole class of people? You might be surprised to learn what the Bible says on this question.

GENTILE LIFESTYLE

I'm going to make a comparison between Gentiles in the Bible and today's LGBTQ community. Even as I think about it, I realize that this might seem like a weak comparison at first. That's what I thought too. Paul's theological reasoning for including Gentiles is quite different from affirming theology. Yet, the more I learned about Gentile inclusion and the church's decision-making around it, the more the parallels jumped out at me. We can learn about how the early church addressed Gentiles and the question of their inclusion.

In Acts 15, early Christians met in Jerusalem to discuss a significant theological and practical shift. Before being excluded from synagogues, early followers of Jesus were considered a Jewish sect. They probably saw themselves as Jews. The inclusion of uncircumcised Gentiles threatened that identity. Circumcision was the mark of God's people for millennia, and now it was challenged.

Gentiles who called themselves followers of Jesus were receiving the Holy Spirit without being circumcised. This led many to believe the requirement of circumcision shouldn't be necessary. Others pushed back, saying Gentiles still needed to be circumcised and that if the church ignored this law, they would be disregarding the Scriptures. The disagreement threatened to rupture the church. They met to decide what to do.

When they met, most churches still required Gentile men to go under the knife to be Christian. For most Gentiles, that was too great a barrier. Though some complied, many would never have become Christians with such requirements. Circumcision wasn't only about the pain and risk of the procedure; it was also about self-identity. Gentiles wanted to follow Jesus. Did they have to be Jewish to do so? Did they have to be circumcised and follow Jewish law? Doing so would alienate them from their Gentile communities and families.

To say they no longer had to be circumcised was to say they could remain Gentile and still follow Jesus. This was genuinely radical. Tribalism, persecution, and theology had led Israelites to think of the children of Abraham as the people of God and Gentiles as enemies.

Gentiles did not obey the law. Their lifestyle was unclean and sinful. They didn't act like God's covenant people. The food they ate, how they ate it, the things they touched, the activities they engaged in, and their very bodies were unclean. They weren't children of Abraham and didn't follow the law of Moses.

But Jesus was a Jewish rabbi who kept the law. If Gentiles wanted to follow Jesus, they should change their behavior. This was not merely some cultural idea; it was central to their understanding of Scripture. They were covenant people, children of Abraham through the covenant (Gen. 17:10-14) that was renewed with the law of Moses (Lev. 12:3; Ex. 12:44, 48).

These early Jewish Christians didn't require perfection. Forgiveness was built into the law itself. They did require a good-faith effort to keep the law that was the covenant God's people had made with God. Grace and mercy come through the covenant, the very covenant sealed by circumcision. Those outside of the covenant were sinners in need of redemption.[92]

Could Gentiles ever access this redemption? Yes, if they were converted, Gentiles could be saved. They could be circumcised as adults and leave their unclean lifestyles. That would be enough to make them part of God's covenant people.

None of this explicitly excluded Gentiles from the church. Early Christians only required that Gentiles keep the same laws the Jews were keeping. Gentiles were no exception. Everyone had the same rules. *Gentiles were welcome; their lifestyle was not. They loved the Gentiles; they forbade the Gentile lifestyle. They loved the sinner; they hated the sin.*

Though for Gentiles, keeping the same law had a much different impact. For Jewish Christians, that law affirmed who they were. For Gentiles, it condemned who they were. The law of circumcision required a greater burden and a heavier sacrifice of Gentiles. These rules amounted to a total change in their lives, the very meaning of being Gentile.

PARALLELS AND DIFFERENCES

In some ways, this is an excellent parallel to the situation of sexual minority Adventists; in some ways, it's not. From a theological perspective, the differences are dramatic. Gentile inclusion and the inclusion of gay, bisexual, and transgender people in the church involve different texts and theological ideas. That's why most of this book is dedicated to those theological issues.

But there is another consequential difference. Jewish Christians were political subjects of Rome and at the bottom of the food chain of nations in the Roman Empire. They had every reason to believe they were morally entitled to their own separate place and religion. Making space for Gentiles who oppressed them was a lot to ask. Heterosexual Christians are in a much different position concerning gay, bisexual, and transgender Christians.

Looking back on these events as Christians, we must carefully take our history into account. Jewish Christians ultimately accepted Gentiles with an openness rarely matched in human history. In turn, Christians have terrorized, victimized, murdered, and exploited Jews for millennia. As we have this discussion, remember that the Jewish Christians became our model to be emulated. Let's not judge them harshly, as we often have.

Even as there are differences to acknowledge, there are also important similarities. These similarities don't do the essential theological work, but they inform us how the Holy Spirit might begin the transformation process. How did God declare that "the time had come" for Gentile inclusion? How might God communicate that "the time has come" to open the door to gay, bisexual, and transgender people to accept the gospel without requiring celibacy or gender conformity?

First, Gentiles were not entirely excluded from fellowship. They were required to embrace behaviors that were both a heavy burden and against their identity as Gentiles. Specifically, they were required to be circumcised and keep the law.

Disapproval of this specific behavior, refusing to be circumcised, is about much more than the behavior; it's about excluding the person. Failure to affirm those who were uncircumcised was failure to affirm Gentiles. Of course, this is the same claim most LGBTQ Christians make. Failing to affirm our gender, sexual orientation, and relationships are failing to affirm us. Behavior and identity can't always be neatly separated.

Second, Christians in the early church (especially in Jerusalem) had a strong preference for their identity as Israelites and children of Abraham. It was the cultural and religious frame of reference that defined the behavioral requirements of Christians. On the other hand, they saw Gentiles as outsiders at best. Prejudice against Gentiles was common, and it was typical to consider Gentiles sinners and separate from God.

Perhaps we don't see prejudice against gay, bisexual, and transgender people in the church. I've spoken to several people who don't believe it exists in any pervasive way. Perhaps we are also confident that we hold no prejudice against sexual minorities. I understand this and remember wanting LGBTQ people to know that I still loved and cared for them even though I agreed with my church's views.

That's probably why it surprised me when, after accepting and affirming my own sexuality, I discovered a shift in how I felt around LGBTQ people. I'd felt sorry for them; I'd thought they were deceived; I wanted to show them the way. There was a barrier between us. That barrier consisted of my idea of what life decisions they should make. I felt they were further from God than I was, and I longed to show them the way through mercy and grace.

When I accepted my sexuality, I realized how patronizing I had been. Instead of thinking I had all the answers and could show them the way, I suddenly realized that they had a lot to teach me. I admired their strength of character and authenticity in the face of prejudice, including my own prejudice.

As months went by, I learned that I had a lot of internalized heterosexism. We all do. I struggled with feelings of embarrassment and shame simply over being bisexual. My gay, bisexual, and transgender friends who grew up in churches teaching accepted theology also experience internalized heterosexism. We spend a lot of time in therapy, prayer, and self-care to work through it all. If we are heterosexist, what are the chances that heterosexuals are free from prejudice?

Since coming out, I've had many experiences in which Adventist pastors attempt to show me they care by using analogies from the gospel. They say they see me the way Jesus saw Zacchaeus (Luke 19:1-8), the woman caught in adultery (John 8:2-11), or a leper (Luke 5:12, 13). Jesus treated them with kindness and grace and showed them what they should do. But when they used these analogies, they were always in the position of Jesus, and I was always the sinner.

I recall one specific conversation. A pastor I knew was comparing LGBTQ people to Zacchaeus, and he was trying to be like Jesus. I had the presence of mind to reply, "Perhaps we should allow Jesus to be Jesus and we should all be equal." In the decades before coming out, no one ever made these types of comparisons with me. They implicitly saw me as equal. Such a comparison would have seemed prideful, the opposite of gracious. But as soon as I came out, people treated me differently.

These are examples of people who are making a genuine effort to be better and show love. Many make no such effort. Many people use harsh words with me. I've been told that I'm disgusting, stupid, and evil again and again. Usually, because I'm bisexual, there is a sense that I'm an outsider. I don't belong anymore. I'm "other." Whether the "othering" is subtle or overt, it prevents some

Adventists from seeing that I have something valuable to say from my experience and study. This is similar to what many Jewish people must have felt toward Gentiles.

The third important parallel between the early church Gentiles and sexual minorities of today has to do with the Bible and theology. The position of the Jerusalem Christians was grounded in Scripture and was the only viewpoint God's people held for thousands of years. Its truth was evident. Though the inclusion of Gentiles and the LGBTQ community are different topics theologically, both were uniformly accepted in historical theology.

God made a covenant with Abraham and his descendants. That covenant stipulated that anyone not circumcised was cut off (Gen. 17:9-14). This requirement became part of the law (Lev. 12:3; Ex. 12:44). Circumcision was also required of those who participated in the Passover (Ex. 12:48). Passover was the meal at which Jesus inaugurated Communion as an ongoing Christian sacrament (Matt. 26:17-30; Mark 14:12-26; Luke 22), which is why we still serve unleavened bread in Adventist Communion services. This also meant that all those in attendance were circumcised Jews. If that isn't enough, Jesus himself was circumcised (Luke 2:21).

Any student of Scripture knows that theology has changed dramatically on this point. Hebrews, Galatians, and Romans especially teach the theological interpretations of the Old Testament that allow for inclusion. But Paul didn't articulate this theology until after Gentiles were baptized without circumcision. The practice preceded the theology.

This conversation is difficult for many Adventists. We are afraid of going soft in our interpretation of Scripture. We're torn between a desire to include and a fear of betraying our loyalty to Scripture. Doctrines believed so long and by so many are difficult to question, let alone to change.

I once heard that to make a significant change, people must believe the new way will be twice as good as the old one. Change feels perilous because it's untested. It's hard to even think about making a theological change before there is an emotional reason to do so. That's just a human reality.

As we are about to see, the Jerusalem church needed to work backward. It's not that theology isn't essential, but they had to feel the tension of the moment before they could understand the theology. They needed a change of heart before they had a change of mind. They couldn't see Scriptures clearly until, in compassion, they appreciated the humanity of Gentiles. Theology alone wasn't enough. The story of how that happened is crucial. It was left for us so that we could learn from them.

For the current debate, the removal of prejudice is necessary but not sufficient. Scripture must support inclusion. But to see Scripture clearly, heterosexual Adventists must also deal with their prejudice. Otherwise, they won't understand LGBTQ people, which means they will be asking all the wrong questions. Adventists need the same thing Peter needed, equal relationships characterized by respect. They must learn (as I had to learn) to see gay, bisexual, and transgender people not as outsiders but as part of us. Until this happens, the log in their own eye will obstruct their view from seeing the Scriptures clearly (Matt. 7:3-5). Understanding the Bible is not only about intellect. The Spirit must guide us with love and compassion.

ANTIOCH

What changed in the early church to bring about the full inclusion of Gentiles? Before the Council in Jerusalem, it was business as usual. The church was predominantly Jewish and seen by many as a sect of Judaism. Yet a different ideology was arising 300 miles north of Jerusalem. Something new was happening in Antioch. A few people had decided to share the gospel with the Greeks instead of only with Jews. These Greeks had eagerly accepted Jesus, becoming part of the church. But these were inconvenient conversions. The Greeks weren't circumcised, and they didn't keep the law the way Christians in Jerusalem did.

Antioch was the beginning of a multiethnic group of Jesus followers. It was also where they were first called Christians (Acts 11:19-26). And it was a problem for Jews in Jerusalem who remained "zealous for the law" (Acts 21:20).

What did this mean for the early church? A pivotal decision arrived. What would they require of Gentiles? Of course, we all know what that decision was. After all, most of us Christians began as Gentiles. Today, the only ritual required for church membership is baptism, not circumcision. This is undoubtedly a welcome change. Ellen White reflected on this decision:

> The time had come for an entirely new phase of work to be entered upon by the church of Christ. The door that many of the Jewish converts [to Christianity] had closed against the Gentiles was now to be thrown open. And the Gentiles who accepted the gospel were to be regarded as on an equality with the Jewish disciples, without the necessity of observing the rite of circumcision (*The Acts of the Apostles*, p. 136).

At first, it seems obvious why this change happened. Paul explained theologically why circumcision is no longer needed. Jesus had removed the requirement.

But it might surprise us to know that this was not the reasoning given in the book of Acts. The early church didn't refer to Paul's theology when it decided to remove the requirement of circumcision and include Gentiles. The story about how and why this dramatic changed happened is deeply relevant to us.

THE CATALYST

In Acts 10, Peter receives a vision in the middle of the afternoon. Unclean animals descended on a sheet, and (it must have been shocking to him) God told Peter he should eat them because God had cleansed them. This went against everything he knew about avoiding what was unclean. Peter didn't understand the meaning of the vision.

Unknown to Peter, the Holy Spirit had given a Gentile named Cornelius a vision the day before. Cornelius' message was much more direct. "Send for Peter." He was even told where to find him. Cornelius' messengers arrived just as Peter was trying to understand his dream. At the prompting of the Spirit, Peter immediately left to meet Cornelius.

Many of us have received divine appointments, moments when we know that the conversation was directed and timed. Peter's encounter with Cornelius was a divine appointment in the extreme.

Ellen White wrote that even arriving at Cornelius' home was agonizing for the apostle. Peter was violating ideas of uncleanness simply by being in that home. He brought witnesses for he "knew that he would be called to account for so direct a violation of the Jewish teachings" (*The Acts of the Apostles*, p. 137).

On arriving, Peter met a Gentile so overcome with humility and a willingness to know God that he fell at Peter's feet, only rising at Peter's insistence. Cornelius was uncircumcised but wholly devoted to God. Surely this was a man who loved God enough to be circumcised. But Peter never asked.

Why not? Peter's mind must have been racing. After the dream of the unclean animals, God brought him to Cornelius. Cornelius lived an unclean lifestyle. Cornelius was uncircumcised. But in the dream Peter was told, "What God has cleansed, no longer consider unholy" (Acts 10:15, NASB).

By not requiring Cornelius to be circumcised, Peter violated a long-held scriptural teaching with centuries of theological history. Yet Ellen White tells us that the actual problem was obscured. For Peter, it seemed to be about the Bible, but it was really about prejudice.

> How carefully the Lord worked to overcome the prejudice against the Gentiles that had been so firmly fixed in Peter's mind. . . . He sought to divest the apostle's mind of this prejudice and to teach the important truth that in heaven there is no respect of persons; that Jew and Gentile are alike precious in God's sight; that through Christ the heathen may be made partakers of the blessings and privileges of the gospel (*The Acts of the Apostles*, p. 136).

Sometimes the theological question that seems so pertinent is only the surface. In this case, the real issue was one of preconceived ideas. What Peter knew to be unclean, what seemed vile and unholy to Peter's understanding, could be made holy by God.

Equally important, the inclusion of Gentiles meant theology had to change. This doesn't mean the Bible had to change. Theology is merely our understanding of the Bible, and sometimes we get it wrong. We are fallible.

Peter grasped all this. Saying nothing of the requirement of circumcision, he told Cornelius and all his friends and family about Jesus. And "while Peter was still speaking these words, the Holy Spirit fell upon all those who heard the word. And those of the circumcision who believed were astonished, as many as came with Peter, because the gift of the Holy Spirit had been poured out on the Gentiles also" (Acts 10:44, 45).

They baptized people who, moments ago, were considered unclean. They baptized them in the name of Jesus without circumcision. A barrier to church membership was set aside at the leading of the Holy Spirit.

What if Peter had instead said, "I love the Gentiles, but I disapprove of their lifestyle. They have to be circumcised and keep the law." Would that have been genuinely loving? Would that have opened the door for Gentiles interested in learning about Jesus? Or would he have prevented Gentile inclusion?

THE CHURCH DECIDES

A few chapters after Peter's encounter with God and Cornelius, the church at large met in Jerusalem to decide the question of Gentile inclusion. They began with a direct report from Peter. Then they listened in silence as Barnabas and Paul shared similar stories from Antioch (Acts 15:6-14).

This is so simple that it's easy to miss. They practice silence and listening. I'm amazed by what they didn't do. They didn't jump immediately to their accepted theology. They didn't object with theological reasoning from Genesis, Exodus, Leviticus, and the rest of the Bible. They didn't assume that what has always been clear to the people of God in the past will still be present truth for the church.

I suspect their humility came from their recent humiliation. Imagine what it would have been like for Jesus' disciples. They followed Jesus for years in utter certainty that they understood His mission. Jesus was the Messiah. He had come to restore Israel and set it free from Roman rule. This is what all the law and the prophets pointed to. They gave up everything for this dream.

Then, in a night of shocking horror, their Messiah was killed. After a brief period of total disillusionment and fear, Jesus rose from the dead. God's plan had been entirely different from what they imagined. They expected God to elevate those who were holy and pure above those who were unclean and cruel. Instead, God sacrificed Himself for everyone.

So why would they be surprised to find that they were wrong again? Why would they be surprised to find that Jewish identity was unnecessary for follow-ers of Jesus? It's just like Jesus to pass right over ideas about which people are acceptable and which are not. It's just like Jesus to forgo pride of religious and ethnic superiority and make Gentiles equal to Jews.

These Jewish followers of Jesus inspire me. Realizing that God was ignoring their requirements, instead of digging in their heels, pointing to the Scriptures as they had always understood them, and creating roadblocks for the gospel, they allowed themselves to see the message the Holy Spirit was giving them. When fellow Christians questioned Peter about why he would baptize uncircumcised Gentiles, he told his story about Cornelius. Ellen White described it:

> On hearing this account, the brethren were silent. Convinced that Peter's course was in direct fulfillment of the plan of God and that their prejudices and exclusiveness were utterly contrary to the spirit of the gospel, they glorified God, saying, "Then hath God also to the Gentiles granted repentance unto life."
>
> Thus, without controversy, prejudice was broken down, the exclusiveness accepted by the custom of ages was abandoned, and the way was opened for the gospel to be pro-claimed to the Gentiles (*The Acts of the Apostles*, p. 142).

God began with a vision instead of an explanation of Scripture. Jesus often taught this way. He used parables, allowing the truth to sink in through story rather than clearly explaining the text. He was thin on exegetical and hermeneutical discourses but heavy on stories. First, ears must be open to hear (Matt. 13:10-17). He even allowed His disciples to see Him crucified, buried, and raised from the dead before making it clear from Scripture why it must happen (Luke 24:13-53).

Theological and scriptural fidelity are crucial. But theological reasoning is insufficient. Our problem is not merely theological. We have a soul problem. Our need for God is spiritual.

That's why the unfolding of truth and openness to Scripture requires more than a Bible study or academic understanding. Our hearts must be made ready. The Spirit must work in us. This is part of what it means to prioritize love.

As the story of Peter, Cornelius, and the early church unfolds, it takes surprisingly long for a theological explanation supporting the inclusion of those who are uncircumcised. God knew what God was doing. The church needed to see Gentile believers not as unclean sinners but as family. Until then, they could never grasp the message of Scripture.

Peter found that they had placed a burden on the Gentiles by their demands and that the burden was so great it amounted to exclusion. He said:

> So God, who knows the heart, acknowledged [the Gentiles] by giving them the Holy Spirit just as He did to us, and made no distinction between us and them, purifying their hearts by faith. Now therefore, why do you test God by putting a yoke on the neck of the disciples which neither our fathers nor we were able to bear? But we believe that we will be saved through the grace of the Lord Jesus Christ we shall be saved in the same manner as they (Acts 15:8-11).

In this, Peter was probably alluding to his Rabbi, Jesus, who said:

> For my yoke is easy and my burden is light (Matt. 11:30).

> For they bind heavy burdens, hard to bear, and lay them on men's shoulders, but they themselves will not move them with one of their fingers (Matt. 23:4).

> Woe to you also, lawyers! For you load men with burdens hard to bear, and you yourselves do not touch the burdens with one of your fingers (Luke 11:46).

This was Peter's theological grounding for including Gentiles. Circumcision was a burden to lift. God makes no distinction. All people are equal.

BURDEN OR CROSS?

If only it were simple to apply this principle about lifting burdens. If only we could easily recognize requirements to remove and make the yoke easy. But what does it mean to have an easy yoke when following Jesus is not about having an easy life? Jesus said to His followers:

> If anyone desires to come after Me, let him deny himself, and take up his cross, and follow Me. For whoever desires to save his life will lose it, but whoever loses his life for My sake will find it (Matt. 16:24, 25).

How do we distinguish a burden to be lifted from a cross to be carried? Jesus describes disciples as people who are willing to lose their lives for God's sake. One would think that the willingness to give one's life for the cause would mean that no sacrifice is off the table, yet that's not the case.

Jesus often spoke of burdens that must be removed and described His yoke as "easy" and His burden "light." Circumcision is a yoke that the New Testament church didn't want to place on Gentiles. So even though we know faithfulness could demand our lives, paradoxically, there are still burdens that should not be born. How do we know the difference?

Perhaps some of it has to do with what the Bible says elsewhere. If it's biblical, it's a cross. If we made it up ourselves, it's a burden. This is an essential part of the discussion, and much of this book is about this question. It's also not the entire discussion. The church in Acts 15 didn't go about it that way.

Peter didn't clarify theology. What he said was that "neither our fathers nor we have been able to bear [it]" (Acts 15:10). Jesus emphasized that those placing the burden were "not willing to move it with one of their fingers" (Matt. 23:4) and "you yourself do not touch the burdens" (Luke 11:46). The burden itself was the reason. The yoke was manifestly too heavy to carry. Despite the fact that some Gentiles were circumcised, circumcision was seen as a requirement too heavy to place on the necks of all Gentiles.

In other words, it matters whether theology is bearable. Does it work in the practical, day-to-day lives of Christians? The results of theology matter. That isn't an antibiblical view. It is the biblical view. Compassion is biblical. Jesus put it this way:

> You will know them by their fruits. Do men gather grapes from thornbushes or figs from thistles? Even so, every good tree bears good fruit, but a bad tree bears bad fruit. A good tree cannot bear bad fruit, nor can a bad tree bear good fruit (Matt. 7:16-18).

At some point, we must look directly at the results of our theology and ask whether it's life-giving. We must not make excuses or turn away from the suffering of others. We must not pick and choose the stories that fit our theology, amplifying narratives that make us feel good about our theology and muting the multitude of those whose experiences present a challenge.

We know they are burdens if they prop up the status quo, bring stability to the organization, and reduce change for religious leaders, but don't bring life. This was the same dynamic of the burdens religious leaders imposed in Jesus' day. They are weights that are born for no compassionate purpose. They aren't centered on the gospel itself. They don't inform us of who Jesus is or what He did for us.

When someone places a burden on you, you can tell because they describe God as an eternal miser. Their vision of God is a withholding parent who wants your obedience, not your joy. God doesn't owe us anything, they insist. We are called to sacrifice. Contrasted to burdens, taking up our cross is entirely about sacrificing for those we love. Jesus said, "Greater love has no one than this, than to lay down one's life for his friends" (John 15:13). This is the Cross. It is sacrifice motivated by love for others.

In contrast to sacrificing for those we love, burdens are about requiring sacrifice as a cost of admission. The cross bridges divides, burdens create them. The cross is the quintessential symbol of the gospel. It represents reconciliation. Burdens represent religious requirements that divide us. They make life harder for some so that others can feel reassured that all is well, holy, and pure. That was the nature of the requirements the religious leaders of Jesus' day demanded, and the same is true today.

Requirements do nothing to bring about redemption, compassion, and peace to the world. There was nothing esoteric about Jesus' willingness to die for us. His sacrifice directly impacted the lives of all who came after Him and all who came before. When we willingly take up our cross and follow Jesus, our religion becomes redemptive, not restrictive.

We're talking about competing ideas. On the one hand, we have religion focused on rules. Rules create meaning in this system, so they multiply. Burdens benefit legalistic religion. In these systems, no rules mean no purpose. Sacrifice is inspiring for its own sake, not for what it accomplishes. Sacrifice and pain become our way of feeling loved by God. If we suffer, we know that we are good and that God approves of us. If we struggle to sacrifice, we feel wretched and sinful and pray to God for forgiveness.

There is some truth to this. If we live our lives for our own pleasure and benefit, we lose our connection to God. When we sacrifice nothing, our spiritual lives atrophy. All those things are true. But if we participate in the suffering of Christ, the suffering itself must not be the point. We don't seek out suffering and sacrifice as a way to connect to God.

Sacrifice must not be our inspiration. Love must be our inspiration. We sacrifice *for* others. There is a purpose for the sacrifice. The sacrifice itself is not the purpose. We are willing to take our stripes and bear our shame, just as our Rabbi did because we are compelled by love to do something good in the world.

BURDENS PACKAGED AS CROSSES

Even as I write this, I know there is another side. For several years I denied my romantic attraction to women. I was committed to following the church's teachings, which I believed to be biblical and the will of God. Even if that meant I would never marry, I was content. It was hard, but I was content. There was meaning and purpose in my decision, as well as acceptance within my Adventist community. Because I believed I aligned with truth and the will of God, the sacrifice was bearable.

Many people are inspired by the stories of gay people who choose celibacy, who take and bear that burden with a sense of purpose. Voluntary suffering can be inspirational. It reminds us of the value of our faith. In fact, at its best, that's exactly what it looks and feels like when the sacrifice of a few reinforces the status quo. It's inspirational.

Suppose a few people find this religion so valuable that they would even give up the opportunity to be a husband and father, a wife and mother. How valuable must that religion be? It reinforces the value to the collective. It also lets them know their theology is just fine and their beliefs are worthy. No problems here. And if people are willing to give so much, it's even better for those who get to be part of the religion and still be a wife, mother, husband, or father. It's inspirational! The vast majority of the church that is straight and cisgender gets all the inspiration and none of the sacrifice.

The problem is that the Bible says we are supposed to look out for the most vulnerable. The powerful are called to sacrifice for the vulnerable, not the vulnerable for the powerful. When gay, bisexual, and transgender people are called to make a huge sacrifice to benefit most of the church, it's a heavy burden on a small group of people. It doesn't redeem those who look at the sacrifice of others. It leads them to self-satisfaction.

Even though for me it was a bearable burden, it isn't for most people. Jesus said that not everyone could be celibate (Matt. 19:10, 11). The apostle Paul agreed (1 Cor. 7:9). Church founders who wrote about the value of celibacy also didn't believe it was possible for everyone (i.e., Ambrose of Milan, John Chrysostom, Augustine, Thomas Aquinas, Martin Luther, John Calvin). The modern church also denies that celibacy is possible for everyone (i.e., Westminster Larger Catechism, Focus on the Family, *Christianity Today*, Albert Mohler).[b]

Heterosexuals have never believed celibacy was possible for all heterosexuals. Requiring celibacy of all heterosexuals would be an excellent way to close church doors forever. They would never stand for it. Neither do most gay, bisexual, and transgender people, and that's why so many leave. Celibacy is no easier and no more possible for LGBTQ people than heterosexual people. Requiring it creates two different experiences of Christianity. In one, your community supports your life and family. In the other, your community forbids them.

This makes life more difficult for those whose lives are already difficult while simultaneously inspiring and requiring nothing of those whose lives are already the easiest. If our religion makes the most sense for people whose lives are already the easiest, it's broken. The religion of Jesus is good news, especially for those who struggle. He brought hope to those who hurt and challenged those who were comfortable. He told us the first would be last (Matt. 20:16). Today's church does the opposite. If the greatest sacrifice falls on the struggling shoulders of a few, it's not the religion of Jesus or the prophets.

Male pastors who are married with children have often told me that they understand the struggle of LGBTQ people because they have sexual temptations as well. They explain that their struggles with pornography or lust help them understand my struggle as a bisexual person. But if a man who is granted the privilege of being a husband and a father still struggles with pornography, that tells me he would not be able to bear the burden of life-long celibacy. He would not be one of the few to accept and live with that burden for a lifetime. As a result, he would not be a pastor or a member of his own church.

I was able. Yet even though the burden was bearable, I ultimately changed my views. I've come to believe that every biblical principle of love, inclusion,

---

b. These examples come from a blog by Karen Keen, "Is Life-Long Celibacy Possible for Everyone? Quotes from Christian Tradition." Keen's research on celibacy made her realize that Christians have never believed everyone is capable of celibacy, and never until the modern era has celibacy been used as a solution for sexual or romantic desire. Keen was a celibate gay Christian until, through study and prayer, she became affirming. Read more of her insights and more about celibacy in her book, *Scripture and the Possibility of Same-Sex Relationships*. Her blog is available at karenkeen.com.

and justice cries out for affirmation, though no specific text explicitly does so. Those who emphasized particular texts about same-sex sex over the Golden Rule easily and confidently conclude that accepted theology is biblical. But I believe I read the Bible as the early church did, as the prophets did, as Jesus did, and (as we will see in a later chapter) as abolitionists did.

We can find those who overcame poverty and say that since they overcame poverty, everyone can. We don't have to care for the poor. We can find someone who says that they prayed away cancer, so no one needs chemo. We can find someone who says they trusted God to overcome their depression, so no one needs to take medications or go to therapy for their mental health.

We can accept that their experience is genuine, but we shouldn't believe them when they say everyone must do as they did. We should try to understand why we have so much wealth and so much poverty. We should focus on preventing and treating cancer, not forbid chemo for those who want it. We should encourage people who need medications and therapy.

We can find those who say they "prayed the gay away." We can find those who say they used to be transgender. We can find someone who says the church's accepted theology about sexuality and gender works well for them, even though they are same-sex attracted or experience gender dysphoria. I used to be one of those "success stories." So did most of my friends. But the fact that some can bear it doesn't mean we should pretend that the problem is solved.

REDEMPTION

What does it mean to take up our cross? Jesus went to the cross *for* us. As the song goes, "When he was on the cross, I was on his mind." Jesus' suffering was redemptive. There was a clear purpose. People needed Him. Jesus didn't take up His cross because there was a rule to do so. Jesus died for those He loved. He was crucified because, in advocating for those He loved, Jesus threatened the religious establishment of the day. He died for us to help us and save us. He died to redeem us from our sin.

That's the difference. Crosses redeem, burdens merely constrain. When we are told to take up our cross, it doesn't mean that we look for ways to suffer. We should expect suffering as a natural result of being like Jesus. We will experience suffering because we follow Jesus' example of building the kingdom of God on earth. We love all people and advocate for those society has thrown aside. In the course of loving the people Jesus loved, we should experience the same kind of rejection Jesus experienced.

Circumcision had no redemptive purpose. It was only about following a law that was no longer meaningfully connected to love and life. The real-world impact of circumcision was to keep most Gentiles out of the church. It served the status quo. It kept people comfortable. It allowed Christians to think of Gentiles as gross and impure.

Removing circumcision required Jewish Christians to confront their prejudice. It took away their theological justifications for feeling superior. No longer could they think of themselves as the fulfillment of God's plan and Gentiles as deviations to be corrected.

Likewise, opposing same-gender marriage is suffering with no purpose. It's about a rule that some believe was God-given. But there is no real-world impact other than preserving the status quo and keeping most gay, bisexual, and transgender people out of churches.

The church's requirements bear little resemblance to Jesus' act of taking up His cross. It doesn't fulfill the aspirational goals Jesus set out. Staying celibate without a calling to celibacy or traditionally presenting one's gender doesn't help anyone; it's not a sacrifice *for* anyone. There is no laying down of life for our friends. At best, it's a sacrifice for an idea; at worse, it's a sacrifice that lets the church off the hook. No longer do they have to welcome people who make some church members uncomfortable. It's a sacrifice that has no redemptive purpose.

SACRIFICE FOR...

But isn't sacrifice ultimately for God? Can't God ask anything of us? Yes, of course. But God's law isn't arbitrary. A willingness to follow God shouldn't be an excuse to ignore the consequences of our beliefs. God's law is ultimately an expression of the character and love of God for our own good. Ellen White wrote:

> God's laws are not merely an expression of His selfish or arbitrary authority. He is love, and in all He did, He had the well-being of humanity in view (*Pacific Health Journal*, Feb. 1, 1902).

For a long time, my thinking had a big question mark in the middle of it. On one side, I had the law of God, which is an expression of God's love for us. On the other side, I had the lived experience of LGBTQ people. I didn't know how to reconcile the two.

The more I learned about the experiences of gay, bisexual, and transgender people in the church, the less our theology looked anything like an expression of God's character. The more I dropped my old prejudice, the less sense my theology made. This disturbed me. Good theology doesn't need to be propped up by prejudice.

Here's how prejudice can support accepted theology: I believed sexual and gender minorities were broken. I thought this was usually a result of sexual abuse.[c] I thought there was something uncomfortable or distasteful about same-gender sex. I thought same-sex couples were inherently unstable and that relationships didn't last.[d] I believed too many stereotypes and bought into vague and shadowy concepts about the gay lifestyle.

I thought of heterosexuals as making their own sexual decisions. But when I thought of gay and bisexual people, I stripped them of their individuality and personal agency. It didn't occur to me that some gay and bisexual people, particularly Adventists, were willing to abide by the same sexual standards as everyone else. Nor did I realize that if we raise gay kids to think this was a possibility for them, there would be even more. I know it's wild that I had these thoughts even though I am bisexual, and I knew they didn't fit me. Such is the nature of compartmentalization, self-deception, and shame.

The process of living chipped away at my prejudice. Some chipping away came through others, and some through self-knowledge. My desires for women were not craven compulsions for sexual encounters. I wanted a life partner. I realized I could find that in someone regardless of gender. I didn't want to know it, but I did.

Why is this kind of love wicked? Why is it evil when two women choose to be life partners, but good if a woman and a man make the same choice? What does this prohibition teach us about the love of God? How does this help us build the church, spread the gospel, or serve the kingdom of God? It didn't make sense.

I took my big question and simply accepted it in faith. Maybe I would never know the answer. Perhaps I would never understand. Maybe it's like the fruit from the Tree of the Knowledge of Good and Evil, a matter of faith, a test; it's not supposed to make sense.

But now I see that the problem is much larger than I thought it was. This prohibition isn't a neutral requirement of all God's followers. Unlike the command

---

c. Now I realize that that's prejudice against both gay people *and* sexual abuse survivors.

d. I confess that this belief lasted a long time. I was even a bit surprised after coming out when I got to know so many same-sex couples who had been together for decades.

not to eat from the tree, which applied to everyone, this asks a lot of a few while protecting most from discomfort and change. This is the same as the requirement of circumcision. This requirement is not harmless. It keeps LGBTQ people out of the church, just like circumcision kept Gentiles out. It also restricts the ability of the church to spread the gospel, just as the requirement of circumcision did.

The early church could have labeled circumcision a test of faith. If Gentiles didn't want to be circumcised, they weren't dedicated enough to follow Jesus. They weren't willing to take up their cross. It would have been easy for those early Christians. But they thought differently. Look again at Peter's reasoning:

> Men and brethren, you know that a good while ago God chose among us, that by my mouth the Gentiles should hear the word of the gospel and believe. So God, who knows the heart, acknowledged them by giving them the Holy Spirit, just as He did to us, and made no distinction between us and them, purifying their hearts by faith. Now therefore, why do you test God by putting a yoke on the neck of the disciples which neither our fathers nor we were able to bear? But we believe that through the grace of the Lord Jesus Christ we shall be saved in the same manner as they (Acts 15:7-11).

The early church believed equality between Jews and Gentiles was only accomplished by allowing Gentiles to remain Gentiles and Jews to remain Jews. They could have taken the few Gentiles who were circumcised and held them up as examples of faithfulness. They didn't choose to do that. They accepted Gentiles as Gentiles, uncircumcised and all.

Jesus may not have commented on circumcision, but He laid the groundwork for the church's decision. He was well aware of the religiosity of His day that taught Christians to withhold good things from one another.

> Or what man is there among you who, if his son asks for bread, will give him a stone? Or if he asks for a fish, will give him a serpent? If you then, being evil, know how to give good gifts to your children, how much more will your Father who is in heaven give good things to those who ask Him! Therefore, whatever you want men to do to you, do also to them, for this is the Law and the Prophets (Matt. 7:9-12)

Yet in the next breath, Jesus speaks of sacrifice:

> Enter by the narrow gate; for wide is the gate and broad is the way that leads to destruction, and there are many who go in by it. Because narrow is the gate and difficult is the way which leads to life, and there are few who find it (Matt. 7:13, 14).

This is the balancing act of Jesus' teachings. Restriction is not inherently good, and permission is not inherently good. God gives us good things. God's way is narrow and difficult. God's burden is light, His yoke is easy, and you will find rest for your soul. To follow Jesus, we must give up our lives. We are called to deny ourselves for the sake of others, following Jesus' example. Yet sometimes we're called to give and receive good things and priceless treasures. We need to tear down the barriers that keep people from the gospel for no good reason, those that create divisions and harm among us. We must be willing to sacrifice and suffer to do so. We must be willing to take up our cross.

The crux of the matter is whether the behavior in question is inherently consistent with the kingdom of God. I hope that most who read this have no sympathy for this comparison, but some believe that accepting same-gender marriage will lead to pedophilia. They say this because they associate same-gender marriage with desire fulfillment as if affirming us will mean affirming anyone with any desire. That's a fundamental misunderstanding of the issue. Pedophilia is selfish and harmful. Same-gender marriage is a loving commitment to making another person's life better, and like all successful marriages, it requires self-sacrifice. Same-gender marriage is compatible with the joy that Jesus promises and the sacrifice that Jesus calls us to.

CHANGE IN BELIEFS

To accept Gentiles, the church had to change its beliefs; there was no other way. This is the nature of belief itself. When we believe something, we act on it. Beliefs are not mere thoughts or ideas; they inform our decisions and how we treat others.

I recall the first time I learned this lesson. During a week of prayer, the pastor brought someone up on stage. He blindfolded him and told him there was a chair behind them.

"Do you believe it?" He asked.

"Yes," said the student.

"Well then, sit down."

We learned quickly, from the squirming and squatting, that the student did not believe that the chair was there, at least not with enough confidence to fall back into it.

Beliefs are important because they inform our actions. Beliefs aren't neutral; they influence our decisions. It might be tempting to imagine a scenario in which someone's beliefs about someone else's sexuality wouldn't impact their decisions or behavior. What about the grandmother who disagrees with her granddaughter's sexuality but never says anything about it and just loves her?

These scenarios might be comforting, but they aren't true-to-life. Beliefs impact the way we treat people. It could be glaring omissions in conversations. It could be outright statements of judgment. It could be a subtle separation that is felt by all. It could be exclusion from a church. It could be a subtle attitude of treating a gay church member as a project.

Whatever the scenario, sincerely held beliefs don't remain mere beliefs. They aren't disembodied thoughts that never find their way out of the mind. Beliefs are inseparable from actions. Sometimes changing our beliefs changes the actions we choose. Sometimes it works the other way around, and we subconsciously adapt our thinking to justify our words or actions. Either way, they're connected.

And if beliefs are relevant to the words we say and the actions we take, that means beliefs are relevant to how we treat others. Beliefs are relevant to our relationships. This inevitably means that beliefs are relevant to love. They impact our ability to love others well. They impact the ability of our communities to embody the loving influence of God in our world.

The beliefs of some early Christians about circumcision impacted their ability to love. The requirement made them exclude Gentiles from baptism and church participation. It served as a cover for prejudice and a justification for their sense that they belonged to God in a way that Gentiles did not.

Removing the requirement of circumcision made them able to love Gentiles better. It helped them make the shift from thinking of Gentiles as unclean people with sinful lifestyles to full participants in the kingdom of God.

Since our beliefs impact our ability to love, how could we ever separate the two? How could we ever say that we can always love someone no matter what we believe? We can't. It's not true. Some beliefs do impact our ability to love.

Imagine an Adventist church that believes fully in affirmation. Imagine that same-sex marriages are supported equally. Imagine transgender people fully supported in their gender. Imagine if Adventist churches regularly had same-sex couples and trans people in their congregations. Imagine them treated as fully equal and integral to the life of the church. Imagine if some were leaders and pastors.

This would be the result of fully affirming theology, and it's not hard to realize that gay, bisexual, and transgender people would have a dramatically different experience in such a church. LGBTQ children growing up there would not struggle with belonging, anxiety, and fear. A change in belief would fuel all these changes. Our belief is more than an opinion. Beliefs carry real consequences.

DESPITE IT

It's also true that people are multifaceted, and relationships are complex. There are many points of connection and disconnection in any relationship. It's impossible to say that we can't love someone at all unless our beliefs are correct. But what is true is that sometimes our beliefs make love more difficult. Sometimes we must learn to love despite our beliefs. That's not as it should be. Our Christianity should make us love better.

At a minimum, here's what it looks like to hold beliefs that are harmful to someone: We disagree with their most life-giving decisions. We hope they will make choices that harm them. We support organizations that oppose their best interests. We want them to change fundamentally good or neutral aspects of themselves before they can have full acceptance and equality.

Maybe it's different for others, but for me, I can never stop wanting full affirmation from my closest relationships. How can you understand me if you don't see what is good in me? How can you understand me if you can't understand the pain the status quo has caused for me and those I love?

To love someone, we must be interested in their well-being. There's no way around it. No law of God disregards our well-being or seeks our harm. To love gay, bisexual, and transgender people, we must be concerned about the impact that our lives and beliefs have on their lives. That impact is the question we will turn to in the next chapter.

CHAPTER 9

God's Guidance is Good and Trustworthy

> *"It doesn't mean I'm hard-hearted or mean-spirited, but I cannot offer false charity in the form of encouraging people to seek that which I know from experience and the teaching of the church to be harmful and destructive."*[93]

> *"God's law is the law of love, and those who put their faith in the Lord will find the healing, peace, and joy God promised. True happiness is only found in faithfulness. Compared to that, the gay lifestyle has nothing to offer."*

One of the pillars of my beliefs is that affirming same-gender marriage and transgender identity is life-giving for gay, bisexual, and transgender people. Affirmation saves lives and changes people for the better. It's good for LGBTQ people, our families, and our churches.

If affirmation harmed people, I would oppose it. But how do we really know? And how do we know that accepted theology isn't best for LGBTQ people and for society at large? And really, how clear is any of this, or is it just a matter of opinion?

I know that those opposing same-gender marriage and transgender identity aren't doing so to harm people. That's not their motivation or intention. They are not often hateful, though admittedly some are. Most of those who support the church's accepted theology have mixed feelings and know they don't have it all figured out. Most people feel torn; full affirmation doesn't feel right to them.

I distinctly remember wrestling with this myself. Years ago, a friend asked for my thoughts on the subject. We were both students at Union College in Lincoln, Nebraska. We were on a road trip and stopped for gas. She asked me out of the blue what I thought about the church's teachings about gay people. "I don't understand why it's wrong for gay people to get married."

It was something I was wrestling with, and clearly so was she. These conversations were just beginning when I was in college. They are now common as young people try to fit all the pieces together. It's important not only that our theology is *biblical* but that it is *good*. We can talk about exegesis all day long, but our theology must express the loving character of God. It must also be ethical. That's what my friend and I wrestled with that day.

I told my friend, "I think of it as a matter of being holistic. It's about healing people so that they can live as God created them to live. If we short-circuit that process, we take away an opportunity for holistic and healed humanity. Maybe God wants to heal gay and lesbian people?"

It seemed to me that psychologists and society at large were shying away from certain facts. The truth was that LGBTQ people were more likely sexually abused as children. There were higher rates of mental health problems and risky behaviors in LGBTQ populations.

I thought that maybe healing the trauma should be the goal. Who's to say that by accepting their sexuality we aren't selling them short? Who's to say that we aren't taking the easy path instead of the hard path that leads to wholeness? Maybe it's best not to approve of this behavior; maybe healing is needed, not affirmation.

This chapter is about these human factors, taking what we've learned from the Bible and looking at how it's working in people's lives. My position has shifted a lot since those days. I know a lot more than I did then, and that knowledge has shifted my thinking. But doing so was time consuming and emotionally demanding. Remembering my own story reminds me of just how hard it was.

We all want to be the heroes of our own stories. We know we're flawed, but it's another thing entirely to imagine we've taken the wrong side and become a villain instead of a hero. When we try to be helpful and compassionate, we don't want to find out that we've been the opposite. It's hard to think about what I said and what I believed, because I've come to see that I was the villain, though I sincerely thought I was doing the right thing.

The emotional and intellectual reckoning necessary to see myself as the villain was slow and arduous. It meant acknowledging that I was part of the problem, recognizing that my Adventist community and those I loved and respected were perpetuating the problem. I had to learn and grow on the subject, shifting everything in my life to be on the right side of this question.

Having walked that path, I know what a big ask this is. The claims I make in this chapter may be the most difficult to consider. Anyone would be expected to be defensive and look for any possible alternate explanations for the challenges I'm going to describe.

Your intentions are good. Those who believe accepted theology rarely want to harm gay, bisexual, or transgender people—quite the opposite. I know this because I didn't hold my viewpoint through hate or ill-intent. I was even willing to apply it to myself, convinced that it was best for me. I could point to myself and others as examples of people who didn't seem to be harmed. I knew the claims about the harm churches were causing, but I didn't think it was our fault.

Eventually, I was no longer okay assuming I was right. I had to be humble enough to ask the question in bald honesty. Could I be harming people unknowingly? There is no easy way to do this. No matter what, it's going to take courage and vulnerability. I almost didn't write this chapter because I knew how difficult it would be.

Many people are furious with churches that don't affirm same-gender marriage or transgender identity. I don't question their right to that anger. Many have survived unspeakable heartache. I've been consumed by that anger myself through my process of grief and loss. Yet, I strive to embody humility and forgiveness, especially when convinced that I'm on the right side of a question. I strive to show the same grace I want to receive from others, the grace I've needed and been given many times.

So, I hope you know that though I believe this theology is innately harmful, I'm not interested in blaming anyone. I've been there. I understand. I even appreciate those who may disagree with me even after hearing me out. My goal is to offer something to consider, not to blame or shame. I hope we can look at the problems with as much curiosity and openness as possible, seeking understanding and a better future for LGBTQ Adventists.

SELF-CONCEPT

When we think about the overall experience of gay, bisexual, and transgender people in the church, the concept of cognitive dissonance is helpful. Cognitive dissonance is when two competing ideas exist together in our minds. It's common in LGBTQ Christians from conservative backgrounds. In moving towards a positive identity as a person of faith and also a positive understanding of one's sexuality or gender identity, most (but not all) people develop cognitive dissonance. How can I be both a faithful Adventist and a gay, bisexual, or transgender person?

As people of faith, it's easy for Adventists to see the benefit of feeling positive about being a believer. It might also be easy to imagine that it's important to positively view one's gender. It might be harder to see why it's important to have a positive view of oneself as a sexual being.

Christianity has not always been good at helping us think of our sexuality positively, but the problem is not all there. The word "sexuality" implies that it's all about sex. When we speak of sexual orientation and sexuality, it's somewhat natural for us to think about the act of sex and the desire for sex because it's right there in the word. That is a challenge with the language.

When I first realized I was not entirely heterosexual, it wasn't because I had sexual thoughts about women. This may sound strange, but a lot of heterosexual people experiment sexually with the same sex. They desire a sexual experience with the same sex, seek out that experience, and remain heterosexual. It's not really about sex. The basic difference is this: heterosexuals won't fall in love with someone of the same gender. They won't want to build a family with someone of the same gender.[94]

When we talk about the struggle to positively accept one's sexuality, we're not talking about sex. We're talking about having a positive identity around one's ability to have and form a family unit based on intimacy with a partner. It's about our relational, romantic, and familial orientation more than any specific sex act. Even those uninterested in a committed relationship generally acknowledge that their sexual orientation is about connection and intimacy, even casual intimacy. Sometimes, because of the sexualization of gay and bisexual people, it can be difficult even to acknowledge that one's sexual orientation is not raw lust. That acknowledgment is part of the process.[95]

Christians accept that they are sinful, so discussing positive self-concept can sometimes seem out of step with our theology. But the Bible often speaks of God's followers as "saints" (Rom. 1:7; 8:27; 1 Cor. 1:2, 12; 14:33; 2 Cor. 1:1; Col. 1:1, etc.). While we recognize our sinfulness, we also recognize that our best impulses are either good or redeemable through God. Heterosexual people don't see their desire to have a family as an impulse to evil, even as they recognize it's imperfect and only God can help them pursue love in a holy way.

Speaking from personal experience, I can say that it is incongruent to regard your desire for a family as an evil desire. It's one thing to recognize that we have many desires for sin, but to believe that our impulse for love is an impulse for sin is another matter entirely.

Yes, we can love the wrong person. Yes, we can love someone who's unavailable and deny our desire for that individual. These are circumstances in which forming a family with an individual is impossible without collateral damage. That's very different from having a desire to love someone for their good, knowing that you could make their life better by caring for them, and calling that impulse evil. As a bisexual person, it took a psychological toll for me to believe that half of my sexuality was holy and the other half was profane. It numbed me to all love. I see that in retrospect.

Of course, we make all kinds of sacrifices for God and our faith. We should be willing to lay down our lives. Is this psychological pain simply the cost of discipleship? Regardless of how we answer that question, we shouldn't ignore or explain away the reality of that cost by pretending that it's psychologically beneficial for gay or bisexual people to believe that their sexuality is sinful. There is typically a real sense of dissonance, a painful rejection of one's sexuality, and a lonely resignation for those who embrace accepted theology. The psychological research reflects this, as we shall see.

DISSONANCE

There are four main ways of responding to this dissonance: rejection of sexuality, rejection of religion, compartmentalization, and integration. The first three are strategies for mitigating the discomfort, anxiety, and depression associated with cognitive dissonance.[96]

This research underscores the experiences of many of us who are gay, bisexual, and transgender. Like many people, my first reaction on realizing I experienced romantic feelings for women was to reject that part of myself, believing it was a sin. After I came out, I went through a period of intense anger at all the pain caused by Christianity. For a while, I wanted to renounce my faith altogether.

I remember talking to a friend who said, "Even after everything, it's like you have an Adventist inside of you, and you need to…"

At this moment, my mind raced ahead of her words and finished her sentence with *you need to kill it*. I felt I wouldn't have peace until I killed all that was Adventist inside me. But that's not how she finished the sentence.

She said, "make peace with it."

She was right. Eventually, I realized this and did make peace. I held onto my faith and God. But it makes sense to me that making peace with our faith applies to all LGBTQ people from all faith communities. Even those who ultimately reject religion would do well to make peace with their religious past and what they carry with them. This is the process of integration.

Integration is that holistic place of *shalom* I once thought was accessible through changing or rejecting a gay or bisexual orientation. An integrated person is whole and at peace. Without integration and the peace it brings, cognitive dissonance understandably exacts a price on mental health. When one can resolve the dissonance, the resolution leads to resilience and mental health. Integration takes time; those who achieve it are often older. It's also more likely that they attend fully affirming churches.[97]

This helps explain why churches that teach accepted theology are difficult for LGBTQ people. Yet not everything about the church experience is bad. It's a mixed bag. Church may also bring many of the positive benefits it brings to all people. For example, church attendance may protect against suicide by providing a sense of community and moral grounding yet cause difficulties in other areas.[98]

This is probably what's behind the impulse of many LGBTQ people to compartmentalize their identities. Personally, I'm terrible at compartmentalization, but I've seen it in action and talked to friends who walk that line. It's a way of trying to ignore the conflict that defines one's existence. Rather than bringing all of yourself to church, you try to leave an important piece at home. Rather than bring all of yourself to your experience of sexuality, you try to forget about your religious convictions. It's easy to see how this could be a painful place to live and why it could make it hard to find either healthy sexuality or healthy spirituality. Yet, it can be impossible for those who see no way to reconcile the two to give up either sexuality or faith.

In a sense, for LGBTQ people in the pews, the church gives with one hand while taking with the other. This is markedly different than the experiences of heterosexual and cisgender people at church. For them, church is beneficial to health and happiness. Those who attend church experience less stress and depression and "greater satisfaction with life, happiness, and well-being."[99]

In one study, when young adults left churches that were not affirming, they experienced less internalized homophobia. Since internalized homophobia is associated with suicide risk, researchers predicted this would result in reduced suicide risk. However, the stress of leaving itself was associated with even greater risk. The loss of church community and the rejection often experienced by LGBTQ people when they come out is consequential. This study was in a population that was primarily white.[100] Church can be even more important for minorities. The cost of leaving one's church community may be higher for Black and Latin gay and bisexual people.[101] Also, none of this research includes transgender people, who likely have a more challenging experience.

CHURCH

With these difficulties in mind, it probably is no surprise that dramatically fewer LGBTQ people attend church than straight and cisgender people. Many have left church entirely because of painful experiences. Yet almost half of us still believe religion is an important part of life. Of this half, more than three-fourths consider themselves Christians. Of the total population of LGBTQ people, 31.3 percent attend church at least monthly.[102]

Despite the difficulties related to gender and sexuality, church communities can be life-giving in other ways. As the community that sustained me until recently, the Adventist Church was my extended family. My identity and strength came in large measure from being part of the church, even when I knew I wasn't heterosexual. I saw the problems, but it still made sense that Jesus said, "The gates of Hades shall not prevail against [my church]" (Matt. 16:18).

The realization that my time as an Adventist pastor was about to end caused a flood of grief. I entered a time of deep mourning for the friendships, the community, and the belonging I enjoyed. The Adventist Church can be wonderful. Despite myself, I still love it, miss participating, and believe in its potential.

I also believe in marriage. Even as a teenager, I remember my peers saying that marriage is "only a piece of paper," and thinking they were foolish. I agree with Dietrich Bonhoeffer, who said, "It is not your love that sustains your marriage, but . . . your marriage that sustains the love."

Because I believe in the church and I believe in marriage, I'm not surprised when I see struggling people excluded from both or either of these institutions. The mental health problems, drug problems, and risky sexual behavior that happen at higher rates in the LGBTQ community make sense. It also makes sense that these numbers are going down as society becomes more accepting. There is real value in the acceptance and support of a church family.

Because the church is important, being rejected by the church has a serious impact. Because marriage is important, those who can't be legally married or don't get full support from their communities are likely to struggle. Because gender matters, transgender people struggle when their gender is not affirmed. Because gay, bisexual, and transgender people cannot bring all of themselves to church in a positive way, the church may be giving with one hand but taking away with the other. None of this is surprising. It's an affirmation of the importance of gender, marriage, and church.

THE CHILDREN

The research mentioned so far applies mainly to adults. We need to switch gears and talk about the experiences of children and adolescents. Most of us feel the same way I do about the safety and thriving of children in the Adventist Church. Our children should be protected and loved. We want them to thrive and grow in life and faith. We tend to frame the question about LGBTQ inclusion in terms of adult couples or adult individuals who are not members but wish to participate. But it's more common and more important to understand how gay, bisexual, and transgender children in our Sabbath school classes and church schools are doing.

As we look at these questions, it's easy for the discussion to feel abstract. I think an analogy will help. Imagine trying to choose between two different academies for your children. You compare two schools. You look at curriculum, graduation rates, class size, and so on. It seems pretty equal. Then you find some new information.

School A has one big problem. It has consistently, since its founding, had a high number of suicides. Not a little bit higher, but 8.4 times the average suicide rate. Digging deeper, you discover that this school also has a problem with children running away and becoming homeless. As you wonder what happens behind those walls, you aren't surprised to discover that kids at this school are also six times more likely to be depressed.[103]

Then you look at School B. The kids seem to do well. They have typical teenage problems. They seem perfectly well adjusted.

Does this change your mind about which school is best for your children? Of course it does. You would never allow your precious children to walk the halls of a school that was breaking the hearts of its students. You immediately enroll your child in School B.

But what if School A had great testimonials? What if the school recruited a handful of students to travel the country talking about how it was an excellent school? What if these few kids seemed to genuinely benefit from the school? What if the people at School A said that the suicide rates weren't really about the school but that those kids had underlying problems? What if your pastor highly recommended School A? Would you be willing to send your children to School A, even though you know about the suicides and depression? Absolutely not. You love your children and would never put them in a place that steals the hope and lives of so many students.

Of course, these numbers are unrelated to specific schools. They're related to specific families. The families that produce these terrifying results for gay and bisexual children are families where minority sexual orientation is rejected. On the extreme end, these kids are bullied, harassed, called names, excluded from family activities, and/or told their families are ashamed of them. These behaviors may be extreme, but they are not uncommon. A friend of mine was told by his father, "I'd rather have a dead son than a gay son." Many people I know personally have experienced extreme rejection from their families.[104]

Mild forms of rejection also correlate with serious problems. Mild rejection is defined as rejection of children's choices to live and date openly as gay or bisexual. Kids who are told God disapproves, who are kept from dating people of the same gender, who are advised not to appear or dress "gay," who are brought to their pastor because of these concerns, who are told not to tell others about their orientation, who are kept from associating with other LGBTQ people, and who pick-up on signs that their parents are ashamed or disappointed, also face higher rates of depression and suicide.[105]

Both the highly rejecting and the mildly rejecting characteristics are found in School A. Though mild rejection is less harmful, it is still quite harmful. Whether the rejection of orientation is severe or mild, there are clear and well-documented negative impacts on teenagers.[106]

What's happening at School B? These kids have dramatically different experiences and different outcomes. The best adjusted kids have parents who actively support and affirm their children's orientation. They talk openly with them about their orientation, support and love them when they come out (even if they feel uncomfortable), help them connect with the affirming LGBTQ community in a healthy way, bring them to clergy who support and affirm them, welcome LGBTQ friends and dating interests, and believe that they can have a wonderful future as they embrace their orientation.[107]

OUR IMPACT

Rejection of LGBTQ orientation and gender identity is often motivated by religious beliefs.[108] The Adventist Church is no exception. We are generally not producing families that accept and protect gay, bisexual, and transgender children. The children are living the consequences.[109]

Research shows that if children go to a non-affirming pastor or other religious leaders for counseling or guidance, they are more likely to commit suicide than if they had never met with the pastor.[110] When someone brings their children to pastors for help, the impact of their words is greater than we imagine.

None of this is as it should be, nor is it intentional. No one wants these outcomes. Church is supposed to be an excellent place to raise a child. The Adventist school system and Adventist home help children develop strong foundations, making them resilient, joyful Christians.

For cisgender, heterosexual children, the Adventist Church is a beautiful place to grow up. Kids connected with the Adventist Church and strong Adventist families are usually far less likely to attempt suicide, suffer depression, or struggle with substance use disorders.[111]

The same cannot be said for kids who are gay, bisexual, and transgender. In terms of their mental health and behavioral outcomes, these kids would be better off with no religion at all than a religion that rejects their sexuality. That is a huge red flag that we can't continue to ignore.

If we apply Jesus' Golden Rule to empathize with their experience, this isn't surprising at all. Anyone might despair at being told as a child that their first innocent crushes are, in fact, temptations to sin. It would be crushing to know that you could meet the perfect person, fall madly in love, yet be expected to remain merely friends forever. Then, as you nurse your wounded heart, it dawns on you that this could happen again and again; no one you fall in love with will ever be acceptable. It would be confusing to experience the desire to love and be loved but believe the desire was evil. How can we embrace the God of love who also tells us that our impulses for a loving marriage are forever irredeemable?

High school is hard enough. Figuring out who we are, what to do with our lives, making friends, and moving into adulthood are difficult tasks. Adding the stress of being an LGBTQ Adventist makes things exponentially more difficult.

BEHIND THE STRUGGLE

LGBTQ kids have a different set of worries. Will they be expelled? Will they be bullied? Will they be rejected? Are they masculine enough or feminine enough? What will their parents do? Are they acting straight and cisgender enough? If they dress, talk, and walk the way they want to, will they be discovered? If they're discovered, will they be kicked out of school? Will they be sent to conversion therapy? Will their family be disgusted by them?

Not surprisingly, these kids struggle. How do you believe that God loves you, that God is for you when one of your biggest fears is being rejected by your church, family, and Christian friends?[112]

The situation is worse for those who are told their very way of existing in the world is unacceptable. Being told the way they move, the clothes they wear, how they describe themselves, and their very identity is sinful in the eyes of God makes living itself a heavy burden.

That's probably why two-thirds of transgender youth have self-harmed in the last year. Two-thirds. Don't miss that number. Don't skip over that number; it's intolerably large. The pain and despair behind this simple statistic should overwhelm us. We must allow it to overwhelm us. Somewhere between 22 and 42 percent of transgender people attempt suicide in their lifetime. We should be in emergency response mode the moment we hear these numbers.[113]

There is something we can do. What helps bring those numbers down? Not surprisingly, transgender kids thrive on support and affirmation from their communities, confidence in their transgender identity, and access to medical transitioning (if they want it). If we believe them and support them, we can change their lives—even save them.[114]

Because of research at Andrews University, we have insight into what happens specifically in our Adventist churches and families when Adventists come out to their families. The research reveals challenging relationships between Adventist parents and their LGBTQ children.

Four out of five LGBTQ Adventists were "scared to come out because I knew my family would think I was sinful and/or disgusting." Nearly half agreed that "I knew that I would be rejected if I shared my sexual orientation and/or gender identity with my family." Another quarter of participants weren't sure whether they would be rejected or not.[115]

When they did come out, their parents often weren't attentive to their vulnerability and fear of rejection, with only one parent in four assuring their children that they "loved [them] no matter what." In contrast, 42.1 percent were "ridiculed" by their family. Their families used demeaning language to describe them in 37.5 percent of cases.[116]

Religion played a role. When they did come out, 75.3 percent of participants reported that "my religious beliefs triggered feelings of guilt and shame." In 82.4 percent of cases, the religious beliefs of parents meant they had "difficulty accepting [their child's] orientation and/or gender identity."[117]

Even though only a third of participants were under 20, 29 percent had financial support cut off when they came out. Sixty-five percent of parents expressed disappointment because they believed their children coming out reflected poorly on them as parents. More than one-fourth of LGBTQ children were blamed for the mistreatment they received.[118]

The researchers at Andrews University concluded that "the majority of LGBT+ individuals in this study have not experienced consistent love from their families or the [Seventh-day Adventist Church]. They have been considered by others, and often by themselves, as being different and least in the kingdom, if members of it at all."[119]

WHAT TO DO?

Some of these reactions by parents and experiences of LGBTQ children are to be expected, even if they are harmful. A church that teaches that same-gender marriage and transgender identity are wrong will not be an easy place for gay, bisexual, and transgender people. There are bound to be difficulties, even in ideal situations. But we can make the situation better for LGBTQ people growing up in Adventist churches and families.

This research on Adventists was published not long before I came out. I decided to preach a sermon at my church about how Adventists are doing with this issue and how we could do better. I didn't talk theology and didn't question the church's doctrine. I simply spoke of our shortcomings and failures to respond in love and how we can do better.

All Adventist pastors and leaders should immediately start telling their congregations that parents must, if their child comes out, tell them that they love them unconditionally, and they must follow through by continuing to act from love. Regardless of theological convictions, this must happen. Don't make financial support dependent on the child hiding who they are. Don't try to coerce them into deciding one thing or another. Don't make this about you and your feelings or embarrassment. Be the adult and put your children first.

I know this must be hard for parents. Their child has been thinking about this moment for years, and parents are often caught off guard. Impulses to control and manage the situation are natural, but pressure won't help. This is a time to trust God and pray.

The most vulnerable times for gay, bisexual, and transgender people are before and right after they come out. Navigating changes in relationships and religious participation can be painful. Don't give your loved one any reason to lose hope. Believing in them and trusting in God will go a long way.

Be careful not to make a big issue about changes in how your child presents. Don't make fun of changes in hair, dress, or behavior that follows coming out. This kind of mocking might be a natural response to the discomfort a family feels at changes in how LGBTQ loved ones express themselves, but these changes often signify self-acceptance. Criticizing or mocking these changes will cut like a knife and create separation in relationships.

These specific suggestions need to be shared near and far with Adventist parents and congregations. Regardless of theological conviction, these are steps that everyone can take. We can and should be clear and specific about things that need to change.

Further, we should say clearly and definitively that stereotyping and mocking the LGBTQ community is wrong. We can and should create churches where LGBTQ people can sit in the pews without fear of harassment. Unfortunately, harassment is common, and church members don't know how to respond because their leaders give little guidance.

After I preached on this subject, even though I didn't challenge Adventist theology, I was questioned closely. Did I agree with the theology of the church? Why would I talk about these things without making it very clear that homosexuality is a sin? This had happened to me on many other occasions as well. When I challenged people to be more loving and accepting of LGBTQ people, they jumped to questioning my theology.

I used to think his questioning was a way of dealing with the discomfort people felt. By falling back on the certainty they had in their theology, they could avoid the discomfort of the challenges I was bringing up. Though that may still be true, I've begun to wonder whether there's more to it.

Maybe accepted theology creates a space in which rejection and fear fester and grow. Perhaps compassion and acceptance lead naturally to affirmation. Judging by results only, this is impossible to disprove. Rejection and fear do fester and grow in all denominations where same-gender marriage and trans-gender identity are considered sinful. This is another compelling reason for the church to re-examine its theological convictions.

Still, there are certainly individuals and even some churches or organizations where accepted theology is maintained in a loving and understanding atmosphere. They are exceptions. For those who subscribe to the accepted theology in the Adventist Church, I hope you strive to be the exception. But even if you are the exception, there are still risks.

BAIT AND SWITCH?

A friend told me about getting involved with her church and being open from the beginning about being gay. She liked the church. Everyone was kind to her, and they never spoke from the pulpit about sexual orientation. She felt accepted and started attending every week. She attended for two years, making friends and feeling that she was part of the community.

As a musician, she wanted to get involved with the praise team. She kept asking about it and being put off without understanding why. Then one day, she got an email from someone on the team. "I need to do the right thing and tell you why you can't be on the praise team. We can't have someone who is openly gay leading worship."

This was the first she'd heard in two years that her sexual orientation was a problem. She'd grown closer to God in that church and never had that made her question whether she was wrong for affirming her sexuality. God wasn't convicting her now, but she experienced rejection.

She'd made friends and built her life around this church. People she trusted and a community she relied on suddenly revealed that she wasn't living up to their standards. I can hardly imagine how she felt. She had felt acceptance and love in a community, but the whole time she was being judged and excluded by people who never thought she belonged. They hoped she would change naturally as she got closer to God. Then she could participate fully. But they didn't want to tell her upfront for fear of not appearing loving. But getting closer to God didn't change her in the way the church hoped it would. She was still okay with being gay. She ended up leaving that church and now is fully involved in the leadership of an affirming faith community.

Another friend I'll call James went to a large megachurch in the South with his husband, Chris, and their daughter. They were nervous at first, but they wanted the best youth program for their daughter. After a shaky start, everything seemed fine. The senior pastor of this megachurch even took a personal interest in them. Every week after the service, the pastor and his wife sought out this couple to chat.

Their families became friends. They texted often. They shared meals in each other's homes. James and Chris felt accepted, even though they seemed to be the only same-sex couple in the church. They got to know elders in the church, they participated in groups, and their daughter made friends in the youth ministry.

After church one week, James was given a theological paper by a church leader. It was about homosexuality, and he wanted his opinion. James felt honored and thought this was a chance to give back. After reading it through, James realized why the leader had given him the paper: "He was telling me I was unnatural and disgusting to God."

James was suddenly terrified that he was leading Chris to hell. But he loved his husband and family deeply; the thought of divorce was excruciating. Chris said he would do whatever James needed. If they needed to stop being intimate, he would do it. He just wanted them to live the rest of their lives together.

James didn't know what to do. He entered a period of deep depression and suicidal thoughts. He got counseling, stopped attending his church, and met some people who helped him see an affirming view of Scripture. He began to recover.

James now attends an affirming church with his husband and daughter, but occasionally he falls back into depression and anxiety. When he does, he thinks about his experience at that church and the fear that he could be leading the love of his life to damnation.

Too often, those who advocate waiting to talk about sexuality and focusing on building a relationship believe it's kindness. But it's no kindness to withhold this information. Something is wrong with theology that must hide. Something is wrong when Christians think they must hide the truth in order to love. It's much more loving to be upfront. But when being upfront, don't be surprised if gay, bisexual, and transgender people believe the theological position is restricting and harmful. It's what most of us believe who have lived this theology.

TUNE-UP

The loving approach is not always about waiting to speak; sometimes, it's about speaking with more love. Basic content doesn't change, but it's balanced with sympathy for the difficulties gay, bisexual, and transgender people experience. Many Adventists assume this is enough. They tune up their approach, making tweaks and trusting these are adequate. But are they? How do they know? They don't know for sure.

Most LGBTQ people, speaking from experience, know it's not enough. The theology itself is what hurts us. It's not only us. One research study focused directly on the impact of theology. It found that "opposition to same-sex sexuality on religious grounds" was harmful in and of itself. Because the research sample was large, with 1,600 participants, it could statistically control for other factors and isolate the impact of theology itself.[120]

Not surprisingly, the results for the gay and bisexual community were "higher levels of anxiety, stress, and shame; more instances of physical and verbal abuse; and more problematic alcohol use." What caught me off guard when I read this study was that exposure to this theology *also* caused problems for heterosexuals in every category studied, though to a lesser degree than the impact on sexual minorities. In other words, the accepted theology on this subject isn't good for anyone. When a pastor preaches a sermon teaching that same-sex sexuality is wrong, it harms all members, regardless of sexual orientation.[121]

Why is this? Perhaps it's because theology is ultimately the study of God. That's what the word "theology" means. All theology teaches us something about who God is. Accepted theology teaches us a picture of God that is less inclusive and less loving, and that's not good for any of us.

When I think about this research and look back on how I used to think about this subject, I realize how many voices I had to ignore when I believed that accepted theology wasn't harmful. I had to assume that mental health professionals and healthcare communities are influenced by bias and politics. I couldn't believe their research or their recommendations. I had to believe that every professional medical and psychological organization was wrong. Those most dedicated to helping gay, bisexual, and transgender people thrive were deceived about what harms them and what helps them. I had to believe LGBTQ people were mostly self-deceived and selfish. I had to believe the research was wrong. I had to believe that most gay, bisexual, and transgender people were wrong about what they said about themselves and their needs.

Most of all, I had to disbelieve the gnawing compassion in my own heart. It told me something was wrong with my church's theology. As hard as I tried to ignore it, it wouldn't go away. I wasn't the first to discover that the gnawing compassion was the voice of the Holy Spirit.

It took me a long time to discover this because I never listened carefully or deliberately enough to anyone who disagreed with me. As someone once told me, "If the voice of God had spoken from heaven and told you that it was okay to date women, you wouldn't have believed it." She had a point. It's not that I was stubborn or self-righteous. Looking back, it was because I loved and trusted my church so much. Yet despite my fastidious denial, when I was honest with myself, I still had doubts. My trust became an unwillingness to believe anyone outside the church, as if the denomination was above reproach.

When we accept that LGBTQ people are simply people, like all other people, the harm of accepted theology becomes obvious. It would harm anyone to label the ability to love as an impulse to sin. It would hurt anyone to tell them they must live as one gender when they can't deny or escape the knowledge that they are a different gender.

Recognizing this takes empathy and understanding. The church has continually struggled to respond to gay, bisexual, and transgender people this way. They have failed to understand that the restrictions on our lives have the same adverse effects that the same limits would have on anyone's life.

Mental health professionals maintain that LGBTQ people need affirming therapies. We need to be told that our sexuality and gender identity are equally valid. That's what the research says. That's what gay, bisexual, and transgender Christians have been trying to communicate to church and society for decades.

My firm conviction is that it's not enough to be more loving in the *delivery* of our theology. We need to be more loving in the *content* of our theology. Anything else is superficial. Compassion is biblical, not only in style but in substance. Love is not the sauce on top of our theology; love is the whole enchilada. Love is not the spin we put on our policies; love is the source of our policies. Love is the beating heart of the gospel and the only thing that brings life to religion. Love is not superficial; it gets down to the marrow. Love is biblical. Compassion is biblical. To believe anything else is to disbelieve what God says about God. To believe otherwise is to disregard God's authority.

Right now, our theology is terrible for the well-being of gay, bisexual, and transgender people. We don't need to hide that reality to justify the truth. Truth doesn't need to hide. Truth doesn't need to dodge or be explained away. Truth stands on its own. I know that intentions have been good, but I hope that the church I love will have the courage to go beyond intentions and embody the community God calls us to be. Our responsibility as a community is to strive towards the ideals God has given us.

REAL LIVES

Knowing how to integrate the impact of our theology with our theology can be difficult. I don't want to pretend there's an easy answer. I understand why people don't want to throw their theology out the window even if they are genuinely concerned about the impact it seems to be having. Yet, no matter how difficult it is to reconcile our theology with these realities, we should avoid acting as if these statistics aren't theologically relevant. This isn't a matter of balancing theology against mental health. Theologically and biblically speaking, mental health matters because compassion is biblical. It is in the character of God to care for the suffering of others.

When we get it right, there is no need for balance. God is for us (Rom. 8:31). God loves us (John 3:16). Following God may cost us in a world that doesn't know God, but the act of following God brings joy and life (Matt. 13:44). Just as God made Sabbath for us, not us for the Sabbath (Mark 2:27), God also made marriage for us, not us for marriage. As difficult as it can be to understand the meaning of the theological primacy of love and the Golden Rule, we can't care about someone without caring that they are depressed and suicidal. We are not living up to its ideals.

I know that acknowledging this leaves those who believe in the accepted theology in a difficult situation. What if my best understanding of Scripture harms people? I've observed that those who recognize that accepted theology is harmful eventually change their theological beliefs. I've watched this shift slowly over years; I've seen it change in a moment; I've experienced the shift myself. For many of us, it's this recognition that drives us back to the text with the humility to learn. People don't often knowingly practice a theology that makes the world less just and less compassionate.

The opposite is also true. Those who believe accepted theology are convinced the theology itself is not harmful. People who follow accepted theology often doubt or minimize the statistics or place the blame somewhere other than on the theology itself. Often, they blame discrimination and hate. The church is called to love better, not to question theology. Few can reconcile the idea that theology is both correct *and* causes pervasive hopelessness and depression to a group of people.

This is a strong biblical reason for this. God is a good parent who give good gifts. God doesn't refuse good things from those who ask or give harmful gifts (Matthew 7:7-12). That doesn't mean life is easy (Matt. 7:13, 14). It does mean that following God will produce good fruit in one's life (Matthew 7:15-20).

But I would argue that the research is in. We know the answers. We know what's happening. To disbelieve or misapply the research, to ignore the lived experience of so many, is a mistake we should no longer make.

Is it protective to affirm children in their sexuality and gender? Yes. Is it harmful to discourage them from dating the gender they are attracted to? Yes. Is it dangerous to discourage them from expressing their gender with internal congruence? Yes. Is it protective to support someone's gender transition? Yes.

The weight of evidence agrees. Every legitimate professional organization supports affirming therapies for members of the LGBTQ community.[a] The vast majority of those of us who are gay, bisexual, and transgender say the same. Those who listen to our stories will hear it.

Still, it's easy to ignore or misunderstand this evidence when we live and work in an environment where accepted theology is a requirement of belonging. I've seen good, loving, and kind people ignore the evidence. I know people who would give you their last meal if you were hungry; they embody the love of God. Yet these same people, because they believe accepted theology, dismiss the multitude of people who cry out in pain. It's time for the church to start listening.

I'm not asking you to agree with what I've written in this chapter. It may be new for many of you. What's most important, and what I am asking, is that you open yourself to the possibility of deeper understanding. We don't need statistics and research studies to understand the issue in the most basic way.

I suggest the following spiritual imagination exercise in the spirit of Jesus' command that we love others as we love ourselves. Prayerfully spend at least 15 minutes imagining in detail how your life would be different if you were gay or transgender. This small investment of time will pay off.

If you were gay, how would your life be different? What would be different for you, starting with your first crush? What would you do as a teenager when your friends were getting crushes? What would you do when everyone was talking about it, and you couldn't share? Would you make things up? Would you stay quiet? What if you decided to come out? What would be different if there was no possibility of falling in love with someone you could marry? Would you

---

a. There is often a belief that mental health professionals practice affirming therapies because of cultural pressures. This is historically unsupported. Mental health organizations were once the biggest drivers of non-affirmation. For many years mental health professionals even ignored the research of Evelyn Hooker, which showed that sexual orientation didn't correlate with mental disorders. They changed their minds primarily because of research and did so long before LGBTQ people gained broad acceptance in culture. See Kathy Baldock's book, *Crossing the Bridgeless Divide*, for more information on this, or investigate the history of Evelyn Hooker and her research.

marry without sexual attraction? Would you stay single? How would you explain it to the people around you? Would you try to hide? What would it be like for you, today, to start telling your friends and family you were gay? What would you say? How would that conversation go? What would change about how they related to you?

What if you were transgender? If you are a woman, what would it be like if you had to live, behave, dress, and date as a man? What if you had to use the men's restroom? If everyone called you by a male name? What if you are a man and had to behave as a woman? How would you, a man, be treated if you put on makeup and a dress and went about your day? What would you do if you knew you were one gender, but the world insisted you were not? How would that impact your life? How would that affect your ability to marry and have a family? Would you be accepted in the church the same as you are today? Would you hide and pretend? What if pretending isolated you and eventually made you crushingly depressed or even suicidal?

Of course, even if you do these exercises, you won't know what it's like, but you'll have more empathy. Even though we will never understand what it's like to be someone else, there are bridges of understanding. We all know pain, joy, rejection, acceptance, depression, hope, and despair. We all know the feeling of trying to fit in when what we want is to belong.

THE VIRTUE

There is more to this than the harm of accepted theology. I believe that same-gender marriage is good and moral on the face of it. When we consider what the Bible teaches in general about what is good and what is sinful, same-sex marriage doesn't fit the sin category, and I'm not sure how transgender identity ever could.

When two people of the same gender choose to get married, making a life-long commitment to one another is an act of love. It's not an act of selfishness. Marriage is innately difficult even as it's inherently beautiful. All the complexities of two adults joining their lives in partnership have the same mix of difficulty, joy, beauty, challenge, and risk, no matter the gender. It's a wild ride regardless of your partner's gender.

Yet, there are extra difficulties for same-gender marriages, particularly in years past or where people don't have equal rights. I'm struck by how exceptional it is that same-gender couples ever stay together under these circumstances. I often meet couples who have been together for decades. What must it have been like for them to forge a relationship when they had to do so in secret?

They couldn't enjoy the simple pleasure of going out to celebrate an anniversary. They needed cover stories for neighbors, family, coworkers, and friends. They could be arrested, thrown in jail, or fired at any time. Until the Clinton administration, it was illegal to be gay and have a government job. Until 2003, sexual intimacy between men was a crime in 19 states and between any same-sex partners in four states. Until 2015, same-sex marriage wasn't available nationally. Until 2020, people could legally be fired for being LGBTQ. Imagine how many adjustments couples needed to make daily just to stay safe, employed, and housed.

Yet, many of these relationships endured. This love inspires me. It's a choice to love and be faithful despite constant opposition. These couples help me understand the love of God. Choosing love when everyone in your life supports the endeavor is a beautiful thing. Choosing love despite rejection from one's community seems impossible and demands sacrifice, suffering, and danger—that's divine love.

When I first started thinking these thoughts, I'd already been through all the theology. I'd already changed my mind about the Bible and same-gender marriage. The theological barriers were down. For the first time, I felt like I was seeing through a clear lens. In the LGBTQ community, which I finally recognized as my own, I found a community that was flawed yet also breathtaking in its sacrifice and love. Once we see same-gender couples in this light, it's difficult to unsee, because it's so true.

Same-sex marriages have the same struggles with selfishness as heterosexual couples. We have the same ego-centered desires that pull us away from each other. But we also have the same cords of love that draw us together. When we choose love, when we allow marriage to make us better people, we experience shining moments when our love reminds us of the love of God.

That's because same-gender marriage is not intrinsically evil. It doesn't compare to anything else we consider a sin. God's love is not revealed through alcoholism, adultery, divorce, pedophilia, incest, or bestiality. Many times, I've heard these compared to same-gender marriage. It's false on the face of it. No analogy rightly compares this love to sin.

Same-gender marriage is simply the form marriage naturally takes for many of us. It harms no one. It doesn't harm society. It doesn't take away from something more beautiful that God had otherwise planned. Gay people can't be made heterosexual, and if they could, it wouldn't make them more holy.

HARD DIFFERENCES

One of my Adventist pastor friends lives nearby; I adore her. She is funny, wry, committed to her faith, and a good listener. She's a strong and kind woman. She has opinions. She has empathy. She's my type of person. Since I came out and lost my position as a pastor, we've tried to stay in touch, sharing meals and catching up on life regularly.

It's not always easy navigating our differences, but it's worth it. I'm grateful it seems worth it to her as well. Yet, there are challenging moments to navigate.

One such moment[b] came after she attended a training for pastors on how to reach people like me. She was excited to tell me about it. Her voice was hopeful, and I got the impression that she felt it would be a connecting point between us.

She shared one of her take-home messages. "He told us that it's possible to love LGBTQ people even if we disagree with their behaviors."

My brain instantly went in five different directions. How could I tell her? How could I share with her the pain I've experienced as a direct result of this theology? How could I tell her the pain inflicted by a church that teaches love is sin? How could I convince her?

I thought of many of the things I've shared with you in this chapter. Then I realized I didn't want to convince her. I wanted her to put herself in my shoes and understand how devastating such theology is and has always been in my life and the lives of so many others. I wanted her to think about how much her marriage and family mean to her and think about what it would be like not to have them. I wanted her to think about what it would be like to be told as a child that her crushes were sinful, not innocent. And if she wouldn't know through empathizing with me, I hoped she would know by listening to me. I didn't want to get into an argument; I wanted to share my life experiences with a friend and be believed.

Then I thought about the conversations I'd had before. I thought about the defensiveness I've encountered in friends when sharing plainly how destructive the theology has been to me. I thought about how they said they felt judged or trapped. I thought about a different friend who'd had a conversation with me, then shared what I said in unflattering terms on a web forum he didn't realize I was reading. I watched the pastors jump all over this "judgmental" attitude of mine, saying how coercive and unkind it is.

---

b. I've since shared my recollection of this moment with her, and she remembers it differently. She feels that I misunderstood her. But she graciously allowed me to keep the story, as it does reflect a relational reality, and it is genuine in my memory. Happily, we're still friends, and even more so a couple years after this conversation.

I thought about another pastor who private-messaged me saying he didn't understand why I would say that non-affirming churches were unloving places for LGBTQ people. I decided to take the direct approach and talk to him on the phone. I shared honestly and openly from my experience. I did my best to be non-defensive, open, and candid. He dismissed me. Then he blocked me on Facebook for several months.

There is a shared belief that seems to be growing. Christians seem to believe their judgments should be met without judgment. They take for granted that they can keep their theological beliefs without negatively impacting the lives of gay, bisexual, and transgender people. I hear this repeated endlessly.

I know many pastors want to do the right thing for all people. There was a time that I found hope in the idea that I could love LGBTQ people well without changing my theology. I had no intention to harm, and neither did they. I knew they operated from sincerely held beliefs and loyalty to the church. But I also knew that they weren't listening to us.

As I sat with my friend over breakfast tacos, all these things flashed through my mind. I saw her hope and eagerness to bring seemingly disparate worlds together. I knew her desire to bridge the gap between us as we sat at that table, trying to be good friends to one another.

What could I say? I didn't want to argue. I wanted to share the reality of my life, and I wanted her to understand. I wanted her to see my scars and acknowledge the pain they represent.

That morning, I didn't have the energy to try again. My friend was relieved and excited. I didn't want to tell her how devastating the theology had been to so many people I know. I didn't want to argue about it.

Not knowing how to respond, feeling overwhelmed and discouraged, I started to cry. It was the last thing I wanted to do. I cried because her conclusions hurt me deeply. The church believes the way I desire a family is a desire for sin and my sexuality is unacceptable. I lost so much as a direct result of the theology of the church. Having shared so much of my story with her, I had hoped she would understand.

I couldn't bring myself to try again at that moment. Maybe she would have listened. Perhaps it would have been a turning point. I don't know. I couldn't muster enough hope that day. Maybe I should have, but I didn't.

It's not just me having this experience. It's repeated in restaurants, homes, and churches all over the world. Even though I know I'll be okay, I'm afraid every day for the children. They're growing up in the Adventist Church and feel as if they don't belong. They are taught that they can't romantically love someone of the same gender in a holy way. They are told that their gender must conform to expectations, not be expressed with congruence. They don't have examples to follow and don't see people like themselves who thrive.

They need someone to tell them they're okay. They need models and mentors. I'm afraid for the shame they will feel over innocent crushes and for what it will do to their young hearts and their will to live. When my friend, a compassionate and kind person, still couldn't see that my life was blown to pieces by theology, what hope is there that someone will listen to these children? Will you listen to them?

That's probably why writing this section of the book has involved countless drafts and hours of painfully staring at my computer screen, fruitlessly willing the right words to appear. I knew I had to provide statistics and reasons. The truth needs to be told. But I didn't want to argue. I've seen how easily arguments can be dismissed. I don't want to merely offer statistics. Too many people quickly decide that statistics don't apply to them.

I want what most of us want. I want to be believed. This theology is not working. It's not doing what theology is supposed to do. It's not producing goodness in my life or in the lives of hundreds of people I know. It's not reflecting the character of God.

I say this not because I hate the church; I love both the LGBTQ community and the church we are still part of. I'm not trying to be judgmental, I offer grace and understanding, but I will tell the truth. We need you to listen. I know how hard it is. I know how complicated it can be. But to be quite candid, I am afraid for the gay, bisexual, and transgender children growing up in Adventist churches, schools, and homes.

For some time, Adventists have asked, "How can we minister to LGBTQ people?" In reading this chapter, you may have discovered the beginning of the answer to that question. Before we can imagine doing good for gay, bisexual, and transgender people, Adventists need to focus on stopping the harm they are causing. The question should be, "How can we stop our churches, members, and families from harming LGBTQ people?" Before asking how the church can minister to LGBTQ people, the church must recognize that it is often part of the problem.

CHAPTER 10

The Bible Says "Homosexuality" Is Wrong

> *"Paul referred to homosexuality in the language that was used in his time. They knew and were familiar with same-sex couples, and Paul would have known about it. He used the language that most closely matched our understanding of homosexuality today, and that's why that word is used in our Bibles."*
>
> *"I'm sure you are aware of what Paul says will be the results of the homosexual lifestyle. You have already made your choice."*

When someone says the Bible speaks against "homosexuality," they are most directly referencing two passages from Paul. These are the only places we find the words "homosexuality" or "homosexual" in the Bible. They are both lists of sins (traditionally called vice lists).

Do you not know that the unrighteous will not inherit the kingdom of God? Do not be deceived. Neither fornicators, nor idolaters, nor adulterers, nor *homosexuals*, nor sodomites, nor thieves, nor covetous, nor drunkards, nor revilers, nor extortioners will inherit the kingdom of God. And such were some of you. But you were washed, but you were sanctified, but you were justified in the name of the Lord Jesus and by the Spirit of our God (1 Cor. 6:9-11, italics supplied).

We know that the law is good if one uses it properly. We also know that the law is made not for the righteous but for lawbreakers and rebels, the ungodly and sinful, the unholy and irreligious, for those who kill their fathers or mothers, for murderers, for the sexually immoral, for *those practicing homosexuality*, for slave traders and liars and perjurers—and for whatever else is contrary to the sound doctrine that conforms to the gospel concerning the glory of the blessed God, which he entrusted to me (1 Tim. 1:8-11, NIV, italics supplied).

From time-to-time friends in the Adventist Church express frustration with me and others in the queer community. They feel like we are backing out of the deal we all signed up for. All Christians have to make sacrifices for our faith. Why should we make exceptions for people tempted by homosexuality? We all struggle with sin; we should all be willing to sacrifice in obedience to God. We don't make excuses for other types of sexual immorality, nor do we make exceptions for liars, adulterers, thieves, greedy people, or drunkards.

"So why," they ask, "do you get a pass?"

People who understand themselves as having "left homosexuality" often find inspiration for their decisions in these verses. They take it on faith that they can overcome when they read 1 Corinthians 6:11: "and such were some of you." God promised them that their homosexuality could become their past and no longer their present or future. By leaving their homosexuality behind, they can become "righteous" (1 Cor. 6:11; 1 Tim. 1:8). They accept this as true, even if they have ongoing desires for a relationship or sexual experiences with someone of the same sex, and even if they slip from time to time. We all make mistakes. I say this sincerely, all of us striving to overcome sin will do so imperfectly.

Before we dive into all the details, I assure you that you don't have to remember every detail. I'm going to give a lot of information, but don't worry, there won't be a quiz. Many of you will find the details as fascinating as I did, but they are also there to show that I did my homework and that what I write is accurate and well-attested. I'm not asking anyone to take my word for it. I'm showing my work, not just my conclusions, so that others can make their own decisions. So, here's my conclusion upfront, so that you can know where I'm headed:

No form of the word "homosexuality" was used in the Bible until 1946, because it's an anachronistic translation. This is one of the rare times in the Bible when an accurate translation is difficult to come by. We can say for sure that "homosexuality" is a poor translation, and the best understanding we have is that Paul meant something else entirely. At the very least, we can affirm that these texts are not an unambiguous condemnation that applies to same-gender marriage.

TRANSLATION

We all tend to trust our English translations, and with good reason. They are excellent. Still, no translation is a one-to-one correlation to the original language. Sometimes translators can't find an English word that's equivalent to the original because of differences in language and culture. That's why we often find different translations with different nuances.

The Greek word *dikaiosune*, for example, has a meaning that overlaps our concepts of "righteousness" and "justice." We don't have one word that combines those meanings. So, translators often have to make a choice.

Occasionally, cultural and political realities motivate translations. Considering people's powerful interests in what the Bible says, it's amazing how few there are, yet they exist. They aren't the norm, but it does happen.

The Greek word for "submerge" is *baptizo*. When the Anglican Church was working on its translation commissioned by King James of England, it had a problem. The Anglican Church didn't submerge people for baptism. It only sprinkled. The Anabaptists, critics of the Anglican Church, pointed out that sprinkling wasn't biblical. So instead of translating the word *baptizo* into English with the most obvious word, which would have been "submerge," translators kept the Greek word that no one understood. They used "baptize."

This translation made it less obvious that the Anglican Church wasn't following the Bible. It would have been absurd to say, "we submerge by sprinkling," but they were able to get away with saying, "we baptize by sprinkling." That's how "baptism" ended up in the King James Version of the Bible. Later translations followed, and all our Bibles use this approach today.

Of course, the word we are particularly interested in today is "homosexual." No one could rightly say that there has been no political or cultural influence behind this word. It shows up in English translations of both 1 Corinthians 6:9 and 1 Timothy 1:10. The New American Standard Bible says "homosexuals." The English Standard Version says, "men who practice homosexuality." The

New International Version says, "men who have sex with men." The New Living Translation says, "those who . . . practice homosexuality." The Contemporary English Version says, "behaves like a homosexual." The New King James Version says, "homosexuals, nor sodomites."

But older translations never use any form of the word "homosexual." The King James Version says, "abusers of themselves with mankind." Similarly, the American Standard Version says, "abusers of themselves with men." Older translations typically used this type of formulation, a statement about being abusers with men. The word "homosexual" didn't show up in the Bible until 1946. Before that, homosexuals were not mentioned in the Bible; there was no mention of sexual orientation at all.

Why did it take so long? If it's always meant "homosexual," why didn't it always say "homosexual"?

"HOMOSEXUAL"

Let's start with how the word first got into our Bibles and the change it brought about in Christian thinking. Kathy Baldock and Ed Oxford first asked this question and determined to find the answer. Why did the first translation team choose the word "homosexual"? Who were they? What reasons did they give?

Baldock and Oxford went to the Yale Archives to examine the notes of the original translation team for the 1946 Revised Standard Version, where the word "homosexual" first appeared. They looked at tens of thousands of pages, some typed, some handwritten. The team had taken meticulous notes.

They'd also received a lot of correspondence related to their translations of one word or another. Bible translations can sometimes be controversial, and this translation was exceptionally so. People get upset when the words in their Bibles change. But as odd as it might seem today, their choice of the word "homosexual" stirred little controversy at the time.

The team itself seemed to make the change with minimal disagreement or analysis. It began with a comparison translation for 1 Corinthians 6:9. They used the Moffat Bible (1925) as their starting point. The words "sodomite" and "catamite" were used for two Greek words—*arsenokoitai* and *malakoi*. A catamite was a young boy enslaved and raped. "Sodomite," of course, was based on the story of Sodom and Gomorrah. It had become a term referring to anal sex, often in the context of sexual assault.

"Catamite" and "sodomite" aren't perfect translations. These are challenging translation choices, for which there may be no perfect answers. Yet despite its drawbacks, Moffat's translation was not about sexual orientation. They chose words that referred to sexual aggression, assault, and coerced sex.

So why the change? Significant changes in word choice often came along with copious notes from the translation team. They left records of lengthy conversation and careful deliberation of countless translation choices. Their notes were meticulous. Surprisingly, Baldock and Oxford at first found no such record in this case. Only after days of digging through tens of thousands of pages, most of which they could tell had never been looked at before, did they finally find a letter.

A young seminarian named David had written the lead translator, Luther Weigle, challenging the choice of the word "homosexual." This insightful young man brought up all the relevant questions. Would the word "homosexual" imply more than intended? Aren't there some people who innately experience these desires? Don't many such people desire a loving and committed relationship just as heterosexuals do? Isn't that quite different than a catamite or sodomite, or from *arsenokoitai* or *malakoi*? Won't this translation be weaponized against homosexuals?

David's understanding was rare at the time, especially among conservative Christians. They still thought of same-sex sex in terms of sexually deviant behavior that anyone can fall into. They thought about exploitation, anonymous sex, and unrestrained lust, not about people who take partners and lovingly care for one another. Increasingly, homosexuality was also seen as a psychiatric disorder that could be treated by psychoanalysis and often cured. How did this young seminarian have this insight? It raised the question of whether he might be gay himself.

Disappointingly, Weigle replied that they chose the word "homosexual" simply because it was a modern word. They were updating the language without understanding the implications. They did this quickly and innocently because of ignorance and cultural influence, not malice. After they read David's letter, it seemed from correspondence that they would reconsider their translation, but the publisher's deadline for changes expired before they could do so. They did change it in a later addition, but the damage was done.

Their translation choice was not unexpected when we think about the ideas they would have been exposed to in the culture they grew up in. They probably didn't understand the word "homosexual" the way we do now. Sexual orientation wasn't the controversial topic it is today. It wasn't an acceptable topic for Christians at all, especially in polite company. "The culture war" wasn't yet declared, and the church didn't see LGBTQ people as an enemy. They lived in the shadows of society. Christians didn't think about them much at all.

PASTOR DAVID

What happened to David, the young seminarian? He had written his letter from a post office box and used a fake last name. Half a century had passed since he'd written his letter.

It might be a miracle, but through grit and persistence, he was recently located. Needless to say, he's not young anymore. He is part of the LGBTQ community, identifying as a homosexual. The story of his life and the letter he wrote is fascinating and has many twists and turns.

I was able to meet him and hear him speak at The Reformation Project's annual conference. He said something that surprised me. When he was a young man discovering who he was, it was easy for him to see that nothing was wrong with him. No one was teaching that homosexuality was a sin. No one was talking about sexual orientation. He simply looked at the Bible and could tell those verses such as 1 Corinthians 6:9 and Romans 1 weren't describing people like him.

He wasn't an idol worshiper, a sodomite, or a catamite. He couldn't see himself in those texts. The topic hadn't been politicized. So, he simply accepted himself and lived many years with a partner whom others assumed was his cousin. He lived a fascinating and productive life as a pastor. Read more about the translation, and David himself, in Kathy Baldock and Ed Oxford's upcoming book, *Forging a Sacred Weapon: How the Bible Became Anti-Gay*. An upcoming documentary film called *1946* chronicles their discovery.

With this knowledge of how the word "homosexual" got into the Bible, we have a new reason to question the translation. Yet because Bible translators base new translations on older translations, the influence of this word-choice has been broad. It influenced future translations and the entire dialogue. It's time to consider what the original translation team took for granted.

In Summary: Paul uses two Greek words in 1 Corinthians 6:9, and one word repeats in 1 Timothy 1:10. These words only came to be understood as "homosexuality" in 1946. Before that, there was little to no conversation on the topic of homosexuality in Christian churches.

RARE VOCABULARY

What do we make of these Greek words? Why the controversy about their translation? What do they mean? Let's start with the word *arsenokoites*.[a]

Usually, the translation of the Bible we have is beyond excellent. Understanding the original Greek behind our translation usually adds nuance but doesn't change the meaning. However, there are exceptions. Sometimes there is genuine ambiguity. One common exception is when a text contains a rare word. If the word wasn't used often, it's hard to understand and translate with confidence.

Arsenokoites is one such word. It only appears twice in all of Scripture. That's right, that word is only used in the two chapters under discussion. Not only that, it wasn't used in any contemporary Greek writings we have from that time. Only Paul used it, only in these two places. Nowhere else.

Yet Paul assumes his readers understood it. Where did they get their understanding? I hate to say this, because it's not the type of answer we want to hear about the Bible, but we really, genuinely don't know. That's the honest answer. I know that answer is incredibly unsatisfying.

Why do I say we don't know the meaning? I rely on Dale B Martin's[122] work most heavily for this conclusion, but scholars universally acknowledge the principles. The only way to reliably determine the meaning of a word is through context. How was the word used? Since we have no examples for comparison, we can't be confident about its meaning. Even in the two verses we're discussing, *arsenokoites* was used as part of a list of vices, providing very little contextual information to base our meaning on.

What about the occurrences of the word that we have? Most of the examples come from at least 100 years after Paul. They generally fall into two categories: first, people who simply quote Paul's list of vices, which doesn't help us; second, people who use the words in the context of some type of injustice or financial exploitation that may or may not have included sex. It's unclear.

On a personal level, I detest saying "I don't know" in this situation. A lot of people will tell you they are sure about this word. I'm afraid the desire for answers will mean my approach doesn't seem convincing. Rather than leave areas of uncertainty or unknowing, I prefer to explain everything and tie it all up

a. For a detailed analysis of the translation issues in these texts, I'd recommend chapter 3 of *Sex and the Single Savior*, by Dale B. Martin. It's the best analysis I've found, and it compellingly dismantles some of the most accepted approaches to these words. It's a must read.

in a neat little bow. In fact, I have spoken and written with a great deal of clarity and confidence on these texts before, but I was wrong. There's just no way to know what this word means.

ASSUMING I'M WRONG

Knowing that it's unsatisfying to simply not understand what an important word means in the Bible, I'll explore other possibilities. Besides, what if I'm wrong? If I am wrong, what is the best explanation for what it *could* mean? There is another possibility worth exploring.

Just as the English Bibles we use are translations of Hebrew and Greek, New Testament churches used a Greek translation of the Hebrew Bible. Their translation was called the Septuagint. When Paul quotes the Old Testament, he's usually using the Septuagint.

The Septuagint has two verses that some scholars believe tell us what *arsenokoites* means. Leviticus 18:22 and 20:13, verses we carefully studied already, both read, "you shall not lie [*koite*] with a man [*arsenos*] as with a woman."

It doesn't take a Greek scholar to understand that *arsenokoites* is a combination of *arsenos* and *koite*. Some assume that this means Paul was referring to Leviticus. He used a new word to refer back to Old Testament passages he was thinking about; passages that say a man should not lie with a man as with a woman. He either coined the word or someone else did with the same intent.[123]

I would love to believe that this is true. It sounds good on a surface level. I also think it makes the affirming case stronger. As a former member of the Sanhedrin and a student of the respected Rabbi Gamaliel, Paul was an expert in the Hebrew Scriptures. This would mean he understood the context of these verses and saw behavior in his time as similar to the behavior described and forbidden in the Hebrew Bible. He saw Christians as standing in the position of the ancient Israelites, called apart from this behavior.

By referring to Leviticus 18 and 21 on lists of sins, Paul wouldn't be speaking to abstract ideas. He observed behaviors that were real and immediate in the lives of his readers and the surrounding culture. Those behaviors reminded him of the reprehensible behaviors described in the Hebrew Bible that we looked at closely when we examined homoerotic behavior in the Torah. As we learn more about the Roman understanding of sex, that will only make more sense as we see parallels to the exploitation and dominance we found in the narratives of the Torah.

Even so, I no longer agree with the argument that *arsenokoites* refers to Leviticus, because this view rests on one huge assumption. It's never good to assume a compound word can be defined by its parts. Its usage must define it. An accurate meaning isn't determined by pulling the word apart, defining its pieces, then putting it back together. Nor is it defined by how those pieces are used elsewhere. We only know a word by understanding how it's used.

Strawberries aren't berries made of straw. Aboveboard doesn't mean something is above a board. Jackpot doesn't have anything to do with pots or a guy named Jack. Bluegrass music isn't about blue grass. Parkways are for driving; driveways are for parking.

We can't tell the meaning of a word by sewing together its constituent parts; we simply can't. That's not how language works. Sometimes words mean what the parts mean, but they often mean something either slightly or entirely different.

Allow me to speculate about how that could happen with this word. In Rome, financial exploitation (and other controlling behavior) was frequently referred to in sexual terms. It's similar to slang and expletives common in every language today, like "he screwed me over." Considering that later usage of *arsenokoites* referred to financial exploitation, it's feasible that this word could have described people who cheat or otherwise exploit others. Or it could more directly refer to someone who trades in catamites, possibly kidnapping and enslaving young boys, a definition that might fit well with 1 Timothy 1:10. If we are going to speculate on the meaning based on the two words in the compound word, there are multiple possible meanings. But again, this is only educated speculation. I don't know what the word means.

I know it's tempting to choose the explanation we prefer, but it's just a guess. I know pastors love to pull apart compound Greek words and make a point based on the meaning of the individual words. I've been guilty of it myself. But it's unreliable.

Still, our question is whether same-sex marriage is acceptable for Christians. For that question, it ultimately doesn't matter which side we land on. If *arsenokoitai* refers to Leviticus, it was talking about the same exploitation described in the Torah. If it's not, we have the most frustrating answer: we don't know. Either way, it's not an indictment of same-gender marriage and doesn't refer to sexual orientation like the word "homosexual" does.

In Summary: We aren't sure what one of these Greek words means because it's not used anywhere else. If it refers to sex, it refers to Leviticus 18 and 20, which are about shaming others through domination. But we can't be sure that it refers to anything sexual.

COMMON VOCABULARY

What about the other word? In 1 Corinthians 6:9, Paul uses the word *malakoi* along with *arsenokoitai*. Fortunately, this word is not rare at all. It's a widespread word in Greek and Roman culture, but not in Jewish culture. We have lots of information about what *malakos* meant and about the cultural values surrounding this meaning.

It's essential to understand some aspects of Greco-Roman culture to understand the word malakos. This information will come in handy in the next chapter when we look at Romans 1. I will also dispel some myths along the way.

The first myth is that Paul was criticizing something called pederasty. Pederasty was a socially sanctioned practice in which older men had a sexual and mentorship relationships with boys. Plato believed pederastic relationships were a virtuous pursuit of ideal beauty. They were a way of mentoring privileged young men of the upper class, and sex with a boy was often considered morally superior to sex with a woman. Pederasty was also deeply tied to political life in ancient Greece, rather than family life.

The idea that Paul was (at least in part) referring to these relationships both here and in Romans 1 used to make sense to me. I've probably even repeated the idea. But as I've learned more about Roman sexuality, I've learned that it's unlikely. Pederasty was illegal during Paul's lifetime and came with immense social stigma. No one could legally have a sexual relationship with a young boy who was a Roman citizen. These boys even wore unique clothing to indicate they were off-limits. Any pederastic relationship would bring permanent shame to the boy and criminal punishment to the man.

I was frustrated when I learned this. I'd been exposed to this idea many times. People on both sides of the conversation frequently refer to pederasty, especially those on the affirming side. I wanted reliable information, so I went to people whose life's work is studying Greek and Roman sexuality.

My eyes were opened to the sexual ethics of Rome by reading Marilyn B Skinner's *Sexuality in Greek and Roman Culture*,[124] the most complete scholarly work available. It's a historical work without a stake in the biblical questions we are considering. She's not writing from a Christian perspective but a historical one, so she doesn't have an agenda in this conversation. She does have a lot of relevant information.[125]

Skinner points out that the sexual ethics of Rome developed from the broader social values of Rome. Their sexual values didn't exist in a vacuum. They were only one of many reflections of the foundational principles and values of Roman society.

Romans were intensely hierarchical. Complex and rigid rules governed every aspect of society. Everyone had a place. Everyone's opportunity and value were based on their place in society. Those with a high station were honored; those with a low station were shamed.

Perhaps most foreign to our understanding, gender was impacted by birth, rank, and status, not just biological sex. Being born male was one contributor to rank and status, but far from the only one. Biological males were considered feminine if they were from a lower class. For example, enslaved men, the poor, actors, gladiators, or convicted felons were feminine even if they were men. Such men were called *malakoi* in Greek. A woman who was wealthy and powerful, on the other hand, could be somewhat masculine, within limits.

This all has to do with the Roman ideal of humanity. The ideal human was undoubtedly male, but also masculine (Latin: *vir*). He had control of his life and decisions. He was hard, impenetrable, decisive, and sought out difficulty and challenge. No one ever had the upper hand against him. No one could make him do anything. He rejected luxury and softness. He was powerful, and his decisions carried influence. He controlled his own life and the lives of others. He was a philosopher, warrior, and leader. He didn't get tired and rarely rested. He didn't have emotional problems. He was never afraid. He was never hurt. If someone tried to force him, or he was in a position of shame, as a last resort, he would die honorably by committing suicide rather than be defeated or controlled. Like Plato, he would end his own life rather than surrender.

In summary: The ideal person was a *vir*, a male Roman citizen with power, strength, and self-control. Even though men had a natural advantage toward being *vir*, women could also possess *virtus*, particularly if they were wealthy and commendable. *Virtus* was virtue itself and was also masculinity. It was related to the characteristics an individual embodied more than biological gender. It just so happened that men were the ones who Romans believed primarily held these virtues. Women were defective in body and morality. Masculinity was integrity and moral fortitude. Morality itself was masculine. Weakness and immorality were feminine.

SOFT

When Paul used the word *malakoi*, he was using a word in Greek that was the opposite of *virtus*. *Malakoi* were feminine, soft, and morally weak. They had no self-determination. They were dishonest, conniving, lacking control. They couldn't be trusted because they had no consistency. They were mush, filling their lives with luxury and avoiding hardship. They loved makeup and fine clothing. They ate before they were hungry. They slept before they were tired. They were afraid of a fight. They would endure shame before they would commit suicide. They embraced disgrace.

Some people degraded themselves voluntarily by taking this role for the pleasure of it. As funny as it might sound to us today, actors were one such class. They were viewed as shameful and weak but were also popular and received gifts and benefits from wealthy Romans. They dressed up and played roles rather than having self-determination.

A *malakos* was not necessarily a man who had sex with other men. On the contrary, he was more likely to dress himself up in lavish style to attract and have sex with women. He would likely have a lot of sex with women because such uncontrolled indulgence was part of being a *malakos*. A *malakos* would possibly perform oral sex on a woman since the woman was considered dominant in this position. His primary characteristic when it came to sex was indulgence. His primary characteristic was not having sex with men. This indulgence was related to over-indulgence in spending on luxuries and gluttony in eating as well as sexual indulgence.

Dale B. Martin put it best:

A man who allowed himself to be penetrated—by either a man or a woman—could be labeled *malakos*. But to say that *malakos* meant a man who was penetrated is simply wrong. A word existed that had that narrower meaning: *kinaedos*. *Malakos*, instead, referred to this entire complex of femininity. This can be recognized by looking at the range of ways men condemned other men by calling them *malakoi*.

As I mentioned, a man could, by submitting to penetration, leave himself open to charges of *malakoi*. But in those cases, the term refers to the effeminacy of which the penetration is only a sign or proof; it does not refer to the sexual act itself. The category of effeminate men was much broader than that. For example, in philosophical texts, *malakoi* are those people who cannot put up with hard work. Xenophon uses the term for lazy men. For Epictetus and the Cynic Epistles the term refers to men who take life easy rather than enduring the hardship of philosophy. In Dio Cassius, Plutarch, and Josephus, cowards are *malakoi*. Throughout ancient literature, *malakoi* are men who live lives of decadence and luxury. They drink too much wine, have too much sex, love gourmet food, and hire professional cooks. According to Josephus, a man may be accused of *malakoi* if he is weak in battle, enjoys luxury, or is reluctant to commit suicide. Dio Chrysostom says that the common crowd might stupidly call a man *malakos* just because he studies a lot—that is, a bookworm might be called a sissy.[126]

It should be clear that *malakoi* was not a sexual term. It referred to men who were effeminate. Indeed, nearly every translation before the twentieth century used some version of the word effeminate.

Men penetrated by other men would be *malakoi*, but that was neither the most common nor the most morally salient understanding of the word. As Martin says, "all penetrated men were *malakoi*, but not all *malakoi* were penetrated men."[127] *Malakoi* could just as easily be men who slept with a lot of women. If Paul was referring to sexually penetrated men, he chose a particularly unclear way of doing so. He chose a word with layers of additional meaning. Other terms were available that would have referred to men who are submissive in sex.

Allow me to use a contemporary example. If someone says, "I hate hippies," I don't hear "I hate tie-dye," "I hate marijuana," or "I hate outdoor concerts." That would be a misunderstanding of the original statement. Back in the 1960s, parents who were afraid that their children would become hippies were not specifically afraid that they would buy a VW van.

Likewise, to condemn *malakoi* is a big picture statement about a group for whom many assumptions were made. It's simply false to pull out one characteristic and use it to define the word, particularly when that one characteristic is not at all universal. Paul's word choice simply doesn't call out same-sex sex as a moral weakness. *Malakoi* are also willing to express emotions openly. Would we assume that's what Paul meant? I hope not.

CHALLENGING TRANSLATION

When I first understood the meaning of *malakos*, I was uncomfortable. It presented a difficulty I still don't know how to resolve, but I need to point it out. First, we know that *malakoi* refers to men who are effeminate. We know that in Paul's day, such men were considered weak-willed and immoral.

This belief reflects a culture that dehumanized women and femininity, viewing men as superior. Women, by nature, were lacking in virtue and goodness. Only the most exceptional and privileged woman had *virtus*. Women couldn't be trusted with leadership and couldn't complete difficult tasks. They were unintelligent and couldn't handle the rigor of philosophy. Being a woman was shameful, but in a way that was socially expected. Women were supposed to be soft, weak, and pliable. But when men were feminine, that was despised.[128]

Second, we know that Paul used this word on a list of vices. He said that those who are *malakoi* are bound for eternal destruction. They will not inherit the kingdom of God.

What are we supposed to do with that? Explaining away the misogyny requires contortions and anachronistic readings of the text. How should we apply a word so inseparably tied to problematic cultural ideas about the inferiority of women?

What would we do if we were on the translation team? How would we feel about using the word "effeminate" to describe men who were going to hell? What do we think about the implication that women are weak, and virtue resides in masculinity?

It is perhaps easier to translate the word as "homosexual" than to wrestle with these questions. Whatever the social and cultural pressures, the meaning of the translations noticeably changed in the twentieth century. It used to be translated "effeminate"; now it's translated "homosexual."

I'm not even going to attempt to solve the moral problem imposed by the word *malakoi*. But neither am I going to pretend it doesn't exist or wriggle my way out of it by manipulating the meaning of the word. It is a word we understand, and it does not mean "homosexual."

There is, however, one aspect of Paul's history that makes me question how much of the Roman concept he endorsed. *Vir* were not only protected socially, but also legally. Because their bodies were considered inviolable, it was illegal to penetrate them sexually or harm them physically.

This is the legal background of Acts 16:16-40. Paul, a Roman citizen, allows himself to be beaten. Such an act is illegal. It undermines Roman society by undermining a Roman citizen who is considered a leader in that society. It disgraces the one who takes the beating and has potentially violent consequences to the one who does the beating. Within the cultural thinking behind the word *malakos* itself is the implication that by allowing himself to be beaten, which is something Paul often did (1 Cor. 11:25), Paul was himself behaving as a *malakos*. Shortly after talking about all the times he was beaten, he says something very *malakos*: "If I must boast, I will boast in the things which concern my infirmity" (1 Cor. 11:30). In this statement, Paul is rejecting Roman morality boldly and clearly.

Again, I don't know the answer to these questions. I am committed to being candid about the limits of my understanding, and I don't have a good explanation for these layers of complexity. But they are there. Paul's understanding of *malakos* was nuanced and not always the same as the established cultural understanding. Since *malakos* is only a word that appears on a list, it's difficult to know what he meant. If someone asked how I would translate *malakoi*, my answer in this context would be "indulgent" or "greedy." I know I would be obscuring part of the meaning of this difficult word, but that's my best guess at the meaning Paul intended.

MALE-MALE SEX IN ROME

Let's return to the question of my fallibility. Even though I don't see any reason to apply these texts to male-male sex, what if I'm wrong? What meaning would we draw in that case?

What sexual relationships happened between men in Rome? (They were unheard of among Israelites.) These relationships were rigidly prescribed by society. They could happen only within the accepted hierarchy. High-status Roman men were allowed to sexually dominate those of lower classes and status.

Let's look again at Roman actors. They had low status. Society considered them shameful, feminine, and lacking in self-control. Respectable Roman citizens were free to dominate them sexually. That doesn't mean, however, that the actors didn't consent. A relationship like this would give actors access to resources and luxury, rewards that came with being the favorite of a wealthy noble. Some male actors were popular sex objects for Roman nobility. They were passed around and gossiped about, yet they could be dropped at any time.

The system was complex. The overarching theme of their sexual ethics mirrored the ethics of their society: power, domination, honor, shame, and hierarchy. As Skinner says:

> In Rome, no blame was attached to the man who indulged in sex with either his male slave or a male prostitute, provided that he took the active role and that financial expenditure, if any, was kept within reasonable limits (p. 260).

It's also true that these relationships involved no commitment. They were extramarital because the Roman elite usually also had wives, particularly in this period. These sexual encounters with other men were, by definition, meaningless to the lives of the powerful. If the *vir* committed excessive time or resources to the relationship, it was shameful and undermined his masculinity. No matter how favored, sexually dominated men were vulnerable to the whims of the men who dominated them.

Relationships in these terms are appropriately compared to the types of sexual exploitation described and forbidden in the Torah, those of Ham and Sodom. They are an institutional form of the same impulse for violent domination and control. They always involved the degradation of one man who was shamed and perverse honor for the man who dominated.

Let's summarize and focus on what we know for sure.

1. Same-sex sex in the Roman empire was adulterous.
2. These encounters existed purely for pleasure and did not involve any of the sacrifices or responsibilities of marriage.
3. They brought shame and disgrace to those penetrated.
4. They were based on ideas about some people in society being superior to others and entitled to dominate.
5. They were rooted in misogyny.

Even if Paul referred more generally to common same-sex relationships in Rome, any one of those characteristics would be enough to explain a prohibition. In Paul's day, same-sex sex was inseparable from these dynamics. Same-sex eroticism in Rome was defined by institutionalized dominance and power. Rome was not a good place to be gay.

Keeping this in mind, how should we answer the following question: How many same-sex marriages would have been stopped by a prohibition on same-sex sex? The answer is zero. Even if Paul intended to prevent same-sex relationships in 1 Corinthians 6:9 and 1 Timothy 1;10, such a prohibition would condemn Roman patriarchs from terrorizing the enslaved and the lower classes. It's only reasonable to assume that any prohibition would be intended to prohibit precisely what it actually did prohibit.

In summary: We know the meaning of the second Greek word under discussion. The closest English word we have is "feminine," which would mean Paul is saying it's immoral to be feminine. But this meaning is deeply rooted in Roman culture and particularly attached to the devaluation of women and cultural values of power and shame. It doesn't mean the same thing "feminine" means today. At other times, Paul flatly contradicted Roman ideas about being feminine. He acted in ways that would have been considered "feminine" to Romans, like allowing himself to be beaten and imprisoned, even boasting about it. Paul's audience would likely have understood what aspects of this word Paul meant to condemn, such as moral weakness, extravagant living, and lack of self-control. It certainly doesn't refer to a person being gay, since a "feminine" man would be more likely to indulge in too much sex with women rather than exclusively, or even primarily, with men.

WHAT IS HOMOSEXUALITY?

There is one more reason "homosexual" is a poor word choice. The word is confusing and comes with baggage. Even though I'm immersed in studying these subjects, I'm not always sure what people mean when they use the word "homosexual" or "homosexuality."

Are they talking about a behavior, an ideology, an identity, or a sexual orientation? Does the word "homosexuality" refer to a way of thinking about sexuality? Is it a way of acting? Is it a propensity? Is anyone who has sex with someone of the same sex a homosexual? What if a straight person experiments sexually? Is that homosexuality? What if a straight man rapes another straight man? What if a straight man is a pedophile who rapes boys? Calling all this behavior "homosexuality" seems to put the blame for sinful heterosexuals on the already burdened shoulders of gay and bisexual people.

More to the point, what if the men in Sodom were primarily attracted to women for sex, as most of them certainly were? Many conservative Christians would say that the point is that they committed homosexual acts. Yet when we hear the word "homosexual," we don't think of heterosexuals; we think of gay and bisexual people.

Gay and bisexual people are often called homosexuals in some circles, mainly in conservative Christian churches. Technically, we could talk about heterosexuals having homosexual sex or homosexuals having heterosexual sex. It's very confusing. The word changes its basic meaning based on whether it's a noun or an adjective. Still, no one can help thinking about homosexual people when they talk about homosexual sex.

All this obscures the reality that even today, not everyone who has sex with the same gender is gay or bisexual. Heterosexuals have sex with people of the same gender for different reasons. Some might be experimenting. Some might be addicted to sex and seeking a new rush.[129] Some might be sexually dominating, as happens often in prisons and during war.

It's also true that not everyone who is gay or bisexual has sex with the same gender. Gay people remain celibate. Gay people marry and have sex exclusively with someone of the opposite sex. Gay people may not have sex at all because they don't want to, are called to celibacy, or are single and waiting for marriage. Serious misunderstandings are happening, and the choice of language makes it worse.

Because the word "homosexual" is confusing, it seems like the biblical discussion is about gay and bisexual people, but it's not. It also makes it seem like being gay or bisexual is about who you do or don't have sex with, and it's not. A person is gay, bisexual, or straight, whether or not they have sex. This is accepted and understood within the LGBTQ community. Sexual acts and sexual identity are different categories. Using the word "homosexual" makes this unclear. It makes it very difficult to know what and who we are talking about.

It's also spiritually dangerous for straight people because it makes it seem like this category of sin is about people totally different from themselves. When Sodom and Gomorrah are associated with LGBTQ people, heterosexuals get a pass. They may also get a sense of superiority, thinking that these verses are about gay people and not about them. This is despite the fact that the events of Genesis 19 were committed entirely or primarily by people we would call straight.

Another example, Romans 1:24-27, is assumed to be about gay and bisexual people, but nothing in the passage warrants such an assumption. Only the belief that homosexual acts are only committed by homosexual people would support this belief. But it's not true, particularly in Rome. That in itself is incredibly confusing when we talk about these topics.

There's another reason not to use the word "homosexual": for readers who don't know already, those of us in the LGBTQ community rarely refer to ourselves as homosexual. This is particularly true of younger generations. The use of "homosexual" often comes across as pejorative. The word isn't only unclear, but it usually signals that someone is either connected to older terminology because of their age, because they are unfamiliar with the discussion, or because they are unconcerned with using respectful language.

This is another layer to the problem of this translation. The choice of the word "homosexual" by translators in 1946 was a choice[130] that confused the meaning of Scripture. It made it harder, not easier, to understand the subject. It also made meaningful conversation more difficult.

Conservative churches can do better. Applying ancient words to modern contexts can be challenging, but it's even more complicated on this topic. The language is quite different and the cultures even more so; simplifying it down to the word "homosexual" causes confusion and damage.

FINAL THOUGHTS AND SUMMARY

Paul uses two Greek words in 1 Corinthians 6:9, and one is repeated in 1 Timothy 1:10. These words only came to be understood as "homosexuality" in 1946. Before that, there was little to no conversation on the topic in Christian churches.

We aren't sure what one of these Greek words means because it's not used anywhere else. If it refers to sex, it could refer to Leviticus 18 and 20, which are about shaming others through domination, but there is no certainty that it refers to anything sexual.

The second Greek word Paul uses may be related to the first word, and we know the meaning of the second word. The closest English word we have is "feminine," which would mean Paul is saying it/is wrong to be feminine. But this meaning is deeply rooted in Roman culture and particularly attached to the devaluation of women and cultural values of power and shame. It doesn't mean the same thing that "feminine" means to us. Also, at other times, Paul flatly contradicted these ideas and acted in ways that would have been considered "feminine" to Romans, such as allowing himself to be beaten and imprisoned. Paul's audience would have understood what aspects of this word Paul meant to condemn, such as moral weakness, extravagant living, and lack of self-control. It certainly doesn't refer to a person being gay, since a "feminine" man would be more likely to have sex with lots of women rather than exclusively, or even primarily, with men.

Anytime the Bible is translated, some factors must be considered and understood: the original text, translation challenges, the culture of the Bible, and its moral concerns. The meaning our culture places on a word might be different from the meaning of a similar word in a different culture.

The team that translated the Revised Standard Version of the Bible in 1946 was not equipped for that process. They paid inadequate attention to the original text. But the text itself is also complicated to translate. They haphazardly applied information from Paul's culture, but they also mistranslated because they didn't understand the modern question or modern awareness. They used "homosexuals," a word with enormous implications that they didn't seem to consider. They had no malice, but it still caused harm and misunderstanding. It's a cautionary tale for all of us.

So, when someone asks why gay and bisexual people get a pass in dealing with our sin, my answer is that we don't. We are called to the same virtues that heterosexuals are called to. We are called to a standard just as high. It's only that not being "homosexual" or not acting like a "homosexual" is not one of those standards. "Homosexual" is a modern word, and it doesn't fit the words of Paul.

A lot more goes into the words of 1 Corinthians 6:9-11 and 1 Timothy 1:8-11 than we realize. Maybe the word "homosexuality" never should have appeared in the Bible. But it's not the only thing Paul said on the subject. What about Romans 1? We might think Romans 1 isn't so open to scrutiny about translation. We are right. Translation doesn't play much of a role in Romans 1 when Paul criticizes men who "burned in their lust for one another." This is the text we turn to next.

CHAPTER 11

"Unnatural Exchange"

> "Paul singles out homosexual intercourse for special attention because he regards it as providing a particularly graphic image of the way in which human fallenness distorts God's created order."[131]

> "Romans 1, especially verses 24-28, contains the most frightening lines in Scripture to anyone struggling in sexual sin."

The second quote is from Rosaria Champagne Butterfield, who describes herself as previously lesbian until converting to Christianity. She believes, as many believe, that in Romans 1 they have a smoking gun. If nowhere else, here we have the clarity we have been looking for in the Bible, Romans 1:24-27:

Therefore God also gave them up to uncleanness, in the lusts of their hearts, to dishonor their bodies among themselves, who exchanged the truth of God for a lie, and worshiped and served the creature rather than the Creator, who is blessed forever. Amen. For this reason God gave them up to vile passions. For even their women exchanged the natural use for what is against nature. Likewise also the men, leaving the natural use of the woman, burned in their lust for one another, men with men committing what is shameful, and receiving in themselves the penalty of their error which was due.

Romans 1 is different than other texts for several reasons.

- It's in the New Testament, and therefore more relevant and applicable than texts in the Old Testament.
- Unlike other texts, this one isn't about rape but seems to indicate mutual desire and consent.
- Paul's objection seems to be specifically related to the fact that they are of the same gender, or at a minimum, his objection seems intensified because they are the same gender.
- It includes not only men but women who "exchanged natural relations for those that are contrary to nature."
- There is more context for this verse than for any other. It isn't part of a list or a one-liner, so we know more about what the author is saying and why.
- Creation is mentioned immediately before sexual behavior described as "against nature," meaning men who "burn with lust for one another." This could mean that Paul links same-sex eroticism to a violation of God's creation order from Genesis 1 and 2.

These points lead to the central point: *Romans 1 is a universal prohibition of same-sex sex in any context.* The accepted theology is that this text is not about rape or exploitation. It is about unchanging biblical principles that are applicable in all circumstances. It is universal.

The argument for universality is made in a couple different ways. This chapter will talk about how Romans 1 is (or is not) connected to creation, either through direct reference to Genesis 1 and 2 or through the idea of what is "natural" according to God's creation. Connecting Romans 1 to the Creation account in Genesis 1 and 2 is perhaps centrally important to many Adventists. They believe Paul is accusing these Gentiles of ignoring the creation of men and women for sexual union.

Creation as a topic shows up right before the discussion of sexuality. There is no direct quote from Genesis 1 and 2, but that isn't necessary to show a connection. Scripture often alludes to other passages through shared words and ideas, but not a direct quote. Here's a statement from the Seventh-day Adventist Theological Seminary at Andrews University:

Paul begins by referencing the "creation of the world," and the power and divinity of God seen through "what has been made," but then reflects how the story has changed. Humans now remake the glory of God into an "image" and "likeness" of "corruptible man," as well as of "birds," "animals," and "creeping" things. The human then ends up worshiping these very creatures that humans were meant to have dominion over and abandons the natural use of the "male" and the "female." The inversion is complete. Instead of having dominion over the beasts, humans now worship and serve "the creature rather than the Creator." They remake the image of God, in which both male and female were fashioned, into an intensification of either masculinity or femininity (Rom. 1:20–25).[132]

They believe that in referencing creation, Paul is referring to that which cannot change. Paul is speaking of the violation of the inviolable nature of sex as God intended it, namely sex between a man and a woman. This is the sin of the Gentiles, the reason they need grace. They violate gender norms.

Yet others emphasize a different take on this passage, even those who believe the accepted theology. Paul identifies the original problem not as ignoring the *order* of creation but ignoring the *fact* of a Creator. Gentiles failed to recognize the primary revelation of creation, namely that there is a creation and therefore a Creator. The problem is not that they didn't follow the order of creation in Genesis 1 and 2, but that they failed to look around them at the world and acknowledge a creator existed. So, they failed to worship the Creator and instead worshiped creation itself.

However, they add that Paul is still concerned with God's creation. They believe Paul's use of the word "natural" refers to what the Gentiles should have understood about how God created male and female for sexual union. They say that Paul was referring to what is natural in human anatomy as an indication of the will of God.

A third argument made by accepted theology is that Paul's words must apply to same-sex marriage today because Paul addressed in his day was like same-sex marriage today. They say that ancient Rome included practices similar enough to today's practice of same-sex marriage to be relevant.

Addressing all of these challenges is too much for one chapter. There is too much crucial information to share about Romans 1:24-27. So, this chapter and the next will both address Romans 1:24-27. By the time we finish, we'll have learned not only about this passage but about the structure of the letter to the Romans and Roman culture.

My burden is to show that these words were not a result of the creation of Adam and Eve, did not reflect a biological moral imperative, and (in the next chapter) were not a response to same-sex covenant relationships in Rome. I want to share why I don't believe these texts refer to Genesis 1 and 2, nor does

Paul use the word "natural" to indicate a biological imperative rooted in creation. We'll look at that in this chapter.

In the next chapter, we'll get into Roman culture. What was Paul communicating? What problematic behavior was Paul referencing in Roman culture? This is the chapter where I'll share my beliefs about Paul's moral concern, which is something Paul says directly in his own words.

EXCHANGES

Thomas Shepherd is an Adventist scholar who emphasizes the fact of creation, not the order of creation. He was one of my theology professors during my four years of undergraduate theology education at Union College. He is very good at what he does. My friends and I agreed that we learned the most in his classes. It wasn't surprising that he later was hired by the Seventh-day Adventist Theological Seminary, where he became my professor once more.

Shepherd is hard to forget. He's a somewhat short man who brims with focused energy—an intellectual force. He thrills with the drama and characters of the biblical text, explaining the nuance of the Greek text (which he reads fluently) with theatrical flair. During one class, he acted out the Greek genitive case meaning that Nicodemus came to Jesus not just during the night, but by night, as if clothed in darkness. Then, pretending to be Nicodemus, he acted out the motion of covering himself with a cape and hustled along, yelling, "By night!"

Speaking of flair, he always wears a bow tie; it's part of him. He's the kind of guy who goes all in with passion, intellect, and imagination. It's a unique combination. When it comes to the text, he is clear, precise, and detailed. As a scholar, he's made significant contributions.

Recently I saw him on the Three Angels' Broadcasting Network (3ABN),[133] and though I wouldn't usually quote a television interview, it's too good not to include in the discussion, and try as I might, I couldn't find a paper he'd written on the subject. It serves as a great starting point, so I'd like to summarize Dr. Shepherd's insights:

Paul structures this passage by speaking of "exchanges" that take place. In the first exchange, the Romans in chapter 1 are subject to God's wrath because they have disregarded what they know of God through observing God's creation. It's not disregarding what they know from Scripture, but of what they should know from "the things that are made" (verse 20). That disregard leads to an exchange of the worship of God for the worship of idols.

In the second exchange, because they have made this exchange of worship, they are given up to "uncleanness, in the lust of their hearts" (verse 24) and have "vile passions" (verse 26). As a result of these passions, they exchanged natural sex for unnatural sex.

In the final exchange, God gives them over to a "debased mind" (verse 28). From this mind follow all manner of destructive and selfish behaviors. It all culminates in the final indictment: "knowing the righteous judgment of God, that those who practice such things are deserving of death, [they] not only do the same but also approve of those who practice them" (verse 32).

Our question focuses on the second exchange of natural for unnatural sex. We need to understand Paul's meaning of the word "unnatural." How does this word contribute to his moral reasoning? Shepherd believes Paul is referring to biological processes. He refers to Romans 11:21, in which the natural branch came with the tree through normal growth. The branch that is grafted in is unnatural.

"Natural," in reference to sex, according to Shepherd's thinking, has to do with sexual organs naturally fitting together. This is the usual way of things. The organs fit, and this is how we achieve human reproduction. This is how God created things in Genesis. Just as nature revealed that God should be worshiped, it revealed that sex is between a man and a woman.

CONTEXT

Shepherd has provided an excellent outline of Romans 1. The knowledge of the Creator was evident to the Romans. They should have known to worship God. Instead, they chose ignorance and exchanged worship of the Creator for the worship of creation. This exchange led to a debased mind, which led to exchanging natural sex for sex against nature. This leads to all kinds of immorality. Let's back up and understand the surrounding chapters, because Paul is making a brilliant rhetorical argument for the universal need for the gospel.

Paul had never been to Rome. Paul preached Christ and the gospel everywhere he went, but he'd never had the chance to do so in Rome. So, in this letter, he explains the gospel to the Romans more fully than in any other place in Scripture. The Roman church had both Roman and Jewish members. In larger society, these groups were antagonistic and critical of each other. It wasn't always easy to bring them together in churches, especially since Jewish Christians had recently returned from a time of political exile. They were trying to reintegrate and learn to worship together again. It wasn't easy.

Paul plays up this tension to later undermine it. He begins using the third person to talk about the Romans, as if he's sliding in beside the Jews and criticizing the lawless Gentiles. All the while, the Romans must listen. You may wonder why Paul says "Greeks" instead of "Romans" in a letter to Rome. The reason is self-preservation. He could have gotten into big trouble for criticizing Rome or Romans. His audience knew what he meant.

Jews believed that they were superior to Gentiles, both Roman and Greek, because they were the recipients of the law and oracles of God. They never worshiped idols. They lived in harmony with God's will—at least they tried. Paul plays into their sense of superiority.

And what sins do Gentiles embrace? They are a parable of wickedness revealing the wrath of God. Not recognizing God leads to idol worship. Idol worship leads to unnatural and destructive sexual desires and practices. Unnatural sexuality leads to all manner of wickedness, a total breakdown. It's just the kind of indictment of Gentiles for which the Jewish people were known.

Paul's criticism of Roman sexual behavior is a transparent allusion to a contemporary Jewish book called *Wisdom of Solomon*.[134] Paul's accusations were a well-known trope and a compelling one. Romans felt the shame of it. Jews felt superior. Paul went for the jugular.

Only after thoroughly arguing for the sinfulness of Gentiles does Paul turn the tables. Jewish Christians were listening with a sense of superiority, but then Paul switched to the second person and directly called them on their hypocrisy.

> You who make your boast in the law, do you dishonor God through breaking the law?
> For, "the name of God is blasphemed among the Gentiles because of you," as it is written
> (Rom. 2:23, 24).

Paul wanted the Jews nodding along in chapter 1, feeling self-satisfied and superior, only to be told in chapter 2 that they are no better. Jews and Gentiles are on level ground, all in need of the grace of God.

Finally, Paul made the point we have all been waiting for: "All have sinned and fall short of the glory of God, being justified freely by His grace through the redemption that is in Christ Jesus" (Rom. 3:23, 24).

This was the point of all Paul's words. He identified the sins of the Romans in chapter 1, so they would see their need for salvation. Then came the sins of the Jewish people in chapter 2. The point is that neither being Roman nor being Jewish saves us.

IDOLATRY

Is the sin of the Romans their failure to heed the lessons of God's created order of male and female? Is he coming down on them for ignoring what they know from Genesis 1 and 2, that God created Adam and Eve?

The parallels Paul draws between Roman and Jewish Christians continue throughout the letter. An important one is that the Romans don't have the law, and the Jews do (Rom. 2:17, 18; 3:1, 2; 9:4.). Paul is showing in Romans 1 that Gentiles are "without excuse" (Rom. 1:20), even though they are "Gentiles, who do not have the law" (Rom. 2:14). They are accountable because of what is "understood by the things that are made" (Rom. 1:20). So, their problem cannot be violating the law of God or ignoring information about how God created our genders. They don't have this information.

Since Romans generally didn't have access to the Bible, it's not the Bible that makes them accountable. The fact of creation makes them accountable, not the biblical account of creation but the fact of creation and a Creator.

Yet, I can imagine someone objecting. Couldn't it be that they are accountable for what creation reveals about gender? Maybe Paul was saying that the Romans should have looked at creation and recognized that sex is intended for male and female couples, and not same-sex couples? That would certainly be a possibility except for one thing. Paul was explicit about what lesson they were supposed to take from nature.

"For since the creation of the world His invisible attributes are clearly seen, being understood by the things that are made, even His eternal power and Godhead [or divinity], so that they are without excuse" (Rom. 1:20). We aren't left to guess about the content of the revelation from creation. There isn't space to speculate on Paul's unstated assumptions. We are told what they should have known. God's "eternal power and Godhead" is revealed (verse 20). There is a God who made the world.

This is the information that was supposed to lead them to worship God. Instead, they "changed the glory of the incorruptible God into an image" (Rom. 1:23). Such imagery is familiar in the Hebrew Bible. In Isaiah we read: "I am the Lord, that is My name; I will not give My glory to another, nor My praise to idols" (Isa. 42:8, NASB). The psalmist echoes this sentiment: "They made a calf in Horeb, and worshiped the molded image. Thus they changed their glory into the image of an ox that eats grass" (Ps. 106:19, 20).

Paul isn't referring to Genesis 1 and 2. He isn't referring to gender, either. His Jewish listeners would recognize a common theme about idolatry in the Hebrew

Bible: the glory of God is exchanged for idols. Paul's indictment of unnatural sex also follows this Hebrew understanding of idolatry. Infidelity toward God leads to infidelity toward one another in destructive sexual behavior (Ex. 32; 1 Kings 14:24; Isa. 57; Jer. 2; 11; Ezek. 16:20-34; 23; Hosea 4:12-14; 1 Cor. 6:9-11: Gal. 5:19-21; Eph. 5:5; Col. 3:5; Rev. 2:14, 20, 21:25). Denial of creation leads to sexual immorality.

This unraveling begins but doesn't end with destructive sexual behavior. The Prophets are full of descriptions of how this primary failure to honor God as Creator spreads. There is a broader breakdown of our duties to care for and love one another (see Isa. 1:15-18; 46:6, 7; Jer. 7:5-7; 10:1-25; Amos 5:10-12; Rev. 18:2, 3). Paul also describes this in Romans 1:28-32.

Infidelity to God leads to infidelity to our spouses, which leads to infidelity to others. This is the message the Hebrew Bible sends about the nature of idolatry. This is the same message that's echoed in Romans 1. It's the unfolding of a predictable process, not a failure of the Romans to follow Scripture.

Since their idolatry led to their unnatural sex, how does this apply to gay Christians? How does this apply to bisexual Adventists raised in the church? What about those who have never been interested in the worship of idols?

Shepherd believes that these words apply to today's gay, bisexual, and transgender Adventists. We still have idolatry today; it just comes in different forms. There are other ways we place things before God in our lives, which also fits into Paul's description of idolatry. Therefore, the idolatry in Romans 1 doesn't only mean the actual worship of idols.[135]

I must admit to being confused by his reasoning. Here is what Paul said:

> Professing to be wise, they became fools, and changed the glory of the incorruptible God into an image made like corruptible man—and birds and four-footed animals and creeping things" (Rom. 1:22, 23).

These words don't describe someone who struggles with placing God first in their life. These words aren't about trusting relationships, achievement, or self-reliance rather than trusting God. These words are about people who made physical images of animals, then worshiped them as their gods. Nothing in Paul's language, the context of the passage, or the historical context indicates that he meant this in a metaphorical sense.

In fact, the context negates the idea that Paul was speaking of metaphorical idolatry. The whole point is to catch Jewish Christians feeling superior because they don't worship idols. Surely Jewish people struggled to keep God first and foremost in their lives at times, just as we do. But that's not what Paul was referring to, or his argument wouldn't work. He's talking about actual, literal idolatry. It's clear from the language and context. This approach raises another question: Why view verses 22 and 23 in such a flexible manner but be rigid with verses 26 and 27?

UNNATURAL

Does this change the substance of what Paul said? Paul calls sex between men unnatural and those who engage in it shameless. Maybe the context changes, but undoubtedly this aspect of his meaning would remain.

> God gave them up to vile passions. For even their women exchanged the natural use for what is against nature. Likewise also the men, leaving the natural use of the women, burned in their lust for one another, men with men committing what is shameful [indecent] (Rom 1:26, 27).

The two words with particular meaning are natural (Greek: *phusis*) and dishonorable/shameless (Greek: *atimias*). This is about what is natural and honorable versus that which is unnatural and dishonorable. Paul's use of the word "natural" has led many to conclude that he is speaking about creation, or something revealed through nature and immutable, like the suitability of male and female anatomy to produce children.

I agree with Shepherd and others who say "unnatural" is not referring to sexual orientation. Paul's point is not that homoeroticism is wrong for straight people because it's unnatural for them, but it would be natural for gay and bisexual people. That kind of reading is out of step with Paul's culture. That's what the words might have meant in our culture, but natural and unnatural had a different meaning in Paul's day.

That's because Paul's culture didn't conceptualize sexual orientation the way we do. They didn't believe some people would naturally fall in love with their same gender and be suited best for partnership with their same gender.[136] If Paul spoke to a culture like ours, and to people in the heterosexual and LGBTQ communities today, we might imagine that he intended for his words to apply to straight people for whom same-sex sex is unnatural. But he wasn't.

I also take issue with an understanding, which Shepherd and the seminary support, that *phusis* is a Jewish idea about how God created the world. The word *phusis* doesn't show up even once in the Septuagint (the Greek translation of the Hebrew Bible). Not once is it used in dozens of biblical books spanning hundreds of pages.

Neither is it of much importance to New Testament writers. When they want to speak about creation, they use words such as "creation" and "creatures," which are common. Paul even uses "creature" in Romans 1:25 when referring to God's Creation. In contrast, the word *phusis* never refers to God's creation of the world, not once.

The word *phusis* does show up a few times in the New Testament.[137] Nearly all the examples are in the writings of Paul. Shepherd used Roman 11:24 to define *phusis*.[138]

> For if you were cut out of the olive tree, which is wild by nature, and were grafted contrary to nature into a cultivated olive tree, how much more will these, who are natural branches, be grafted into their own olive tree?

Shepherd said that this instance of *phusis* represents God's creation, how God created the world. Therefore, Shepherd believes Paul uses *phusis* the same way in Romans 1. The Romans are against nature because their sex defies how we are created, our biology as men and women, because the sexual organs don't match properly.

But Paul is saying here that there are two olive trees. One of those trees is cultivated, the other wild. Judaism is cultivated because God uniquely watched over Israel and gave them the Law and Prophets. Greeks are wild because they received no such instruction. This isn't a difference in creation but cultivation. It's not about how God makes olive trees; it's about whether they were watched over and tended or left wild.

To graft a wild branch onto a cultivated tree isn't unnatural because they are different categories in their being or creation, like men and women. It's unnatural because it's a strange thing to do. Why remove a branch that has been selected and bred for productivity only to replace it with a wild branch? It's counterproductive. The wild branch won't produce as many olives. But God did it out of grace and love for Gentiles. Paul's telling Gentiles to be humble because they are late to the game. God has been cultivating Israel for centuries.

God didn't create Jews and Gentiles to be separate by nature. We all share a common creation but are divided by history. The differentiating factor in the olive trees is whether they were cultivated, not how they were created. So, this example does not demonstrate that "natural" means living out the biological reality of our creation.

In this example, the word *phusis* also was not a moral category. God acted against nature, grafting a wild branch into a cultivated tree. Not only is there no reference to creation, there is no reference to morality. God acts against *phusis*, which means that in this case acting against nature is morally good.

If we want to build the argument, as Shephard does, that male/male or female/female sex is wrong because the sex organs don't fit, this is the worst possible text to use for support. God specifically and intentionally did something unnatural by placing together two things that don't fit: cultivated trees and uncultivated branches.

In this text, being unnatural is not inherently wrong. Nor is unnatural a concept rooted in God's creation intent. They are both olive trees, so they do grow together when grafted. It's just an unnatural thing to do. It goes against what seems like the right decision, what seems natural and expected behavior.

PARALLEL USES OF "NATURAL"

A couple other uses of the word natural, translated from *phusis*, are relevant to our text. The first is Romans 2:12-15, one of my favorite texts in the Bible because it shows that God's grace is bigger than religion. God works on the hearts of all people, even those who don't know God by name.

> For as many as have sinned without law will also perish without the law, and as many as have sinned in the law will be judged by the law (for not the hearers of the law are just in the sight of God, but the doers of the law will be justified; for when Gentiles, who do not have the law, *by nature* do the things in the law, these, although not having the law, are a law to themselves, who show the work of the law written in their hearts, their conscience also bearing witness, and between themselves their thoughts accusing or else excusing them).[139]

In Romans 1, Paul spoke in detail about the sins of the Gentiles. He later brought balance to those statements. Being a Gentile didn't equate to being forsaken by God, even before they came to know about Jesus and the Hebrew Bible. I can only imagine the relief Gentile Christians would have felt at these words as they thought about good people they knew who had died before having a chance to learn about Jesus. It turns out there always was a path for them to follow God.

This passage connects with Romans 1 on several points. In Romans 1, "their foolish hearts were darkened" (verse 21), which led to "the lusts of their hearts" (verse 24). But in Romans 2, Gentiles "show the work of the law written in their hearts" (verse 15).

The state of the heart precedes behavior. In Romans 1, Gentiles violate what they should have naturally known, engaging in idolatry, which led to darkened and lustful hearts. Unnatural sexual practices followed these desires. Then at the end of the chapter, they fell into all kinds of sins against one another.

By contrast, the Gentiles did "by nature" the works of the law. They didn't have the Hebrew Bible, but they still did what was right. What was this law they followed intuitively? It must have been a natural sense, a conscience.

The fallen Gentiles are without excuse because they should have known better. Their conscience should have led them as it led the Gentiles in Romans 2. Because of this natural sense of right and wrong, even those without the Bible are accountable. They can't give the excuse, "I didn't have the Bible to tell me what was right and wrong." They are without excuse.

Now we are getting to the heart of it. The Gentiles in Romans 1 should have felt shame. Idolatry should have pricked their conscience. They should have seen how their idolatry insulted their Creator.

Doesn't this mean, by the same token, that they should have seen that men were not made for sex with other men? Since Paul was speaking about their conscience, must he be referencing right and wrong?

He was speaking of right and wrong, but not only in an absolute sense but also in the sense of what they understood despite not having the Bible. To say that "nature" refers to the conscience is to say that it is not a direct reference to creation or biology, but it does still reference morality. We must pay attention to what moral arguments Paul was making. What is the behavior, and why does Paul say it's wrong? What connection does that have to the questions we ask today? We can't simply read into the text a biological reason if it's not stated in the text or alluded to in any way. We should understand what they were doing and why Paul said it was wrong.

We shouldn't quickly and uncritically apply those behaviors to gay and bisexual people who want to marry someone of the same gender. Why not? Because when we apply the same standard to demonstrably different situations, we can end up with opposite results, results that have nothing to do with the concerns of the original passage of Scripture. Consider another passage to illustrate this principle.

SISTER CHAPTERS

We must consider one more use of the word natural. This text uses *phusis* in a context and with a meaning strikingly similar to what Paul has to say in Romans 1:24-28. Here are the similarities:

- Paul is also the author of both texts.
- Both speak of natural (*phusis*) in the context of gender-conditioned behaviors.
- In both passages, the concepts of shame and honor are central.
- Both refer to creation in nearby verses.

> But I want you to know that the head of every man is Christ, the head of woman is man, and the head of Christ is God. Every man praying or prophesying, having his head covered, dishonors his head. But every woman who prays or prophesies with her head uncovered dishonors her head, for that is one and the same as if her head were shaved. For if a woman is not covered, let her also be shorn. But if it is shameful for a woman to be shorn or shaved, let her be covered. . . . Does not nature itself teach you that if a man wears long hair it is a disgrace for him, but if a woman has long hair, it is her glory? For her hair is given to her for a covering (1 Cor. 11:3-6, 14, 15).

Not many of us would be willing to enforce this rule in our church services this Sabbath. Yes, Paul thought the church in Corinth should have known better. Yes, he thought they were behaving disgracefully and unnaturally. He says so directly. Yet when we ask whether Paul believed this unnatural behavior was always wrong, we must conclude that his answer would be no, or we must enforce an uncomfortable code on our church members.

William Loader has published multiple books on New Testament sexuality and contemporary Jewish ideas about sexuality. He is personally affirming but believes Paul did have a moral objection to same-sex sex in Romans 1, and that it was based on something similar enough to modern ideas about sexual orientation to be relevant. He is often quoted by those who oppose same-sex marriage.

But Loader also believes that Paul had a moral point based on creation that he was making in 1 Corinthians 11. Paul thought men must have short hair and women must have long hair and/or a covering. Loader believes that Paul didn't think this was cultural but taught these gender norms as moral. He then appeals to the broader messages and values of Scripture in both cases. He is consistent. He uses the same approach to interpret both passages because they are so similar.[140]

I haven't seen such consistency in accepted theology. If we are consistent students of the Bible, what should we do? There are some differences between the two passages, but the similarities are too striking to ignore. Paul speaks in such similar terms that it seems inconsistent to say that one passage *must not* apply to us in its plain meaning and the other *must* apply in its plain meaning.

How can anyone justify interpreting these passages in different ways? (1) We might look for differences between the two passages[141] and ignore the crucial similarities. (2) We might ignore the parallel entirely and just not mention 1 Corinthians 11. (3) We might project our morality on the Bible, uncritically following our own moral intuition. If we feel that it's not a big deal for women to cut their hair, we dismiss it. If we feel that same-sex sex is a problem, we keep it.

These approaches are unsatisfying. They don't respect the authority of Scripture. They don't help us with Romans 1. But there is another option.

Paul spoke of an unnatural, disgraceful gender violation in two passages. At a minimum, this should give us pause before confidently concluding that anytime Paul uses words such as unnatural and disgraceful, he is talking about moral absolutes rooted in creation that apply to all people, times, and situations. It gives us reason to believe he might be speaking of behaviors with cultural implications. If he is, we must have solid reasons for stating otherwise, reasons that come from the text and context, not our own suppositions.

However we interpret these passages, I hope we use the same rule for both. We shouldn't change the rules at halftime. If we do, we aren't listening to Scripture. We're using selective applications to support our views, even when we're unaware we're doing so. Sadly, it's easy for us to dismiss some passages and universally apply others without good reasons, or without even realizing what we're doing. We need to be diligent and prayerful.

From 1 Corinthians 11, we learn that something can be unnatural in one context and perfectly natural in another. Something that might prick the conscience of someone in the ancient world, like a woman with short hair or a man with long hair, might be perfectly acceptable today. That's because the same action can make different statements in different contexts, and the purposes behind those actions can change. The meaning behind an action can change over time.

That's why it's so important to pay attention not only to the specifics but to the reasons for them. We implicitly understand this when it comes to many passages of Scripture. Most of us have never wrestled with whether we should police hair length in our churches. It's hard to consistently keep the context in mind for all passages, even controversial ones, or even passages in which we might be tempted to follow our own intuition and not dig deeper.

Remember, we can be conservative and still believe that women don't have to wear head coverings. We can take the Bible seriously and say it's not unnatural and shameful for women to have short hair or men to have long hair. We don't take the Bible any less seriously if we say that the connection between creation and these rules about hair doesn't mean these rules are universal mandates for all times and places. Conservatives already consider culture when interpreting a passage like 1 Corinthians 11, in which creation is linked to gendered behavior that is shameful and unnatural.

This approach doesn't dismiss the Bible; it takes it seriously. It's not respectful to take Paul's words out of context. It's not faithful to avoid the difficult work of sifting, working, and prayerfully discerning the meaning of Scripture. All I'm asking is for the same consideration in Romans 1.

SUMMARY AND MOVING FORWARD

I hope that I've demonstrated that Paul's reason for speaking of creation was not to bring to mind the specific *order* of creation, but the *fact* of a Creator. Paul was following a long prophetic tradition from the Hebrew Bible. The prophets taught that idolatry is unfaithfulness to God and can be compared to lusting after other gods. This, in turn, leads to giving oneself over to sexual lust. The ultimate result is a breakdown of human compassion as relationships devolve into exploitation.

Further, had God held the Romans accountable to the *order* of creation and gender, they would have had an excuse. They could have said that God never gave them the Bible, and they were being held accountable to rules they never knew about. That's why Paul pointedly emphasizes that they were responsible for that which was revealed through creation, and he explains precisely what they should have known. They should have known based on what was made, not based on Scripture, that God is Creator and alone worthy of worship.

Neither does the word natural refer to creation. It's never used this way either in the Greek Old Testament or in the New Testament. Neither is natural a word always imbued with moral weight, since God himself violates what is natural in Romans 11. Instead, natural is what one knows naturally, what makes sense. In the context of Romans 1, it's what the conscience says. This is clarified further in Romans 2:12-15. Natural is about personal conviction, whether or not we behave in ways we know to be good and right.

The specific manifestations of these things can change over time. This might be hard to acknowledge for Romans 1, but we already readily accept this for other passages. In 1 Corinthians 11, women were required to wear head coverings, women couldn't cut their hair short, and men couldn't grow their hair long. These behaviors were called unnatural and shameful and were linked to creation.

This passage demonstrates why it's essential to pay attention not only to the specifics but to the reasons for them. Violating social norms about hair and hair coverings might not have been a problem in itself, but if it showed that the church didn't care about offending the rest of society and would just as quickly behave shamefully concerning social norms, then it would be a manifestation of a deeper problem, an impediment to the gospel commission.

Nothing in this passage makes us think that the application is universal. There is no rational pronouncement related to the original creation. There is no statement about biological imperatives related to reproduction. Therefore, we should remain open to the possibility that context could teach us something crucial.

In the next chapter, we will find that Paul makes his moral reasoning plain in Romans 1:24-27. He tells us forcefully what was wrong with same-sex erotic behavior. As we look at Roman society, we'll also see why the particular same-sex behaviors Paul describes fit this moral reasoning.

CHAPTER 12

Paul, the Romans, and Lust

"The Greeks and Romans had open sexual practices. They had gay relationships that were totally accepted and normal in their society. They spoke about
men loving each other. There weren't a lot of rules. It was sexually open."

"We do have examples in the ancient world of loving, committed homosexual
relationships. Sometimes people want to say, 'They didn't have any of that, so
that doesn't' apply to us today, because they didn't have those experiences.' No,
they actually did, and it assumes much to assume that the apostle Paul had
no knowledge of that or any understanding of what was going on among the
Gentiles. He did."[142]

Roman sexuality brings to mind corrupt emperors luxuriating in sexual depravity among columns of marble and the trappings of empire. It recalls explicit
murals on the walls in Pompeii, sexual liaisons of every kind frozen in time
in ashy graves. Guided by these images, we tend to think of ancient Rome in
terms of sexual liberty taken to the extreme. Anything goes. There are no rules.

Wikipedia tells us that same-sex marriage was accepted, citing Nero's alleged marriage to a young man. Wouldn't it be possible for a gay person to live however they wanted in such a culture?

These popular images and impressions dominate Hollywood's portrayal of Rome. They feed our own sexual imagination, so they're good for turning a profit—and they are not without historical documentation. The murals in Pompeii are real. There are ancient descriptions of Roman emperors that are every bit as libertine as anyone could imagine. If we go directly to original sources and read about sex in Rome, we find all this and more.

But what would someone think of our own culture if they read *50 Shades of Grey* and watched porn and *Saturday Night Live*? Would they have an accurate picture? Would they know that most Americans still value marriage and raising families? Would they accurately understand our social norms, taboos, and customs?

Context is everything. *Fifty Shades of Grey* appeals to contemporary women because it's taboo. It doesn't represent a typical dating relationship. The fascination is in the transgression, and only when we understand that can we place it in its social context. Otherwise, we might conclude that most wealthy American men have sex dens and require their girlfriends to sign non-disclosure agreements.[143]

The same is true of Greco-Roman writing. Comedians back then, like comedians today, mocked those in power with outrageous jokes and fabrications about their sexual affairs. The murals in Pompeii were in the dressing rooms, and historians believe they are humorous depictions designed to ease the nerves of people about to get naked in public.

Most important, the fabrication of imperial sexual scandal was a political tool. Scandals threatened the rule of an emperor, or they might help the new emperor trash the last guy to solidify his power. Historians believe the tales of debauched Roman emperors are embellished, if not false. They tell us what Romans despised, not what they enjoyed.

Our modern embellishments of these embellished stories are even worse. Nero didn't marry a young man, as a Wikipedia author alleged. He's said to have castrated an enslaved boy and forced the boy to pledge himself as a permanent sex slave. That's the story anyway. But it's probably ancient propaganda, not history.

To understand Paul and Romans 1, it doesn't matter whether the transgressions of the emperors were historically accurate or just old rumors. All that matters is that these behaviors were considered reprehensible by Romans, and even threatened the legitimacy of the implicated emperors. Far from examples of marriage, they were examples of people who had broken societal commitments and shown weakness of character.

All this underscores the complexity involved in grasping what happened in Rome. There's a world of difference between reading and understanding. Context is king. Unless we understand context, we could be completely wrong. Pornography is not dating advice. Political propaganda is not history. Satire is not literal. Off-color jokes don't teach societal norms. Sometimes the cultures with the most rigidity produce the most profanity in their literature.

THE MUTUALITY PROBLEM

Let me illustrate how desperately cultural context is needed. Both sides often misunderstand the question of the meaning of mutuality in Romans 1:27—they "burned in their lust for one another." This isn't the exploitation of unwilling victims. Mutuality itself was the problem. And this turns out to be a problem for both sides of the question.

First, the classic affirming argument: Paul was speaking about exploitation. Paul's words wouldn't have applied to gay and bisexual people today because he was talking about pederasty, rape, shrine prostitution, and sexual exploitation in general. Gay or bisexual Adventists who want a loving and committed marriage to someone of the same gender do not fit these depictions. They want relationships that are mutual and egalitarian, and that's why they are in different moral categories.[144]

The problem is that Paul's words seem to indicate some degree of mutuality already present. Paul says they "burned in their lust for one another" (Rom. 1:27). The language suggests mutual desire. Paul's stated moral problem wasn't domination or exploitation. Paul says they were lustful, not that they violently attacked one another.

Nor does it seem consistent to say that Paul opposed any sexual relationship where one party had power over another. Marriage, as practiced at the time, typically meant the men had authority and power over women. Men had control in religious, financial, and judicial terms. Marriage was commonly between a man and a girl, rather than a man and a woman. Brides were young. That, in part, is what maintained the uneven power dynamic in marriage.

I don't believe this was Paul's only understanding of marriage. I wouldn't even say it's the ideal for what he thought marriage could be. Yet Paul never spoke clearly and firmly against marriages without mutuality. He didn't say our relationships must be egalitarian. Are we to believe he now says the wrath of God is poured out on Gentiles because their relationships lacked mutuality? Why has he never used this strong language to condemn lack of mutuality in heterosexual marriage? This argument just doesn't work.

Second, the accepted theology argument: Paul understood that same-sex couples had loving and mutual relationships. They were committed to each other. Paul definitely would have known about these relationships because they were common at the time, and Paul was well informed.

Some argue that, in many ways, Romans thought of sexuality similarly to the way we do today. They knew about sexual orientation. Same-sex mutual relationships are precisely what Paul is condemning. That's why he used the language of mutuality.[145]

This argument doesn't hold up well under scrutiny. Recall that Paul is making a broader point about the gospel. Gentile Romans are destined for destruction and in need of the grace of God. They are without excuse. He describes them and their behavior with words like "foolish," "unclean," "vile," "dishonorable," "shameful," and "unnatural." In verses 28-32, he uses dark and derogatory language to characterize them.

In short, Paul is not pulling punches; he's coming for them. Since that's Paul's point and purpose in these verses, why would he choose mutual and non-exploitive sex as his example? It would be easy to identify the more egregious sexual sins in Roman society if I were Paul. I would have talked about how citizens could rape socially inferior people with impunity, particularly enslaved people. As Marilyn Skinner points out, "In Rome no blame was attached to the man who indulged in sex with either his own male slave or male prostitute, provided that he took the active role and that financial expenditure, if any, was kept within reasonable limits."[146]

In Rome, the very city Paul was writing to, at the exact time he was writing, a wealthy citizen could rape an enslaved boy or girl as often as he pleased. He would face no legal repercussions. He wouldn't even face social repercussions. This behavior was as expected and natural to them as taking afternoon tea.

Isn't rape much more offensive than a one-night stand? Isn't the perpetual and unending rape of a defenseless boy with the full support of society even more offensive? I shudder to think of the lives of enslaved people in Rome when Paul wrote this letter. I can't imagine trying to hold onto hope and dignity while being regularly raped by the man who has absolute power over my life in a society that believes this is perfectly acceptable.

If I were Paul, I would have pointed to this as the reason that the wrath of God was poured out on Gentiles. But Paul does point out the mutuality. From our perspective, he seems to miss the point. Paul seems to be saying that mutuality is the problem. Doesn't it seem a bit strange? Why is it that mutual same-sex erotic encounters were the ultimate sexual sin? Maybe it's because the mutuality indicates something other than mutual love.

SIFTING OPINIONS

Paul's decision makes perfect sense when we understand his culture and Rome's culture. To that end, first, we must address common misunderstandings. There is a lot of misinformation.

But how to do so? At first, understanding the cultural context of Rome seemed impossible. I turned to popular and scholarly books on the topic of sexuality and Christianity. No matter its perspective, every book I read made significant points about what happened in Greco-Roman culture. Everyone thought it was necessary for understanding the passage, but it seemed that everyone had something different to say.

This part of my study quickly became the most frustrating. Writers painted diametrically opposing pictures of Roman culture at the time Paul wrote to Christians in Rome. Some said that Paul definitely would have known about same-sex relationships that were mutual and committed, like marriages. Some went far enough to say that this was common. Others said same-sex relationships only showed up in pederasty and shrine prostitution. They say there was always exploitation.

Of course, many gave references to back up their statements. It was time consuming, but I made a practice of looking up the references. Some of them were terrible. Sometimes literature centuries removed was said to be contemporary to Paul. Many quotes were out of context or flatly contradicted in the next paragraph of the cited document. I once looked up a passage that was supposed to be about same-sex sex only to find a discussion about bestiality. This was not in a fringe book, but a popular book written by a pastor with a Ph.D. These are supposed to be trustworthy people. I felt disillusioned.

The most often quoted ancient text for those who oppose same-sex marriage comes from Plato's *Symposium*. In it, a discussion is happening between philosophers. Aristophanes tells a story about couples who always seek completion in one another, some same-sex and some opposite sex. At first blush, it sounds like the silver bullet, proof of sexual orientation in Rome, and that's how it's used. But there are multiple problems with this reference. First, Plato wrote it 400 years before Paul wrote to the believers in Rome. Second, it was from Greek culture, not Roman culture. Third, it was a joke that relied on absurdity.

The fictional monologue described ridiculous creatures with four arms, four legs, and two heads. They couldn't move quickly on their legs because of their round shape, so they ran by rolling their spherical bodies. The gods became angry and separated them, creating modern humans with two legs, two arms, and one head, longing for the missing half. Some of those couples became two men, some two women, and some a man and a woman. The other characters in Plato's *Symposium* took this monologue as a joke and treated it as absurd. Aristophanes is also treated humorously in other parts of the dialogue. He's the comic relief. The humor of the joke relied on its absurdity because it was in opposition to their values, not because it was an expression of them.

Even though this was a 400-year-old joke from a different culture, those who argue against same-sex marriage often quote Plato's *Symposium* as proof that same-sex monogamous couples were present in Rome and known to Paul. It would be the equivalent of using comic relief from Shakespeare to define twenty-first-century American sexual ethics.

Reading all these explanations left me frustrated. How could I know who to believe? How could I find a trustworthy source? So many people were confident about their conclusions but without adequate references. So, I stopped paying attention to people on either side arguing their point and turned to scholars of Greek and Roman sexuality.

To my great relief, I found scholars who weren't trying to make a theological or moral point, but simply trying to understand the culture. They explained Greek and Roman sexuality in the context of the broader culture and helped me place various genres of literature into their cultural context. It was clarifying. I found more definite answers than I expected. Relying on these scholars, I will point out a few misconceptions, then discuss what we know of the culture.

For those who want to follow up on this research, I suggest the following sources, on which I'm basing most of the information in this chapter. *Sexuality in Greek and Roman Culture* by Marilyn B. Skinner is an in-depth book that represents the latest scholarship by one of the top scholars in the field. *Roman Sexualities*, edited by Judith P. Hallett and Marilyn B. Skinner, is a bit older but is a collection of chapters by different authors that allows for a breadth of input.

As we dive into contextual information, keep in mind that there is no test to pass at the end of the chapter. This information is simply to show my work and illustrate my points. The details are for illustration, and because I find them interesting, and hope others might as well.

My point throughout this chapter is this: *The Romans had a structure for their society, and it was rigid. It applied to sex as well as to every other area of life. Those who didn't cooperate were assumed to be out of control, overcome by desire, morally compromised, and destructive to themselves and the empire. There is every indication in Roman writing, Jewish writing, and Paul's own words that this lack of self-control and destructive desire was the point of Paul's message. Paul was not talking about same-gender marriage. He was observing something in Roman culture and commenting on that behavior.*

GREECE AND ROME

First, Greek and Roman sexuality were different in meaningful ways. This is something scholars say often and prominently as a corrective to previous scholarship that tended to lump together 1,000 years of history, calling them "Greco-Roman." Distinct characteristics reflected how Greek and Roman social and political structures operated differently. This is especially true of same-sex sexual behavior, usually known in scholarly circles as homoeroticism.

There were also significant differences within Roman culture at different periods and with different governments. There were substantial differences between the Roman Republic and Imperial Rome. This historical shift happened when Julius Caesar conquered Rome and undermined the Senate. Augustus Caesar followed Julius Caesar. He brought stability to Rome as well as marriage reform mere decades before the birth of Christ.

The most pertinent example of differences between Greek and Roman culture, and within Roman culture, is the shifting attitudes and laws about pederasty. Pederasty was encouraged in Greek culture but was illegal in Roman culture during Paul's lifetime. Pederasty was a sexual mentoring relationship between an early pubescent boy and an adult male on the same social level. The men initiated boys into sex. Today we call this statutory rape. There were some significant variations in how these relationships were understood,[147] but they were seen as positive in Greek culture.

Pederasty was the most common, established, and visible form of same-sex eroticism in Greek culture. These relationships occasionally continued into adulthood, but this was frowned on. Had the New Testament been written in Plato's day, it would have been reasonable to think that Paul was referring to pederasty, the dominant form that same-sex relationships took at the time.

Yet, in first-century Rome, having sex with a social equal was taboo, and having sex with a Roman boy was a felony. It was considered "*stuprum*, a criminal sexual act."[148] This wasn't an arbitrary difference between Greek and Roman culture. It reflected systemic differences between the way Romans viewed the world, the government, and all social relationships. Sex was only one way these differences were revealed.

Greek city-states had relatively simple social structures and limited hierarchy compared to Rome. The sprawling Roman Empire that came hundreds of years later brought complex social and political challenges that were met with equally complex social and political systems. Maintaining control and managing an empire with so many people, cultures, and governments was a colossal challenge; loose social structures would never accomplish the task.

Order was maintained through complicated social hierarchies that encoded systems of violence as a natural part of life. Those at higher levels of society could violate and dominate those at lower levels with impunity but were untouchable by lower classes. Roman citizens were at the top. Conquered people, enslaved people, the poor, criminals, gladiators, actors, and other unfortunates were at the bottom. To be at the bottom was not only to be poor or lacking in influence, but to be at risk of socially sanctioned violence and exploitation. Poignant among many examples of this violence was in the brutality of the coliseums and gladiatorial games, in which the lower classes bled and died for sport.

This approach was not devoid of virtue. Citizens were supposed to gain manliness through acts of goodwill. If they gave money to the poor, built monuments, freed those they had enslaved, worshiped the gods, and refrained from beating their family members, men would gain reputation and influence. These behaviors also demonstrated manliness and virtue. It's not hard to see how this concept brought stability to their social system.

Sex was part of this system as well. Any sex act of penetration was considered domination. Sex must only take place within the established hierarchy of who dominates and who is subjugated. Sex was one of many cultural expressions of domination, indicating status and gender. A person's role in sex could permanently change the perception of their gender, whether masculine or feminine, even if the perception of the person's sex as male or female remained.

For a boy who was a Roman citizen to be dominated by anyone else would have brought life-long shame of femininity. This is why pederasty was impossible, and sex with Roman boys was criminal. Since pederasty was a socially acknowledged mentoring relationship with a sexual component, it was impossible in Rome. Such sexual relationships wouldn't help young men get ahead in life but prevent them from doing so. Behaviors that amounted to pederasty in the past were, in the Roman context, sexual shaming and domination.

Boys thus treated were not considered victims and treated with compassion; they were deemed feminized and tainted with the shame of women. They carried the stigma of weakness, foolishness, and immorality. This wasn't only a personal shame but a threat to the empire. In theory, any male citizen could rule some part of the empire, even as the emperor himself. It was unthinkable to give such a responsibility to someone weak and shameful. Since Roman male citizens were in demand for ruling the empire, they couldn't afford to ruin them through pederasty and feminization.

SEX AND MUTUALITY

Why did society respond with enduring shame for these sexual violations? Sex was one expression of the system of domination, and society depended on rigidly maintaining these power dynamics. If sex was mutual, something had gone badly wrong. It takes effort to imagine what it would be like to live in such a society:

> Every sexual act is based on the distinction between active and passive. Every sexual act encodes power relations: dominator and dominated. Each carries a burden of aggression or humiliation, power or powerlessness. The dominant ideology is the ideology of domination.[149]

Romans had strong ideas about gender, as we described in the last chapter. Grown men, especially adult male citizens, were supposed to be hard, strong, dominant, and active. They demonstrated this partly by playing the active (penetrating) sexual role, whether with a man or a woman. It was unnatural for a dominant man to play a passive role.

The sexual distinction made was not whether someone was gay or straight but dominant or passive in sex and society. It wasn't about the gender of one's partner but about the sexual position one took. The active partner had honor; the passive partner had shame. So long as a Roman man was sexually dominant, sex with men or women demonstrated masculinity and virility. Both were perfectly acceptable, establishing his dominance and control.

Passive men were considered feminine. Romans thought women didn't have control, and neither did feminine men. They were weak and controlled by their urges. They slept with too many partners. Though some might try to equate feminine men with gay men, keep in mind that it was more likely that most of their partners were women, and masculine men were just as likely to have sex with men. Secular society today thinks of men who have a lot of sex as virile and manly, not so in ancient Rome. Such men were weak, with no control and no honor.

All this reflects larger cultural narratives that emphasized self-control and dominance as masculine (therefore virtuous) qualities. Having same-sex sex was not particularly relevant ethically, so long as it was within the patterns of dominance and submission and was in moderation. The problem was those who lost control, showed weakness, or stepped out of prescribed social roles. Male Romans should always be the penetrators in sex.

Does this domination mean that marriages were loveless? It sounds that way to modern ears. But for them, and for most people throughout time, there was no contradiction between love and dominance. A man can love his wife, he can think she's beautiful and captivating, but he shouldn't let her have power over him. She is there to be protected and cared for as weak and vulnerable. His love for her enhanced his strength in guarding and protecting her. His love for her should not cause him to make poor decisions or lose control. "Being at a woman's beck and call was a flagrant sign of unmanliness."[150]

In fact, during the early imperial period when the New Testament was written, Romans were increasingly marrying for love. When the republic fell, the inheritance of property became less important for political influence. Consequently, marriage became less politically motivated.

When Caesar Augustus took control after a period of unrest, he instituted marriage reform to ensure stability and the growth of Roman citizenry. Incentives were awarded for having legitimate children and penalties for those who weren't married, much like many modern tax codes. With marriage becoming more beneficial and less politically calculated, love was undoubtedly part of Roman marriages. This meant no diminishment of the requirement for men to be dominant, invulnerable, and in control. Nor were men in any sense bound to monogamy.

Though the coexistence of dominance and love may seem foreign and strange, it's not. The trope of a damsel in distress harmonizes with Roman ideas about sexual relationships. According to this view, women are weak and should be dominated. Admirable women embraced this view of themselves, their world, and their husbands. They kept their place and didn't try to step beyond it. They may wield influence, but it should be in support of the men in their lives. Women who didn't overstep were honorable, but it would never be honorable for men to behave this way. Women were expected to be diminutive in public life, but such hiding was virtuous. They could love their husbands relentlessly, but their love must be admiration from a lower social station, not from equality. One could imagine that Roman men would be turned on by a woman's weakness and naiveté but turned off by strength and self-possession.

I would argue that such social roles persist today, though with greater flexibility and more exceptions. There is social value for women being young, naive, and innocent. It can be cute for women or girls to be weak, embarrassed, or sentimental. Boys like it when girls ask them for help. If the roles are reversed, men or boys may be accepted when they ask for help, but they still risk being shamed or accused of not being "man enough" simply because they need help. On the other hand, women risk being seen as intimidating or controlling if they lead in situations where men might be expected to lead. These Roman values, though diminished, are still with us today.

Because sex was about dominance, every sex act followed rules of who was masculine and dominant and who was feminine and submissive. That's why mutual sexual encounters were unacceptable and degrading, especially for those who were expected to maintain dominance. They were a violation not only of sexual taboos but of the basic order of society and the hierarchy that made Rome strong. They were moral lapses of destructive desire.

THE CURSE OF STRENGTH

How important was it for male Roman citizens to maintain this masculine dominance in sex and all areas of life? Weakness was forbidden. Those who can't be weak must always be strong. A moment of vulnerability could expose someone to ridicule. Lose control, lose respect. Invulnerability was the watchword. This was the life of Roman male citizens in the imperial court, where influence and social standing were everything. The requirement of extreme masculinity was oppressive and dangerous. Those who fell from favor could suffer greater losses than pride. They could lose property. In extreme cases, they could lose their lives.

Sex was important politically because failures in self-control indicated an inability to lead. Sexual lack of self-control happened in many ways: having too much sex, paying too much for sex, spending too much of one's income on sex, having non-dominant sex, having sex with someone who was off limits, or having a mutual sexual relationship—especially with another man—because both parties would compromise their manliness. The act of "burning in their lust for one another" indicates that both parties are active in pursuit and implies a breakdown of rules, interpreted as a breakdown of self-control and an inability to be masculine and virtuous. Romans didn't see sexual behavior in a vacuum. Sex was conceptually tied to social standing and moral obligations.

Sexual domination was also often used metaphorically to illustrate control. The poet Catullus (who pushed the envelope of social acceptability) described the political limitations placed on him by governor Memmius with graphic metaphorical sexual imagery: "Oh Memmius, while I lay on my back you slowly rammed me in the mouth with that whole beam of yours well and at length."[151]

Controlled sexual behavior, character, masculinity, and the ability to lead were closely connected in the Roman mind. Lack of self-control could show up in many ways. Weakness showed up in eating too much, too often, and spending too much money on food. The same "feminine" types of men were prone to all manner of excess. Immoderation in eating or in sex demonstrated a fatal character flaw. This flaw meant incapacity to govern. They couldn't make sound and prudent decisions. Impulses controlled them. Loss of self-control was the primal sin in the Roman Empire.

All these rules about domination, all this social hierarchy, was so that male Roman citizens could serve their families and their kingdom. They were expected to do so. Their restraint had a purpose.

EMPERORS WERE NOT EXEMPT

Catullus didn't reserve his invective humor for Memmius. He also dared to go after Julius Caesar and his ally, Mamurra. Skinner quotes Catullus: "Two little eggheads in one little bed, neither one nor the other the Keener seducer."[152] This line was from a poem that, according to Skinner, "strikes at the jugular by imputing an unhealthy egalitarianism to Caesar and Mamurra's purported liaison."[153]

The punch line was in the mutuality. Skinner explains, "Taking the active sexual role is a metonym for 'natural' exercise of rank and privilege, allegations that Caesar reciprocally services his henchman cancel out his patrician birth and his authority as proconsul, reducing him to the level of his creature."[154]

Historians don't believe that Caesar and Mamurra had a sexual relationship. The outrage of a mutual sexual relationship was Catullus' off-color and rule-breaking brand of humor. Perhaps owing to Catullus' notoriety as a comic, maybe simply because it's safer to ignore a critic, Caesar let the comments go.

Tolerance was short-lived in the time of the emperors. Later emperors sought to curtail criticism. Tiberius Caesar (a contemporary of Jesus) extended treason laws to criminalize slanderous or damaging speech. Any statements against the emperor or well-placed citizens could result in property confiscation or even execution. (This is probably why Paul used the word "Gentile" throughout the book of Romans instead of referring directly to Romans.)

Yet rumors still flew, often published in pamphlets with anonymous authors. Such rumors could take down powerful men, but so could false (or real) accusations of slander. During this time, the atmosphere in the court was of heightened paranoia, with power and security depending on social ties and reputation.

Scandalous stories about powerful Romans and their sexual trysts were popular among commoners. They were like tabloids. Everyone knows the headlines are likely fabrications, but they are scandalous enough to sell copies. Except in Rome, they were politically dangerous and illegal. These rumors undermined the reputation of these men as leaders and, by proxy, the empire itself. These scandals could turn people against their rulers.[155]

Such rumors became a significant part of Emperor Nero's unpopularity.[156] He was despised partly because he was sexually indulgent. But even before Nero, not long before Paul wrote his letter to the Romans, emperor Gaius Caligula was said to indulge in reckless, shameful, and destructive sexual activity. Relevant to Paul's statement, Caligula was also known for idolatry. He almost put an idol in the Jewish temple, which would have incensed the Jews and probably led to war. He was cruel and violent. He sexually humiliated high-ranking Roman citizens and military men. He embodied all of Paul's many criticisms of Gentiles in Romans 1. Roman people were ashamed of him. Paul's description may even be an intentional reference to Gaius Caligula.[157]

It's hard to know what was true and what was libel. Though the modern mind associates Roman emperors with sexual indulgence and deviance, historians suspect most of these stories were fabrications for political gain. They are too improbable and too politically convenient. They could have been attempts to take down emperors, but it's even more likely that slander was used as a political tool to discredit past emperors and strengthen the rule of the current emperor.

For our purposes, to understand Paul's meaning, it doesn't ultimately matter whether these stories were true or false. They were probably believed, at least in part, by the people. These accusations struck at the heart of the legitimacy of imperial rule, and they were the first thing anyone would think of when they thought of the shame of Romans. This was Roman rulers failing to live up to Roman sexual morality. They were examples of people too overcome by vile passions to follow their conscience. They were perfect examples of the sinfulness of Rome and the foolishness of trusting in one's Roman identity for salvation.

The most damning aspect of the accusation was the mutuality itself. We return to Marilyn B. Skinner, one of the foremost experts on Roman sexuality. Commenting on Caesar and why accusations of sexual mutuality with another man were a challenge to his leadership, she wrote, "The active sexual role is a metonym for 'natural' exercise of rank and privilege."[158]

A metonym is a word that stands in for another word or concept. "Washington" is a metonym for the federal government. "The pen" is a metonym for the written word. "Heart" is for emotion. "Hand" is for help. "Natural" sex is controlled, follows rules of dominance and submission, and is never mutual. "Unnatural" sex is uncontrolled, burning with lust, destructive, and mutual.

Skinner wrote these words without Romans 1 in mind. She's a scholar of Roman sexuality, not a theologian. Her sphere of study is unrelated to the Bible. Yet, her words perfectly explain Paul's meaning and purpose in Romans 1:24-27.

JEWISH LITERATURE

Jewish people characterized Roman sexuality in ways that are remarkably similar to the Romans' own self-criticism. Philo was a Jewish writer in Alexandria, one of the learning centers in ancient Rome. He sought to harmonize Jewish religion with Greek philosophy, but he was also a cultural critic. He reflected well Jewish sentiments about Roman sexuality:

> As men, being unable to bear discreetly a satiety of these things, get restive like cattle, and become stiff-necked, and discard the laws of nature, pursuing a great and intemperate indulgence of gluttony, and drinking, and unlawful connections; for not only did they go mad after women, and defile the marriage bed of others, but also those who were men lusted after one another, doing unseemly things, and not regarding or respecting their common nature, and though eager for children, they were convicted by having only an abortive offspring; but the conviction produced no advantage, since they were overcome by violent desire.[159]

The criticisms Philo levels are not unique. He connects "intemperate indulgence of gluttony" with uncontrolled sexual behavior, just as the Romans did.

Lust leads first to adultery with women, and then the desire progresses to mutual sex with other men. When these men wanted to have children, they were unable to conceive. Philo believed impotence was a physical consequence of men who "lusted after one another." This is reminiscent of Paul saying, "men, leaving the natural use of the woman, burned in their lust for one another, men with men committing what is shameful, and receiving in themselves the penalty of their error which was due" (Rom. 1:27).

Note that Philo describes men who begin by "discard[ing] the laws of nature" by "indulgence of gluttony." The laws of nature are temperance; their violation is gluttony. Over-indulgence and loss of self-control are unnatural. They are also destructive. When Philo points to the laws of nature, he is not referencing the creation of male and female in Genesis 1 and 2. Nature calls for temperance.

Philo described them as "mad after women" before they go after other men. They were overwhelmed entirely with aggressive "violent desire." Why did he believe these behaviors would lead to infertility? Probably because he believed, as did the Romans, that semen reflects the character of the man. These men are so weak in character that their children are stillborn. Philo continues:

> And so, by degrees, the men became accustomed to be treated like women, and in this way engendered among themselves the disease of females, and intolerable evil; for they not only, as to effeminacy and delicacy, became like women in their persons, but they made also their souls most ignoble, corrupting in this way the whole race of man, as far as depended on them.[160]

When I first read this, I thought Philo was simply being misogynistic. He's saying women are inferior. That's why he used the phrase "disease of females." The men are "treated like women" in that they are penetrated sexually by other men. If men allow themselves to be treated like women sexually, they become as degraded as women.

Philo also talks about the same gender categories that were common in Rome. Adult males who are made the passive partner by a masculine man take on the shame of being passive and feminized. Women have a kind of shame, a hiding and passivity that would have been viewed as natural for them, even if it was inferior to the nature of men. In their thinking, women were naturally inferior. But for men to take on this shame when they could have been masculine shows weakness and degradation.

I've seen people look at this parallel between Paul and Philo and fall into the trap of equating their ideas, interpreting Paul through the lens of Philo's words. It's important to note that Paul did not echo Philo in all he said. Paul does not refer to a feminizing disease. He avoids comments about the inferiority of women that were common in Philo's writing and other writing of the times. Rather than seeing Paul as derivative from Philo, we should see both as engaging in a similar conversation that many others were also having.

Philo and Paul were both disgusted by the sexual excess that also disgusted Romans. It was perhaps a source of superiority for Jews to think of how disordered and disgusting the Romans were in their sexual practices. The Romans claimed superior discipline and order but couldn't control their urges. Many Jewish and early Christian writers made strikingly similar statements.[161]

Philo doesn't speak of dominating, aggressive sexual assault visited on the lower classes, though he must have known how common this was. The victims of this violence were not Philo's concern. No, what was most sickening was that they lusted after one another. This mutual lusting is what degraded them by feminizing them. The mutuality itself showed that they were out of control, willing to shame themselves and each other.

Paul was not reinventing the wheel. He was picking up on and repeating a common Jewish criticism of Gentiles. His reflection on mutual sex between men as a reflection of destructive and consuming lust was in harmony with Jewish and Roman thinking.

For the most part, Jewish criticism of Roman excesses mirrored the Romans' criticisms of themselves. There was one key difference. For the Romans, neglecting the gods could lead to sin. For the Jews, worshipping pagan gods was the source of sin. Romans believed their "good fortune and right to govern other nations came directly from the gods."[162] Jews were indignant at being ruled by a nation that worshiped idols.

It was common in Jewish literature to attribute Roman moral failures to their idolatry, notably in *Wisdom of Solomon*.[163] *Wisdom* is a Jewish book written pseudonymously in the first century B.C. The parallels between *Wisdom* and Romans 1 are so strong that many scholars believe Paul had this text in mind. *Wisdom* and Romans both say that the Gentiles should have discovered God through creation, so they are without excuse. In their ignorance, they worship idols, and this leads to all manner of immorality. The parallels are undeniable.[164] Paul entered an ongoing conversation using widely understood imagery and values.

It's idolatry that led to degrading acts and threatened the authority of Rome. *Idolatry* led to *unnatural sex* and other sexual sins that exploded into every sin imaginable. Paul wasn't the first to level this accusation. He drew upon well-established ideas of gender, sex, idolatry, sin, and shame.

Some say that Jewish opposition to same-sex erotic behavior was based on God's intent in the creation of man and woman. However, I have never seen a footnote referencing the words of these Jewish teachers and have not been able to find any such teachings myself in Jewish literature contemporary to Paul. We see no such reasoning in the influential quotes above, either. I am open to these references if anyone can show them to me, yet I suspect they would have been referenced and quoted if they did exist and easy to locate if this was a common Jewish belief.

Perhaps we are failing to recognize that for Jews and Romans alike in the first century, they didn't associate same-sex eroticism with marriage in any sense, so the association with Adam and Eve would not have been intuitive for them. Opponents of same-sex marriage make the association today. But opponents of same-sex erotic behavior in the past had different moral concerns because same-sex erotic behavior was synonymous with sexual excess and destructive lust.

MUTUALITY WAS THE PROBLEM

Now we are well equipped to answer the question posed at the beginning of the chapter. Why did Paul use mutual sexual encounters between men as the highest example of sin? Why not use the routine and socially sanctioned rape of enslaved people?

We now know more about the type of mutuality Paul was describing. It was mutuality, but not the mutuality of love. It was a mutual desire to exploit one another. There was no trace of concern for the humanity of the other. It wasn't rape, but had there been refusal, it may have become rape. It was an embodiment of selfishness.

Loss of control in lustful indulgence was the height of immorality in Roman thinking. It found its most stark expression in this type of destructive sexual mutuality between male citizens who should have been the first to exercise self-control and dominance. Mutuality was the point, but not mutual love, care, and commitment. It was mutual loss of control and mutual self-destruction. Why would someone behave as Paul describes in Romans 1:24-27? Because they allowed themselves to be defeated, taken prisoner by sexual desire, losing self-possession. Yet, it was only the canary in the coal mine. It indicated much broader moral failings that went far beyond sex to the very ability of Rome to govern the world.

This criticism would have hit a chord with both Jews and Gentiles in Rome. Had Paul mentioned the rape of enslaved boys, it would have impacted Jews but not Romans. Had he spoken of adultery, he'd have the same problem. Romans had no problem with adultery. He wouldn't be able to make his point as forcefully with both audiences. Paul used the example that would be effective with both Jewish and Gentile Christians, and even with non-Christians in Rome. It's a brilliant evangelistic tool because it resonates with all possible audiences, demonstrating Paul's deep understanding of presenting the gospel to all people and cultures.

Accepted theology makes very different arguments about why this sex is wrong. They argue that it's innate in the mechanics of homoerotic sex or that same-sex sex is inherently and categorically impure. Such arguments would not resonate in Rome. Paul's words emphasize the same problematic behaviors the Romans themselves would emphasize, consuming and uncontrolled desire that is mutually destructive.

They equated mutual same-sex sex with loss of control because that's how it showed up in their society. Much like assuming long hair was shameful on men because of what it signified. Paul moved with the cultural values in both cases, making arguments based on the underlying moral reasoning. Paul found the point of agreement. He described people who had really lost control. But he didn't describe gay people who were asking for the blessing of marriage. He didn't describe mutual love, commitment, and sacrifice.

Based on everything we've learned, people in Roman culture who were prone to fall in love with the same gender would not be free to act on that impulse for lasting love. They would be limited to extramarital affairs, relegating to a small corner of life a relationship that they might wish was the center of their family. That's not what Paul described in Romans 1:24-27.

WHAT ABOUT WOMEN?

But what about the lust of women? Weren't they also having sex with one another? "Even their women exchanged the natural use for what is against nature" (Rom. 1:26). What is meant by "natural use"? Accepted theology assumes this refers to women forsaking heterosexual sex for same-sex sex.

It might be surprising to learn that Christians understood this text differently for the first three centuries of Christianity. Christians who lived closest to the time of Paul believed he was referring to "noncoital or nonprocreative forms of *heterosexual* intercourse."[165] They didn't automatically think of same-sex sex when they thought of "unnatural."

Romans had many ways of thinking of women's sex as unnatural. A woman having any non-vaginal sex was unnatural, even if it was with her husband.[166] Women were supposed to be passive in relationships and sex. It was unnatural for her to be the initiator. It was also unnatural for men to perform oral sex on women. Yet Romans in the first century gave little thought to the possibility of women having sex with one another. It was a male-centered society. They generally thought of the sexuality of women, natural or otherwise, as being related to men.[167]

Today, we don't tend to think of oral sex (or other forms of non-coital sex) as unnatural, even in Christian circles. At the very least, we don't think of Paul's words in Romans 1 as referring to these kinds of sex. We view sexual intimacy between married people as a way of strengthening their bond. It's hard to express how different our assumptions are from the beliefs and values in Paul's day. For them, women having non-procreative sex was about lustful lack of control.

Still, I don't claim to know for sure what Paul refers to. We don't have enough information to be entirely certain, nor do I think the actual behavior is his point. His point remains that their lust is out of control and leads to their behavior, which was probably non-vaginal sex, but the main point is that it was fueled by destructive lust.

If we believe Romans 1 forbids all same-sex sex, not only the kind characterized by unrestrained lust, then there are other implications for heterosexuals as well. It would be strange in his context for Paul to describe women having unnatural sex and not at least in part be referring to non-vaginal sexual practices with men, practices intended to experience sexual pleasure without risking pregnancy.

Some want to say that Paul's context and moral intent aren't relevant. He forbade same-sex sex, which applies equally to imperial Roman sex parties and married same-sex couples. If so, then we should make the same context-free applications to heterosexuals. Married heterosexuals should never engage in sexual behavior that isn't vaginal sex.

More than that, birth control would also come under scrutiny since it is a way to avoid pregnancy. Indeed, the Christian church has considered non-procreative sex as unnatural and sinful for most of its history. When we consider Romans 1 as a prohibition on same-sex marriage, we shouldn't ignore the reality that unnatural sex for women was usually a means of getting sexual satisfaction without risking pregnancy. Consistency demands heterosexuals who oppose same-sex marriage at least wrestle with the implication that birth control and non-vaginal sex is off-limits for heterosexuals. These are the implications of literalism. Or we can follow Paul's moral reasoning by paying attention to Paul's words themselves.

UNRESTRAINED AND DESTRUCTIVE LUST

I've argued from a cultural perspective. But am I getting this from the text itself? Or am I simply imposing it on the text?

The emphasis on uncontrolled and destructive lust is absolutely in the text. Paul didn't mince words or risk misunderstanding. In his New Testament letters, Paul often spoke about sexual sin, but nowhere else does he speak with such intensity of the desire that motivates sexual sin. He used the strongest language to communicate that this desire was extreme, intense, unrestrained, and destructive.

In just three verses (Rom. 1:24, 26, 27), Paul used four different synonyms for lust: *epithumia, pathe, ekkaio,* and *orexis.*

> The lusts [*epithumia*] of their hearts . . . vile passions [*pathe*] . . . burned [*ekkaio*] in their lust [*orexis*].

These words and their combination are unique in all of Scripture. No other passage combines more than two of them at once. They are not words for healthy sexuality. Never in the New Testament are any of these words used to describe a sexual passion related to marriage. None of these words describes the feeling, purpose, or meaning of marriage by Paul or any other New Testament writer.

The first word, *epithumia,* is a common word for passion or lust. Paul uses the word almost exclusively in a negative context and often associates it with "the flesh" and sexual sin. Often, *epithumia* contrasts with life according to the Spirit (Rom. 6:12; 7:7, 8; 13:24; Gal. 5:16, 24; Col. 3:5; Eph. 2:3).

The word *pathe* is not used as often but is associated with Gentile sexual sins (Col. 3:5; 1 Thess. 4:5). *Ekkaio* is used only here but appears to be a more emphatic form of the verb "burn," meaning "burn up." It indicates utter destruction. *Orexis* is also used only here and connotes strong desire. Together, *ekkaio* and *orexis* convey "burned up in strong desire." One respected lexicon puts it this way: "In some languages the equivalent idiom is 'to boil with desire' [or] 'to feel hot in the genitals.'"[168]

This is about uncontrolled and destructive passion. Paul emphatically communicates that this is not a healthy, controlled sexual appetite. This is lust, passion, desire, and craving, unbridled and immoderate. They are consumed, burned alive with covetous lust. It is inherently destructive.

Why is mutual sex between men the best example of lust? Because it was not their right. They had a right to have sex with their wives. They had a right to have sex with anyone they'd enslaved, male or female. They had a right to have extramarital sex with men or women. They had a right to buy sex. They were supposed to keep all these desires in moderation, but they were their right. There were few limitations, and one of the only limitations was mutual sex with other citizen men. They did not have that right. To take it anyway showed weakness, vulnerability, and sinfulness.

Though Paul didn't say it outright, his words would have immediately recalled the accusations leveled against Roman emperors such as Gaius Caligula. Why wouldn't Paul have said it outright? Why wouldn't he have come out and said that he was speaking about Roman emperors and their sexual excess?

Paul spoke of "Gentiles" instead of "Romans" and alluded to familiar narratives instead of stating the object directly because it was unsafe for Christians to criticize Rome directly. Rome was a violent empire, and Christians were a small, vulnerable, and persecuted religious sect. This is what I learned when I took a seminary class on the book of Romans, and conservative commentators widely accept it. Plus, treason laws imposed by Tiberius Caesar made any criticism of the emperor or high-ranking Romans a criminal offense, potentially punishable by death.

It makes sense that Paul's words were a veiled but discernable allusion to the excesses of the imperial court, real or imagined, which shamed all Rome. This was the perfect cultural illustration of Paul's point: *The Roman world is given over to lust and in need of redemption.*

THOU SHALL NOT COVET

This point connects not only with Roman culture, not only with the words of Romans 1, but also with Paul's overall arguments about sin. Though in our text it's translated as "lust," in Romans 7:7, 8, *epithumia* is translated "covet." "For I would not have known covetousness unless the law had said, 'You shall not covet.'" Paul is quoting the Ten Commandments. The first commandment ("Thou shalt have no other gods before me") and the last commandment ("Thou shalt not covet") together form the moral underpinning of all ten commandments (Exod. 20).

Behind every sin we commit against one another is the sinful desire of *epithumia*, the covetousness that puts our desires above our neighbors' desires. And behind every sin is the denial that there is one God, and we are all God's creation. Lust is covetousness; both words are translations of *epithumia*. The implications go far beyond sex.

Paul's theology in Romans 1 is one sinew in the body of his theological think-ing. Lust and covetousness are of the flesh and against the Spirit. Paul's theology of sin is closely linked with our human tendency to do precisely what we know is wrong because we follow our covetous, lustful flesh and its desires.

> For I know that in me (that is, in my flesh) nothing good dwells; for to will is present with me, but how to perform what is good I do not find. For the good that I will to do, I do not do; but the evil I will not to do, that I practice. Now if I do what I will not to do, it is no longer I who do it, but sin that dwells in me (Rom. 7:18-20).

In Romans 1, Paul describes people who do what they know is wrong. First, they violate the first commandment. They fail to recognize and worship the creator. As a result, they lose self-control through not worshipping God, not having their mindset on things of the Spirit. They are given over to the flesh. They violate the last commandment through their covetousness. By implication, they've broken the whole law.

Sexual desire is good within the context of a commitment to love and care for the person we desire, understanding that they are whole persons, deserving of love and protection. Sexual desire is not good when it is pure desire, burning and uncontrolled. It's not good when it is mutually destructive yet indulged regard-less. When passion overwhelms our sense, we are living from the flesh, not the Spirit; we are in the mindset of Romans 1:24-27.

When we attempt to apply these words to same-gender marriage, the people accused don't meet this description. Paul has given us a complete picture. We aren't meant to take it apart piece by piece and apply the parts without refer-ring to the whole. Such an approach is not biblical faithfulness. If we take it apart, even sexual desire itself is forbidden in all contexts. The problem isn't sexual desire; sexual desire is a gift from God. The problem is desire that's all-consuming and destructive.

DESIRE AND SEXUAL ORIENTATION

Recognizing Paul's obvious emphasis on desire changes how we interpret the text for today. In the interview with Thomas Shepherd, discussed at the beginning of the last chapter,[169] he said that Paul makes a distinction between desire and behavior. The behavior is sinful, not the desire. Shepherd is in har-mony with the seminary and other Adventist institutions, emphasizing the difference between desire and behavior. Therefore, a person might be attracted to the same gender by no choice of their own, but Paul calls them not to act on their desire.

Accepting that people don't choose and can't change their sexual orientation is progress. The distinction between orientation and behavior creates some space for LGBTQ Christians. It acknowledges a reality that should be obvious by now: there is a burden that comes with hiding fundamental aspects of our human experience.

Distinguishing between desires and behavior could alleviate the need to hide or pretend to be straight. If the church could come to the point of not discriminating against people who are gay but committed to celibacy, it would be good for LGBTQ Adventists. I appreciate this perspective. It's honest and helpful.

What I can't accept is that Paul taught this in Romans 1:24-27. The condemnation of the Romans was not only about engaging in sinful behavior; it was about sinful desires. They are condemned by their desires, and the desires themselves were part of God's judgment. "God also gave them up to uncleanness, in the lusts of their heart. . . . God gave them up to vile passions" (Rom. 1:24-26).

Paul describes a progression first from idolatry, then to destructive sex, and finally to all kinds of exploitations and cruelties. First, they "became futile in their thoughts, and their foolish hearts were darkened [in idolatry]" (verse 21). As a direct result of their futile thinking, God gave them over to "the lusts of their hearts" (verse 24). They had "vile passions" (verse 26) and "burned in their lust" (verse 27). The desires themselves are a sign of the judgment of God.

The Gentiles in Romans 1 contrast with the Gentiles in Romans 2. Paul describes "good" Gentiles as having pure desires and hearts (Rom. 2:12-16). Paul describes people who either have good desire and are good, or have vile desires (as a result of idolatry) and are evil. He doesn't describe people with desires that were no fault of their own. These people were directly responsible for their desires. The desires convey guilt. Paul also makes no separation between desire and action.

The opposite of the sinful Gentiles is not Gentiles who resist vile desires, but Gentiles who have pure hearts without these desires. The good Gentiles are faithful to the knowledge they have; they develop an understanding of God, and the law of God is written on their hearts. They never develop impure hearts; they never develop consuming lust.

This is all part of Paul's overall theme. Corrupted understanding leads to corrupted desires that lead to corrupted behavior. On the flip side, correct understanding leads to pure desires that lead to pure behaviors. It's a direct line.

Paul doesn't give any off-ramps, no separation or distinction between belief, desires, and behavior. There isn't even a category for people who have the desire but don't act on it. Nor are there people who worship and believe in God but have these desires anyway. Christians who worship God but experience same-sex attraction are nowhere to be found in this passage. The guilty Gentiles all worship idols, not metaphorically but literally.

As a result, there isn't any advice in this passage about what Christians should do should they find themselves doing their best to follow God, yet also wanting a life partner of the same gender. Paul describes people who worship idols and are overcome with lust, not people who worship God and desire marriage.

If this condemns all same-sex behavior for all time and all people in all circumstances, it condemns those who engage in it and those who desire it. If this passage applies to people who are gay and bisexual, it's not just a condemnation of acting gay but of being gay or same-sex attracted. The desire itself is a sign that "God gave them up to uncleanness, in the lust of their hearts" (verse 24) and "God gave them up to vile passions" (verse 26). I can't see any other way to read it.

SEXUAL MORALITY

Paul is speaking of people whose lust has hijacked their judgment. His language is quite clear on this subject, and that language matches Paul's words about sexual sin throughout his writing. But why can't it be both? Might it be that Paul condemns same-sex sex precisely because it is characterized by just such destructive and uncontrolled lust?

One of my favorite seminary teachers is New Testament professor Richard Choi, one of the most careful and thorough teachers I've ever had. His classes were small because he had a reputation for asking a lot of his students. His expectations were high, not only for his students but also for himself. I had the privilege of taking a class in Romans from him. I'll never forget the paper I wrote. He inspired me. Wanting to do my best, I spent 40 hours of intense study and writing on that one paper.

Choi's understanding of Romans 1 was this: natural sex is sex with one's spouse. Paul condemned the Gentiles not only because of same-sex sex but because of all kinds of unnatural sex. It's about a destructive desire to defile ourselves sexually. Of all these behaviors, "homosexuality is the bloom."[170] It's the ultimate act of degradation. He said that sex is like fire. If we allow it, it burns out of control and consumes us. Choi pays close attention to Paul's words because this is his language exactly—lust that burns a person alive.

Choi was asked to do a presentation for the seminary on the topic of homosexuality.[171] He put up a slide during his presentation that succinctly and accurately described Paul's overarching moral teachings about sex from all his writings. Paul says we are drawn to sin, heterosexuals and homosexuals alike. This desire is toward what he described as "immorality sex," which he defined as having a "great number and variety of partners." That's certainly what was happening in Romans 1.

On the other hand, if we want to follow God and be moral, the model is "marriage sex," defined as "only with your spouse forever." Of course, Paul also mentioned celibacy as the preferred state, but if we're going to have sex, it should be the married kind: "only with your spouse forever."

As much as I admire him, when Choi spoke about Romans 1, describing gay people as consumed by the fire of lust, I remember making a mental note: this was another of my seminary professors who didn't understand. I knew that my struggle was not about letting my sexual desire go wild but about a desire for monogamy and self-sacrificial love. I just wanted a life partner.

We need to get the question right. Gay and bisexual Adventists are not asking for what Paul described in Romans 1:24-27. We are asking the church to help us be faithful in marriage. By God's grace, we are all capable of the kind of "only with your spouse forever" relationship that Paul defined as moral and good.

That's the crux of the matter. How do Paul's words apply to gay and bisexual people? Paul was describing precisely what Choi said he was describing: sex as a fire that can burn out of control and consume a person.

Those who believe in stereotypes about the "gay lifestyle," and think that the essence of same-sex sex is a consuming fire of vile lust logically see gay people in Romans 1. I don't say this lightly. The Adventist Church (and nearly all churches) once saw gay men this way.

One example: *Adventist Review* once had an article that said, in part: "Homosexuality is death oriented; it's not life-oriented." It described sexual intimacy between men as "an almost beastlike relationship. It's a perversion." It went on to decry a report that said sex between men should be decriminalized, adding that "most of homosexual behavior is learned. And if it's a learned response, it can be unlearned."[172]

This attitude is still present in Adventist thinking. Gay and bisexual people are often portrayed as sexually uncontrolled and destructive. Our desire for a loving relationship is often seen as a spiritual disorder resulting from the indulgence of sexual sin. Functionally, Christians have often behaved as if minority sexual orientations were contagious and could become epidemic, as if heterosexuality were fragile and easily lost. If one believes such things, it's easy to apply Romans 1 to gay and bisexual individuals.

I don't believe these stereotypes, and I'm guessing most of you reading this book don't buy them either. If we recognize that gay and bisexual people ask for support in their marriages, we realize they are different from those described in Romans 1. If we acknowledge that someone can know their sexual orientation before having a sexual experience, we are not on board with this old-school stereotyping.

If Paul had intended to advise gay and bisexual people, he would have accurately described them. I don't see myself in these descriptions. I don't see other gay and bisexual people in these descriptions.

I stand by the claim I made early in this chapter about the point of Romans 1:24-17: *The Romans had a structure for their society, and it was rigid. It applied to sex as well as to every other area of life. Those who didn't participate in that structure were assumed to be out of control, overcome by desire, morally compromised, and destructive to themselves and the empire. There is every indication in Roman writing, Jewish writing, and Paul's own words that this lack of self-control and destructive desire was the point of Paul's message. Paul was not talking about same-gender marriage. He was observing something in Roman culture and commenting on that behavior.*

This leaves gay and bisexual people with an open question about living out their sexuality with holiness. This is the irony of Richard Choi's categories. Many of us strive to fit into the "only with your spouse forever" category of holy sexuality, not the "great number and variety of partners" category of immoral sex so deftly described in Romans 1. And we are all free to take up such a goal. So, it's not a stretch to believe that Paul's description doesn't fit us. I humbly suggest that gay and bisexual people may also be capable, by God's grace, of living into holy sexuality.

WHAT WOULD PAUL THINK?

"Let's be real. If we could talk to Paul right now, and we could ask him whether homosexuality was sinful, he would say 'yes.'" I remember hearing this argument and finding it compelling at one point. What is the value of all this cultural stuff? We all know Paul wouldn't be a gay-rights activist, don't we? We all know he would be against same-gender marriage, don't we?

This is a gut check. It boils things down to their essence. The problem is, so much of that essence has to do with our gut, not with Paul himself. When I heard this rhetorical question, it got me thinking. What if we took it seriously?

How would Paul, under the influence of God, answer our questions if he showed up in our church today? Would he hear about same-gender marriage (something he never spoke about and probably never considered) and immediately forbid it? Some people are confident that he would, that he already has. I disagree.

Paul was an evangelist. He didn't compromise the law or the Bible for the sake of the gospel. Yet, he didn't bury his head in a Bible and ignore what God was doing in the world. Paul questioned his theology when he saw the Spirit working. As a Jew, Paul looked forward to the return of the Messiah. He expected the Messiah to come with military or spiritual might. But to die on a Roman cross as a cursed man? This was different than every expectation Paul had.

And further, to be called to minister among Gentiles? Those who were unclean? Paul had to completely rethink his theology because of what happened in his life. Because of an encounter with God (Acts 9:3-9), he took three years to re-evaluate what he thought he knew (Gal. 1:15-18).

Based on what the Bible tells us of Paul, I can only imagine that he wouldn't jump to conclusions when he saw sincere followers of Jesus asking the church for a blessing on their marriages. I don't imagine he would have seen the same degradation in us that he saw in the Romans. I suspect that Paul would want to understand what God was doing in the world and compare that with the Bible, with the openness that a new awareness could mean a new understanding.

This is how Paul conducted himself in the first century, and I imagine he'd do the same in the twenty-first century. We should do the same. This is the kind of deliberative process we learned about in earlier chapters. The Bible teaches us that we should apply the law of God with compassion and understanding for the real impact it has on people's lives.

During the question-and-answer session after Richard Choi's presentation, a student asked about the terminology he used, asking if he correctly identified people in the LGBTQ community. Choi responded, "I am ignorant about what goes on today. I'm not ignorant of what went on in the Bible, but I am ignorant about what goes on today."

As much as I respect Richard Choi, he missed an opportunity and a critical element of this whole conversation. We must understand the modern context if we are to apply the ancient text to our lives. Ignorance of that context is not a virtue, and having no understanding is never admirable.

Sadly, ignorance of who we are as gay, bisexual, and transgender people leads to pejorative assumptions about us. It's far too easy to read those assumptions into the text. We find an example of that here. In Choi's own words, Paul speaks of people who have sex with a "great number and variety of partners." That's not what I'm advocating for in this book. I'm advocating for same-sex marriage. By Choi's own definition, same-sex marriage does not fit Paul's moral category of sin.

We want to be faithful and monogamous to one person for the rest of our lives. We understand that it isn't easy. We aren't looking for the easy way, but what we believe is the right and best practice. We are not people who Paul described with "vile passion" who "burned in their lust for one another." To understand how Paul's words do (or do not) apply, Adventist scholars need to learn more about the LGBTQ community and understand that many simply ask for the same burdens and privileges heterosexuals already enjoy in our churches.

I don't believe Paul would have jumped to conclusions, and he certainly wouldn't have valued ignorance. He would have gotten to know us. He wouldn't have labeled us with a "homosexual lifestyle" any more than he labeled Gentiles with a "Gentile lifestyle." Paul would have looked at what the Spirit was doing and re-examined the Bible, knowing he always had something to learn. He would have taken time to understand both the text and the people. I know Paul would do that today because that's what he did in his lifetime. That's also what the Adventist Church should do.

WAS PAUL IGNORANT?

At one point, I found the argument I just made unsatisfactory. I thought it was suspect to root any of our conclusions in Paul's ignorance. In so doing, aren't I questioning the inspiration of Scripture itself? Paul wrote it, but God inspired it. The Bible isn't just the opinions of Paul and Moses. The Bible is the Word of God. We don't call it the Word of Paul.

Unlike Paul, God is all-knowing. God didn't have to be informed about sexual orientation. God didn't have to wait until humans revealed the issue of same-gender marriage or transgender identity. Paul might not have known, but God knew, and God inspired Paul. Why wouldn't God have explained the whole situation since the Bible was meant to instruct everyone for all time?

That's a good question, but I'm not going to answer it. At least, I'm not going to speculate that God didn't speak directly to sexual orientation. We don't always know why God does what God does. I could give it a shot, but others might have different ideas, which would be fine. We cannot always know with certainty when it comes to the all-knowing God because we're far from all-knowing. Yet we often can describe with certainty what the Bible includes and what the Bible doesn't include. Some examples:

The Bible advised the Israelites to bury their excrement outside the camp (Deut. 23:12, 13) but never explained germ theory or that we would have indoor plumbing one day. The Bible advises us to be subject to ruling authorities (Rom. 13:1-7) but never warns us about totalitarianism and never recommends democracy. The Bible talks about how we spend our time (Eph. 5:15-17) but never about engaging with social media. The Bible talks a lot about money but never about whether Christians should invest in the stock market or what kinds of companies Christians should invest their money in. The Bible talks about churches and being the church but never about denominations; we have no instruction on how to think about being a denomination and what relationship this has to the Biblical descriptions of churches. Paul wrote to churches in a specific city; we write to churches in a particular denomination.

These differences are consequential. We would have loved to have a heads-up about fascism and communism. We'd love some guidance today on capitalism, democracy, and socialism. It would be very helpful if the Bible talked about the consequences of social media on society. In saying that the Bible doesn't address these topics directly, I'm not making a value statement about the knowledge of biblical authors or the omniscience of God. I'm just making observations from a place of trust that the Bible we have is the Bible God wants us to have.

God's foreknowledge on these things didn't mean all things of future consequence were referred to directly in the Bible. We'd have a tough time coming up with a single example in which the Bible included instruction about something that would come up in the future but was irrelevant to the immediate audience. Every word of the Bible is relevant to the audience to which it was written.[a] A discussion about same-gender marriage would have been irrelevant to them.

Look at the beginning of the epistle, "Paul . . . to those who are in Rome" (Rom. 1:1, 7). We are listening in on a conversation between him and the Christians in Rome in the first century. *We* are listening in on *their* conversation. This letter has been preserved and canonized by the church because it is inspired

---

a. The one possible exception to this could be apocalyptic prophetic writings in which the meaning only became apparent over time. Yet even here, we don't find descriptions of thoroughly modern things, such as airplanes, democracies, or television. Even apocalyptic writing is written with the words and images of the day.

and of enormous value. This doesn't change the fact that it was addressed to the Christians in Rome in the first century. He used their language, Koine Greek. He spoke of their concerns. He addressed individuals in their congregations.

There is wisdom in this. There is no such thing as a culturally neutral language or setting. The only way to make the Bible applicable in the first, fourth, fourteenth, and twenty-first centuries at the same time is to write to the original culture. To expect a Bible written to our twenty-first-century thinking is the height of self-obsession. Once we know its cultural setting, we can understand the purpose better and apply it to our own time and place.

We must realize our responsibility. Paul isn't here; you and I are. We've been searching diligently for a "thus saith the Lord," but what if we don't have it? Maybe if we could go back in time and thank Paul for telling us that same-gender marriage is wrong, he would wonder what on earth we were talking about.

If that's the case, what should we do about it? How do we move forward to make consequential moral decisions in areas not directly addressed in the Bible? That's not an easy question, but neither is it as new and foreign as it might seem. We do this all the time without realizing it, and the Christian church has engaged in these questions time and time again.

There are different recommended approaches for these questions. One method is to ask what is modeled in Scripture. On this question, we'd see that every marriage in the Bible was between a man and a woman. How does that influence our thinking on the subject? What else might be important to consider? How do we answer new questions in ways that are biblical? Those are questions for the next chapter.

CHAPTER 13

The Biblical Model

"If God intended homosexuality, why not give some instructions about it in the Bible?"

"We can easily point to the many passages in which man and woman are united as one with God's sanctification and blessing. Yet the Scriptures are silent regarding same-sex unions. It seems that such an important union would be mentioned somewhere in Scripture. Our opinion doesn't matter. The Word of God is everything. If a verse elevated same-sex marriage in a positive and holy light, this would all be a nonissue. But there isn't."

We've looked at all the passages that are often quoted as direct prohibitions of all same-sex sexuality. That is important because I take the Bible seriously, and I imagine you do as well. If you accept my conclusions in this book, even if you are uncertain, an important question remains. Is it enough to say there is no prohibition? Where is the permission? Where is the example? Even if we accept that there is no red light in the Bible, that's not the same as having a green light.

There are topics on which Bible authors debate. Divorce is handled differently in different passages and at different times in Scripture. There is movement and dialog about whether, when, and why divorce may or may not be acceptable.

There are debates around topics of violence. Many Old Testament texts speak of using violence, while Jesus often speaks of not using violence. Deuteronomy 28 promises blessings for obedience and curses for disobedience; the book of Job is about a man who was cursed despite his obedience. Within Scripture, we find contextual considerations and dialog within the text itself. This happens on many different topics, acknowledging the complexity of life and faith.

Yet, there is no dialog about same-gender marriage. There are probably hundreds of examples of married people, all of them men and women. Solomon may have married hundreds of women and had hundreds more concubines, but he never married a man. David may have told Jonathan, "Your love to me was wonderful, surpassing the love of women" (2 Sam. 1:26), but most people agree that this was probably not romance, let alone marriage. Marriage shows up in the text in terms of male and female. This is the assumed paradigm—instructions on marriage address to husbands and wives.

Neither does the bible mention gender transitions. There may be different ideas about living as a man or a woman, but no one identifies as transgender. Their identity never struggles to match their external physiology. There are eunuchs whose anatomy has been changed or who may have been born with non-normative anatomy. Yet, we don't have explicit examples of someone appearing male at birth and later identifying as a woman. That doesn't appear in the pages of the Bible. Isn't that definitive enough? Doesn't it cast doubt on affirmation?

When we have this kind of reasonable doubt, even if we acknowledge that the waters are muddy, isn't it better not to risk it? "When in doubt don't" is an approach many Adventists use on various topics. Prohibition certainly seems like the safer route in the absence of biblical permission. If God wanted us to know there were different ways of doing marriage or gender, God would have told us as much. This is too important to be left to chance.

Add to that the texts that seem to oppose same-sex sex in various contexts. Yes, the contexts are dramatically different from our own. Yes, none of the biblical authors were asked about same-gender marriage. Yes, none of these statements would have stopped same-gender marriage when they were written. But don't they mean something? The only information the Bible gives is negative, even if it's in a different context.

I understand this objection. Like many others, it's one I once held. I remember saying that it was more than a matter of an individual verse or two; it was the unified witness of Scripture. When seen all together, the picture of marriage is consistent, and opposition to same-sex sex is also consistent.

HISTORICAL PERSPECTIVE

What shifted my understanding? I realized that this principle, though compelling, is one we apply only selectively. It overemphasizes situational descriptions in the Bible at the expense of more important principles. It risks importing the *culture* of Bible times instead of the *ethics* of the Bible.

Historically, those who emphasize this approach to Scripture have been on the wrong side again and again. They tend to neglect our responsibility to respond to new awareness and human need. The more I examined these topics and saw them through the lessons of church history, the more clarity I found.

The church has significantly amended its theological understanding on many topics. We all know there were significant shifts in cosmology because of Galileo's work. His book was banned, and he was placed on house arrest for the rest of his life by people who wanted to take the words of Scripture literally when it spoke of the sun moving in the sky or the earth being firmly established (Josh. 10:13; 1 Chron. 16:30; Ps. 93:1; Ps. 96:10; Ps. 104:5; Eccl. 1:5). When we talked about gender roles, women were once seen as intellectually and morally inferior to men. That didn't shift because of Bible study but because of the growing role of women in society.

In the last 100 years, another seismic theological shift has taken place. Antisemitism was propped up by theology for 19 centuries. The gospel of John especially speaks negatively of "the Jews," and this language fueled prejudice. Literal understandings of other texts led Christians to blame the Jewish people for killing Jesus (e.g., Matt. 27:25; 1 Thess. 2:14-16). Judaism became a foil for Christianity; Jews were disparaged as "Christ killers" and spawns of Satan. Supersessionism was the theological framework of centuries, teaching that Christians replaced Jews as God's people.

Only after the Holocaust did Christians see the sins they had been committing against the Jewish people. Shocked by the results of antisemitic theology and understanding at last that they had fueled its flames, theologians en masse changed their theological approach to Judaism.[173]

Half a century later, I listened as my seminary professors explained this history. The best ones told us to be cautious about how we speak of Jews. Again, this wasn't because of a new theological insight arising from the text. Even as they pointed out good theological reasons to support the shift, my professors at the Seventh-day Adventist Theological Seminary were clear that this shift arose from the events of world history, not from Bible study. Enough Christians were horrified by the results of Christian antisemitism that we changed. Blatant antisemitism was once mainstream, and though antisemitism persists, the improvements are evident.

It's happened again and again. Those who stick to literalistic interpretations at the expense of human suffering or new information wind up on the wrong side. On some of these topics, in retrospect, there is plenty of reason to debate the text. As we look back, knowing which perspective won the day, it's easier for us to see clearly than it was for them. For some texts, even this retrospective view of theology isn't simple. On some subjects, it's still hard to understand the Bible.

One subject has been a topic of study for me these last few years. The more I've learned, the more I've realized what a wonderful lesson it can be for our current debate. That subject is slavery.

THEOLOGY AND SLAVERY

It may seem like an unlikely parallel at first, but we can learn a lot by delving into the church's response to the question of slavery. How did the church change and grow on this topic theologically and historically?

For most of my life, I had only a vague impression of what the Bible says about slavery. I came across disturbing texts, but I got used to dismissing them. It was all too easy to say that slaveholders used the texts to justify their behavior. It was all too easy to accept that the Bible is anti-slavery on closer examination. But in all honesty, I never looked closely.

I read one particular book that soothed my doubts. William Webb's *Slaves, Women, and Homosexuals*[174] taught the trajectory approach to Scripture. The Bible constantly moved away from slavery and toward abolition. Our duty as Christians is to continue that trajectory by doing what was never done in the Bible, outlawing all slavery. The Bible might never have advocated such a move, but it moved in that direction, and we should continue that movement.

Webb claimed that Israel was moving in a positive direction relative to its surrounding cultures. It was the only culture in the Ancient Near East that treated enslaved people as humans instead of property, giving them rights and protection. It also didn't allow fellow Israelites to be enslaved. It moved towards growth and redemption, and we should keep moving further in that direction.

Slavery may not have been abolished in the New Testament, but according to Webb, Paul spoke of the spiritual freedom of those enslaved. These were "breakout texts" in which the truth shined through, even if it didn't yet bring the desired change. Shouldn't this lead naturally to the conclusion that enslaved people should be free? Paul asked Philemon to free Onesimus, who Philemon had enslaved. Doesn't that mean Paul is on the side of abolition?

Here was an elegant explanation for those uncomfortable texts. I was eager to believe these arguments. It strengthened my faith in the Bible. The problem wasn't the Bible but our failure to understand it. We just weren't reading carefully enough. God was working for abolition all along. The Bible supported abolition all along.

But the devil is in the details. I later learned the explanation I loved so much doesn't hold up well to scrutiny. As I read more broadly, I saw that Webb's book involved a lot of cherry picking. Moreover, it also wasn't the reasoning that inspired Christian abolitionists.

Ancient Israel was not moving away from slavery relative to surrounding nations. Surrounding nations often treated enslaved people like people, not merely property. For instance, the ancient *Code of Hammurabi* (*CH*) is contemporary to ancient Israel and the most complete legal code outside Israel. In *CH*, citizens could sell themselves as indentured servants just like in Israel, but the servitude was only three years instead of six. Some of Israel's contemporaries allowed enslaved people to bring lawsuits, a right not extended in the Bible. Some nations freed enslaved people when they conquered foreign cities, something Israel never did. Israel did speak of protecting the weak, helpless, and enslaved, but so did other nations. Israel was better than some in some ways but worse in others. They didn't stand out. They weren't moving in an abolitionist direction.[175]

The New Testament brought no improvement to the Hebrew Bible. Paul spoke about the equality of all people, but this never meant that enslaved people were owed their freedom (1 Cor. 12:13; Gal. 3:28; Col. 3:11). When Paul spoke about liberty for enslaved people, he meant this only in a spiritual sense, never in a legal sense. The spiritual freedom of those enslaved was meant to encourage them to submit to their slaveholders (1 Cor. 7:21-24). In Paul's teaching, spiritual freedom and personal dignity existed within the system of slavery and were not a threat to the system.

Slavery was even expanded from the Hebrew Bible to the New Testament. God's people could now own one another in the Hebrew Bible. Christians enslaved one another in perpetuity. Rather than being more anti-slavery than surrounding culture, New Testament authors went along with majority culture. There were abolitionists among Stoics, but not among Christians. Tragically, because of perceived biblical support for slavery, any movement in the direction of abolition ended when Christianity became the official religion of Rome. The world struggled with slavery for nearly another 2,000 years.[176]

I'm saddened by this legacy of slavery perpetuated by the faith of Jesus. It all seems so out of character with the major themes of Jesus' teachings. But as I studied the topic of slavery historically and theologically, I began to realize that advocates of slavery were on more solid ground when it came to the Bible than I imagined. I also learned that the way slavery advocates explained the text was eerily similar to the way I had always approached the text, particularly on the subjects of sex and gender.

CHRISTIAN SLAVERY

Christians who supported slavery[a] centered their lives on Scripture. They believed the Bible was a clear guide to life. They believed Scripture was direct and straightforward, accessible to all, giving all the instruction necessary. God's plan is understood through the Bible.

Though we wonder how Christians could ever support slavery, they wondered how any Bible-believing Christian could support abolition. Scripture did not sanction abolition, and slaveholders were never reprimanded anywhere in the Bible. Slavery was always acceptable if enacted according to the proper legal process and divine permission. The viewpoints of those who supported slavery aligned with nearly 2,000 years of Christian teaching about slavery.

Their basic biblical understanding[177] was as follows:

- God was the one who originally established slavery on the earth through Noah's prophetic statement to his sons. Because of the sin of Ham, the Canaanites, Ham's descendants, were cursed with slavery as a punishment (Gen. 9:20-25).
- Abraham, father to Jews and Christians alike, purchased and enslaved people and was blessed by God in doing so (Gen. 17:12). Further, God blessed Abraham by giving him more people to enslave (Gen. 24:35).
- People could be legally enslaved by conquest (Deut. 20:10, 11), if purchased from other nations, or if purchased from foreigners living in Israel (Lev. 25:44-46).

---

a. I'm focusing primarily on the United States, where the result of a failure to resolve the theological battle was an actual civil war. To my knowledge, the theological elements were similar in other times and places, some of which we will touch on.

- Enslaved foreigners and their descendants could be legally owned in perpetuity and passed down for generations. Only Israelites could not be permanently enslaved (Lev. 25:44-46).
- Jesus challenged Old Testament laws such as the equal retributional justice of "an eye for an eye" (Matt. 5:38-42), but He never challenged the widespread practice of slavery. Instead, He used slavery as a metaphor in many parables, and even in those parables, it wasn't negative (e.g., Luke 17:7-10; Matt. 25:14-30).
- Paul taught that though enslaved people should welcome emancipation, they should be obedient if it didn't happen (1 Cor. 7:21).
- Slaveholders and all those in power were given authority by God (Rom. 13:1-7).
- Paul and Peter advised slaveholders to treat well the people they enslaved. They didn't say to release them. Slaveholders were given these instructions as full participants in Christian communities and weren't barred from serving as elders or deacons. Enslaved people were instructed to submit no matter what (1 Tim. 3:1-13; Col. 3:22; 4:1; Eph. 6:5-8; Tit. 2:9, 10; 1 Pet. 2:16-18).
- Though Paul and Peter both described enslaved people as spiritually free, this spiritual freedom did not change the legal situation on earth in which slavery was honored (1 Cor. 7:20-24; 1 Pet. 2:16-18).
- Even when converted to Christianity, slaveholders were not expected to free those they were keeping in slavery, even fellow Christians (1 Tim. 6:1, 2). This is a movement in the direction of increased slavery when compared to the Hebrew Bible, in which God's people could not enslave each other. Sadly, God's people did not move toward ending slavery.
- Though Paul pleaded with Philemon to free Onesimus, who had escaped Slavery, Paul did not appeal to the immorality of slavery. He simply said that Onesimus' freedom would be useful for the gospel. By pleading with Philemon and requiring Onesimus to return to Philemon, Paul was honoring the legitimacy of Philemon's choice about whether or not to exert his legal right to own Onesimus (Philemon 1:1-25).
- Lordship and slavery were common metaphors for God and God's people. This metaphor is so common that we often refer to God as "Lord."

How could we build a clear biblical case stronger than this one? What plain biblical texts argue for universal emancipation? Slavery was consistently modeled throughout both testaments. Using only a strict reading of the text, how could we possibly convince Christian slaveholders that slavery was a moral evil to be renounced at significant personal cost? Slaveholders were a regular and established part of the church. Many Jewish and Christian people were slaveholders, including Abraham, the father of Israel. On what basis would we exclude slaveholders from the Christian church when they were always included in the Bible?

God's people were instructed about how to enslave people properly. Instructions were given to enslaved and enslavers. How and when someone should be enslaved was often clarified. Kidnapping was not the right way to enslave someone (Ex. 21:16; Deut. 24:7). When Joseph was kidnapped by his brothers and sold into slavery, that was the wrong way to go about it. God also sometimes ended slavery in specific situations. Deciding that Israel should no longer be enslaved, God freed them from Egypt. Yet after being freed, Israel was also free to enslave others. There was a right and wrong way to enslave people, but never was slavery categorically immoral.

CHRISTIAN HISTORY

Christian history doesn't help. Origen, a third-century church father, supported race-based slavery of dark-skinned people. Augustine (d. 430) advocated for slavery and the need for kings to protect the ownership rights of slaveholders.[178] For example, Augustine said in *The City of God*:

> The condition of slavery is justly imposed on the sinner. Wherefore, we do not read of a slave anywhere in the Scriptures until the just man Noah branded his son's sin with this word, so he earned this name by his fault, not by nature. . . . The prime cause of slavery, then, is sin, so that man was put under man in a state of bondage; and this can only be by a judgment of God, in whom there is no unrighteousness, and who knows how to assign divers punishment according to the desert of sinners.[179]

Slavery is a historical, biblical teaching of the church. This theology was not new or unique to West African shores or the American South. Christians didn't challenge slavery for nearly 1,800 years. During the medieval period, slavery took the form of serfdom for most European peasants. It was essentially slavery under another name.[b]

---

b. Serfs were essentially enslaved. The difference is that they were legally tied to a piece of land owned by their lord rather than being directly legally owned. Yet, their labor was owned, and they could not marry, sell property, or travel without permission. It was essentially slavery by proxy. (www.britannica.com/topic/serfdom)

This is the context in which Martin Luther spoke, vigorously defending slavery against its critics:

> You assert that no one is to be a serf of anyone else, because Christ made us all free. That is making Christian freedom a completely physical matter. Did not Abraham and the other patriarchs and prophets have slaves? Read what St. Paul teaches about servants, who, at the time, were all slaves. This article, therefore, absolutely contradicts the gospel. It proposes robbery, for it suggests that every man should take his body away from his lord, even though his body is the lord's property. A slave can be a Christian, and have Christian freedom, in the same way that a prisoner or a sick man is a Christian, and yet not free. This article would make all men equal, and turn the spiritual kingdom of Christ into a worldly, external kingdom; and that is impossible. A worldly kingdom cannot exist without an inequality of persons, some being free, some being imprisoned, some lords, some subjects, etc.; and St. Paul says in Galatians that in Christ the Lord and servant are equal.[180]

I found this quote of Martin Luther's particularly disturbing because of how closely it tracked with the words of Paul in the New Testament. Paul spoke of spiritual freedom for the enslaved but never applied that freedom to physical, legal slavery. Luther is not explaining away the text but paying close attention to its plain meaning.

In many ways, abolitionists fought an uphill battle. There is no alternative explanation for texts about slavery. In the Old Testament, Israelites could enslave foreigners for generations. In the New Testament, enslaved people were the property of their owners in perpetuity. Texts about slavery are about actual slavery that happened in the real world. Throughout Christian history, support for slavery was real, lasting, and included the same basic legality of Slavery in the American South.

Sometimes I try to imagine whether I would have become affirming if the tables were turned. What if all cultures of Bible times spoke directly against same-gender marriage and transgender identity? What if the Bible justified these words? What if the Bible specifically described same-sex marriage as a curse, as Abraham's growing household of enslaved people was described as a blessing? What if the statements in Romans 1 and Leviticus 18 had served to stop or end same-gender marriages? Would I have become affirming? I doubt it.

But this is not the case with same-gender marriage or transgender identity. Same-gender marriage and transgender experiences are never addressed in the Bible or Christian history. There are solid arguments for why the texts that address same-sex eroticism speak to something entirely different. No texts reference transgender people. It's much easier to conclude that the uniformity of cisgender heterosexuality in the Bible reflects biblical culture, not biblical morality, because there was no awareness of same-sex marriage or transgender people. There was biblical awareness of slavery.

The same is true of Christian history. Until the late twentieth century, no Christian ever talked about ex-gays, having your identity in Christ, or gay people remaining celibate. Before that, all people were considered heterosexual, and same-sex eroticism was considered an act of perverted lust, unconnected to commitment and love.[181]

One could make the argument that abolitionists had a more difficult task, biblically and historically. I believe that's true, particularly from a literalistic framework. This is probably why, as we shall see, so few abolitionists even discussed the texts that refer to slavery. Their biblical foundation was in something else entirely.

WHO GOT IT RIGHT?

Despite the preponderance of biblical arguments, supporters of slavery lost. This is remarkable. If the source of morality is Scripture, and if the text is clear, why such a dramatic change? In a relatively short time, Christianity went from universally believing that slavery was biblical to universally believing it wasn't.

The Bible didn't change. So, why such a dramatic departure from historical Christian doctrine? It would be helpful to think of the one and only group of Christians who got this issue right before anyone else. The Christians who got it right were enslaved people. The Christians in the American South who were right about the evils of slavery—and ignored—were Black Christians.[182]

Why were they dramatically ahead of their time? Was it because of their excellent theological training? No, teaching a Black person to read was illegal. Was it because they better understood the plain meaning of Scripture? No, they often had limited access to the text. The texts they were taught were about enslaved people submitting.

They got it right not because of what they found in the text but because of what they brought to the text—and what they didn't bring. They didn't bring bigotry, economic advantage, and tradition. They instead embodied the longing for freedom, equality, and a desire for their people to thrive. They lived every day the harsh reality of pro-slavery theology, and they knew it had nothing to do with the love of God.

Harriet Tubman was one of the most remarkable people in history. She was a devout Methodist and believed she experienced visions from God. She certainly seemed to have divine protection. Tubman didn't need to do a Bible study on slavery. She knew God, and she knew God loved her. So, she knew God wanted her and her people to be free.

By contrast, scholars, experts, and leaders of respectable churches in the South were all white. Whether slaveholders themselves or in solidarity with white slaveholders, they were not invested in the quality of life of those they enslaved. They were invested, financially and otherwise, in forcing enslaved people to work as hard as possible with as few resources as possible. The privileged lives of slaveholders depended on the grueling lives of the enslaved. As a result, it was easy for slaveholders to accept the plain meaning of Scripture when it came to slavery.

Black Christians were not respected. They were dismissed as brutish, ignorant, and self-serving. It was too easy for slave owners to teach a theology they believed was a hard and unfortunate truth. They believed Black people were inferior by nature and needed to be cared for by white Christians. Wealthy Southern Christians convinced themselves that the institution of slavery was loving and beneficial for enslaved people.[183]

Yet, the enslaved saw themselves in the story of Israel. David Walker was an abolitionist. His father had been enslaved, but he was free. In his pamphlet, *Appeal*, Walker cast a theological vision for liberating his people through the story of Israel's escape from Egypt. He wrote prophetically before the Civil War about the hundreds of thousands of Egyptians who died because of enslaving God's people. Walker's theological vision was of liberation. He saw his people's story in the story of the enslaved Israelites and looked forward to a day when God would deliver them.

Enslaved people in America identified with Israel under Egypt. Israel was displaced, forced into slavery, and ultimately freed by God through Moses. Negro spirituals embody this hope. God was with them, and they would one day be free. Their faith in God sustained them. Only through faith did they sustain the hope that was essential to survive the brutal and dehumanizing conditions of slavery.[184]

Enslaved people didn't see themselves as less human or less worthy than Europeans or white Americans. They saw themselves as God's people. They believed they had the right to a better life, not only in the by and by but in the here and now.

What is the biblical basis for enslaved people's theology? Why see themselves in the Israelites rather than in the people the Israelites enslaved? Why not follow New Testament instructions to submit even when they were beaten and treated unjustly (1 Pet. 2:16-18)? Was their approach exegetically sound? Did it fit within the grammatical/historical interpretation of the Bible? Or was it based on liberation, love, and the character of God?

THE LAW CLARIFIES THE GOLDEN RULE

Christian abolitionists, Black and white, enslaved and free, made their arguments based on broad ideas about human value, not on specific texts about slavery. People like David Walker, Henry Ward Beecher, Thomas Clarkson, Frederick Douglass, William Wilberforce, and Sojourner Truth repeatedly spoke about the broad spirit of Scripture over and above the specific letter of the law about slavery. They spoke of universal human value and the Golden Rule.[185]

White abolitionists joined black people. In England, William Wilberforce became interested in abolition only after his conversion to Christianity. His faith motivated his abolitionism. Not only was he not convinced by pro-slavery theology, he didn't feel the need to meet this theology on its own terms. He didn't attempt an explanation. He was motivated by the broad meaning of Scripture, its command to care for and love all people. He ignored the biblical proofs for slavery. These verses weren't important to him.

Another example is Ellen White. Her abolitionist ideals were based on humanity and dignity for enslaved people. Her broad view of Christianity made her an Abolitionist, not her interpretations of texts that referred to slavery.

Slavery supporters understood that proponents of slavery appealed to the humanity and wellbeing of enslaved people. James Henry Thornwell, one of the more prominent defenders of slavery, recognized this. "The incompatibility of Slavery with the spirit and temper of the Gospel is not unfrequently attempted to be made out from the injunction of the Saviour to love our neighbour as ourselves."[186]

He said that we should love people, not question biblical doctrine. Love had limits. We can't simply do whatever seems loving. Slavery was a limit for Thornwell because it was universally practiced and taught in the Bible. He encouraged Christians to apply the Golden Rule through the lens of the Bible's teachings on slavery. "We should treat our slaves as we should feel that we had a right to be treated if we were slaves ourselves."

Love was seen through the lens of laws about slavery. Any act that might seem to benefit the enslaved was filtered out if it didn't fit the model of slavery that pervaded Scripture. Christians would not accept universal abolition because they could find nothing in the Bible that directly supported it. In the Bible, God determined who was enslaved and who was free. God did not abolish slavery. God made Israel free, and Canaan enslaved.

Thornwell and others concluded that abolition came from somewhere other than the Bible. It was cultural, sentimental, and ungodly:

> We think there can be little doubt, that, if the church had universally repressed the spirit of speculation, and had been content to stand by the naked testimony of God, we should have been spared many of the most effective dissertations against slavery. Deduct the opposition to it which has arisen from *sympathy* with imaginary sufferings, from ignorance of its nature and misapplication of the crotchets of philosophers—deduct the opposition which is due to *sentiment*, romance or speculation, and how much will be found to have originated from the humble and devout study of the Scriptures? Will any man say that he who applies to them with an honest and unprejudiced mind, and discusses their teachings upon the subject, simply as a question of language and interpretation, will rise from their pages with the *sentiments* or spirit of a modern Abolitionist? Certain it is that no direct condemnation of slavery can anywhere be found in the Sacred Volume.[187]

Abolitionists prioritized the Golden Rule: "love others as you love yourself." They took it at face value. They made this the most important text for the question of slavery, even though this text doesn't mention slavery. They asked slavery supporters, "Does enslaving people seem loving to you?"

Slavery supporters responded: "If God made me a master, I should treat my slaves with love. If God made me a slave, I should obey with love."

Abolitionists saw this through the lens of love and human dignity. Their sympathy with the enslaved was theologically significant. Defenders of Slavery saw love and human dignity through the lens of the specific texts about slavery. Sympathy with suffering was not theologically persuasive. First, you decide on your theology; then, you implement it lovingly. Love doesn't determine theology; We must follow the law.

Specific texts on the topic of slavery spoke clearly and directly to slavery. The Golden Rule doesn't specifically address slavery, so it wouldn't come up in a systematic study of the subject. The Golden Rule and the major themes of Jesus' ministry were too vague and emotional for the proponents of slavery. They wanted a "thus saith the Lord" on the subject. But they were wrong because they read the Bible in the wrong way.

THE BIBLE IS NOT FLAT

I just saw a book titled *The Soup Bible*. If this book resembled the actual Bible, it would be a collection of history, poetry, legal code, lament, and prophecy about soup. I would also expect a healthy portion dedicated to both the love of soup and how soup is sometimes confusing, disappointing, and painful. But I bet it's just a bunch of recipes.

The title of this book makes the same mistaken assumption about the Bible that we often make. The Bible is not a cookbook with holiness recipes. It's not a list of rules. It's not ingredients for a good life. Instead, it's a small library of not only different books but different types of books.

We treat Scripture like a cookbook or manual of rules and theology because we prefer it that way, not because God does. If God wanted us to have a manual, we would have a manual. The Bible is a witness to the work of God in diverse places, with diverse people, in diverse times. It is a collection of poetry, history, gospels, law, lament, erotic love, wisdom, apocalyptic, and letters from pastors to their congregations.

This diverse and complicated collection of works can't be read as if each verse were the same in meaning, context, and importance. In other words, God didn't mean for us to read the Bible as if it's flat, as if each passage is just as important as any other.

Judges 19 is not as important as Matthew 28. We shouldn't take Judges 19 as our great commission. Jesus is more important than Paul. It's called Christianity, not Paulianity. Paul read the entire Old Testament through his understanding of who Jesus is. That's the point of Galatians and Romans. Should we not also read Paul through the knowledge of the teachings of Jesus? Would Paul not be mortified to read his words placed on the same level as the words of his Savior?

Besides, the Bible looks nothing like a manual, despite our attempts to turn it into one. Pull out your car's manual. Now pull out your Bible. Compare the two and tell me that they're meant to be used and understood in the same way.

We sure try, though. We try to flatten the variegated landscape of Scripture. This approach favors rules and regulations over the more critical themes highlighted in Scripture. In short, we prefer the truth clear, simple, and easily packaged with proof texts that sound like simple answers. We want clarity and simplicity. But God gave us the kind of book that requires us to wrestle, pray, and struggle through with the guidance of the Spirit.

This doesn't mean that one part of Scripture contradicts another. I'm not trying to create a conflict between one text and another. It's only a literalistic approach that sees contradiction in difference. Some passages of Scripture clarify other passages of Scripture. We get our interpretive key for less central verses from the truth revealed in more central verses. We shouldn't reverse the process. Even this explanation is an oversimplification. We can't understand this concept unless we understand the Bible in its totality and know how to apply it today.

The goal is not to throw out some texts and keep others. The goal is an understanding that harmonizes Scripture and is grounded in God's character. Only this approach honors God's ultimate authority to interpret the Bible. God's character is on display particularly in the life of Christ and in the key texts that the Bible itself tells us are most important. We don't want to ground our understanding of slavery in texts that speak directly to slavery. We want to ground those texts, and all texts, in the big picture teachings and values of the Bible, seeking harmony between these greater themes and the specific texts.

If we don't put first things first, we're letting the tail wag the dog. Slavery supporters tried to scrutinize and modify their understanding of love to fit their teaching of slavery. They should have scrutinized and modified their understanding of slavery to accommodate the teaching of human worth and dignity. They would have realized slavery had to go.

PARALLELS

What does this have to do with same-gender marriage and transgender people? There are many meaningful similarities, both theological and institutional.

But there are differences as well. I would rather be an LGBTQ person growing up in the church today than be enslaved. As devastating as the mental health problems are in LGBTQ Christians, they are nothing to the exploitation and hopelessness of slavery, particularly American chattel slavery. No question. I have no desire to equate the two or claim they are morally equivalent. They are not.

On the other hand, I'm certainly glad I didn't have to defend abolition 200 years ago. Bible texts about slavery are really and clearly about actual slavery. The texts about same-sex sex are all about something very different from same-gender marriage. The words in the Bible sanctioned the enslavement of real people when they were written. They did not stop same-gender marriage when they were written.

An article written in an Adventist publication is worth mentioning when discussing the parallels and differences between slavery and affirmation. James Standish claimed that the two subjects were dramatically different in ways that invalidate comparison. He mentioned three differences:

First, he claims that biblical laws limit slavery; they don't mandate it. So, Scripture wasn't trying to say slavery was okay, but trying to reduce the practice. As we've seen, this doesn't hold true to the text. The first time slavery appears in the Bible, a man of God prophesies that an entire people group will be enslaved as a way of dealing with their sin. In other words, a plain reading of the text mandated it. God also "blessed" Abraham with the opportunity to enslave people. The law gave explicit permission. Even the limitations themselves were not particularly stringent compared to those of neighboring countries. With this approach, how do you distinguish between God's permissiveness and God's true law?

Second, Standish states that slavery was not in any way related to salvation. But isn't this the problem? Slaveholders could participate freely and fully in the life of the church. Their souls were unstained by enslaving fellow humans. The problem is that slavery was allowed and was not a matter of sin or salvation.

Third, Standish says slavery was different in the Old Testament and much better than in the American South. His examples are overstated and not always accurate. Yet even assuming he was entirely correct, does this mean he would be willing to return to slavery if it was practiced as in the Old Testament? Is it okay to own people and pass them down from generation to generation? I don't think so.[188]

There are enough similarities between the two situations to be meaningful and instructive, keeping in mind the differences. Here are some parallels between the current debate about sexuality and gender and the historical debate about slavery:

1. Theology that would be good for LGBTQ people (as we understand what is good for us) would challenge the institutional church. They would experience financial and membership losses, at least in the short term. Theology that would be good for enslaved people (as they understood what was good for them) threatened Southern religious institutions and all religious institutions for the first 1,800 years of Christian history.
2. Those who write theological position papers are not part of the LGBTQ community. Policy and doctrine are set by theologians who are insulated from having relationships with openly gay and transgender people that are respectful, close, and on equal power levels, if they have those relationships at all. Those writing pro-slavery theology were not enslaved themselves. They were insulated from relationships with enslaved people that were respectful, close, and on equal power levels.

3. Theology that affirms same-gender marriage and transgender people would be a departure from historical Christianity. Theology that supports abolition was just as radical a change with respect to historic Christian teaching.
4. There are no biblical examples of same-gender couples or transgender people, and there are sufficient texts that, on their face, support accepted theology. There are no examples of universal abolition or abolitionists in the Bible. There are sufficient texts that, on their face, affirm slavery.
5. A small minority of LGBTQ people say accepted theology is good and good for them. The church chooses to listen to these people and ignore the majority, believing there is a way to be loving without theological change. A small minority of enslaved and Black people said that slavery was good—and good for them. The church listened to these people and upheld the idea that they could be loving without theological change.

Are we in a historical situation similar to that of slavery? Could we be importing the *culture* of Bible times instead of the *morality* of the Bible?

THE MAIN THING

If you ask how I could support same-gender marriage and transgender affirmation with no biblical precedent, the answer is similar to that of the abolitionists. I follow the morality of the Bible. My guide is "the spirit and temper of the gospel," the call for justice, the overriding principle of love, and God's concern for the wellbeing of those mistreated. God's church should always stand for these values.

The moral arguments for affirming theology are based on wellbeing, the Golden Rule, and human dignity. Affirming the gender of trans people is an obvious good. Supporting and encouraging everyone to experience sexuality in the monogamous marriage commitment is an obvious good that conservative churches have long championed for heterosexuals.

Providing this kind of support isn't a carte blanche for LGBTQ people to live as they please. It simply puts us on the same level as heterosexuals. It enables us to go about the business of living our sexuality in healthy ways. It allows us to stop pouring energy into trying to fulfill rules about gender and marriage that help no one. Instead, we can pour our energy into being like Jesus and making a meaningful difference in the world. It helps us live out our sexuality and gender in ways that honor ourselves, our families, and those in our communities.

Affirming theology draws from the prophets who spoke against the exploitation of widows, orphans, and the poor. We side with Isaiah, who foretold the inclusion of eunuchs in the assembly of God's people, though the law forbade them. We side with Peter, who baptized Cornelius with no more justification than the moving of the Spirit. We side with Philip, who baptized the Ethiopian eunuch who would have been cast out from the assembly of God's people. We side with Jesus, who rejected religious exclusiveness and called a bunch of rejects to be His disciples. In this way, affirming theology is an expression of the gospel itself.

Affirming theology also believes in a church whose love is pure. No longer are there two different versions of faith—one for cisgender heterosexuals and the other for LGBTQ people—one in which we have been given the gift of family, and the other where the desire for a family is a temptation to sin. No longer do rules manifest in cruelly unequal ways. Faith communities can be made whole again when sexual minorities are treated as vital and given the same high, but attainable, ethical standards.

The theological perspectives of affirming theology are similar to those of the abolitionists. Conversely, those who oppose affirming theology see things in ways eerily similar to those of slavery supporters.

Affirming theology draws upon the Golden Rule and asks of heterosexual Christians, "Would you want your marriage and gender to be rejected the way they are for LGBTQ people?"

Accepted theology responds, "My job is to treat LGBTQ people as I would like to be treated if my marriage and gender identity were forbidden." These words echo James Henry Thornwell's words from nearly three centuries past. Rather than considering the impact of our theology on real people, we simply obey, no matter the cost to vulnerable people.

Affirming theology places love, compassion, and justice in the driver's seat. Love is more than *how* we communicate our beliefs. Love is about *what* we believe. The fact that same-gender marriage was never modeled or mentioned in the Bible is less important than the Golden Rule, because the Bible was never meant to cover every possible scenario for all times and all places. It didn't cover the essential moral imperative of abolition.

This theology that places love at the foundation is not what we find when Adventists approach the question of same-gender marriage. Ángel Manuel Rodríguez was director of the Biblical Research Institute of the General Conference, the church's highest theological authority, when he published the following:

The church would betray the will of the Lord by allowing *sentimental sympathy* and *loving understanding* to become *sentimental* permissiveness. We all need divine wisdom to minister to such individuals and families without negotiating away biblical teachings, norms, and principles.[189]

Thankfully, Rodríguez has a different tone than Thornwell, but both focus on the harm done by a theological belief as "sentimental." Both dismiss love and understanding as insufficient reasons to question our beliefs. It's hard to read this quote and realize that what Rodríguez dismisses as "sentimental" is the concern that many have about our responsibility to care for the wellbeing of children in our communities. It's not sentimentalism to be horrified about children losing hope and committing suicide because of these beliefs.

How could Rodriguez's approach have found the moral strength to fight a civil war and end the institution of slavery? Slavery was an institution written into nearly every book of the Bible. Only a heart touched deeply by sentiment would find the courage for such opposition. Only Christians who saw love, compassion, and empathy as morally strong principles would have opposed Slavery 200 years ago.

THE GOLDEN RULE

"Sentiment" is not anti-Bible. The major themes at the heart of the Bible support the wellbeing and dignity of all people, *especially* the vulnerable with the least power. The Golden Rule and the highest Christian principle of love are explicitly given as the source of every single bit of the law (Matt. 22:40).

"God is love" means that love is the core of God's nature. "Love your neighbor as you love yourself" is more than nice words; it's a principle with real-world implications. It doesn't mean that enslaved people should be presented the gospel so they can be saved. It means that enslaved people should be set free now, in this life. It means that slavery should be outlawed. It means that slaveholders should be expelled from church membership, even if New Testament Christians accepted them in their congregations.

Even Ellen White, who held Scripture in the highest regard, did not base her anti-slavery views on any specific texts about slavery. She appealed to the broad teachings of Scripture. She made no scriptural defense of abolition other than an appeal to love and humanity. She did not clarify the texts cited to support slavery.[c] It was enough for her that this evil system caused suffering, which lingered even after abolition.

> The colored people are suffering the results of the bondage in which they were held. When they were slaves, they were taught to do the will of those who called them their property. They were kept in ignorance, and today there are thousands among them that cannot read. Many who profess to be teachers among them are corrupt in character, and they interpret the Scriptures in such a way as to fulfill their own purposes, and degrade those who are in their power... The Scripture has been perverted, and the people have been so instructed as to be easily seduced by evil spirits... The whole system of slavery was originated by Satan, who delights in tyrannizing over human beings (*Advent Review and Sabbath Herald*, Jan. 28, 1896).

White says that slavery originated with Satan, but there is no text to support this. No verse says that Satan established slavery. No text says slavery is a moral evil. Instead, God's spokesperson, Noah, was the first to establish slavery, and he established it for an entire people group (Gen. 9:25-27).[190]

Where did Ellen White get that Satan originated slavery? What was the source of her support for abolition? Human dignity was enough. Human suffering was sufficient cause to end slavery. The Golden Rule and the importance of loving all people were all she needed, even though these verses about love and the Golden Rule never directly say that slavery is wrong. She believed that the Spirit would help us determine what we should do if we really loved and respected enslaved people.

Let me be clear. The biblical passages cited as prohibitions for LGBTQ people can be overcome. The more their intent is understood, the more apparent it is that they don't apply to same-sex marriage or transgender people. Yet, I recognize that some may not agree. I'm convinced my perspective is the best approach, but it's not the only obvious one. There will be disagreement about the prohibitions. In the absence of the total clarity we might desire, rather than relying on a rule of thumb that always favors prohibition, we should lean on what is most evident in Scripture.

Rather than "when in doubt, don't," we should rely on the Golden Rule as our rule of thumb. The clarity of the command to care for all people should

---

c. A search through the Scripture index of Ellen White's writings indicates that she never mentioned most of the key texts supporting slavery. Others were never addressed concerning the institution of slavery but interpreted allegorically instead.

guide us. I'm not advocating throwing out any text of Scripture: every text, every word, every jot, every tittle matters. Everything matters, but not every Bible text matters equally. Jesus didn't have any qualms about naming two texts as the greatest.

ATTACKING THE BIBLE

For white Christians in the American South, and even many white Christians in the North, sentimentality was an attack on Scripture itself. They argued that to undermine slavery was to undermine the authority of Scripture. They saw abolition as a surrender to relativism and chaos.

James Henry Thornwell said: "Certain it is that no direct condemnation of Slavery can anywhere be found in the Sacred Volume. . . . The Church cannot accept [condemnation of slavery] without renouncing the supremacy of the Scriptures."[191]

This is the same accusation made against affirming theology. I have often heard statements such as these: "Love is no excuse for disobeying the Bible." "LGBTQ people should submit themselves to God's natural order." "From beginning to end, marriage in the Bible is between a man and a woman. Anything else is an attack on Scripture itself."

I understand that they come from a place of reverence for the Bible. I know they are motivated by trust in the wisdom of God over the understanding of fallen humanity. The intentions are good, but they are misguided.

Richard Davidson is a theologian, seminary professor, and advocate of traditional theology. He wrote two chapters in *Homosexuality, Marriage, and the Church* released by the Seventh-day Adventist Theological Seminary. He was one of my favorite professors at the seminary. I had him for two classes, including one with only a few brave souls gathered around a table for an intensive look at Old Testament law. I probably learned more in that class than in any other. I know him to be a tender, humble, careful, and sincere follower of Jesus who encourages and listens to his students.

Yet, I can't reconcile myself to his understanding of affirming theology. He dedicated an entire chapter to the thesis that expanding marriage to same-gender couples threatens our dependence on the Bible and that "most fundamentally, what is at stake in this discussion is the authority of Scripture" (p. 187).

When Christianity shifted its viewpoint on slavery, it wasn't because we found a Bible verse explicitly supporting abolition. We changed because we took the Bible's core values seriously—seriously enough to accept abolition though Scripture never modeled abolition and consistently modeled slavery. Seriously enough to say that even though slavery was always present in the economic labor systems of the Bible, we were compelled to abolish it. We broke the model, creating something new that better matched the character of God and the major scriptural themes of justice, love, and humanity.

Why is the dignity of enslaved people and the universal command to love primary when we look at slavery but dangerous when applied to gay, bisexual, and transgender people? Why would we destroy the model of slavery without destroying the Bible, but we can't expand marriage to include same-gender couples or affirm transgender people?

Supporters of Slavery knew Abolitionists were appealing to the major themes of Scripture over and above specific verses about slavery. They considered it a way of excusing the clarity of certain biblical texts and of justifying the personal behavior and beliefs of abolitionists:

> Finding it impossible to deny that slavery... is actually sanctioned by Christ and His apostles, those [abolitionists] who would preserve some show of consistency in their veneration of the Scriptures, and their condemnation of us, resolve the conduct of the founders of Christianity into motives of prudence and considerations of policy. *While they admit that the letter of the Scriptures is distinctly and unambiguously in our favor, they maintain that their spirit is against us.*[192]

Those who focus on "the letter of Scriptures" above "their spirit" supported slavery. William Wilberforce himself summed up Scripture this way:

> Is it nothing to be taught that all human distinctions will soon be at an end; that all the labors and sorrows of poverty and hardship will soon exist no more; and to know, on the express authority of Scripture, that the lower classes, instead of being an inferior order in the creation, are even the preferable objects of the love of the Almighty?[193]

This is the reasoning that supporters of slavery dismissed as sentimental disregard for Scripture. Why? Because Wilberforce ignored verses about slavery. I couldn't find a single place where he explained why abolition is consistent with texts supporting slavery. I found no exegetical arguments. Like Ellen White, he never addresses these texts.[194]

Slavery supporters had absolute confidence in their theology because they could quote chapter and verse. God's law said enslaved people must submit.

If abolition didn't follow the law, they undermined Scripture. Any appeals to love in this context were simply excuses for dismissing the Bible. James Henry Thornwell called the slave's desire to be free "passions and selfishness" and the abolition of slavery "the sanction of the grossest wickedness."[195]

The irony in this is that the proponents of slavery who thought they were defending Scripture are the very ones who most threatened the integrity of scriptural authority. They are still the cautionary tale used by opponents of Christianity, arguing that we can't trust the Bible.[196] Slavery proponents thought they were defending the Bible, but they were slandering it. It's shocking to think how callous they were to human suffering.

We should not be ignorant of the realities of our own time. One of the number one reasons people, especially young people, leave conservative Christian churches is that the church doesn't accept LGBTQ people. One of the most common criticisms of Christians is that they are anti-gay.[197]

This comes as a surprise to no one who works with young people. Accepted theology makes people question whether the church is a force for good in the world. Too often, churches serve those whose lives are already easiest in society, rejecting marginalized people.

It's difficult for people to believe in the Bible when they are taught to explain away the suffering of neighbors, friends, and family who happen to be gay, bisexual, or transgender. It's equally difficult for them to deal with the cognitive dissonance created by trying to harmonize the reality that affirming theology helps people thrive with the traditional insistence that such thriving is sinful. None of these justifications should be requirements of biblical faithfulness.

ALREADY THERE

A lot in this chapter may seem new, but it's not as new as it seems. One way or another, we've often taught that despite a few misunderstood texts, the Bible is anti-slavery. Slavery supporters were only justifying their terrible behavior. That's how we talk about the subject, but most people haven't studied it in depth. What are our real reasons for opposing slavery?

Imagine if we became convinced that the Bible taught that slavery was right, and abolition was wrong. I know, I'm asking a lot. But let's say we decided to do an objective Bible study to discover whether slavery was evil or moral because we believe our morality should come from the Bible. We were careful to ignore our intuition and cultural ideas about slavery. We did our best to see the text.

What if we came to the same conclusion that has been the majority opinion in Christian history? What if we decided the Bible presented slavery as a normal part of God's ordering of society, a response to sin in the world, and the only question is how to figure out who is enslaved? I believe this is the conclusion we would reach if we were interpreting the Bible in the same way today's church interprets Scripture related to LGBTQ people. Would we then decide that slavery is morally acceptable and advocate reinstating it?

Absolutely not. The very thought is disgusting. The idea that one human should own another human as property is abhorrent. We don't consider slavery a moral option because we know that compassion is biblical. Human dignity is scriptural.

We are unwilling to preach the supposed virtues of slavery from the pulpit on Sabbath mornings. No matter what theological explanation we devise for why slavery is wrong and why Scripture opposes it, our conclusion is inevitable: Slavery is wrong.

Today's Christians sometimes argue over which explanation is better, yet all assume slavery is wrong. In truth, the explanations themselves are afterthoughts because even if they were found wanting, we wouldn't start preaching the virtues of slavery. We believe slavery is wrong because it's a violation of the fundamental dignity of all people created in the image of God. That's the theology conservatives have already accepted when it comes to slavery, and it's a whole lot better than what Christendom has believed for most of its history.

Today's conservative theology accords with that of the abolitionists. Using the same approach, we could affirm same-gender marriage and transgender people. We wouldn't need to radically change to affirm. The pieces are already there. We only need to apply them to a new situation.

Angel Rodríguez, who cautioned against "sentimental permissiveness" in the face of the suffering of LGBTQ people, had something very different to say about slavery:

> God did not proscribe [Slavery], but He did regulate it in order to protect slaves from abuse and exploitation. God does not uproot us from our culture but takes us where we are and makes us better persons.[198]

Rodríguez says this despite Noah's prophetic judgment that Canaanites would be enslaved. He said this despite the Bible's explanation about when people can be legally enslaved. He says this despite the Bible saying God rewarded Abraham with the ability to enslave people. He said this despite Peter's admonition for enslaved people to submit even to cruelty. Ellen White concurs with Rodríguez:

> It was not the apostle's work to overturn arbitrarily or suddenly the established order of society. To attempt this would be to prevent the success of the gospel. But he taught principles that struck at the very foundation of slavery and which, if carried into effect, would surely undermine the whole system (*Acts of the Apostles,* p. 459).

We believe that apparent endorsements of slavery in the Bible were only a reflection of the culture of Bible times, not the morality of the Bible. Why can't we accept that the absence of same-gender marriage and transgender people in the Bible is also a cultural reflection? Another respected Adventist scholar has a straightforward explanation of why conservative Christians reject slavery.

> The Bible does not contain an explicit prohibition of slavery; yet, by looking at biblical principles that stress human dignity, freedom, and fundamental equality as well as by studying Paul's treatment of slavery in letters such as Philemon, many Christians, including Adventists, came to realize that slavery had to be abolished.199

In my research, I also came across an article by another professor of mine at Andrews University. When I was a student there, Darius Jankiewicz was a professor in Historical Theology at the Seventh-day Adventist Theological Seminary. I had the privilege of taking one class with him but wish I could have taken more. He's not only a skilled historian but one of the best communicators I've had in the classroom. He could bridge the past and the present so we could learn from the mistakes and failures of those who came before us.

I recall the detailed approach he took in class to walk us through the history of how ordination entered the Christian church. Ordination was not a concept from the Bible, particularly not as we practice it today. I knew people who entered his class believing women shouldn't be ordained as pastors and left believing no one should be ordained and that women could serve equally. He teaches in a way that challenges paradigms.

After writing most of this chapter, I came across an article Jankiewicz wrote on slavery. He didn't make any connections to LGBTQ affirmation and may disagree with that parallel. Yet, we are certainly in agreement about the main points of the historical debate between abolitionists and slavery supporters. Jankiewicz says of abolitionists, "Their focus was on Scripture's grand themes, such as the love of God, His moral law, creation in the image of God, freedom, equality, redemption and restoration—'abstract principles' reviled by their pro-slavery colleagues."[200]

In fact, in his article, he makes many of the same points I do, quoting many of the same sources. He advocates for a "dynamic" approach to interpretation that takes culture and the themes of Scripture into account, rather than a "literalistic" approach that focuses on the strict meaning of words stripped of context. I couldn't agree more.

Jankiewicz ends his article with the stunning admission that there are times when the culture gets it right, and Christians get it wrong. Sometimes Christians can be shamed by a culture that grasps a moral good before the church does. "One of the more peculiar lessons that Christians may learn from faith in slavery in the antebellum South, is that God can use culture to help, lead, teach, and even shame us."[201]

I'm advocating the same theological approach for gay, bisexual, and transgender Adventists that is already in place for slavery. It wasn't sentimental to believe that enslaved people should be free. It's not sentimental today to say that the church should support same-gender marriage and transgender people.

Adventism is demanding of the LGBTQ community what it would never demand of cisgender, heterosexual members. The church wouldn't survive one month if it did. Members would flee if the church banned all heterosexual marriages and demanded married people get divorced. Nor would it survive requiring cisgender people to behave and identify as a gender different than they know themselves to be. It simply wouldn't work. It's no less harmful to demand such things of gay, bisexual, and transgender people. It's no less cruel, no less dehumanizing. We should take this seriously because Jesus commands us to love others as we love ourselves.

It's a conservative approach to Scripture to recognize when something is cultural. It's a conservative approach to rely on the major themes of Scripture, giving them greater moral weight. Conservative theology cares about human suffering and human wellbeing. Conservative theology builds a society where all people can participate and contribute to their best abilities, where people have rights and responsibilities. I know this because conservatives do this with slavery and many other topics.

Conservatives care about people. Compassion is biblical. The only difference between someone who believes in affirming theology and someone who doesn't is that the same approach to slavery has not yet been applied to same-gender marriage and transgender identity. Most conservatives simply haven't gotten there yet with LGBTQ people, but I believe they will.

The positive theological reason for same-gender marriage and transgender affirmation is human dignity, the Golden Rule, and love. This is much more important than the fact that there were no same-gender couples and no transgender people in the Bible. There were no abolitionists in the Bible either.

PERMISSIVENESS

But what about that danger of permissiveness? If we center our theology on love and the Golden Rule, what's to keep us from simply allowing everything that sounds good? What's to keep us from permitting anything that feels right?

Once, while talking to some friends from church, I started to say that the church's requirements of LGBTQ people were burdensome. "Can you imagine what it would be like?" I asked. "It seems like a lot to ask, and it's hard to understand why."

One friend spoke up: "I think it's wrong to put ourselves in their place. We shouldn't think about what sin is like. We're supposed to focus on what is good."

The appeal of his advice is its simplicity. If it's wrong, don't think about it. It reminds me of a rule of thumb I often followed in my life when I was particularly legalistic, the same rule I spoke of in the introduction: "When in doubt, don't."

If we reject this advice, what's to keep us from swinging the other way? What's to prevent us from simply avoiding hard things? What prevents us from becoming a weak and permissive religion?

Let's step back and think about it for a moment. Does empathy lead naturally to permissiveness? If I place myself in someone else's shoes, do I automatically want the easy choice for them? Or does empathy, especially for someone caught in sin, lead me to want them to make the difficult choice?

When I empathize with alcoholics, I don't become permissive. I know recovery from alcoholism is hard, and I hope that alcoholics make those hard decisions. If I didn't care about the person, I wouldn't care that they were harming themselves. Compassion makes me less permissive and more restrictive. If we don't care if an alcoholic keeps drinking, we aren't caring for them at all.

For a time, I worked in juvenile corrections. I conducted intake interviews and wrote psychological reports and treatment recommendations for hundreds of adolescents. The hardest interviews were with youth who had sexually assaulted children. Even if I was compassionate for their (often horrific) personal circumstances, I had zero desire to be permissive about their compulsions. Few life choices are more soul-crushing than compulsive behaviors that victimize other people. My wish for them is that they would do absolutely anything to prevent themselves from harming children. Love makes me restrictive.

Compassion doesn't make me wish people would have affairs because they feel like it. Identifying with someone's pain doesn't make me hope they will resort to physical violence. Understanding the compulsion to waste money causes me to value contentment, not consumerism.

Empathy and love are not paths to permissiveness. Momentary satisfaction is not high on our list of hopes for those we love. We hope they will make choices that are healthy and life-sustaining for themselves and others. That more profound level of desire comes from love and empathy. That's how Jesus loves us, and how He loved His disciples. That's why He loves so deeply and demands so much. Jesus doesn't just want things to be easy for us. Jesus wants us to live lives of meaning, purpose, sacrifice, and joy.

This is what Jesus was talking about when He said we should love others as we love ourselves. Our hope for ourselves is not simply that we have it easy. It's certainly not that we choose destructive self-gratification. We want to live our values. We want to make a meaningful difference in the world. We hope to live lives of purpose and joy.

When Jesus spoke about love, His words showed confidence that conservative churches today rarely reflect. Jesus didn't give caveats. He didn't hedge or qualify his statements about the importance of love as the wellspring of Christian morality. Jesus wasn't afraid that an emphasis on love would water down ethics. In Jesus' understanding, love is demanding, even to the point of death if necessary. Reading passages like Luke 6:17-49, Matthew 5-7, 25:31-27, and John 15:9-17, you will find a very different conversation about love than the one we often engage in today. Jesus taught the rigor of an ethic of love.

I hope we all learn to embrace that rigor, so we can make hard decisions that lead to good outcomes for ourselves and others. I hope we all know and love Jesus. I hope we sacrifice for others even when we don't know how it will work out. I hope we choose good over easy.

We shouldn't be afraid to get close to the experience of gay, bisexual, and transgender people, because empathy doesn't lead to permissiveness. Empathy and understanding may lead us to ask ourselves difficult questions, but we should do it anyway. Love for others doesn't make us compromise the law. Love clarifies the law. The law is there for our good and the good of others. Love helps us understand that.

Through empathy and love, we see what is plain to see: that transgender people are beautiful, strong, and brave. We have nothing to fear from them.

They are simply people who experience their neurological gender differently than cisgender people. Their gender doesn't make them scary or sinful. We have maligned, feared, and slandered them for no good reason. There is no redemption, goodness, or love in mandating alignment with external anatomy over neurological gender.

Through empathy and love, we see what is plain to see: that same-gender couples are just as capable of having loving marriages as heterosexuals. Same-gender couples are not marrying out of selfishness or rebellion against God. Same-sex marriages are at least as demanding and sacrificial as any others. When the church refuses to support these marriages, tells gay and bisexual children that their love is sinful, and opposes full equality under the law, the church is causing untold harm. Love is love.

The reputation of Christ and the church has suffered because of how Christians treat gay, bisexual, and transgender people. Intending to defend the authority of Scripture, accepted theology has nonetheless caused the world to doubt the goodness of God and the Bible.

Conservative Christians have done much of this with good intentions. They haven't intended to cause harm or ignore the major themes of Scripture. They haven't meant to major in minors and minor in majors. But they have. It's time to change. For the sake of a new generation of Christians, for the sake of the reputation of Christ, it's time to change.

I spent much of this book on the texts used as prohibitions because I take the Bible seriously. I imagine you do, too. We need to keep looking closely at every text and passage of the Bible. In the final analysis, we might have questions. We might not have total certainty. Maybe after carefully considering my arguments, you just won't agree. Or maybe after reading this book, you'll have more questions. This is hard stuff.

When this is the case, we must ask ourselves what our priorities are. What kind of communities do we want to build? What types of relationships do we want to have? What help do we offer (or withhold) from people who ask for our support? What kind of space do we want to give to those who believe in affirming theology?

I hope that even those who disagree with affirming theology can make space for those who believe it. I hope we can acknowledge that conservative people can believe in the Bible, trust in Jesus, and affirm same-gender marriage and transgender identity.

CHAPTER 14

Now What?

This book focused on theological and biblical questions. We looked at a lot of information. It's a lot to absorb. Take your time, and don't feel rushed in thinking it through. We Adventists often approach the subject of affirmation from a theological and biblical angle. We pretend that this is *only* a theological and intellectual challenge. But that's not true. Our theology is not a detached academic exercise. Theology is not a personal matter, either. Our beliefs exist in relationships within the institution of the church.

As we close this book, let me put my experience and the general topic of affirmation into context. We need to talk not only about theology but where theology leads. Where do we go from here? What are the challenges facing us as Adventists? What are our opportunities?

First, let's talk about the challenges and opportunities in the big picture. To do that, we need to look back at how we got to where we are today. Then we can see more clearly where we are. The challenges are real. Even having an open conversation about theology on this topic requires facing those challenges, but there are opportunities if we see them for what they are and seize them.

Second, let's talk about challenges and opportunities on a personal level. This is especially for those who have become affirming. Drawing on my own experience and the experiences of others I know, I have some insights that I hope are helpful as we wrestle with how to live out these beliefs.

Finally, I will share my own experience. I'll share a bit about what it was like for me to become affirming and what it was like to come out.

LOOKING BACK

I'm not going to sugarcoat this story. It's rough. This doesn't mean the people involved were bad people or that they intended to cause harm, but some of them could have done better.

For a long time, Adventists didn't do much to address same-sex sexual orientation. The first article I could find that focused on sexual minorities was a brief opinion piece in 1970 by Miriam Wood, who used to have a regular column in the *Review and Herald*. She spoke of "one of the ugliest of all words, one of the ugliest of all moralities—homosexuality."[202] The same author later praised Anita Bryant, who led the campaign to maintain the criminalization of same-sex sexuality and make sure employers could continue to fire people for being gay.[203]

There was also a scathing editorial by Robert Parr, a long-time editor for *Signs of the Times*, in 1974. "We categorically state that homosexuality is evil and disgusting." He called for authorities to take away the civil right to protest and gather publicly from LGBTQ people. "We will not concede that these Gay Liberation people have any right to parade themselves before the young . . . to preen themselves in the glare of respectable publicity."[204]

This was not a good start for the Adventist Church. Other than these few scattered articles, there were few other references. Homosexuality was usually cited as a sign of how corrupt the world had become. Other statements dehumanized gay people. But there was no serious attempt to address the subject, no humble attempts to understand the gay and lesbian community, and certainly no advice for gay Adventists, let alone bisexual or transgender people. There seems to have been an attitude that homosexuality did not exist in the Adventist Church. It was something that existed outside, in "the world."

Perhaps it goes without saying because we all assume this to be the case, but I found no articles that were sympathetic to affirmation. I doubt such articles would have been allowed. There were brief theological statements about why homosexuality was wrong, often focusing on Sodom and sometimes on Genesis and Paul's writings. None were more than a couple of sentences. The question of studying the Bible more closely on the topic, or trying to expand our understanding, didn't seem to be under consideration.

In 1976 the Adventist Church made a more concerted effort to acknowledge the existence of gay Adventists. *Insight* magazine announced that Colin Cook, a former homosexual, had become heterosexual with God's help. Cook outlined how he had become heterosexual through the use of 12-steps recovery and how others could as well.[205] Two years later, an article in the *Review* by an anonymous woman claimed that her son was cured of homosexuality. She offered a three-step process to cure anyone and claimed that Cook had made more than 200 people "completely heterosexual."[206]

While these claims might seem wild today, they show that Adventists were starting to realize that some Adventists are gay. They see that they need to have some alternative, some kind of ministry for them. They wanted to make them heterosexual as soon as possible. Within their belief system, Colin Cook seemed like the answer to their prayers.

As a result of the publicity, Cook received national recognition (if not international) and thousands of requests for help. He used his elevated profile to do seminars in churches around the country, gathering donations. With this and significant financial assistance from the General Conference, he founded the Quest Learning Center in 1980. The center claimed to cure homosexuality using a modified 12-step program, calling the new program "homosexuals anonymous." All told, the General Conference gave his ministry donations totaling more than six figures, a large sum even by today's standards.[207]

Meanwhile, outside the institutional church, Seventh-day Adventist Kinship International was formed. The "International" in the name was a grandiose embellishment at the time, as it was just a few LGBTQ Adventists in the United States who had found one another. The institution did not support them.

In 1979 they held their first Kinship Kampmeeting, asking theologians and pastors to attend and give spiritual guidance. The Adventist Church agreed to send the representatives they requested and to pay their airfare. In return, Colin Cook was also allowed to come and present his "cure."[208]

The Adventist Church continued to give Colin Cook favorable press. I spoke to a woman named Dorothy who went to the seminary with Cook. She said they gave him time in classes to talk to seminary students about how he was healed of homosexuality and had a program for healing others. When she later found out her own son was gay, she immediately thought of Cook.

Dorothy called and spoke to Cook, interested in getting her son into his program. Cook said he would have his wife call back in a few days. Waiting for the call, Dorothy didn't feel peace about Cook's ministry. Something didn't seem right. As a deeply spiritual woman, dedicated to prayer, she brought the matter to God. Soon she had a sense of peace about her son. She didn't need to try and change him. She didn't pursue the matter any further.

Warning signs about Cook's ministry appeared from the beginning. The participants at Kinship recognized it right away. They found his presentation at their first Kampmeeting utterly incompatible with their experiences. Listening carefully, they realized Cook said that being heterosexual was a gift from God to be received by faith. Those who have faith can claim heterosexuality even if their feelings and behaviors haven't changed. That accounted for a discrepancy with a man Cook brought to Kinship to testify about how he had become heterosexual. Talking to him later, Kinship members found this supposedly heterosexual man had recently spent a weekend having sex with a man he'd just met.

They tried to speak with church leaders about their concerns, but the leaders didn't listen. Kinship asked to have a regular channel of communication with the General Conference, but it was never granted. Two years later, the General Conference issued a letter to pastors forbidding attendance at Kinship events. They also said it was impossible to open communication and expressed a desire to stop Kinship from using "Seventh-day Adventist" in their name. That same year the church filed to copyright the name "Seventh-day Adventist."[a]

While refusing to communicate with Kinship, the General Conference continued to fund Cook and give him positive press. They did not provide any oversight or accountability for his program. They left him alone and took his word that all was well and that people were being cured of homosexuality by the hundreds.

Ronald Lawson, a Kinship founder and sociologist, was alerted to problems in Cook's program. He investigated, talking to as many counselees as he could track down. He soon found that Cook was sexually abusing his counselees, masturbating while on the phone with nearly all his long-distance counselees, and giving naked erotic massages to others, including minors. This happened for the entire six years the ministry was in operation. Lawson sent a detailed report to then General Conference president, Neal Wilson (Ted Wilson's father).

---

a. SDA Kinship is still around. You can join from anywhere in the world if you are LGBTQ, a family member of an LGBTQ person, or simply an ally interested in supporting and learning. For more information, visit sdakinship.org.

To make sure it wouldn't be ignored, Lawson sent it to 20 other leaders as well. Quest was closed within the month.[209]

Sadly, that wasn't the end of it. A few months later, *Ministry* interviewed Cook. They allowed him to apologize and regain credibility. He was contrite and humble. Anyone who didn't know what happened could be excused if they were impressed by how he took responsibility.

Cook and the interviewer described his sins with vague and minimizing words. They said he "slipped," and Cook said he engaged in "physical intimacy with some of my counselees," but that it was not "sexual intercourse." His confession took only a handful of lines. The rest was dedicated to Cook explaining his theories, how he changed, and why his program still worked. Nowhere was it disclosed that Cook had exploited most of his counselees for the entire time the ministry was in operation. Cook maintained that he had only had sexual contact with his wife for the last eight months. He said he was back on track. When asked about his future plans, Cook said, "this trial was permitted by God" and outlined a vision for a vast ex-gay organization.[210]

The Adventist Church minimized Cook's predatory behavior and allowed him to redeem himself. This put Cook in another position of trust. At the end of that year, Cook opened Quest II and was back at it. He eventually gained the support of Focus on the Family and national recognition in two appearances on *The Phil Donahue Show.* Cook hadn't changed. He sexually abused more vulnerable men who had come to him for help. Eventually, Ronald Lawson exposed him again, this time to the *Denver Post.*[211]

While they were defending and supporting Colin Cook, the General Conference tried to stop Kinship from using the name "Seventh-day Adventist." After filing a copyright for the name in 1981, the General Conference told Kinship to stop using it in 1985. In 1987 they hired a legal team for top dollar and sued Kinship. The General Conference lost in Federal District Court in 1991. Realizing they would risk their copyright on a national level if they pushed the matter, they chose not to appeal. A judge ordered the General Conference to pay Kinship's legal fees of $200,000.[212]

When I talked to Kinship members who lived through this experience, they expressed sadness. Though continually reaching out to the denomination, they were told they weren't worthy of dialogue. The same happened after the lawsuit. Kinship sent an olive branch and asked for dialogue. They also asked for a theological study with members selected by both Kinship and the church.

In response, the General Conference sent a letter stating: "It would seem quite obvious that as long as your organization finds a homosexual relationship to be an acceptable lifestyle, it will be impossible for it and the church to develop any meaningful relationship." The letter closed with the words: "I hope this old saying indicates the church will continue a kind and compassionate ministry to everyone: 'God hates the sin but loves the sinner.'"

Candidly, I'm disheartened by the self-satisfaction of General Conference leaders. They failed to live up to our ideals as Adventists. To reject any "meaningful relationship" with Kinship because of the perceived sinfulness of Kinship's position shows a lack of awareness of their own sin or humility about their fallibility. Kinship has been right many times when the General Conference was wrong. The institution badly needed the perspective of Kinship, especially when it came to Colin Cook. They didn't know what they didn't know, and they were too proud to realize that they could have learned quite a bit from the "sinners." They could have avoided not only scandal, but the sexual abuse they enabled. Though claiming compassion, their compassion was sadly lacking. I wish they could learn from these mistakes and start open dialogue with Kinship and LGBTQ people they might theologically disagree with. It would be a healthy step for them to take.

Today the relationship is marginally better. Every year a few Adventist pastors quietly attend Kampmeeting. Behind the scenes, conversations are happening. The North American Division of the General Conference has made strides, recently publishing a book called *Guiding Families of LGBT+ Loved Ones: Adventist Edition*. It's available through AdventSource. The book doesn't question Adventist doctrine but promotes a more open and understanding approach that prioritizes relationships. It avoids language that implies that people can change their orientation. This has been welcomed by Kinship and many LGBTQ Adventists. But the General Conference continues to endorse problematic ministries opposed by Kinship.

Though the name SDA Kinship International sounded grandiose at the time, the organization has lived up to its name. It now has a global presence. As of this writing, 3,770 individuals claim membership worldwide. More than 1,600 members are outside the United States, and international membership is experiencing considerable gains in Brazil.

INSTITUTIONAL BARRIERS

This troubled history should inform us going forward. Our past can be understood when we think about the institutionalization of Adventism. The institution has been taking shape for more than a century. Global, continental, regional, and local administrators are part of this system. We have school systems. We have theologians and professors. We have authors and publishing houses. We have magazines, both church-sponsored and independent. We have the Adventist Development and Relief Agency (ADRA). We have missionaries and missions. We have clinics and hospitals. We have a medical school. We have churches large and small. We have independent ministries and television stations. We have Oshkosh, Silver Springs, and Loma Linda.

The presence of the global church is almost beyond comprehension. The church feels deceptively small, but it's huge. As of this writing, there are more than 94,000 churches, 9,000 schools, 21 million members, 20,000 ordained ministers, and 300,000 employees.[213] The church rakes in about $2 billion in tithe each year,[214] plus offerings.

Our lives intersect with this behemoth. We shouldn't fool ourselves into thinking anyone is in charge of it, though some have more influence than others. Anything this large doesn't change quickly, or easily, or at the will of any one individual. We all play our roles in this institution, relying on one another to play their parts well. We trust one another to help build collective understanding, and the institution helps us each understand our roles and responsibilities.

Though we often think of institutions as inherently negative, they aren't entirely. There are benefits to the Adventist institution. No one can do or understand everything. Having experts who share our foundational values on essential subjects is helpful for all of us. Having leaders with shared values multiplies impact. This collective effort has vast benefits.

The Adventist Church accomplishes incredible acts of humanitarianism globally. It operates schools in places where there wouldn't have been educational options. It runs clinics for those with little access to healthcare. Because of our collective action, the Adventist message, only 160 years old, has spread to every corner of the globe. This kind of reach is only possible because the institution exists. Ideas, ideologies, and movements simply do not stand the test of time unless they organize themselves. Even though we sometimes think "institution" is a bad word, our institution has been successful on many levels.

Unfortunately, there are downsides. A disadvantage is the dilution of responsibility. When I came out, my local church never had to wrestle with whether or not they would allow me to stay on as their pastor. Such questions were not their responsibility. They supported me as a person but accepted that I would no longer be their pastor.

Whose responsibility was it to decide? The local conference didn't have to decide. The North American Division tied their hands. The North American

Division is not free to go against the General Conference because the many global divisions of the church would fight tooth-and-nail to stop an Adventist church in Chandler, Arizona, from keeping me on as a pastor, even though they don't know me and will never meet me. Besides, none of these administrative levels would go against biblical theology.

Who helps us understand the Bible? We have scholars who help us have confidence in our understanding of the Bible. They make theological statements that are used for setting policy. They help us decide who can be a pastor, who can be married, who can be baptized. They train our pastors. They write many of our theological books. Yet even they are not free to follow their convictions about what the Bible says.

If they don't support accepted theology, they usually lose their jobs. For this reason, those who disagree either keep their mouths shut, quietly find different employment, or never sign up in the first place. The Adventist Church is wary of indulging any more Desmond Fords, facing the fallout of a theologian who departed from the accepted collective theological understanding. They know the political disaster and loss of tithe and membership that could follow. So, institutional concerns inevitably outweigh any moral weight individuals would otherwise feel.

The suppression of individual responsibility and individual voices works against our ability to question our collective theological understanding. After decades of this, our doctrines have crystallized. Everything is a fundamental theological assumption. We now have hundreds of pages of them. We've gone far beyond the pillars and landmarks of theology given to us by our founders. We hold tight to everything instead of just holding tight to the center. There's no room for any growth but numerical. Our prophetic voice is silenced. Even subjects that should be outside the theological center are considered essential. We can't differentiate between those beliefs that make us who we are and those that don't.

So, who was responsible for deciding I could no longer be an Adventist pastor or employee? Who made this an unquestionable reality? I don't know. Everyone's hands are tied, so everyone feels justified to wash their hands of responsibility. No one feels the moral weight of the decision. No one is responsible. The buck never stops.

Questions about my employability are comparatively trivial. What about the 12-year-olds who walk into their youth pastor's office with an ashen face and shaking voice to share the secret they've always kept carefully hidden? They've been trying to change, but they can't. They hope you can tell them what they should do. What does God think of them? Is there a reason to hope beyond the false promises of change? Can they have a marriage and a family one day? Can they live a life that's not devastated by gender dysphoria? Is the precious piece of their humanity so broken that it's irredeemable and must be denied?

Who carries the moral weight of these questions? Whose shoulders are bent by the heaviness of questions about this child's future? The way we do things today, no one but this child will feel that weight. The institution has given everyone else a reason to wash their hands of responsibility. Even the pastors, looking into the eyes of those children, trust that they are getting good advice from their church. They understand their responsibility to stay within denominational guidelines. They are assured that everything will work out fine. So, where does the weight fall? The weight that should fall on faithful and mature Adventist leaders falls silently on the small shoulders of those children who carry it in silence, shoulders bend and hearts heavy as they walk our halls.

The problem is not with the intentions, kindness, or intelligence of these leaders. Adventists and Adventists leaders (mostly) have these in spades. "Don't blame the church for what people have done to you." This advice is standard for those who are tempted to leave the church. Even though there are hurtful people in the Adventist Church, the church itself has value and shouldn't be abandoned.

In many ways, this is true, but it's not when it comes to the treatment of LGBTQ people. The institution is the problem. It constrains members' compassion. If Adventist individuals felt the moral responsibility to make their own decisions, everything would be different. In this instance, Adventist people are better than their institution. Adventist people would suffer longer and study deeper if the decisions rested on them alone. This is the problem, now what's the solution?

HOW CHANGE HAPPENS

As I was coming out, I gained an intimate understanding of these dynamics. I also realized something else: institutional change will never come from the institution. If we wait for institutional employees—pastors, teachers, administrators, and publishers—to lead the way in biblical exploration as I've done in this book, we'll wait forever. We all know Pacific Press Publishing Association won't publish a book like the one you're holding, even if the people who work there want to.

Don't give up hope. When an institution changes, it's usually because members have already changed. One example is the administrators who champion women's ability to serve equally in pastoral ministry. They are always in locations where members in the pews support them overwhelmingly. It still takes courage on their part, but without the support of the members who vote them into office, they could never do it. The institution only changes when its members want it to.

None of this is an accident. The Adventist Church is organized from the ground up. We've forgotten this. Too many layers of administration make it seem that only administrators make decisions. But that isn't true.

The Adventist Church is a representative organization. Church members elect the people who run the church. Power ultimately comes from members who change rules and change officers in their conference constituency meetings. They select the Executive Committee that is ultimately responsible for all significant decisions outside of those meetings. That means members, and only members, empower administrators to make changes.

That's why this book exists. Members need tools. We need theological teaching that doesn't come from the institution because the institution's resistance to change means many new ideas are suppressed. Independent publishing allows for unconstrained Adventist biblical exploration. Plenty of material produced by the institution supports accepted Adventist theology, and I'm confident this book will inspire even more explanations from the institution. Read those, too. Study it all. Take it all in. Read, pray, wrestle, and learn. We must take the Bible more seriously and study it more thoroughly on this subject, and we must do it together.

Church members cannot wait for local church pastors to start a Sabbath school class that studies this book. Members must do it. Members must create small groups, share the book with friends and family, and spread the word on social media. Members must ask LGBTQ people to share their stories. Members must lead discussions, plan events, and seek out the truth. Elders, church board members, and students in our schools have this ability and this responsibility.

Before publishing this book, I shared it with at least a dozen people. They all said it could make a difference. It has the power to raise the quality of our conversations on this topic. Even those who continue to believe the church's accepted theology told me that this book contributes meaningfully to the conversation. Even those who are fully affirming told me that this book helped them understand and appreciate the other side better, to have more respect for those who hold accepted theology.

Many Adventists want a better conversation. We're tired of vitriol, fear, anger, and coercion overwhelming any potential for understanding. We're curious to understand both sides with generosity. We know the conversation is past due.

I hope this can be more than a book. I want this to be a movement for deeper biblical understanding, but that's entirely up to you, my reader. This discussion can begin wherever we find ourselves. We can start study groups in schools, churches, local communities, and social media. We can give books as gifts to people who need them, especially LGBTQ people and their families. Ask pastors to read it. Study it in your Sabbath school class (it's just about right for one quarter, one chapter a week).

These ideas won't be shared from the platform of your local camp meeting, they won't be shared in *the Adventist Review*, and it's unlikely that your pastor will promote them from the pulpit, so it's going to have to be you. Use the book to break the silence and start dialoguing and learning. This is something tangible to do.

I'M AFFIRMING, NOW WHAT?

Having this conversation is essential, and if that's all this book does, I'm happy. But at some point, as you prayerfully turned these pages, some of you became fully affirming. Your interest isn't only in promoting the conversation but also in being faithful in affirming your beliefs.

There's no one way to do this. There are many "right" ways to be affirming and be an ally to gay, bisexual, and transgender people. You need to find your right way, and even that can change with time and circumstance. It depends quite a bit on whether you are a church member, an employee of the church, and/or whether you are LGBTQ yourself.

Church members, not employees, and not LGBTQ, have the most options. If you remain in the Adventist Church and vocally promote change, you don't have to worry about a career like employees do. No matter how vocal you are, you're unlikely to lose church membership.

Recognize your freedom and be bold. It requires boldness to get this message out. It won't happen if we wait for institutional support or if we shrink back when facing resistance. Be persistent and unyielding in promoting conversation and prayerful study of the Bible. Some will work quietly because that's your style. Some will work vocally because that's your style. But in whatever way is natural, find a way to be bold. Let's make our convictions known.

Many have family members in the LGBTQ community. If so, and if we embrace affirming theology, our gay, bisexual, and transgender family members want to know about it. In your relationship, there may be pain and wounds that need healing, or maybe not. But knowing that we support them will make a difference.

FOR AFFIRMING CHURCH EMPLOYEES AND PASTORS

Church employees have different choices and consequences. Your entire career may be tied to Adventism, and you don't know how to shift into a different field, not to mention that you have a calling. Financial decisions are also real and immediate, especially if you have a family to support. If you choose to remain publicly silent on affirmation because of these realities, you can still do many things.

Many people in our schools and churches work as quiet allies. I used to feel conflicted about anyone who was affirming and working for the Adventist system despite seeing the harm done. How can they support a system that causes so much pain?

I asked this exact question of a friend who works at one of our schools. Without a moment's hesitation, she said, "Because those LGBTQ kids need me. Who are they going to talk to if I'm not there?"

How could I argue with that? I listened as she told me stories of gay and transgender students she had helped navigate the Adventist system. She helped them accept themselves. She helped them be realistic about the future they may or may not have within Adventism. She spoke to them and helped them in ways she never could if she had left.

I can't criticize her. In fact, I'm grateful for her work. She's not the only ally I know who quietly works within the system to help gay, bisexual, and transgender kids navigate it. I know pastors, administrators, and university professors who do the same, many of them. As a result of their work, the Adventist Church is much safer for LGBTQ kids.

I also know that there are claims upon our loyalty other than affirming theology. For Adventist pastors, leaving that employment for any reason is thought of as "leaving the ministry." I felt that way when I came out. I knew I needed to come out, but how could I leave the ministry? This was my calling, a lifelong calling. Pastors have to wrestle with these difficulties, and there are no easy answers.

Leaving Adventist pastoral ministry is much more than losing the benefits of employment. It's about community, identity, and vocation. I don't pretend that these are easy decisions because I know how real they are for those who read these words. That's why for some, affirming theology is a heavy weight. There are no universal answers.

For some people, silent affirmation is no longer tenable. They need to speak out. Some Adventist pastors openly support affirming theology and keep their jobs, but they are few. They know the lines they can't cross, and they go right up to them. It helps to have a local church that is affirming. Such pastors have expressed to me that they are ready even if they lose their jobs.

Then some just have to do that baptism, perform that marriage, or speak out about affirming theology so that it can't be ignored. I was obviously in this category. Those who are pastors or employees and LGBTQ probably won't last forever working for the church. You might quietly slip away. Maybe coming out or speaking out will be part of your exit strategy.

For those thinking about speaking out or coming out in a vocal and public way, as I did, I have some thoughts. Only do this if you are called to, because it will be harder than you imagine. It's not going to be easy if your message goes viral and many people see it. But your impact for good will be incalculable.

For several months after I came out, each day started the same. I woke up disoriented from the forgetfulness of sleep. I felt like myself for a moment, as if I were still an Adventist pastor with the belonging and purpose of the Adventist community. Then I would be hit with the realization of everything that had happened and how everything was changed.

I had come out publicly as bisexual. Everyone I had ever known and everyone I ever would have met in the Adventist Church, tens of thousands of people, had seen my video. I had lost my ability to be an Adventist pastor or employee ever again. I was now known in the Adventist community for this one thing, not for everything I had been and done before. I was free to follow my conscience, but that freedom was costly.

During this time, I read an online thread in which Adventist pastors spoke about my coming-out video and didn't realize I was reading. Someone shared that he had been working with some gay youth in his church for years, encouraging them not to affirm their sexuality. He expressed his anger at me that "in one fell swoop," I had undone all his work. Of course, this calls into question how compelling his message was. It only took a 27-minute video to undo years of effort. I'm so grateful that those kids heard a message of hope.

There are many more stories like this. I heard about Adventist youth and young adults coming out and affirming themselves in the most unexpected places. So many people came out to me, asked for my help, and thanked me for my work that I couldn't keep up. I hardly responded to those messages because I was so flooded with emotion and overwhelmed by it all. The hunger for affirmation is overwhelming because of the steady diet of shame many people have received in the church. Many have languished in desperation for a word of hope that God could affirm their way of being and loving.

Some people saw me as a hero. But some saw me as a devil. People made wild assumptions about me and my sex life based on nothing other than my orientation. I had my spirituality, my dignity, and my intelligence questioned regularly. There was even a bizarre conspiracy theory that maintained I wasn't a genuine pastor at all. I was planted in my position so that I could come out and cause disruption.

Reactions were extreme. I had to cultivate the spirit of Jesus. Even when people believed in Him, He "would not entrust himself to them, for he knew all people" (John 2:24, NIV). We can't find our identity in the opinion of others, though I was tempted to.

I lost my identity when I came out. Rather than being an Adventist pastor, I was a controversial former Adventist pastor. I had switched sides, betraying my church family. I was a turncoat. It felt as if the earth was moving under my feet, and I struggled to stay standing.

If you're thinking of coming out in a big way, make sure you're committed. It's probably impossible to be ready. You'll just have to take that ride without knowing where it will lead. The cost will be high, but the rewards will be boundless. I've never done anything better.

During this time in my life, I often thought about Jesus' parable of the pearl of great price (Matt. 13:44). A man discovered a treasure hidden in a field. Its value was beyond compare. He immediately sold everything to buy the pearl. Not only that, he sold all his earthly belonging with "joy." I recognized my path in this parable. I knew the loss, but I also knew the joy.

Jesus spoke of the promise of a seed. If it's willing to die and be buried, it will grow through the soil, into the sunshine, producing multitudes more than its own small life would seem to promise (John 12:24).

God may be calling you to this kind of sacrifice. This might be what Jesus meant when He said to "take up [your] cross and follow me." (Matt. 16:24) Only you and Jesus can answer that question, though if you have a spouse, you'll want to include them, of course. Make a plan, and be bold.

FOR THE LGBTQ COMMUNITY

Beloved, I especially hope you've become affirming. If so, your journey will be the most challenging and most rewarding of all. When I accepted my sexual orientation, the sky was bluer, and the flowers sweeter. Life opened up in a way I hadn't foreseen.

Some of it was about new dating possibilities, but mostly it was internal. I discovered the weight of internal conflict I'd unknowingly carried for so many years. I discovered it in a delightful way, through its absence. I could feel again. Shame I thought I had banished, had only driven deeper, but was now actually gone.

I began to see God differently. I'd always believed God loved me, but I'd never realized how much. I'd always known God cared about love and justice, but I'd never realized how completely God cared for humanity. I knew God loved the world, but I'd never realized how extravagantly God loved *all* the world.

Over time, things got much harder in other ways. My internalized shame wasn't gone. The roots were gone, but years of mental habits meant it kept showing up again and again, especially as I began dating. I was also shamed by well-meaning (and sometimes not-so-well-meaning) Christians. My sense of identity was in constant flux. I felt adrift in my career for much of the last few years.

While my faith was so much stronger and easier at first, it later became harder to hold onto at all. I was horrified when I daily discovered more about how severe the harm is to the LGBTQ community. For so many years, I'd had no idea just how bad things were. I worried that there wasn't a way to do religion that was safe. I realized how wrong I'd been and wondered what else I was getting wrong. I realized how wrong the Adventist Church was about sexual orientation and gender identity, and I wondered what else could be wrong.

With no faith community to stabilize me, I struggled with anger, disillusionment, and pain. They've labeled this process. They call it "deconstruction." The term sounds intellectual, but it's more visceral than that. When the house you live in begins to deconstruct, you start worrying about survival. No wonder research says that leaving your church because of your sexuality can be hazardous to your mental health, at least in the short term.

Rather than taking this process seriously, even though it is serious, I decided to wait it out. I knew a lot of my reactions to church and religion were rooted in pain, even trauma. I knew I wasn't thinking clearly. I've slowly been healing and recovering spiritually, intellectually, and emotionally.

I've spoken to many people who have been through this process, so I know I've experienced nothing unique. Sadly, we have to go through this. It's a difficult spiritual path, but there's hope, and things do get better. I encourage you to intentionally separate the actions of Christians from the character of God. I also encourage you to remember that even when you don't have a place in your home church, you do have a place in God's kingdom. Adventism, Christianity, and the Bible are worthy of the effort to reclaim them.

I look at my life now, and I marvel at how what seemed impossible turned out to be possible. I didn't realize I could do this. I didn't realize I could come out, accept myself, and pursue relationships. I didn't know I could make peace with God again. But with God all things are possible.

LGBTQ Adventists have a lot of difficult decisions to make. Do you continue attending an Adventist church? Do you attend a Sunday church? Is it more important that the church is affirming or otherwise theologically consistent with your beliefs?

I don't attend an Adventist church, and here's why: my understanding of being part of a church is not attendance only. We should all contribute to the building-up of the church (Eph. 4:16). We should all serve in ways we are gifted to serve (Rom. 12:6–8, 1 Cor. 12:8–10, 28–30, Eph. 4:11, 1 Pet. 4:11). Being a perpetual pew-warmer is not biblically being part of the church. Why attend somewhere I have few options to participate?

I'm also a pastor at heart. I'm not pastoring a church as of this writing, but I may again someday. Even if I'm not on staff, having the opportunity to teach and lead is an integral part of my spiritual gifts. I've chosen not to attend a church where I can't teach, lead, and have a potential future as a pastor. Though if I lived near enough to one of the few Adventist churches that are affirming in local church leadership, I might attend there.

I don't believe it's wrong to go to church on Sunday, although I prefer Saturday. The Bible has no prohibition on attending church on Sunday. I keep Sabbath in my home, and sometimes with friends. It works for me for the time being. What you do in your church attendance is, of course, entirely between you and God.

WHEN I BECAME AFFIRMING

Know two things as you come to the end of this book. First, I respect you even if you don't accept affirming theology. Second, affirming theology is an inseparable part of my Christianity. It's hard for me to understand God and faith apart from affirming theology. It makes so much sense on the deepest levels of faith and scriptural teachings. It's healing, loving, and beautiful.

My drive to share this theology is nothing short of a calling. I believe whole-heartedly that God wants gay, bisexual, and transgender children to grow up in our churches and experience affirmation. I hope they can experience this from as many people as possible. In fact, I'll tell you a secret: If you are LGBTQ, I wrote this book mostly for you. You are the reason I pressed on when writing made my heart ache. I want you to have a moment with God like the moment I had.

After highlighting hundreds of passages, painstakingly examining Greek and Hebrew texts of Scripture, praying and crying out to God, my theological understanding finally came into focus. I'd been wrong to be against same-gender marriage and transgender identity. It became clear that God saw things differ-ently than I did.

This may sound strange, but only then did I realize the personal implications. If God does not oppose same-gender marriage, God must see beauty in it. If God affirms same-gender marriage, who am I to refuse it just because it's easier to act heterosexual? I began to see that it was wrong for me to stay out of the struggle, but so far, I only encountered these ideas intellectually, and my heart was unmoved.

It was time to get away with God. I went to a cabin in the woods, and I prayed. The idea of surrendering to God is one we don't take seriously enough. Sometimes I wonder how many moments of total surrender I have really had in my life. How often have I genuinely been open to any word the Lord would speak to me? I don't know, but I know it's not a lot. I also know that this was one of them.

My past and my future were in suspense. I let go of attachments and obli-gations. I only wanted to know what God would have me do. My focus and intention were on being open to whatever God might say. Sitting with my jour-nal and my Bible, I looked out huge picture windows onto a forest of Ponderosa Pine and waited.

At first, there was nothing. No words. No guidance. No peace. Then I was suddenly overwhelmed with a feeling of pure joy. There was nothing but the feeling, and it seemed to come from outside of me. I laughed out loud, because what else do you do when overcome by joy? Then I asked God, *What is this?* God didn't speak audibly, but the words came forcefully to my mind: *It's okay.*

With those two words, years of shame, dismay, and fear fell to dust. I knew what the Bible said. I'd studied it prayerfully and openly. Now I had the confir-mation and strength I needed. It was okay for me to embrace affirming theology; okay to accept myself and the feelings I had long ago quarantined to a deep corner of my subconscious.

I'm reminded of a story from the life of David, before he was king of Israel. He and his small battalion of fighters returned to their village to find their belongings looted and their women and children taken. All was in jeopardy, and they didn't know if they could get it back. Maybe all was lost already. David's people were so angry that they spoke of stoning him. Scripture records that at that moment, he "strengthened himself in the Lord his God" (1 Sam. 30:1-6).

That's what happened to me that day in the cabin. I was strengthened in the Lord for the battle that was ahead of me. I sometimes think that every moment since has been a struggle to help others know that joy and that strength.

So, to you, my LGBTQ family, I pray that you can know this joy and find the strength God offers. I hope that you can also find free and full affirmation. Of course, this doesn't mean that all standards go out the window. It doesn't mean we get to do whatever we want, far from it. We are called to the same sexual fidelity and much more sacrifice and courage.

That's what's required of us to live well as gay, bisexual, and transgender Christians. But we are up to the challenge. The LGBTQ Christian community is unimaginably strong and loving. For those wrestling with your sexuality or gender identity, you are not alone. You can do this. God is with you. I am with you.

When you are shamed and excluded, may you find encouragement in this text that has encouraged me: "I sought the Lord, and He heard me, and delivered me from all my fears. They looked to Him and were radiant, and their faces are not ashamed" (Ps. 34:4, 5).

Acknowledgments

This book was born from the ashes of grief and loss. How do you say thank you to the multitudes of people who helped you put your life back together so you could begin the arduous task of writing a book like this? How do you say thank you to the people who believed in and supported this essential work? No word of thanks is sufficient. But I will try.

My brother Mike and his wife Stephanie have always accepted and loved me. They gave me immediate and full-hearted support from the moment I came out to them. How can you write a book like this without family who affirms you completely? My mother and my late father introduced me to Jesus, raised me in the Adventist church, and taught me to live a spiritual life of purpose. They gave their children the example of a faith rooted in genuine love for God and joy in the Christian life. For them, I am forever grateful.

Publishing is a daunting task, particularly with a book as complicated as this one. So many have given feedback on my writing or even donated valuable services proofreading and editing. First of all, Stephen Chavez donated his time editing the entire book. If you know anything about publishing, you know there couldn't have been a better editor and that his donation was extravagantly generous. Marygrace Coneff, David Potter, and Caroline Laredo also donated time proofreading the document.

Aphelandra did the design work that made this book so beautiful. She was terrific to work with, and the results speak for themselves. I'm also grateful for CCPM's work adapting and designing social media materials. Steve McCarthy helped me in a million ways to refine my language and figure out how to get past difficult sections. He also generously volunteered to record and produce my Kickstarter video.

RA is an Adventist scholar who gave me feedback on an early outline of the book. I'm immensely grateful for his help. His scholarship is of the highest caliber. He helped make this a better book and me a more confident writer. Randi Robertson was a valuable sounding board and editor for transgender and intersex content in this book. She has always been there to help me understand these sometimes complicated questions and her own perspective and experience. A team of beta readers, many of whom are pastors and elders in the Adventist church, gave me valuable feedback for the final version of the book and helped me know the book was effective.

This book would not be possible without many people who prepared the way in the Adventist church by speaking about the LGBTQ community and telling our stories. Daneen Akers and Stephen Eyer worked tirelessly for many years to increase LGBTQ visibility and understanding in the Adventist church. Their documentaries, *Seventh-Gay Adventist* and *Enough Room at the Table* (find them at sgamovie.com), had an incalculable influence. Because of their work, I knew that many in the church were ready for the kind of theological conversation this book invites. They have also been constant in friendship, supporting me from the first moment I met them. They filmed and produced my coming-out video. Without their help, it wouldn't have been half what it was. I turned to them for guidance and advice on a million questions over the last few years. I wouldn't be where I am without them.

My work also benefits from decades of tireless work from Seventh-day Adventist Kinship International. They have persevered to support and advocate for LGBTQ Adventists for 40 years. The Reformation Project also works tirelessly for LGBTQ inclusion in the broader Christian church. Their materials helped me become affirming. Since coming out, through both of these groups, I formed relationships, had opportunities to present my ideas, and rediscovered a sense of shared purpose and community. This went a long way towards restoring my sense of place and belonging without which this kind of book would be nearly impossible to write. I would run out of space if I mentioned everyone who deserves acknowledgment. I will mention Floyd Poenitz, Kathy Baldock, and Matthew Vines. All three have helped me learn, develop sharper arguments, and believe in myself and my capacity to make a difference in this conversation.

So many people have challenged, supported, and loved me in necessary and redemptive ways. Herb Montgomery challenged me to be affirming when I wasn't there yet, even though I didn't make it easy for him. When I told him I was coming out as bisexual and would be losing my job, he supported and cared for me. He has been a tireless advocate for the LGBTQ community regardless of personal cost, and I have all the respect in the world for him. MW has been a constant support in my life and helped me through many tear-filled conversations. She was one of the first people to know I was queer and helped me through many a desperate hour. Her expertise on the book itself was also invaluable. DW has been there from the beginning, when we first started laughing about the appeal of a certain TV character, unaware that there might be more to the story. She has constantly shown me kindness, understanding, and non-judgmental support. Jenn Ogden has been a relentless advocate for me, and I've had the great joy of watching her become an incredible ally. She also helped by giving me feedback on early drafts.

Daniel and Jokatama interviewed me about my book and blessed me with laugher and joy. Brian and Steve commiserated with me over pizza on Monday nights and provided friendship and understanding. Beth helped in a million ways, and was one of the first to believe in this project. She helped me begin in earnest and supported me along the way. First Church UCC Phoenix welcomed me with open arms and no agenda. Their love and worship healed many wounds.

I was afraid that when it came time to ask for financial support, I wouldn't get it. My Kickstarter backers really came through. They showed up for me and helped make this book a reality. Thank you so much to those of you who believed in this project, saw how important it was, and helped me make it a reality.

Endnotes

1. Nicholas Miller's remarks during his introduction to the "Marriage, Homosexuality, and the Church" conference at the Seventh-day Adventist Theological Seminary in 2009.
2. It was a footnote that briefly critiqued a point made by James Brownson. Roy Gane, "Old Testament Principles Relevant to Consensual Homoerotic Activity – Part 1 of 3," *Ministry*, Sept., 2005.
3. Ronald Lawson, "The Adventist Church and its LGBT Members – Part 2," *Spectrum*, spectrummagazine.org/news/2021/adventist-church-and-its-lgbt-members-part-2.
4. Ibid.
5. psychologyandchristianity.wordpress.com/tag/gay-marriage
6. Adventist News Network, "'In God's Image' summit on sexuality opens in Cape Town."Mar.17,2014,adventist.news/en/news/in-gods-image-summit-on-sexuality-opens-in-cape-town
7. The International Board of Ministerial and Theological Education (IBMTE). "Handbook of Seventh-day Adventist Ministerial and Theological Education." Department of Education–Ministerial Association, General Conference of Seventh-day Adventists, Silver Springs, MD, 2001, p. 91-93, education.eud.adventist.org/file-admin/education.eud.adventist.org/files/resources/IBMTE-Handbook_2001.pdf
8. www.youtube.com/watch?v=dC8oGrQHUF0

9. Lawson, *Spectrum*. I tried to find an official record of this and reached out to someone who followed up with Adventist Archives. I was told that the papers were not where they should have been. Apparently, it's not uncommon for documents to be misfiled. Maybe that's all there is to it, but there are reasons to be skeptical. If my information is wrong, I'm willing to be corrected if these documents can be located.

10. Ibid.

11. Ibid.

12. Some people make slight changes to this doctrinal list, but there is consensus around its basic outline.

13. Seventh-day Adventist Theological Seminary. "Delimitation of Academic Freedom for the Faculty and Staff of the Seventh-day Adventist Theological Seminary at Andrews University," www.andrews.edu/sem/about/statements/delimitation-of-academic-freedom.pdf

14. Ellen G. White (CW 35.2).

15. Richard M. Davidson, "Homosexuality and the Bible," *Homosexuality, Marriage, and the Church: Biblical, Counseling, and Religious Liberty Issues,* Eds. Roy E. Gane, Nicholas P. Miller, and H. Peter Swanson. Andrews University Press, 2012, p. 196.

16. Seventh-day Adventist Theological Seminary, "An Understanding of the Biblical View on Homosexual Practice and Pastoral Care." Voted Oct. 9, 2015. www.andrews.edu/sem/about/statements/seminary-statement-on-homosexuality-edited-8-17-jm-final.pdf

17. The story is retold in Genesis 2:20-25.

18. See his book, *The Sabbath,* Farrar, Straus, and Giroux, 2005.

19. Ángel Manuel Rodriguez, "Adventists and Homosexuality: The Central Issues in the Debate," *Biblical Research Institute of the General Conference of Seventh-day Adventists (BRI),* Aug., 2017, adventistbiblicalresearch.org

20. The two English words, "sanctified" and "holy," come from the same Hebrew word, *kodosh.*

21. See James Brownson, *Bible, Gender, Sexuality,* for more about the phrase.

22. References are taken from Ron du Preez's exceptional book that demonstrates Colossians 2:16, "Therefore let no one pass judgment on you in questions of food and drink, or with regard to a festival or a new moon or a Sabbath," refers to ceremonial sabbaths, not the seventh-day Sabbath. He also shows in this book how linguistic clues indicate definitively in which sense the word is being used. Ron du Preez, *Judging the Sabbath: Discovering what can't be found in Colossians 2:16,* Andrews University Press, 2008.

23. Seventh-day Adventist Theological Seminary. "An Understanding of the Biblical View on Homosexual Practice and Pastoral Care." Voted Oct. 9, 2015, www.andrews.edu/sem/about/statements/seminary-statement-on-homosexuality-edited-8-17-jm-final.pdf

24. Quote edited for clarity. Taken from an interview with David Blankenhorn and Jonathan Rauch on the *On Being* podcast, onbeing.org/programs/david-blankenhorn-and-jonathan-rauch-the-future-of-marriage

25. General Conference of Seventh-day Adventists. "Responding to Changing Cultural Attitudes Regarding Homosexual and Other Alternative Sexual Practices," www.adventist.org/articles/responding-to-changing-cultural-attitudes-regarding-homosexual-and-other-alternative-sexual-practices. There are also many examples around the world of the Seventh-day Adventist Church encouraging persecution of LGBTQ people, including arrest and even violence. Here is one example: www.modernghana.com/news/1064477/legalising-lgbt-will-dehumanize-ghanas-social.html

26. There are both differences and similarities between Genesis 1 and 2 and Revelation 21 and 22 that can be seen by reading the passages together.

27. adventistbiblicalresearch.org/materials/bri-ethics-committee-releases-statements-on-transgenderism

28. executivecommittee.adventist.org/wp-content/uploads/2017/04/111G-Statement-on-Transgenderism.pdf

29. It's hard to see this belief as anything but a misunderstanding on a couple of levels. First, being transgender involves much more social pushback and difficulty than being gay or bisexual in most countries. In other countries, especially Iran, transgender people are widely supported, but gay and bisexual people are not. But for the context of most reading this book, it would be much easier to be in a same-sex relationship than to surgically alter your anatomy, particularly when those alterations are unwanted. Second, gay and bisexual people don't want to change genders. Doing so would be like straight people changing their gender. It would involve dramatically altering every aspect of who we are and how we experience ourselves and our identities. So, it's hard to understand this statement or imagine what evidence or support there could be for it.

30. I first recall hearing this from Megan DeFranza, who wrote about it in her thorough and insightful book *Sex Difference in Christian Theology: Male, Female, and Intersex in the Image of God*, Eerdmans, 2015.

31. An article from the Biblical Research Institute defines "merism" as a statement that "combines two words to express a single idea; it expresses 'totality' by combining two contrasts or two extremes." Randall Younker, "Crucial Questions of Interpretation of Genesis 1," *BRI*, Oct., 2009, adventistbiblicalresearch.org/wp-content/uploads/Crucial-Questions-of-Interpretation-in-Genesis-1.pdf

32. Geoffrey is his real name, but his last name is withheld. See openbiblepodcast.com, Episode 1, for his story.

33. For a helpful discussion on this topic, see Karen Keen. *Scripture, Ethics, and the Possibility of Same-Sex Relationships*, Eerdmans, 2018.

34. C. E. Roselli, "Neurobiology of Gender Identity and Sexual Orientation," *Journal of Neuroendocrinology,* vol. 30, no. 7, 2018.

35. Canyon Walker Press, 2014.

36. Jody L. Herman, et al., "Age of Individuals Who Identify as Transgender in the United States." Williams Institute of UCLA School of Law, Jan, 2017, thewilliamsins. wpengine.com/wp-content/uploads/Age-Trans-Individuals-Jan-2017.pdf

37. Leonard Sax, "How Common is Intersex? A Response to Anne Fausto-Sterling," *Journal of Sex Research,* vol. 39, no. 3, 2002.

38. Learn more about sex and female athletics in the BBC Article: Matt Slater, "Sport and Gender: A History of Bad Science and 'Biological Racism,'" www.bbc.com/sport/athletics/29446276

39. Pia Baldinger-Melich, et al., "Sex Matters: A Multivariate Pattern Analysis of Sex- and Gender-Related Neuroanatomical Differences in Cis- and Transgender Individuals Using Structural Magnetic Resonance Imaging," *Cerebral Cortex,* vol. 30.3, Mar., 2020, p. 1345–1356. doi.org/10.1093/cercor/bhz170

40. Megan DeFranza was the first person to point this out to me.

41. Austen Hartke, *Transforming: The Bible and the Lives of Transgender Christians.* Louisville, Westminster John Knox Press, 2018.

42. PFLAG is a national organization that offers support for the families of LGBTQ people and LGBTQ people themselves. It has free support groups all over the country, and I highly recommend them. Find out more at Pflag.org.

43. Jaime M. Grant, et al., "Injustice at Every Turn: A Report of the National Transgender Discrimination Survey," *Washington: National Center for Transgender Equality and National Gay and Lesbian Task Force,* 2011. transequality.org/issues/resources/national-transgender-discrimination-survey-full-report

44. For a thorough discussion of eunuchs and their meaning in ancient culture, see DeFranza. *Sex Difference in Christian Theology,* p. 68-106.

45. Ángel Manuel Rodríguez wrote an article for the *Biblical Research Institute* entitled "Deuteronomy 23:1-4, and Isaiah 56:3-8." In it, he argued that exclusion from "the assembly of the Lord" referred not to exclusion from worship or belonging with God's people, but only exclusion from the assembly of leaders. After reading the article, I don't think he made his case convincingly. Yet even if eunuchs were excluded only from leadership, this is still a significant statement about their relative worth compared with those without "defect," as the text describes.

46. DeFranza, Sex Difference in Christian Theology.

47. See also Mark 10:2-12.

48. William J. Webb, Slaves, Women and Homosexuals: Exploring the Hermeneutics of Cultural Analysis. IVP Academic, 2001.

49. Matthew 4:4, 7; 5:21, 27; 15:1-6; 19:17-20; 22:31, 32, 37-39; Mark 7:10; 10:19; 12:26-34; Luke 4:4, 12; 18:20; 20:37, 38; John 8:12, 13, 17, 18.

50. Cheryl Anderson, *Ancient Laws and Contemporary Controversies.* Oxford University Press, 2009, p. 12. For a deeper understanding of the ways biblical laws impacted women and foreigners, this is an excellent resource. It may be challenging for those who have grown accustomed to approaches to the Old Testament that smooth over the difficulties. For this reason, I recommend it for gaining a fuller understanding of Scripture.

51. "The Heart of God," *Truthlink*, lesson 2, Truthlink.org.

52. Ty Gibson, "The Image of God." *Truthlink,* lesson 3, Truthlink.org.

53. Ty Gibson, "The Apocalypse of Human Sexuality," *Lightbearers*, Dec. 22, 2015, lightbearers.org/the-apocalypse-of-human-sexuality.

54. DeFranza. *Sex Difference in Christian Theology,* p. 147. Though Karl Barth talked about marriage as part of the reflection of the image of God, he did not take it to the extreme that it must be taken to exclude same-sex marriage. For him, it was one possibility for fulfilling the image of God, but he also believed that people individually could embody that image.

55. Miroslav Kiš, "The Christian View of Human Life," *Ministry*, Aug., 1991. ministrymagazine.org/archive/1991/08/the-christian-view-of-human-life

56. Kiš, Miroslav, "Return to Innocence: Biblical ethics of homosexual relations." *Homosexuality, Marriage, and the Church: Biblical, Counseling, and Religious Liberty Issues,* Eds. Roy E. Gane, Nicholas P. Miller, and H. Peter Swanson. Berrien Springs, Mich: Andrews University Press, 2012, p. 180. Some who believe in accepted theology have a problem with Kiš' statements. I've been told this explicitly. Even though I never had a class from Kiš, he taught while I was at the seminary. Seminary students regularly pushed back on statements he made about gay, bisexual, and transgender people. They told him it was dehumanizing and theologically problematic. I would point out that many believe in accepted theology and would take issue with his statement. Yet this viewpoint is well respected. His statement did show up in a book that listed three different editors who are also well respected in Adventism. The chapters were based on presentations given at a conference, so there were a lot of eyes on this statement and significant institutional support.

57. Christians did this to Jewish people, women, left-handed people, Black people, Muslims, and others. It's nothing new.

58. Nov. 2, 2015, www.nadadventist.org/sites/default/files/inline-files/NAD%20Statement %20on%20Human%20Sexuality-Nov%202%202015.pdf

59. See, for example, the official Seventh-day Adventist theological statement on "homosexuality." www.adventist.org/articles/homosexuality

60. James Brownson, *Bible, Gender, Sexuality: Reframing the Church's Debate on Same-Sex Relationships.* Eerdmans, 2013. I first learned about this idea by reading Brownson's book. Find a more in-depth conversation about these concepts in his book.

61. Ty Gibson, "The Apocalypse of Human Sexuality," lightbearers.org/blog/the-apocalypse-of-human-sexuality

62. "Marriage," *Merriam-Webster.com.* Accessed Mar. 4, 2021.

63. This is the approximate number of same-gender marriages based on the number of lesbian, gay, and bisexual people in society. The estimate for marriage might be high because most bisexual people marry someone of the opposite sex even when they accept same-sex relationships. There are more potential other-sex partners available.

64. It's worth noting that in the early church, the first couple generations of Christians had egalitarian views of women that were rejected when the church became more political and more Roman. To learn about this and more about women's roles in the church historically, see Beth Allison Barr, *The Making of Biblical Womanhood: How the subjugation of women became the gospel truth,* Brazos, 2021.

65. In Ephesians and Colossians, children are also on the list, and in Titus and 1 Peter, the household itself is also called to submit to ruling authorities. Wives and enslaved people appear on all lists.

66. Gibson, "The Apocalypse of Human Sexuality."

67. *Ibid.,* emphasis his.

68. Roy Gane, *Old Testament Law for Christians.* Baker, 2017, p. 28, 29.

69. For a thoughtful, candid discussion about these moral quandaries in the Torah, particularly for women and foreigners, I recommend Cheryl Anderson, *Ancient Laws and Contemporary Controversies: The Need for Inclusive Biblical Interpretation.*

70. Gane, Old Testament Law.

71. Karen Keen, Scripture, Ethics, and the Possibility of Same-Sex Relationships. Eerdmans, 2018.

72. Roy E. Gane, Nicholas P. Miller, and Peter H. Swanson, editors. *Homosexuality, Marriage, and the Church: Biblical, Counseling, and Religious Liberty Issues.* Andrews University Press, 2012.

73. Roy E. Gane, "Same-sex Love in the 'Body of Christ'?" *Christianity and Homosexuality: Some Seventh-day Adventist Perspectives.* Adventist Forum, 2008, p. 63-72.

74. Gane, Old Testament Law, p. 31.

75. Ibid., p. 30.

76. Keen, *Scripture and the Possibility of Same-Sex Relationships.* It's well worth reading this book for Keen's take on the Torah alone, but she has many other valuable insights.

77. Gane, *Old Testament Law,* p. 32-33, emphasis mine.

78. *Ibid.,* p. 34.

79. Roy E. Gane, "Old Testament Principles Relevant to Consensual Homoerotic Activity—Part 3." *Ministry,* Jan., 2016, emphasis mine.

80. Roy E. Gane, "Prohibitions of Homosexual Practice in Leviticus 18 and 20: Moral or Ceremonial?" *Biblical Research Institute.* Available at: adventistbiblicalresearch.org

81. Seventh-day Adventist Theological Seminary, "An Understanding of the Biblical View on Homosexual Practice and Pastoral Care." Voted Oct. 9, 2015.

82. www.adventist.org/articles/birth-control/

83. Ibid.

84. For most of the church's history, this has been the majority view about sex. Only since the sexual revolution have Christians begun to think of sex as a pleasure worth seeking within marriage, independent of whether it resulted in children.

85. Gane, Old Testament Law, p. 63.

86. See Richard Davidson's explanation for a conservative Adventist perspective that considers connotation and original language, reaching the same basic conclusion I have reached here. Richard M. Davidson, "Homosexuality in the Old Testament." *Homosexuality, Marriage, and the Church: Biblical, Counseling, and Religious Liberty Issues,* Roy E. Gane, Nicholas P. Miller, and H. Peter Swanson, editors. Andrews University Press, 2012, p. 7-11.

87. Robert Alter, *The Five Books of Moses,* p. 623-624.

88. Babylonian Talmud, Yevamot 76a. Available at: https://www.sefaria.org/sheets/115282?lang=bi.

89. For an influential example of this, see Augustine, *On the Good of Marriage.*

90. You can read the history of the churches' conflict and adaptation to the culture during the 20th Century in R. Marie Griffith, *Moral Combat: How sex divided American Christians and fractured American politics,* Basic Books, 2017.

91. All national professional associations support affirming therapies, meaning therapies that affirm one's sexual orientation and gender identity. This includes the American Medical Association, the American Academy of Pediatrics, the American Psychiatric Association, the American Psychological Association, the American Counseling Association, the National Association of Social Workers, the National Educational Association, and the Association of American Educators. These organizations all have educational materials and scientific support for affirming approaches, which are easily found on their websites. I found no exceptions, though a couple of organizations appear to be professional organizations but are not. They don't provide educational materials for CEUs, members are only a tiny portion of professionals in the field, and they are formed for ideological and political reasons, but given names that imply they are professional organizations. Another apparent exception is the American Association of Christian Counselors, but this is a for-profit organization, not an association. Members don't decide on policies, so it doesn't reflect the position of professionals. Timothy Clinton, who owns

AACC, profits from the business and sets all the policies. The Christian Association of Psychological Studies takes no position and has no statements about LGBTQ people.

92. N. T. Wright, *The Climax of Covenant*, Fortress Press, 1993.

93. The words of an anonymous friend of Nicholas Miller, quoted by Miller in introductory remarks during the "Marriage, Homosexuality, and the Church" conference at the Seventh-day Adventist Theological Seminary, 2009.

94. I'm going to make things more complicated for those of you who read the footnotes. There are some very limited exceptions to this because of sexual fluidity. To understand the nuance of sexual orientation and sexual fluidity, the book to read is Lisa Diamond's *Sexual Fluidity*. Her research on this subject is unmatched. One story she tells in her book is of two heterosexual women who have never had any romantic or sexual interest in another woman, who fell in love with each other and only each other. Neither of them thought of themselves as anything but straight. Because one party couldn't imagine being perceived as gay, they ended the romantic aspect of their relationship, and both married men. Every indication is that this type of situation is vanishingly rare, but it does exist. I've also heard stories of straight people who stayed with their transgender spouses after the spouse transitioned. They now appear to be gay or bisexual but still consider themselves straight. They stay together because they honor their marriage and have and always will love their spouse. Others are unable to stay together. So, even the question, "Who do I fall in love with?" is not 100 percent reliable because fluidity exists in addition to sexual orientation, which is more stable. Lisa Diamond's book helps explain these concepts. The language we use to describe ourselves will probably always be imperfect.

95. Those in the "side b" community acknowledge that orientation can't be changed and still believe in and abide by accepted theology. They often embrace their identities as gay or bisexual while still rejecting the behavior of intimacy with the same gender. They believe that being gay or bisexual and accepting oneself is not primarily about romantic or sexual connection to the same gender. I agree that sexual orientation is about much more than sexual attraction. Still, I disagree overall because even though sexual orientation is much more than attraction, it seems strange to parse out one's attractions from being gay. It might not be the only aspect, but it can't be removed from the whole. Not everyone who accepts their sexuality will have sex. Perhaps they aren't particularly interested in a relationship, are called to celibacy, or haven't found the right person. Still, they are open to that part of themselves and don't consider their capacity for romance an urge for sin. Even though there is such thing as gay culture and being gay or bisexual is about more than who you are attracted to, the capacity for love with someone of the same gender can't be separated from being gay or bisexual. It's the defining characteristic. There must be a rejection of one's identity for anyone who rejects the defining characteristic of that identity.

96. Eric M. Rodriguez, "At the Intersection of Church and Gay: A Review of the Psychological Research on Gay and Lesbian Christians." *Journal of Homosexuality*, 2009, 57:1, p. 5-38, DOI: 10.1080/00918360903445806

97. Ibid.

98. Karl Kralovec, et al., "Religion and Suicide Risk in Lesbian, Gay and Bisexual Austrians." *Journal of Religion and Health,* 2014, vol. 53, no. 2, p. 413-423. doi:10.1007/s10943-012-9645-2

99. Dudley Chancey, "How the Church Treats the LGBT Community," *Gender, Sexual Identity, and Families: The Personal Is Political*, Kevin P. Lyness and Judith L. Fischer, eds., Michigan Publishing, 2019. DOI: http://dx.doi.org/10.3998/groves.9453087.0005.001

100. Jeremy J. Gibbs and Jeremy Goldbach, "Religious Conflict, Sexual Identity, and Suicidal Behaviors among LGBT Young Adults." *Archives of Suicide Research,* 2015, vol. 19.4, p. 472–488. doi:10.1080/13811118.2015.1004476

101. Chancey, "How the Church Treats the LGBT Community."

102. Kerith J. Conron, Shoshana K. Goldberg, and Kathryn O'Neill, "Religiosity Among LGBT Adults in the US," Williams Institute of UCLA School of Law, October 2020. williamsinstitute.law.ucla.edu/wp-content/uploads/LGBT-Religiosity-Oct-2020.pdf

103. Family Acceptance Project, "Supportive Families, Healthy Children: Helping Families with Lesbian, Gay, Bisexual, and Transgender Children," San Francisco State University, 2009. familyproject.sfsu.edu/family-education-booklet

104. Ibid.

105. Ibid.

106. Ibid.

107. Ibid.

108. Caitlyn Ryan, et al., "Family Acceptance in Adolescence and the Health of LGBT Young Adults," *Journal of Child and Adolescent Psychiatric Nursing* 2010, vol. 23.4, p. 205-213. See also Dani E. Rosenkrantz, et al., "Cognitive-Affective and Religious Values Associated with Parental Acceptance of an LGBT Child," *Psychology of Sexual Orientation and Gender Diversity,* 2010, vol. 7.1, p. 55.

109. David Sedlacek, Curtis J. VanderWaal, and Lauren Ashley-Mae Lane, "The Impact of Family Rejection or Acceptance among LGBT+ Millennials in the Seventh-day Adventist Church." *Journal of the North American Association of Christian Social Work,* 2017, vol. 44, nos. 1-2, p. 72-92. digitalcommons.andrews.edu/pubs/525

110. Ilan H. Meyer, Merilee Teylan, and Sharon Schwartz, "The Role of Help-Seeking in Preventing Suicide Attempts Among Lesbians, Gay Men, and Bisexuals," *Suicide and Life-Threatening Behavior,* 2015, vol. 45.1, p. 25-36.

111. I am generalizing here, assuming that Adventist homes and schools are at least as good as most religious homes and schools. Y. Joel Wong, Lynn Rew, and Kristina

D. Slaikeu, "A Systematic Review of Recent Research on Adolescent Religiosity/ Spirituality and Mental Health," *Issues in Mental Health Nursing,* 2006, vol. 27.2, p. 161-183. See also Loyd S. Wright, Christopher J. Frost, and Stephen J. Wisecarver. "Church Attendance, Meaningfulness of Religion, and Depressive Symptomatology Among Adolescents," *Journal of Youth and Adolescence,* 1993, 22.5, p. 559-568.

112. Jennifer K. Felner, et al., "Stress, Coping, and Context: Examining Substance Use Among LGBTQ Young Adults with Probable Substance Use Disorders," *Psychiatric Services,* 2020, vol. 71.2, p. 112-120. See also Brian A. Rood, et al., "Expecting Rejection: Understanding the Minority Stress Experiences of Transgender and Gender-Nonconforming Individuals," *Transgender Health,* 2016, vol. 1.1, p. 151-164.

113. Statistics from the Centre for Suicide Prevention. www.suicideinfo.ca/resource/ transgender-people-suicide

114. Ibid.

115. Sedlacek, et al.

116. Ibid.

117. Ibid.

118. Ibid.

119. Ibid.

120. B. J. Sowe, A. J. Taylor, and J. Brown, "Religious Anti-Gay Prejudice as a Predictor of Mental Health, Abuse, and Substance Use," *American Journal of Orthopsychiatry,* 2017, vol. 87.6, p. 690–703. doi.org/10.1037/ort0000297

121. Ibid.

122. Ibid.

123. This is the most common understanding I have found among those who support accepted theology, e.g., Gagnon, *The Bible and Homosexual Practice* and Davidson, *The Flame of Yahweh: Sexuality in the Old Testament,* Hendrickson, 2007, p. 637, 638.

124. Wiley-Blackwell, 2013.

125. In this section, I draw again on Dale B. Martin's work in *Sex and the Single Savior.*

126. Ibid., p. 44, 45.

127. Ibid., p. 45.

128. James Brownson's book, *The Bible, Gender, and Sexuality* has a chapter dedicated to the theme of honor and shame as it relates to gender, sex, and the writings of Paul. It's very illuminating.

129. Michael John Cusick, Surfing for God: Discovering the Divine Desire Beneath Sexual Struggle, Thomas Nelson, 2012.

130. Martin, *Sex and the Single Savior,* p. 38. For those interested in the details of transla- tion issues, I recommend chapter three of this book. It's the best analysis I've found and upends assumptions made in other interpretations.

131. Miroslav M. Kiš, "Return to Innocence: Biblical Ethics of Homosexual Relation-ships," *Homosexuality, Marriage, and the Church*, p. 179.

132. Note that they are repeating the idea that the image of God is related to sex. In their view, the Image of God is corrupted by the "intensification" of one sex through same-sex sex. So, sex or sexual relationships are the place in which we find the image of God, and the image of God is only present if both biological sexes are represented. This leaves questions about how celibacy can ever fulfill God's image, besides the other problems we mentioned about this viewpoint in chapter 4. It's painfully reductionistic, not attested in the text itself, and probably wasn't at all what the authors intended.

133. I wouldn't usually quote a video like this for the book, but what he said and how he approached the topic is too good and too scholarly to ignore. There has been a lack of Adventist New Testament scholars commenting on homosexuality in recent years. At the conference held by the seminary, and the subsequent book based on the conference, rather than using an Adventist scholar for the New Testament, they partnered with a Presbyterian, Robert Gagnon. At the time of writing, I couldn't find an article that Thomas Shepherd wrote on the topic, though he teaches a class on New Testament sexuality, so it seems important to include his work. The dis-cussions were part of the "Heaven's Point of View" series from the Three Angels Broadcasting Network and are entitled "Romans 1, Homosexuality, Part 1" and "Romans 1, Homosexuality, Part 2." Available at www.youtube.com/watch?v=bvHF5jVdI2k and www.youtube.com/watch?v=6FDQfD8WB0o

134. See *Wisdom of Solomon*, chapters 13 and 14. *Wisdom* is widely available online for free. It's also part of the Apocrypha in the Roman Catholic Bible. Solomon didn't write the book, but the author used the name as a pen name, a common practice at the time.

135. Shepherd, "Homosexuality."

136. Proponents of accepted theology often point to the work of William Loader, who believed Paul understood sexual orientation in a way that was close enough to modern understandings. Loader's perspective is much more cautious than the way he is usually represented. He says there were some concepts in Rome at the time that might have been similar enough to homosexuality to be relevant. He also says Paul *might* have been exposed to them, not that he was. Even so, Loader believes that if Paul was familiar with ideas about sexual orientation, he rejected them. Loader believes that in Romans 1, Paul assumed all people were essentially hetero-sexual. He does not believe Paul was referring to sexual orientation. As nuanced as this perspective is, Loader's comments allow for much more understanding of sexual orientation than most historians who study Imperial Rome. Most scholars are clear that ancient Rome did not understand sexual orientation as we do.

137. Romans 1:26; 2:14, 27; 11:21, 24; 1 Corinthians 11:14; Galatians 2:15; 4:8; Ephesians 2:3; James 3:7; 2 Peter 1:4. The adjective form also appears in Romans 1:26, 27; 2 Peter 2:12.

138. Shepherd, "Homosexuality."

139. Italics were added for emphasis.

140. William R. G. Loader, *Sexuality in the New Testament: Understanding the key texts*, Westminster John Knox, 2010, p. 58 (ebook).

141. One context in the Bible in which long hair for men was explicitly mentioned is the Nazirite vow (Num. 6:1-5), which included not cutting one's hair. Samson is the most well-known example of someone who took this vow. In contrast to Paul's direction that men should have short hair, God removed His blessing when Samson cut his hair (Judges 13-16, especially 13:4, 5). Samuel took this vow for life (1 Sam. 1:11). John the Baptist may have taken it as well. Yet even this could be easily explained away as an explicit exception to what is otherwise the rule. Even so, there are no biblical exceptions for women required to have long hair.

   Another difference between the two passages is significant. When one compares the statements about hair length in 1 Corinthians 11 with "men with men" in Romans 1, Paul provides a clear theological argument rooted in creation and the godhead to explain directly why hair length was significant. The chronological order of creation indicates the husband has authority over the wife (or another interpretation is that men are the biological source of women). Hair length is an expression of authority (or origination). No such explanation is given in Romans 1. We are left trying to connect unnatural sex behavior to idolatry, but Paul hasn't laid it out with the same specificity. Even comparing the passages according to their differences doesn't justify applying the plain meaning of one and not the other.

142. Shepherd, "Homosexuality."

143. For the record, I've never read this book and never will. I find it detestable on many levels.

144. Those who pay careful attention to affirming theology realize that, while this argument is often used in a broad sense for understanding the Bible's approach to same-sex eroticism, many make a different argument for Romans 1:24-27, one along the same lines as the arguments I will be making.

145. Shepherd, "Homosexuality."

146. Skinner, Sexuality in Greek and Roman Culture, p. 260.

147. Plato saw them as more likely to embody idealized sex, rational and based on ideal forms instead of relationships with women that were physical and common. Other ancient Greeks experienced pederasty in terms of deep emotional attachment. The Sacred Band were Theban warriors who fought together with other males with whom they were sexually involved in pederastic relationships. The affection they

had was said to motivate them to be superior fighters. So, even within early Greek thought, there was significant variation. All this was long before the time of Paul.

148. Skinner, Sexuality in Greek and Roman Culture, p. 258.

149. Holt N. Park, "The Teratogenic Grid." *Roman Sexualities*, Judith P. Hallet and Marilyn B. Skinner, eds., Princeton University Press, 1997, p. 53, 54.

150. Skinner, Sexuality in Greek and Roman Culture, p. 284

151. Ibid., p. 257.

152. Ibid., p. 285.

153. Ibid., p. 285.

154. Ibid., p. 285

155. Ibid., p. 315-349.

156. Catharine Edwards, "Unspeakable Professions: Public Performance and Prostitution in Ancient Rom," *Roman Sexualities*, p. 67, 68, 86.

157. James V. Brownson, *Bible, Gender, Sexuality*, 2013, p. 156-161.

158. Skinner, Sexuality in Greek and Roman Culture, p. 285.

159. Philo, *On Abraham*, p. 135. Available at: earlychristianwritings.com/yonge/book22.html.

160. Philo, *On Abraham*, p. 136.

161. See Brownson. *Bible, Gender, Sexuality*, chapter 8 for more examples.

162. Skinner, Sexuality in Greek and Roman Culture, p. 315.

163. See *Wisdom*, chapters 13 and 14.

164. Keen, Scripture and the Possibility of Same-Sex Relationships, p. 37, 38.

165. Brownson, Bible, Gender, Sexuality, p. 225.

166. See Diodorus Sicul, *Fragments of Book XXXII*. Writing a first century B.C. medical book, he describes a woman without a vaginal opening who, in having sex with her husband, is "obliged to submit to unnatural embraces." Available at penelope.uchicago.edu/Thayer/E/Roman/Texts/Diodorus_Siculus/32*.html

167. There are some mentions of same-sex female eroticism in Greek writing, but this predates our time period by centuries and is a dramatically different culture. See Skinner.

168. J. P. Louw and Eugene A. Nida, "Orexis," *Greek-English Lexicon of the New Testament: Based on Semantic Domains*, United Bible Societies, 1988.

169. Shepherd, "Homosexuality."

170. My personal class notes from Richard Choi's "Exegesis of Romans" class.

171. Richard Choi, "Tuesday Choice: The New Testament and Homosexuality," www.youtube.com/watch?time_continue=12&v=Tnul1KjkZtI&feature=emb_logo

172. "Ask the Editor," *Ministry*, July 1978.

173. David Gushee, Righteous Gentiles of the Holocaust, Fortress, 1994.

174. InterVarsity Press, 2001.

175. Hector Avalos, Slavery, Abolitionism, and the Ethics of Biblical Scholarship, Sheffield Phoenix Press, 2011.

176. For those familiar with William Webb's work and trajectory theology, I suggest also reading Avalos' book. Trajectory Theology is a post-hoc explanation for why slavery is wrong. It wasn't the theological language of the abolitionists themselves, unless we see trajectory theology in a different light as a general movement of Scripture toward love, equality, and liberation. In this sense, abolitionists would undoubtedly agree. But I could find no evidence that they made most of the arguments in Webb's book as it relates to slavery. In my estimation, Webb's arguments work better for affirmation than abolition because there are so many differences between the culture of their time and ours when it comes to same-sex eroticism.

177. Learn how they thought about Scripture in Mark Noll's book, The Civil War as a Theological Crisis. The summary of the texts and reasoning used begins on page 33. Based on my reading, I've added to them slightly.

178. Ibid., p. 162, 163, 215.

179. Augustine, The City of God, 19.15.

180. Avalos, p. 220.

181. As far as I am aware, no Christian thinker or theologian even used the word "homosexuality" until C. S. Lewis referred to it in a letter in 1954. Christians didn't start talking seriously about the subject until the 1970s.

182. Mark A. Knoll, The Civil War as a Theological Crisis, University of North Carolina Press, reprint 2015.

183. James Henry Thornwell said, "It will be found that the very principles upon which we have been accustomed to justify Southern Slavery are the principles of regulated liberty; that in defending this institution we have really been upholding the civil interests of mankind, resisting alike the social anarchy of communism and the political anarchy of licentiousness, that we have been supporting representative, republican government against the despotism of masses on the one hand, and the supremacy of a single will on the other."

184. To learn about how Black enslaved women survived American chattel slavery, see Deloris Williams, Sisters in the Wilderness.

185. Read more about the particular characters and arguments made in this debate in Mark A. Noll, The Civil War as a Theological Crisis. See especially chapter three, "The Crisis over the Bible." Hector Avalos's book, Slavery, Abolition, and the Ethics of Biblical Scholarship, has examples of abolitionist arguments on pages 243-248. In William Wilberforce's central tract against slavery, "An Appeal to the Religion, Justice, and Humanity of the Inhabitants of the British Empire, in Behalf of the Negro Slaves in the West Indies," he makes no scriptural arguments but only appeals to general Christian sympathy.

186. *Complete Works of James Henry Thornwell.* I suggest this book for those who want to read directly from one of the most popular proponents of slavery. Thornwell was a highly influential Southern preacher and college president. His complete works are available online. Here is the full quote from which the cited quotes are taken: "Beside the arguments drawn from considerations of justice and the essential rights of humanity, the incompatibility of slavery with the spirit and temper of the gospel is not unfrequently attempted to be made out from the injunction of the Saviour to love our neighbour as ourselves, and to do unto others as we would have them to do unto us. The principle, however, upon which the precept of universal benevolence is interpreted in this case makes it the sanction of the grossest wickedness. If we are to regulate our conduct to others by the arbitrary expectations which, in their circumstances, our passions and selfishness might prompt us to indulge, there ceases to be any other standard of morality than caprice... The rule then simply requires, in the case of slavery, that we should treat our slaves as we should feel that we had a right to be treated if we were slaves ourselves."

187. Ibid (emphasis mine).

188. James Standish, "Slavery and Sexuality," *Adventist Record*, Apr. 2, 2014. record. adventistchurch.com/2014/04/02/slavery-and-sexuality

189. Ángel Manuel Rodríguez, "Adventists and Homosexuality: The Central Issue in the Debate," *The Biblical Research Institute General Conference of Seventh-day Adventists.* (emphasis mine) adventistbiblicalresearch.org

190. Christians of European descent believed themselves superior to Africans. They stigmatized Africans as degenerate sinners and intellectual inferiors. They had many ways of justifying this belief, from technological to religious differences, and refused to believe evidence to the contrary. Therefore, they pointed to the Bible when they said that slavery was for the benefit of the slaves. They believed that through enslavement, enslaved people could be improved so that they could be emancipated someday. "The blacks are immeasurably better off here than in Africa, morally, physically, and socially. The painful discipline they are undergoing is necessary for their further instruction as a race, and will prepare them, I hope, for better things. How long their servitude may be necessary is known and ordered by a merciful Providence. Their emancipation will sooner result from the mild and melting influences of Christianity than from the story and tempest of fiery controversy."—Robert E. Lee.

191. Complete Works of James Henry Thornwell.

192. Ibid (emphasis mine).

193. An Appeal to the Religion, Justice, and Humanity of the Inhabitants of the British Empire, in Behalf of the Negro Slaves in the West Indies.

194. Theodore Dwight Weld attempted to prove that the Bible was against slavery by using its plain meaning. He didn't rely on the main themes of Scripture and the Golden Rule, but on the texts about slavery. His book, *The Bible Against Slavery*

(1837), is a valiant attempt in a losing battle. When I read it, I couldn't help but admire his ardor, even though his logic was deeply flawed. Weld himself was an early architect of the abolition movement. Two years later, he co-wrote *American Slavery As It Is* (1839), a collection of stories from those enslaved. This book was one of the most influential books in the abolitionist movement, inspiring *Uncle Tom's Cabin*. Despite Weld's significant influence in the abolitionist movement, his theological defense of abolition never took hold. The biblical arguments he made simply did not withstand scrutiny. Later abolitionists never used them.

195. Complete Works of James Henry Thornwell.

196. Hector Avalos' book, *Slavery, Abolitionism, and the Ethics of Biblical Scholarship,* held as its thesis that the Bible cannot be trusted as an ethical guide because it historically reinforced slavery and discredited abolitionists.

197. See David Kinnaman, *You Lost Me*, Baker, 2011.

198. "A Question of Slavery," adventistbiblicalresearch.org

199. Ekkehardt Mueller, "Hermeneutical Guidelines for Dealing with Theological Questions." *Reflections: The Biblical Research Institute Newsletter*, Oct. 2012, no. 40.

200. Darius Jankiewicz, "Hermeneutics and Slavery," Adventist review OCTOBER 21, 2016 www.adventistreview.org/hermeneutics-and-slavery [check formatting]

201. Ibid.

202. Miriam Wood, "Thou Shalt Not!" *Review and Herald*, Feb. 26, 1970, p. 7.

203. Miriam Wood, "When You're Young: Anita Bryant and Homosexuality," *Review and Herald,* Oct. 6, 1977, p. 8.

204. Robert Parr, "Nice People, Really?" *Signs of the Times*, Jan. 1, 1974, p. 28, 29.

205. Colin Cook, "God's Grace to the Homosexual: Part 1," *Insight*, Dec. 7, 1976, p. 4-8.

206. Meg True (pseudonym), "Homosexuality in the Family: Part 1," *Adventist Review*, Feb. 23, 1978, p. 6-8.

207. Eliel Cruz, "The Seventh-day Adventist Church's Complicated History with the LGBT Community," *Sojourner.* sojo.net/articles/seventh-day-adventist-church-s-complicated-history-lgbt-community

208. Ronald Lawson, "The Adventist Church and its LGBT Members – Part 1," *Spectrum.* Available at: spectrummagazine.org/news/2021/adventist-church-and-its-lgbt-members-part-1

209. Ibid.

210. Robert J. Spangler, "Homosexual Recovery—Six years Later," *Ministry*, Sept., 1997, p. 4-9.

211. Ronald Lawson, "The Adventist Church and its LGBT Members."

212. Ibid.

213. www.adventist.org/statistics/seventh-day-adventist-world-church-statistics-2020

214. adventist.news/en/news/is-the-adventist-church-not-realizing-12-billion